From the fifth edition of *Spring in Action* by Craig Walls

T0341014

Spring in Action, Sixth Edition

Spring in Action, Sixth Edition

CRAIG WALLS

MANNING
SHELTER ISLAND

Manning Publications Co.
20 Baldwin Road
PO Box 761
Shelter Island, NY 11964

Development editor:	Jennifer Stout
Technical development editor:	Joshua White
Review editor:	Mihaela Batinić
Production editor:	Deirdre S. Hiam
Copy editor:	Pamela Hunt
Proofreader:	Katie Tennant
Technical proofreaders:	Doug Warren and German Gonzalez-Morris
Typesetter:	Dennis Dalinnik
Cover designer:	Marija Tudor

ISBN: 9781617297571
Printed in the United States of America

brief contents

contents

preface

Spring entered the development world more than 18 years ago with the fundamental mission of making Java application development easier. Originally, that meant offering a lightweight alternative to EJB 2.x. But Spring was just getting started. Over the years, Spring expanded its mission of simplicity to address common development challenges, including persistence, security, integration, cloud computing, and others.

Although Spring is closing in on two decades of enabling and simplifying enterprise Java development, it shows no signs of slowing down. Spring continues to address Java development challenges, whether it be creating an application deployed to a conventional application server or a containerized application deployed to a Kubernetes cluster in the cloud. And with Spring Boot providing autoconfiguration, build dependency help, and runtime monitoring, there has never been a better time to be a Spring developer!

This edition of *Spring in Action* is your guide to Spring and Spring Boot and has been updated to reflect the best of what both have to offer. Even if you're new to Spring, you'll have your first Spring application up and running before the end of the first chapter. As the book progresses, you'll learn how to create web applications, work with data, secure your application, and manage application configuration. Next, you'll explore options for integrating your Spring applications with other applications and how to benefit from reactive programming in your Spring applications, including the new RSocket communication protocol. As the book draws to a close, you'll see how to prepare your application for production and learn options for deploying.

Whether you're new to Spring or have many years of Spring development to your credit, this is your next step in your journey. I'm excited for you and happy to bring this guide to you. I look forward to seeing what you create with Spring!

acknowledgments

One of the most amazing things that Spring and Spring Boot do is automatically provide all of the foundational plumbing for an application, leaving you as a developer to focus primarily on the logic that's unique to your application. Unfortunately, no such magic exists for writing a book. Or does it?

At Manning, several people worked their magic to make sure that this book is the best it can possibly be. Many thanks in particular to my development editor, Jenny Stout, and to production editor, Deirdre Hiam, copy editor, Pamela Hunt, graphics editor, Jennifer Houle, and the entire production team for their wonderful work in making this book a reality.

As the book was forming, we had several peer reviewers take an early look, give us feedback, and help make sure that the book stayed on target and covered the right stuff. For this, my thanks go to Al Pezewski, Alessandro Campeis, Becky Huett, Christian Kreutzer-Beck, Conor Redmond, David Paccoud, David Torrubia Iñigo, David Witherspoon German Gonzalez-Morris, Iain Campbell, Jon Guenther, Kevin Liao, Mark Dechamps, Michael Bright, Philippe Vialatte, Pierre-Michel Ansel, Tony Sweets, William Fly, and Zorodzayi Mukuya.

I absolutely must give a shout out to everyone on the Spring engineering team. You consistently produce some of the most incredible stuff I've ever worked with, and I am proud to consider you my colleagues.

Many thanks go to my fellow speakers on the No Fluff/Just Stuff tour. I continue to learn so much from every one of you. And many thanks to those of you who have attended one of my sessions on the NFJS tour; although I'm the one at the front of the room, I often learn a lot from you, too.

As I did in the previous edition, I'd like to thank the Phoenicians. You know what you did.

Finally, to my beautiful wife, Raymie, the love of my life and my sweetest dream: thank you for your encouragement and for putting up with yet another book project. And to my sweet and wonderful girls, Maisy and Madi: I am so proud of you and of the amazing young ladies you are becoming. I love all of you more than you can possibly know or words can express.

about this book

Spring in Action, Sixth Edition, was written to equip you to build amazing applications using the Spring Framework, Spring Boot, and a variety of ancillary members of the Spring ecosystem. It begins by showing you how to develop web-based, database-backed Java applications with Spring and Spring Boot. It then expands on the essentials by showing how to integrate with other applications and programs using reactive types. Finally, it discusses how to ready an application for deployment.

Although all of the projects in the Spring ecosystem provide excellent documentation, this book does something that none of the reference documents do: provide a hands-on, project-driven guide to bringing the elements of Spring together and build a real application.

Who should read this book

Spring in Action, Sixth Edition, is for Java developers who want to get started with Spring Boot and the Spring Framework as well as for seasoned Spring developers who want to go beyond the basics and learn the newest features of Spring.

How this book is organized: A roadmap

The book has four parts spanning 18 chapters. Part 1 covers the foundational topics of building Spring applications:

- Chapter 1 introduces Spring and Spring Boot and how to initialize a Spring project. In this chapter, you'll take the first steps toward building a Spring application that you'll expand on throughout the course of the book.

- Chapter 2 discusses building the web layer of an application using Spring MVC. In this chapter, you'll build controllers that handle web requests and views that render information in the web browser.
- Chapter 3 delves into the backend of a Spring application, where data is persisted to a relational database.
- Chapter 4 continues the subject of data persistence by looking at how to persist data to nonrelational databases, specifically, Cassandra and MongoDB.
- In chapter 5, you'll use Spring Security to authenticate users and prevent unauthorized access to an application.
- Chapter 6 reveals how to configure a Spring application using Spring Boot configuration properties. You'll also learn how to selectively apply configuration using profiles.

Part 2 covers topics that help integrate your Spring application with other applications:

- Chapter 7 expands on the discussion of Spring MVC started in chapter 2, by looking at how to write and consume REST APIs in Spring.
- Chapter 8 shows how to secure the APIs created in chapter 7, with Spring Security and OAuth 2.
- Chapter 9 looks at using asynchronous communication to enable a Spring application to both send and receive messages using the Java Message Service, RabbitMQ, or Kafka.
- Chapter 10 discusses declarative application integration using the Spring Integration project.

Part 3 explores the exciting new support for reactive programming in Spring:

- Chapter 11 introduces Project Reactor, the reactive programming library that underpins Spring 5's reactive features.
- Chapter 12 revisits REST API development, introducing Spring WebFlux, a new web framework that borrows much from Spring MVC while offering a new reactive model for web development.
- Chapter 13 takes a look at writing reactive data persistence with Spring Data to read and write data to Cassandra and Mongo databases.
- Chapter 14 introduces RSocket, a new communication protocol that offers a reactive alternative to HTTP for creating APIs.

In part 4, you'll ready an application for production and see how to deploy it:

- Chapter 15 introduces the Spring Boot Actuator, an extension to Spring Boot that exposes the internals of a running Spring application as REST endpoints.
- In chapter 16, you'll see how to use Spring Boot Admin to put a user-friendly browser-based administrative application on top of the Actuator.
- Chapter 17 discusses how to expose and consume Spring beans as JMX MBeans.

- Finally, in chapter 18, you'll see how to deploy your Spring application in a variety of production environments, including Kubernetes.

In general, developers new to Spring should start with chapter 1 and work through each chapter sequentially. Experienced Spring developers may prefer to jump in at any point that interests them. Even so, each chapter builds on the previous one, so there may be some context missing if you dive into the middle of the book.

About the code

This book contains many examples of source code, both in numbered listings and inline with normal text. In both cases, source code is formatted in a `fixed-width` `font like this` to separate it from ordinary text.

In many cases the original source code has been reformatted; we've added line breaks and reworked indentation to accommodate the available page space in the book. In rare cases, even this was not enough, and listings include line-continuation markers (⏎). Additionally, comments in the source code have often been removed from the listings when the code is described in the text. Code annotations accompany many of the listings, highlighting important concepts.

You can get executable snippets of code from the liveBook (online) version of this book at https://livebook.manning.com/book/spring-in-action-sixth-edition. The complete code for the examples in the book is available for download from the Manning website at https://www.manning.com/books/spring-in-action-sixth-edition, and from GitHub at github.com/habuma/spring-in-action-6-samples.

Book forum

Purchase of *Spring in Action, Sixth Edition,* includes free access to liveBook, Manning's online reading platform. Using liveBook's exclusive discussion features, you can attach comments to the book globally or to specific sections or paragraphs. It's a snap to make notes for yourself, ask and answer technical questions, and receive help from the author and other users. To access the forum, go to https://forums.manning.com/forums/spring-in-action-sixth-edition. You can also learn more about Manning's forums and the rules of conduct at https://forums.manning.com/forums/about.

Manning's commitment to our readers is to provide a venue where a meaningful dialogue between individual readers and between readers and the author can take place. It is not a commitment to any specific amount of participation on the part of the author, whose contribution to the forum remains voluntary (and unpaid). We suggest you try asking the author some challenging questions lest his interest stray! The forum and the archives of previous discussions will be accessible from the publisher's website as long as the book is in print.

Other online resources

Need additional help?

- The Spring website has several useful getting-started guides (some of which were written by the author of this book) at https://spring.io/guides.
- The Spring tag at Stack Overflow (https://stackoverflow.com/questions/tagged/spring) as well as the Spring-Boot tag at Stack Overflow (https://stackoverflow.com/questions/tagged/spring-boot) are great places to ask questions and help others with Spring. Helping someone else with their Spring questions is a great way to learn Spring!

about the author

CRAIG WALLS is a senior engineer with VMware. He's a zealous promoter of the Spring Framework, speaking frequently at local user groups and conferences and writing about Spring. When he's not slinging code, Craig is planning his next trip to Disney World or Disneyland and spending as much time as he can with his wife, two daughters, three dogs, and a parrot.

about the cover illustration

The figure on the cover of *Spring in Action, 6th edition*, is "Le Caraco," or an inhabitant of the province of Karak in southwest Jordan. Its capital is the city of Al-Karak, which boasts an ancient hilltop castle with magnificent views of the Dead Sea and surrounding plains. The illustration is taken from a French travel book, *Encyclopédie des voyages* by J. G. St. Sauveur, published in 1796. Travel for pleasure was a relatively new phenomenon at the time, and travel guides such as this one were popular, introducing both the tourist as well as the armchair traveler to the inhabitants of other regions of France and abroad.

The diversity of the drawings in the *Encyclopédie des voyages* speaks vividly of the distinctiveness and individuality of the world's towns and provinces just 200 years ago. This was a time when the dress codes of two regions separated by a few dozen miles identified people uniquely as belonging to one or the other. The travel guide brings to life a sense of isolation and distance of that period, and of every other historic period except our own hyperkinetic present.

Dress codes have changed since then, and the diversity by region, so rich at the time, has faded away. It is now often hard to tell the inhabitants of one continent from another. Perhaps, trying to view it optimistically, we have traded a cultural and visual diversity for a more varied personal life—or a more varied and interesting intellectual and technical life. We at Manning celebrate the inventiveness, the initiative, and the fun of the computer business with book covers based on the rich diversity of regional life two centuries ago brought back to life by the pictures from this travel guide.

Part 1

Foundational Spring

Part 1 of this book will get you started writing a Spring application, learning the foundations of Spring along the way.

In chapter 1, I'll give you a quick overview of Spring and Spring Boot essentials and show you how to initialize a Spring project as you work on building Taco Cloud, your first Spring application. In chapter 2, you'll dig deeper into the Spring MVC and learn how to present model data in the browser and how to process and validate form input. You'll also get some tips on choosing a view template library. You'll add data persistence to the Taco Cloud application in chapter 3, where we'll cover using Spring's JDBC template and how to insert data using prepared statements and key holders. Then you'll see how to declare JDBC (Java Database Connectivity) and JPA (Java Persistence API) repositories with Spring Data. Chapter 4 continues the Spring persistence story by looking at two more Spring Data modules for persisting data to Cassandra and MongoDB. Chapter 5 covers security for your Spring application, including autoconfiguring Spring Security, defining custom user storage, customizing the login page, and securing against cross-site request forgery attacks. To close out part 1, we'll look at configuration properties in chapter 6. You'll learn how to fine-tune autoconfigured beans, apply configuration properties to application components, and work with Spring profiles.

Getting started with Spring

This chapter covers
- Spring and Spring Boot essentials
- Initializing a Spring project
- An overview of the Spring landscape

Although the Greek philosopher Heraclitus wasn't well known as a software developer, he seems to have had a good handle on the subject. He has been quoted as saying, "The only constant is change." That statement captures a foundational truth of software development.

The way we develop applications today is different than it was a year ago, 5 years ago, 10 years ago, and certainly 20 years ago, before an initial form of the Spring Framework was introduced in Rod Johnson's book, *Expert One-on-One J2EE Design and Development* (Wrox, 2002, http://mng.bz/oVjy).

Back then, the most common types of applications developed were browser-based web applications, backed by relational databases. Although that type of development is still relevant—and Spring is well equipped for those kinds of applications—we're now also interested in developing applications composed of microservices destined for the cloud that persist data in a variety of databases. And a new interest in reactive programming aims to provide greater scalability and improved performance with nonblocking operations.

As software development evolved, the Spring Framework also changed to address modern development concerns, including microservices and reactive programming. The creators of Spring also set out to simplify its development model by introducing Spring Boot.

Whether you're developing a simple database-backed web application or constructing a modern application built around microservices, Spring is the framework that will help you achieve your goals. This chapter is your first step in a journey through modern application development with Spring.

1.1 *What is Spring?*

I know you're probably itching to start writing a Spring application, and I assure you that before this chapter ends, you'll have developed a simple one. But first, let me set the stage with a few basic Spring concepts that will help you understand what makes Spring tick.

Any nontrivial application comprises many components, each responsible for its own piece of the overall application functionality, coordinating with the other application elements to get the job done. When the application is run, those components somehow need to be created and introduced to each other.

At its core, Spring offers a *container*, often referred to as the *Spring application context*, that creates and manages application components. These components, or *beans*, are wired together inside the Spring application context to make a complete application, much like bricks, mortar, timber, nails, plumbing, and wiring are bound together to make a house.

The act of wiring beans together is based on a pattern known as *dependency injection* (DI). Rather than have components create and maintain the life cycle of other beans that they depend on, a dependency-injected application relies on a separate entity (the container) to create and maintain all components and inject those into the beans that need them. This is done typically through constructor arguments or property accessor methods.

For example, suppose that among an application's many components, you will address two: an inventory service (for fetching inventory levels) and a product service (for providing basic product information). The product service depends on the inventory service to be able to provide a complete set of information about products. Figure 1.1 illustrates the relationships between these beans and the Spring application context.

On top of its core container, Spring and a full portfolio of related libraries offer a web framework, a variety of data persistence options, a security framework, integration with other systems, runtime monitoring, microservice support, a reactive programming model, and many other features necessary for modern application development.

Historically, the way you would guide Spring's application context to wire beans together was with one or more XML files that described the components and their relationship to other components.

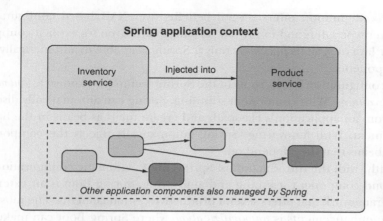

Figure 1.1 Application components are managed and injected into each other by the Spring application context.

For example, the following XML code declares two beans, an `InventoryService` bean and a `ProductService` bean, and wires the `InventoryService` bean into `ProductService` via a constructor argument:

```xml
<bean id="inventoryService"
    class="com.example.InventoryService" />

<bean id="productService"
    class="com.example.ProductService" >
  <constructor-arg ref="inventoryService" />
</bean>
```

In recent versions of Spring, however, a Java-based configuration is more common. The following Java-based configuration class is equivalent to the XML configuration:

```java
@Configuration
public class ServiceConfiguration {
  @Bean
  public InventoryService inventoryService() {
    return new InventoryService();
  }

  @Bean
  public ProductService productService() {
    return new ProductService(inventoryService());
  }
}
```

The `@Configuration` annotation indicates to Spring that this is a configuration class that will provide beans to the Spring application context.

The configuration's methods are annotated with `@Bean`, indicating that the objects they return should be added as beans in the application context (where, by default, their respective bean IDs will be the same as the names of the methods that define them).

Java-based configuration offers several benefits over XML-based configuration, including greater type safety and improved refactorability. Even so, explicit configuration with either Java or XML is necessary only if Spring is unable to automatically configure the components.

Automatic configuration has its roots in the Spring techniques known as *autowiring* and *component scanning*. With component scanning, Spring can automatically discover components from an application's classpath and create them as beans in the Spring application context. With autowiring, Spring automatically injects the components with the other beans that they depend on.

More recently, with the introduction of Spring Boot, automatic configuration has gone well beyond component scanning and autowiring. Spring Boot is an extension of the Spring Framework that offers several productivity enhancements. The most well known of these enhancements is *autoconfiguration*, where Spring Boot can make reasonable guesses at what components need to be configured and wired together, based on entries in the classpath, environment variables, and other factors.

I'd like to show you some example code that demonstrates autoconfiguration, but I can't. Autoconfiguration is much like the wind—you can see the effects of it, but there's no code that I can show you and say "Look! Here's an example of autoconfiguration!" Stuff happens, components are enabled, and functionality is provided without writing code. It's this lack of code that's essential to autoconfiguration and what makes it so wonderful.

Spring Boot autoconfiguration has dramatically reduced the amount of explicit configuration (whether with XML or Java) required to build an application. In fact, by the time you finish the example in this chapter, you'll have a working Spring application that has only a single line of Spring configuration code!

Spring Boot enhances Spring development so much that it's hard to imagine developing Spring applications without it. For that reason, this book treats Spring and Spring Boot as if they were one and the same. We'll use Spring Boot as much as possible and explicit configuration only when necessary. And, because Spring XML configuration is the old-school way of working with Spring, we'll focus primarily on Spring's Java-based configuration.

But enough of this chitchat, yakety-yak, and flimflam. This book's title includes the phrase *in action*, so let's get moving, so you can start writing your first application with Spring.

1.2 *Initializing a Spring application*

Through the course of this book, you'll create Taco Cloud, an online application for ordering the most wonderful food created by man—tacos. Of course, you'll use Spring, Spring Boot, and a variety of related libraries and frameworks to achieve this goal.

You'll find several options for initializing a Spring application. Although I could walk you through the steps of manually creating a project directory structure and defining a build specification, that's wasted time—time better spent writing application code. Therefore, you're going to lean on the Spring Initializr to bootstrap your application.

The Spring Initializr is both a browser-based web application and a REST API, which can produce a skeleton Spring project structure that you can flesh out with whatever functionality you want. Several ways to use Spring Initializr follow:

- From the web application at http://start.spring.io
- From the command line using the `curl` command
- From the command line using the Spring Boot command-line interface
- When creating a new project with Spring Tool Suite
- When creating a new project with IntelliJ IDEA
- When creating a new project with Apache NetBeans

Rather than spend several pages of this chapter talking about each one of these options, I've collected those details in the appendix. In this chapter, and throughout this book, I'll show you how to create a new project using my favorite option: Spring Initializr support in Spring Tool Suite.

As its name suggests, Spring Tool Suite is a fantastic Spring development environment that comes in the form of extensions for Eclipse, Visual Studio Code, or the Theia IDE. You can download ready-to-run binaries of Spring Tool Suite at https://spring.io/tools. Spring Tool Suite offers a handy Spring Boot Dashboard feature that makes it easy to start, restart, and stop Spring Boot applications from the IDE.

If you're not a Spring Tool Suite user, that's fine; we can still be friends. Hop over to the appendix and substitute the Initializr option that suits you best for the instructions in the following sections. But know that throughout this book, I may occasionally reference features specific to Spring Tool Suite, such as the Spring Boot Dashboard. If you're not using Spring Tool Suite, you'll need to adapt those instructions to fit your IDE.

1.2.1 Initializing a Spring project with Spring Tool Suite

To get started with a new Spring project in Spring Tool Suite, go to the File menu and select New, and then select Spring Starter Project. Figure 1.2 shows the menu structure to look for.

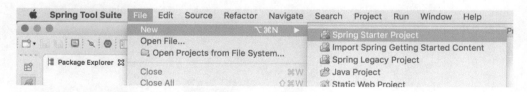

Figure 1.2 Starting a new project with the Initializr in Spring Tool Suite

Once you select Spring Starter Project, a new project wizard dialog (figure 1.3) appears. The first page in the wizard asks you for some general project information, such as the project name, description, and other essential information. If you're familiar with the contents of a Maven pom.xml file, you'll recognize most of the fields as items that end up in a Maven build specification. For the Taco Cloud application, fill in the dialog as shown in figure 1.3, and then click Next.

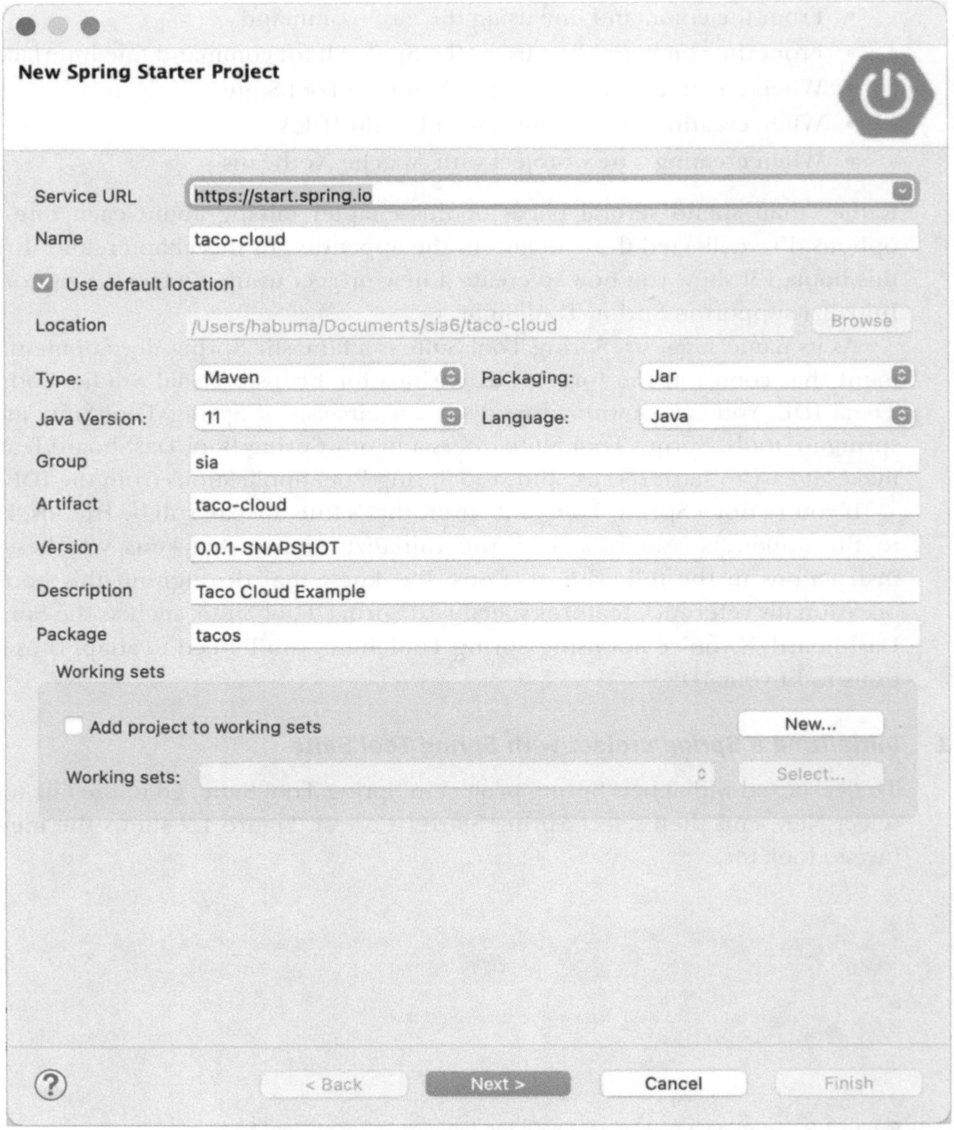

Figure 1.3   Specifying general project information for the Taco Cloud application

The next page in the wizard lets you select dependencies to add to your project (see figure 1.4). Notice that near the top of the dialog, you can select on which version of Spring Boot you want to base your project. This defaults to the most current version available. It's generally a good idea to leave it as is unless you need to target a different version.

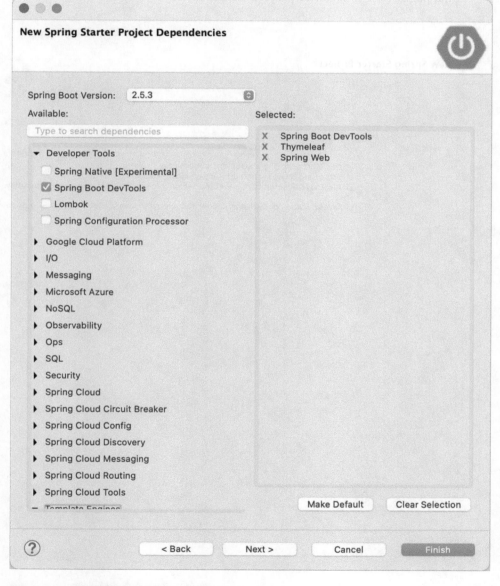

Figure 1.4 Choosing starter dependencies

As for the dependencies themselves, you can either expand the various sections and seek out the desired dependencies manually or search for them in the search box at the top of the Available list. For the Taco Cloud application, you'll start with the dependencies shown in figure 1.4.

At this point, you can click Finish to generate the project and add it to your workspace. But if you're feeling slightly adventurous, click Next one more time to see the final page of the new starter project wizard, as shown in figure 1.5.

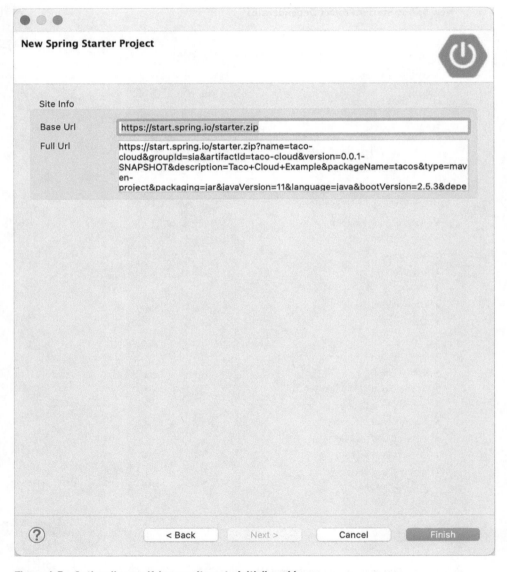

Figure 1.5 Optionally specifying an alternate Initializr address

By default, the new project wizard makes a call to the Spring Initializr at http://start .spring.io to generate the project. Generally, there's no need to override this default, which is why you could have clicked Finish on the second page of the wizard. But if for some reason you're hosting your own clone of Initializr (perhaps a local copy on your own machine or a customized clone running inside your company firewall), then you'll want to change the Base Url field to point to your Initializr instance before clicking Finish.

After you click Finish, the project is downloaded from the Initializr and loaded into your workspace. Wait a few moments for it to load and build, and then you'll be ready to start developing application functionality. But first, let's take a look at what the Initializr gave you.

1.2.2 Examining the Spring project structure

After the project loads in the IDE, expand it to see what it contains. Figure 1.6 shows the expanded Taco Cloud project in Spring Tool Suite.

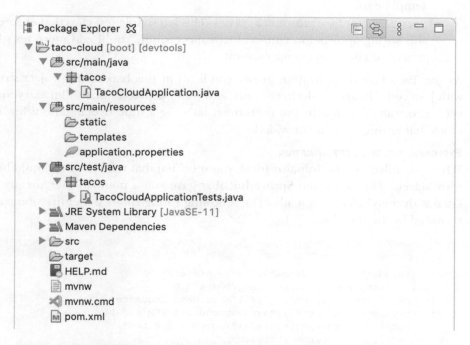

Figure 1.6   The initial Spring project structure as shown in Spring Tool Suite

You may recognize this as a typical Maven or Gradle project structure, where application source code is placed under src/main/java, test code is placed under src/test/java, and non-Java resources are placed under src/main/resources. Within that project structure, you'll want to take note of the following items:

- *mvnw* and *mvnw.cmd*—These are Maven wrapper scripts. You can use these scripts to build your project, even if you don't have Maven installed on your machine.
- *pom.xml*—This is the Maven build specification. We'll look deeper into this in a moment.
- *TacoCloudApplication.java*—This is the Spring Boot main class that boot-straps the project. We'll take a closer look at this class in a moment.
- *application.properties*—This file is initially empty but offers a place where you can specify configuration properties. We'll tinker with this file a little in this chapter, but I'll postpone a detailed explanation of configuration properties to chapter 6.
- *static*—This folder is where you can place any static content (images, stylesheets, JavaScript, and so forth) that you want to serve to the browser. It's initially empty.
- *templates*—This folder is where you'll place template files that will be used to render content to the browser. It's initially empty, but you'll add a Thymeleaf template soon.
- *TacoCloudApplicationTests.java*—This is a simple test class that ensures that the Spring application context loads successfully. You'll add more tests to the mix as you develop the application.

As the Taco Cloud application grows, you'll fill in this barebones project structure with Java code, images, stylesheets, tests, and other collateral that will make your project more complete. But in the meantime, let's dig a little deeper into a few of the items that Spring Initializr provided.

EXPLORING THE BUILD SPECIFICATION

When you filled out the Initializr form, you specified that your project should be built with Maven. Therefore, the Spring Initializr gave you a pom.xml file already populated with the choices you made. The following listing shows the entire pom.xml file provided by the Initializr.

Listing 1.1   The initial Maven build specification

```
<?xml version="1.0" encoding="UTF-8"?><project
    xmlns="http://maven.apache.org/POM/4.0.0"
  xmlns:xsi="http://www.w3.org/2001/XMLSchema-instance"
  xsi:schemaLocation="http://maven.apache.org/POM/4.0.0
        https://maven.apache.org/xsd/maven-4.0.0.xsd">
  <modelVersion>4.0.0</modelVersion>
  <parent>
    <groupId>org.springframework.boot</groupId>
    <artifactId>spring-boot-starter-parent</artifactId>
    <version>2.5.3</version>                    ⟵──┐ Spring Boot
    <relativePath />                                │ version
  </parent>
  <groupId>sia</groupId>
  <artifactId>taco-cloud</artifactId>
```

```xml
<version>0.0.1-SNAPSHOT</version>
<name>taco-cloud</name>
<description>Taco Cloud Example</description>

<properties>
  <java.version>11</java.version>
</properties>

<dependencies>
  <dependency>
    <groupId>org.springframework.boot</groupId>
    <artifactId>spring-boot-starter-thymeleaf</artifactId>
  </dependency>

  <dependency>
    <groupId>org.springframework.boot</groupId>
    <artifactId>spring-boot-starter-web</artifactId>
  </dependency>

  <dependency>
    <groupId>org.springframework.boot</groupId>
    <artifactId>spring-boot-devtools</artifactId>
    <scope>runtime</scope>
    <optional>true</optional>
  </dependency>

  <dependency>
    <groupId>org.springframework.boot</groupId>
    <artifactId>spring-boot-starter-test</artifactId>
    <scope>test</scope>
    <exclusions>
      <exclusion>
        <groupId>org.junit.vintage</groupId>
        <artifactId>junit-vintage-engine</artifactId>
      </exclusion>
    </exclusions>
  </dependency>

</dependencies>

<build>
  <plugins>
    <plugin>
      <groupId>org.springframework.boot</groupId>
      <artifactId>spring-boot-maven-plugin</artifactId>
    </plugin>
  </plugins>
</build>

<repositories>
  <repository>
    <id>spring-milestones</id>
    <name>Spring Milestones</name>
    <url>https://repo.spring.io/milestone</url>
  </repository>
```

Starter dependencies

Spring Boot plugin

```
  </repositories>
  <pluginRepositories>
    <pluginRepository>
      <id>spring-milestones</id>
      <name>Spring Milestones</name>
      <url>https://repo.spring.io/milestone</url>
    </pluginRepository>
  </pluginRepositories>

</project>
```

The first thing to take note of is the <parent> element and, more specifically, its <version> child. This specifies that your project has spring-boot-starter-parent as its parent POM. Among other things, this parent POM provides dependency management for several libraries commonly used in Spring projects. For those libraries covered by the parent POM, you won't have to specify a version, because it's inherited from the parent. The version, 2.5.6, indicates that you're using Spring Boot 2.5.6 and, thus, will inherit dependency management as defined by that version of Spring Boot. Among other things, Spring Boot's dependency management for version 2.5.6 specifies that the underlying version of the core Spring Framework will be 5.3.12.

While we're on the subject of dependencies, note that there are four dependencies declared under the <dependencies> element. The first three should look somewhat familiar to you. They correspond directly to the Spring Web, Thymeleaf, and Spring Boot DevTools dependencies that you selected before clicking the Finish button in the Spring Tool Suite new project wizard. The other dependency is one that provides a lot of helpful testing capabilities. You didn't have to check a box for it to be included because the Spring Initializr assumes (hopefully, correctly) that you'll be writing tests.

You may also notice that all dependencies except for the DevTools dependency have the word *starter* in their artifact ID. Spring Boot starter dependencies are special in that they typically don't have any library code themselves but instead transitively pull in other libraries. These starter dependencies offer the following primary benefits:

- Your build file will be significantly smaller and easier to manage because you won't need to declare a dependency on every library you might need.
- You're able to think of your dependencies in terms of what capabilities they provide, rather than their library names. If you're developing a web application, you'll add the web starter dependency rather than a laundry list of individual libraries that enable you to write a web application.
- You're freed from the burden of worrying about library versions. You can trust that the versions of the libraries brought in transitively will be compatible for a given version of Spring Boot. You need to worry only about which version of Spring Boot you're using.

Finally, the build specification ends with the Spring Boot plugin. This plugin performs a few important functions, described next:

- It provides a Maven goal that enables you to run the application using Maven.
- It ensures that all dependency libraries are included within the executable JAR file and available on the runtime classpath.
- It produces a manifest file in the JAR file that denotes the bootstrap class (TacoCloudApplication, in your case) as the main class for the executable JAR.

Speaking of the bootstrap class, let's open it up and take a closer look.

BOOTSTRAPPING THE APPLICATION

Because you'll be running the application from an executable JAR, it's important to have a main class that will be executed when that JAR file is run. You'll also need at least a minimal amount of Spring configuration to bootstrap the application. That's what you'll find in the TacoCloudApplication class, shown in the following listing.

Listing 1.2   The Taco Cloud bootstrap class

```
package tacos;

import org.springframework.boot.SpringApplication;
import org.springframework.boot.autoconfigure.SpringBootApplication;

@SpringBootApplication                                          ◁─── Spring Boot
public class TacoCloudApplication {                                   application

  public static void main(String[] args) {
    SpringApplication.run(TacoCloudApplication.class, args);   ◁─── Runs the
  }                                                                 application

}
```

Although there's little code in TacoCloudApplication, what's there packs quite a punch. One of the most powerful lines of code is also one of the shortest. The @SpringBootApplication annotation clearly signifies that this is a Spring Boot application. But there's more to @SpringBootApplication than meets the eye.

@SpringBootApplication is a composite annotation that combines the following three annotations:

- *@SpringBootConfiguration*—Designates this class as a configuration class. Although there's not much configuration in the class yet, you can add Java-based Spring Framework configuration to this class if you need to. This annotation is, in fact, a specialized form of the @Configuration annotation.
- *@EnableAutoConfiguration*—Enables Spring Boot automatic configuration. We'll talk more about autoconfiguration later. For now, know that this annotation tells Spring Boot to automatically configure any components that it thinks you'll need.

- *@ComponentScan*—Enables component scanning. This lets you declare other classes with annotations like @Component, @Controller, and @Service to have Spring automatically discover and register them as components in the Spring application context.

The other important piece of TacoCloudApplication is the main() method. This is the method that will be run when the JAR file is executed. For the most part, this method is boilerplate code; every Spring Boot application you write will have a method similar or identical to this one (class name differences notwithstanding).

The main() method calls a static run() method on the SpringApplication class, which performs the actual bootstrapping of the application, creating the Spring application context. The two parameters passed to the run() method are a configuration class and the command-line arguments. Although it's not necessary that the configuration class passed to run() be the same as the bootstrap class, this is the most convenient and typical choice.

Chances are you won't need to change anything in the bootstrap class. For simple applications, you might find it convenient to configure one or two other components in the bootstrap class, but for most applications, you're better off creating a separate configuration class for anything that isn't autoconfigured. You'll define several configuration classes throughout the course of this book, so stay tuned for details.

TESTING THE APPLICATION

Testing is an important part of software development. You can always test your project manually by building it and then running it from the command line like this:

```
$ ./mvnw package
...
$ java -jar target/taco-cloud-0.0.1-SNAPSHOT.jar
```

Or, because we're using Spring Boot, the Spring Boot Maven plugin makes it even easier, as shown next:

```
$ ./mvnw spring-boot:run
```

But manual testing implies that there's a human involved and thus potential for human error and inconsistent testing. Automated tests are more consistent and repeatable.

Recognizing this, the Spring Initializr gives you a test class to get started. The following listing shows the baseline test class.

| Listing 1.3   A baseline application test |

```
package tacos;

import org.junit.jupiter.api.Test;
import org.springframework.boot.test.context.SpringBootTest;
```

```
@SpringBootTest                                      ⟵  A Spring
public class TacoCloudApplicationTests {                Boot test

    @Test                                       ⟵  The test
    public void contextLoads() {                   method
    }

}
```

There's not much to be seen in `TacoCloudApplicationTests`: the one test method in the class is empty. Even so, this test class does perform an essential check to ensure that the Spring application context can be loaded successfully. If you make any changes that prevent the Spring application context from being created, this test fails, and you can react by fixing the problem.

The `@SpringBootTest` annotation tells JUnit to bootstrap the test with Spring Boot capabilities. Just like `@SpringBootApplication`, `@SpringBootTest` is a composite annotation, which is itself annotated with `@ExtendWith(SpringExtension.class)`, to add Spring testing capabilities to JUnit 5. For now, though, it's enough to think of this as the test class equivalent of calling `SpringApplication.run()` in a `main()` method. Over the course of this book, you'll see `@SpringBootTest` several times, and we'll uncover some of its power.

Finally, there's the test method itself. Although `@SpringBootTest` is tasked with loading the Spring application context for the test, it won't have anything to do if there aren't any test methods. Even without any assertions or code of any kind, this empty test method will prompt the two annotations to do their job and load the Spring application context. If there are any problems in doing so, the test fails.

To run this and any test classes from the command line, you can use the following Maven incantation:

```
$ ./mvnw test
```

At this point, we've concluded our review of the code provided by the Spring Initializr. You've seen some of the boilerplate foundation that you can use to develop a Spring application, but you still haven't written a single line of code. Now it's time to fire up your IDE, dust off your keyboard, and add some custom code to the Taco Cloud application.

1.3 Writing a Spring application

Because you're just getting started, we'll start off with a relatively small change to the Taco Cloud application, but one that will demonstrate a lot of Spring's goodness. It seems appropriate that as you're just starting, the first feature you'll add to the Taco Cloud application is a home page. As you add the home page, you'll create the following two code artifacts:

- A controller class that handles requests for the home page
- A view template that defines what the home page looks like

And because testing is important, you'll also write a simple test class to test the home page. But first things first … let's write that controller.

1.3.1 Handling web requests

Spring comes with a powerful web framework known as Spring MVC. At the center of Spring MVC is the concept of a *controller*, a class that handles requests and responds with information of some sort. In the case of a browser-facing application, a controller responds by optionally populating model data and passing the request on to a view to produce HTML that's returned to the browser.

You're going to learn a lot about Spring MVC in chapter 2. But for now, you'll write a simple controller class that handles requests for the root path (for example, /) and forwards those requests to the home page view without populating any model data. The following listing shows the simple controller class.

Listing 1.4   The home page controller

```
package tacos;

import org.springframework.stereotype.Controller;
import org.springframework.web.bind.annotation.GetMapping;

@Controller                       ◁─────  The controller
public class HomeController {

  @GetMapping("/")          ◁──────┐  Handles requests
  public String home() {           │  for the root path /
    return "home";          ◁──┐  Returns the
  }                             │  view name

}
```

As you can see, this class is annotated with `@Controller`. On its own, `@Controller` doesn't do much. Its primary purpose is to identify this class as a component for component scanning. Because `HomeController` is annotated with `@Controller`, Spring's component scanning automatically discovers it and creates an instance of Home-Controller as a bean in the Spring application context.

In fact, a handful of other annotations (including `@Component`, `@Service`, and `@Repository`) serve a purpose similar to `@Controller`. You could have just as effectively annotated `HomeController` with any of those other annotations, and it would have still worked the same. The choice of `@Controller` is, however, more descriptive of this component's role in the application.

The `home()` method is as simple as controller methods come. It's annotated with `@GetMapping` to indicate that if an HTTP GET request is received for the root path /, then this method should handle that request. It does so by doing nothing more than returning a `String` value of home.

This value is interpreted as the logical name of a view. How that view is implemented depends on a few factors, but because Thymeleaf is in your classpath, you can define that template with Thymeleaf.

Why Thymeleaf?

You may be wondering why I chose Thymeleaf for a template engine. Why not JSP? Why not FreeMarker? Why not one of several other options?

Put simply, I had to choose something, and I like Thymeleaf and generally prefer it over those other options. And even though JSP may seem like an obvious choice, there are some challenges to overcome when using JSP with Spring Boot. I didn't want to go down that rabbit hole in chapter 1. Hang tight. We'll look at other template options, including JSP, in chapter 2.

The template name is derived from the logical view name by prefixing it with /templates/ and postfixing it with .html. The resulting path for the template is /templates/home.html. Therefore, you'll need to place the template in your project at /src/main/resources/templates/home.html. Let's create that template now.

1.3.2 Defining the view

In the interest of keeping your home page simple, it should do nothing more than welcome users to the site. The next listing shows the basic Thymeleaf template that defines the Taco Cloud home page.

Listing 1.5 The Taco Cloud home page template

```
<!DOCTYPE html>
<html xmlns="http://www.w3.org/1999/xhtml"
      xmlns:th="http://www.thymeleaf.org">
  <head>
    <title>Taco Cloud</title>
  </head>

  <body>
    <h1>Welcome to...</h1>
    <img th:src="@{/images/TacoCloud.png}"/>
  </body>
</html>
```

There's not much to discuss with regard to this template. The only notable line of code is the one with the `<img>` tag to display the Taco Cloud logo. It uses a Thymeleaf `th:src` attribute and an `@{...}` expression to reference the image with a context-relative path. Aside from that, it's not much more than a Hello World page.

Let's talk about that image a bit more. I'll leave it up to you to define a Taco Cloud logo that you like. But you'll need to make sure you place it at the right place within the project.

The image is referenced with the context-relative path /images/TacoCloud.png. As you'll recall from our review of the project structure, static content, such as images, is kept in the /src/main/resources/static folder. That means that the Taco Cloud logo image must also reside within the project at /src/main/resources/static/images/TacoCloud.png.

Now that you've got a controller to handle requests for the home page and a view template to render the home page, you're almost ready to fire up the application and see it in action. But first, let's see how you can write a test against the controller.

1.3.3 *Testing the controller*

Testing web applications can be tricky when making assertions against the content of an HTML page. Fortunately, Spring comes with some powerful test support that makes testing a web application easy.

For the purposes of the home page, you'll write a test that's comparable in complexity to the home page itself. Your test will perform an HTTP GET request for the root path / and expect a successful result where the view name is home and the resulting content contains the phrase "Welcome to...." The following code should do the trick.

Listing 1.6 A test for the home page controller

```
package tacos;

import static org.hamcrest.Matchers.containsString;
import static
    org.springframework.test.web.servlet.request.MockMvcRequestBuilders.get;
import static
    org.springframework.test.web.servlet.result.MockMvcResultMatchers.content;
import static
    org.springframework.test.web.servlet.result.MockMvcResultMatchers.status;
import static
    org.springframework.test.web.servlet.result.MockMvcResultMatchers.view;

import org.junit.jupiter.api.Test;
import org.springframework.beans.factory.annotation.Autowired;
import org.springframework.boot.test.autoconfigure.web.servlet.WebMvcTest;
import org.springframework.test.web.servlet.MockMvc;

@WebMvcTest(HomeController.class)          ⟵┐  Web test for
public class HomeControllerTest {           │  HomeController

    @Autowired
    private MockMvc mockMvc;    ⟵——— Injects MockMvc

    @Test                                          ┌─ Performs GET /
    public void testHomePage() throws Exception {  │
      mockMvc.perform(get("/"))          ⟵────────┘
        .andExpect(status().isOk())        ⟵         Expects HTTP 200
        .andExpect(view().name("home"))    ⟵——— Expects home view
        .andExpect(content().string(       ⟵
            containsString("Welcome to...")));    │  Expects Welcome to...
```

```
    }

}
```

The first thing you might notice about this test is that it differs slightly from the Taco-
CloudApplicationTests class with regard to the annotations applied to it. Instead of
@SpringBootTest markup, HomeControllerTest is annotated with @WebMvcTest. This
is a special test annotation provided by Spring Boot that arranges for the test to run in
the context of a Spring MVC application. More specifically, in this case, it arranges for
HomeController to be registered in Spring MVC so that you can send requests to it.

@WebMvcTest also sets up Spring support for testing Spring MVC. Although it could
be made to start a server, mocking the mechanics of Spring MVC is sufficient for your
purposes. The test class is injected with a MockMvc object (thanks to the @Autowired
annotation) for the test to drive the mockup.

The testHomePage() method defines the test you want to perform against the
home page. It starts with the MockMvc object to perform an HTTP GET request for /
(the root path). From that request, it sets the following expectations:

- The response should have an HTTP 200 (OK) status.
- The view should have a logical name of home.
- The rendered view should contain the text "Welcome to…."

You can run the test in your IDE of choice or with Maven like this:

```
$ mvnw test
```

If, after the MockMvc object performs the request, any of those expectations aren't
met, then the test will fail. But your controller and view template are written to satisfy
those expectations, so the test should pass with flying colors—or at least with some
shade of green indicating a passing test.

The controller has been written, the view template created, and you have a passing
test. It seems that you've implemented the home page successfully. But even though
the test passes, there's something slightly more satisfying with seeing the results in a
browser. After all, that's how Taco Cloud customers are going to see it. Let's build the
application and run it.

1.3.4 Building and running the application

Just as we have several ways to initialize a Spring application, we also have several ways
to run one. If you like, you can flip over to the appendix to read about some of the
more common ways to run a Spring Boot application.

Because you chose to use Spring Tool Suite to initialize and work on the project,
you have a handy feature called the Spring Boot Dashboard available to help you run
your application inside the IDE. The Spring Boot Dashboard appears as a tab, typically near the bottom left of the IDE window. Figure 1.7 shows an annotated screenshot of the Spring Boot Dashboard.

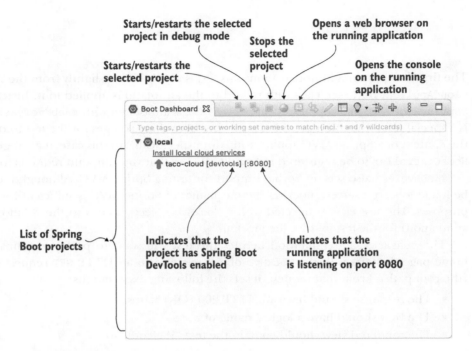

Figure 1.7 Highlights of the Spring Boot Dashboard

I don't want to spend much time going over everything the Spring Boot Dashboard does, although figure 1.7 covers some of the most useful details. The important thing to know right now is how to use it to run the Taco Cloud application. Make sure `taco-cloud` application is highlighted in the list of projects (it's the only application shown in figure 1.7), and then click the start button (the left-most button with both a green triangle and a red square). The application should start right up.

As the application starts, you'll see some Spring ASCII art fly by in the console, followed by some log entries describing the steps as the application starts. Before the logging stops, you'll see a log entry saying Tomcat started on port(s): 8080 (http), which means that you're ready to point your web browser at the home page to see the fruits of your labor.

Wait a minute. Tomcat started? When did you deploy the application to a Tomcat web server?

Spring Boot applications tend to bring everything they need with them and don't need to be deployed to some application server. You never deployed your application to Tomcat—Tomcat is a part of your application! (I'll describe the details of how Tomcat became part of your application in section 1.3.6.)

Now that the application has started, point your web browser to http://local-host:8080 (or click the globe button in the Spring Boot Dashboard) and you should see something like figure 1.8. Your results may be different if you designed your own logo image, but it shouldn't vary much from what you see in figure 1.8.

Figure 1.8 The Taco Cloud home page

It may not be much to look at. But this isn't exactly a book on graphic design. The humble appearance of the home page is more than sufficient for now. And it provides you a solid start on getting to know Spring.

One thing I've glossed over up until now is DevTools. You selected it as a dependency when initializing your project. It appears as a dependency in the generated pom.xml file. And the Spring Boot Dashboard even shows that the project has DevTools enabled. But what is DevTools, and what does it do for you? Let's take a quick survey of a couple of DevTools's most useful features.

1.3.5 Getting to know Spring Boot DevTools

As its name suggests, DevTools provides Spring developers with some handy development-time tools. Among those are the following:

- Automatic application restart when code changes
- Automatic browser refresh when browser-destined resources (such as templates, JavaScript, stylesheets, and so on) change
- Automatic disabling of template caches
- Built in H2 Console, if the H2 database is in use

It's important to understand that DevTools isn't an IDE plugin, nor does it require that you use a specific IDE. It works equally well in Spring Tool Suite, IntelliJ IDEA, and NetBeans. Furthermore, because it's intended only for development purposes, it's smart enough to disable itself when deploying in a production setting. We'll discuss how it does this when you get around to deploying your application in chapter 18. For now, let's focus on the most useful features of Spring Boot DevTools, starting with automatic application restart.

AUTOMATIC APPLICATION RESTART

With DevTools as part of your project, you'll be able to make changes to Java code and properties files in the project and see those changes applied after a brief moment. DevTools monitors for changes, and when it sees something has changed, it automatically restarts the application.

More precisely, when DevTools is active, the application is loaded into two separate class loaders in the Java virtual machine (JVM). One class loader is loaded with your Java code, property files, and pretty much anything that's in the src/main/ path of the project. These are items that are likely to change frequently. The other class loader is loaded with dependency libraries, which aren't likely to change as often.

When a change is detected, DevTools reloads only the class loader containing your project code and restarts the Spring application context but leaves the other class loader and the JVM intact. Although subtle, this strategy affords a small reduction in the time it takes to start the application.

The downside of this strategy is that changes to dependencies won't be available in automatic restarts. That's because the class loader containing dependency libraries isn't automatically reloaded. Any time you add, change, or remove a dependency in your build specification, you'll need to do a hard restart of the application for those changes to take effect.

AUTOMATIC BROWSER REFRESH AND TEMPLATE CACHE DISABLE

By default, template options such as Thymeleaf and FreeMarker are configured to cache the results of template parsing so that templates don't need to be reparsed with every request they serve. This is great in production, because it buys a bit of a performance benefit.

Cached templates, however, are not so great at development time. They make it impossible to make changes to the templates while the application is running and see the results after refreshing the browser. Even if you've made changes, the cached template will still be in use until you restart the application.

DevTools addresses this issue by automatically disabling all template caching. Make as many changes as you want to your templates and know that you're only a browser refresh away from seeing the results.

But if you're like me, you don't even want to be burdened with the effort of clicking the browser's refresh button. It'd be much nicer if you could make the changes and witness the results in the browser immediately. Fortunately, DevTools has something special for those of us who are too lazy to click a refresh button.

DevTools automatically enables a LiveReload server (http://livereload.com/) along with your application. By itself, the LiveReload server isn't very useful. But when coupled with a corresponding LiveReload browser plugin, it causes your browser to automatically refresh when changes are made to templates, images, stylesheets, JavaScript, and so on—in fact, almost anything that ends up being served to your browser.

LiveReload has browser plugins for Google Chrome, Safari, and Firefox browsers. (Sorry, Internet Explorer and Edge fans.) Visit http://livereload.com/extensions/ to find information on how to install LiveReload for your browser.

BUILT-IN H2 CONSOLE

Although your project doesn't yet use a database, that will change in chapter 3. If you choose to use the H2 database for development, DevTools will also automatically enable an H2 console that you can access from your web browser. You only need to point your web browser to http://localhost:8080/h2-console to gain insight into the data your application is working with.

At this point, you've written a complete, albeit simple, Spring application. You'll expand on it throughout the course of the book. But now is a good time to step back and review what you've accomplished and how Spring played a part.

1.3.6 Let's review

Think back on how you got to this point. In short, you've taken the following steps to build your Taco Cloud Spring application:

- You created an initial project structure using the Spring Initializr.
- You wrote a controller class to handle the home page request.
- You defined a view template to render the home page.
- You wrote a simple test class to prove your work.

Seems pretty straightforward, doesn't it? With the exception of the first step to bootstrap the project, each action you've taken has been keenly focused on achieving the goal of producing a home page.

In fact, almost every line of code you've written is aimed toward that goal. Not counting Java `import` statements, I count only two lines of code in your controller class and no lines in the view template that are Spring-specific. And although the bulk of the test class utilizes Spring testing support, it seems a little less invasive in the context of a test.

That's an important benefit of developing with Spring. You can focus on the code that meets the requirements of an application, rather than on satisfying the demands of a framework. Although you'll no doubt need to write some framework-specific code from time to time, it'll usually be only a small fraction of your codebase. As I said before, Spring (with Spring Boot) can be considered the *frameworkless framework*.

How does this even work? What is Spring doing behind the scenes to make sure your application needs are met? To understand what Spring is doing, let's start by looking at the build specification.

In the pom.xml file, you declared a dependency on the `Web` and `Thymeleaf` starters. These two dependencies transitively brought in a handful of other dependencies, including the following:

- Spring's MVC framework
- Embedded Tomcat
- Thymeleaf and the Thymeleaf layout dialect

It also brought Spring Boot's autoconfiguration library along for the ride. When the application starts, Spring Boot autoconfiguration detects those libraries and automatically performs the following tasks:

- Configures the beans in the Spring application context to enable Spring MVC
- Configures the embedded Tomcat server in the Spring application context
- Configures a Thymeleaf view resolver for rendering Spring MVC views with Thymeleaf templates

In short, autoconfiguration does all the grunt work, leaving you to focus on writing code that implements your application functionality. That's a pretty sweet arrangement, if you ask me!

Your Spring journey has just begun. The Taco Cloud application only touched on a small portion of what Spring has to offer. Before you take your next step, let's survey the Spring landscape and see what landmarks you'll encounter on your journey.

1.4   Surveying the Spring landscape

To get an idea of the Spring landscape, look no further than the enormous list of checkboxes on the full version of the Spring Initializr web form. It lists over 100 dependency choices, so I won't try to list them all here or to provide a screenshot. But I encourage you to take a look. In the meantime, I'll mention a few of the highlights.

1.4.1   The core Spring Framework

As you might expect, the core Spring Framework is the foundation of everything else in the Spring universe. It provides the core container and dependency injection framework. But it also provides a few other essential features.

Among these is Spring MVC, Spring's web framework. You've already seen how to use Spring MVC to write a controller class to handle web requests. What you've not yet seen, however, is that Spring MVC can also be used to create REST APIs that produce non-HTML output. We're going to dig more into Spring MVC in chapter 2 and then take another look at how to use it to create REST APIs in chapter 7.

The core Spring Framework also offers some elemental data persistence support, specifically, template-based JDBC support. You'll see how to use `JdbcTemplate` in chapter 3.

Spring includes support for reactive-style programming, including a new reactive web framework called Spring WebFlux that borrows heavily from Spring MVC. You'll look at Spring's reactive programming model in part 3 and Spring WebFlux specifically in chapter 12.

1.4.2 Spring Boot

We've already seen many of the benefits of Spring Boot, including starter dependencies and autoconfiguration. Be certain that we'll use as much of Spring Boot as possible throughout this book and avoid any form of explicit configuration, unless it's absolutely necessary. But in addition to starter dependencies and autoconfiguration, Spring Boot also offers the following other useful features:

- The Actuator provides runtime insight into the inner workings of an application, including metrics, thread dump information, application health, and environment properties available to the application.
- Flexible specification of environment properties.
- Additional testing support on top of the testing assistance found in the core framework.

What's more, Spring Boot offers an alternative programming model based on Groovy scripts that's called the Spring Boot CLI (command-line interface). With the Spring Boot CLI, you can write entire applications as a collection of Groovy scripts and run them from the command line. We won't spend much time with the Spring Boot CLI, but we'll touch on it on occasion when it fits our needs.

Spring Boot has become such an integral part of Spring development that I can't imagine developing a Spring application without it. Consequently, this book takes a Spring Boot–centric view, and you might catch me using the word *Spring* when I'm referring to something that Spring Boot is doing.

1.4.3 Spring Data

Although the core Spring Framework comes with basic data persistence support, Spring Data provides something quite amazing: the ability to define your application's data repositories as simple Java interfaces, using a naming convention when defining methods to drive how data is stored and retrieved.

What's more, Spring Data is capable of working with several different kinds of databases, including relational (via JDBC or JPA), document (Mongo), graph (Neo4j), and others. You'll use Spring Data to help create repositories for the Taco Cloud application in chapter 3.

1.4.4 Spring Security

Application security has always been an important topic, and it seems to become more important every day. Fortunately, Spring has a robust security framework in Spring Security.

Spring Security addresses a broad range of application security needs, including authentication, authorization, and API security. Although the scope of Spring Security is too large to be properly covered in this book, we'll touch on some of the most common use cases in chapters 5 and 12.

1.4.5   Spring Integration and Spring Batch

At some point, most applications will need to integrate with other applications or even with other components of the same application. Several patterns of application integration have emerged to address these needs. Spring Integration and Spring Batch provide the implementation of these patterns for Spring applications.

Spring Integration addresses real-time integration where data is processed as it's made available. In contrast, Spring Batch addresses batched integration where data is allowed to collect for a time until some trigger (perhaps a time trigger) signals that it's time for the batch of data to be processed. You'll explore Spring Integration in chapter 10.

1.4.6   Spring Cloud

The application development world is entering a new era where we'll no longer develop our applications as single-deployment, unit monoliths and will instead compose applications from several individual deployment units known as *microservices*.

Microservices are a hot topic, addressing several practical development and runtime concerns. In doing so, however, they bring to fore their own challenges. Those challenges are met head-on by Spring Cloud, a collection of projects for developing cloud-native applications with Spring.

Spring Cloud covers a lot of ground, and it'd be impossible to cover it all in this book. For a complete discussion of Spring Cloud, I suggest taking a look at *Cloud Native Spring in Action* by Thomas Vitale (Manning, 2020, www.manning.com/books/cloud-native-spring-in-action).

1.4.7   Spring Native

A relatively new development in Spring is the Spring Native project. This experimental project enables compilation of Spring Boot projects into native executables using the GraalVM native-image compiler, resulting in images that start significantly faster and have a lighter footprint.

For more information on Spring Native, see https://github.com/spring-projects-experimental/spring-native.

Summary

- Spring aims to make developer challenges easy, like creating web applications, working with databases, securing applications, and microservices.
- Spring Boot builds on top of Spring to make Spring even easier with simplified dependency management, automatic configuration, and runtime insights.
- Spring applications can be initialized using the Spring Initializr, which is web-based and supported natively in most Java development environments.
- The components, commonly referred to as beans, in a Spring application context can be declared explicitly with Java or XML, discovered by component scanning, or automatically configured with Spring Boot autoconfigurations.

Developing web applications

This chapter covers

- Presenting model data in the browser
- Processing and validating form input
- Choosing a view template library

First impressions are important. Curb appeal can sell a house long before the home buyer enters the door. A car's cherry red paint job will turn more heads than what's under the hood. And literature is replete with stories of love at first sight. What's inside is important, but what's outside—what's seen first—is also important.

The applications you'll build with Spring will do all kinds of things, including crunching data, reading information from a database, and interacting with other applications. But the first impression your application users will get comes from the user interface. And in many applications, that UI is a web application presented in a browser.

In chapter 1, you created your first Spring MVC controller to display your application home page. But Spring MVC can do far more than simply display static content. In this chapter, you'll develop the first major bit of functionality in your Taco Cloud application—the ability to design custom tacos. In doing so, you'll dig deeper into Spring MVC, and you'll see how to display model data and process form input.

2.1 *Displaying information*

Fundamentally, Taco Cloud is a place where you can order tacos online. But more than that, Taco Cloud wants to enable its customers to express their creative side and design custom tacos from a rich palette of ingredients.

Therefore, the Taco Cloud web application needs a page that displays the selection of ingredients for taco artists to choose from. The ingredient choices may change at any time, so they shouldn't be hardcoded into an HTML page. Rather, the list of available ingredients should be fetched from a database and handed over to the page to be displayed to the customer.

In a Spring web application, it's a controller's job to fetch and process data. And it's a view's job to render that data into HTML that will be displayed in the browser. You're going to create the following components in support of the taco creation page:

- A domain class that defines the properties of a taco ingredient
- A Spring MVC controller class that fetches ingredient information and passes it along to the view
- A view template that renders a list of ingredients in the user's browser

The relationship between these components is illustrated in figure 2.1.

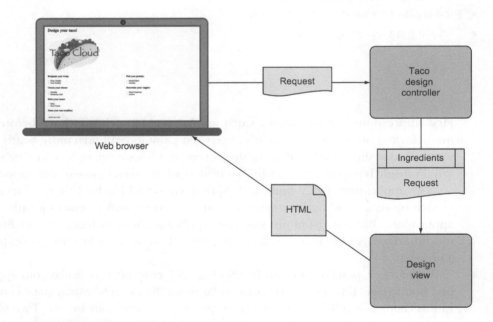

Figure 2.1   A typical Spring MVC request flow

Because this chapter focuses on Spring's web framework, we'll defer any of the database stuff to chapter 3. For now, the controller is solely responsible for providing the ingredients to the view. In chapter 3, you'll rework the controller to collaborate with a repository that fetches ingredients data from a database.

Before you write the controller and view, let's hammer out the domain type that represents an ingredient. This will establish a foundation on which you can develop your web components.

2.1.1 Establishing the domain

An application's domain is the subject area that it addresses—the ideas and concepts that influence the understanding of the application.[1] In the Taco Cloud application, the domain includes such objects as taco designs, the ingredients that those designs are composed of, customers, and taco orders placed by the customers. Figure 2.2 shows these entities and how they are related.

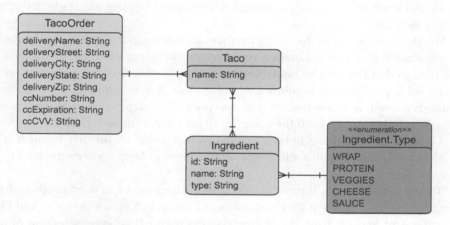

Figure 2.2   The Taco Cloud domain

To get started, we'll focus on taco ingredients. In your domain, taco ingredients are fairly simple objects. Each has a name as well as a type so that it can be visually categorized (proteins, cheeses, sauces, and so on). Each also has an ID by which it can easily and unambiguously be referenced. The following `Ingredient` class defines the domain object you need.

Listing 2.1   Defining taco ingredients

```
package tacos;

import lombok.Data;
```

---

[1] For a much more in-depth discussion of application domains, I suggest Eric Evans's *Domain-Driven Design* (Addison-Wesley Professional, 2003).

```
@Data
public class Ingredient {

  private final String id;
  private final String name;
  private final Type type;

  public enum Type {
    WRAP, PROTEIN, VEGGIES, CHEESE, SAUCE
  }

}
```

As you can see, this is a run-of-the-mill Java domain class, defining the three properties needed to describe an ingredient. Perhaps the most unusual thing about the Ingredient class as defined in listing 2.1 is that it seems to be missing the usual set of getter and setter methods, not to mention useful methods like equals(), hashCode(), toString(), and others.

You don't see them in the listing partly to save space, but also because you're using an amazing library called Lombok to automatically generate those methods at compile time so that they will be available at run time. In fact, the @Data annotation at the class level is provided by Lombok and tells Lombok to generate all of those missing methods as well as a constructor that accepts all final properties as arguments. By using Lombok, you can keep the code for Ingredient slim and trim.

Lombok isn't a Spring library, but it's so incredibly useful that I find it hard to develop without it. Plus, it's a lifesaver when I need to keep code examples in a book short and sweet.

To use Lombok, you'll need to add it as a dependency in your project. If you're using Spring Tool Suite, it's an easy matter of right-clicking on the pom.xml file and selecting Add Starters from the Spring context menu. The same selection of dependencies you were given in chapter 1 (in figure 1.4) will appear, giving you a chance to add or change your selected dependencies. Find Lombok under Developer Tools, make sure it's selected, and click OK; Spring Tool Suite automatically adds it to your build specification.

Alternatively, you can manually add it with the following entry in pom.xml:

```
<dependency>
    <groupId>org.projectlombok</groupId>
    <artifactId>lombok</artifactId>
</dependency>
```

If you decide to manually add Lombok to your build, you'll also want to exclude it from the Spring Boot Maven plugin in the <build> section of the pom.xml file:

```
<build>
  <plugins>
    <plugin>
      <groupId>org.springframework.boot</groupId>
      <artifactId>spring-boot-maven-plugin</artifactId>
```

```
        <configuration>
          <excludes>
            <exclude>
              <groupId>org.projectlombok</groupId>
              <artifactId>lombok</artifactId>
            </exclude>
          </excludes>
        </configuration>
      </plugin>
    </plugins>
</build>
```

Lombok's magic is applied at compile time, so there's no need for it to be available at run time. Excluding it like this keeps it out of the resulting JAR or WAR file.

The Lombok dependency provides you with Lombok annotations (such as `@Data`) at development time and with automatic method generation at compile time. But you'll also need to add Lombok as an extension in your IDE, or your IDE will complain, with errors about missing methods and `final` properties that aren't being set. Visit https://projectlombok.org/ to find out how to install Lombok in your IDE of choice.

Why are there so many errors in my code?

It bears repeating that when using Lombok, you **must** install the Lombok plugin into your IDE. Without it, your IDE won't be aware that Lombok is providing getters, setters, and other methods and will complain that they are missing.

Lombok is supported in a number of popular IDEs, including Eclipse, Spring Tool Suite, IntelliJ IDEA, and Visual Studio Code. Visit https://projectlombok .org/ for more information on how to install the Lombok plugin into your IDE.

I think you'll find Lombok to be very useful, but know that it's optional. You don't need it to develop Spring applications, so if you'd rather not use it, feel free to write those missing methods by hand. Go ahead … I'll wait.

Ingredients are the essential building blocks of a taco. To capture how those ingredients are brought together, we'll define the `Taco` domain class, as shown next.

Listing 2.2 A domain object defining a taco design

```
package tacos;
import java.util.List;
import lombok.Data;

@Data
public class Taco {

  private String name;

  private List<Ingredient> ingredients;

}
```

As you can see, `Taco` is a straightforward Java domain object with a couple of properties. Like `Ingredient`, the `Taco` class is annotated with `@Data` to have Lombok automatically generate essential JavaBean methods for you at compile time.

Now that we have defined `Ingredient` and `Taco`, we need one more domain class that defines how customers specify the tacos that they want to order, along with payment and delivery information. That's the job of the `TacoOrder` class, shown here.

Listing 2.3   A domain object for taco orders

```java
package tacos;
import java.util.List;
import java.util.ArrayList;
import lombok.Data;

@Data
public class TacoOrder {

  private String deliveryName;
  private String deliveryStreet;
  private String deliveryCity;
  private String deliveryState;
  private String deliveryZip;
  private String ccNumber;
  private String ccExpiration;
  private String ccCVV;

  private List<Taco> tacos = new ArrayList<>();

  public void addTaco(Taco taco) {
    tacos.add(taco);
  }
}
```

Aside from having more properties than either `Ingredient` or `Taco`, there's nothing particularly new to discuss about `TacoOrder`. It's a simple domain class with nine properties: five for delivery information, three for payment information, and one that is the list of `Taco` objects that make up the order. There's also an `addTaco()` method that's added for the convenience of adding tacos to the order.

Now that the domain types are defined, we're ready to put them to work. Let's add a few controllers to handle web requests in the application.

2.1.2   *Creating a controller class*

Controllers are the major players in Spring's MVC framework. Their primary job is to handle HTTP requests and either hand off a request to a view to render HTML (browser-displayed) or write data directly to the body of a response (RESTful). In this chapter, we're focusing on the kinds of controllers that use views to produce content for web browsers. When we get to chapter 7, we'll look at writing controllers that handle requests in a REST API.

For the Taco Cloud application, you need a simple controller that will do the following:

- Handle HTTP GET requests where the request path is /design
- Build a list of ingredients
- Hand off the request and the ingredient data to a view template to be rendered as HTML and sent to the requesting web browser

The DesignTacoController class in the next listing addresses those requirements.

Listing 2.4   The beginnings of a Spring controller class

```
package tacos.web;

import java.util.Arrays;
import java.util.List;
import java.util.stream.Collectors;
import org.springframework.stereotype.Controller;
import org.springframework.ui.Model;
import org.springframework.web.bind.annotation.GetMapping;
import org.springframework.web.bind.annotation.ModelAttribute;
import org.springframework.web.bind.annotation.PostMapping;
import org.springframework.web.bind.annotation.RequestMapping;
import org.springframework.web.bind.annotation.SessionAttributes;

import lombok.extern.slf4j.Slf4j;
import tacos.Ingredient;
import tacos.Ingredient.Type;
import tacos.Taco;
import tacos.TacoOrder;

@Slf4j
@Controller
@RequestMapping("/design")
@SessionAttributes("tacoOrder")
public class DesignTacoController {

@ModelAttribute
public void addIngredientsToModel(Model model) {
    List<Ingredient> ingredients = Arrays.asList(
      new Ingredient("FLTO", "Flour Tortilla", Type.WRAP),
      new Ingredient("COTO", "Corn Tortilla", Type.WRAP),
      new Ingredient("GRBF", "Ground Beef", Type.PROTEIN),
      new Ingredient("CARN", "Carnitas", Type.PROTEIN),
      new Ingredient("TMTO", "Diced Tomatoes", Type.VEGGIES),
      new Ingredient("LETC", "Lettuce", Type.VEGGIES),
      new Ingredient("CHED", "Cheddar", Type.CHEESE),
      new Ingredient("JACK", "Monterrey Jack", Type.CHEESE),
      new Ingredient("SLSA", "Salsa", Type.SAUCE),
      new Ingredient("SRCR", "Sour Cream", Type.SAUCE)
    );

    Type[] types = Ingredient.Type.values();
    for (Type type : types) {
      model.addAttribute(type.toString().toLowerCase(),
```

```
            filterByType(ingredients, type));
  }
}

@ModelAttribute(name = "tacoOrder")
public TacoOrder order() {
  return new TacoOrder();
}

@ModelAttribute(name = "taco")
public Taco taco() {
  return new Taco();
}

@GetMapping
public String showDesignForm() {
  return "design";
}

private Iterable<Ingredient> filterByType(
    List<Ingredient> ingredients, Type type) {
  return ingredients
            .stream()
            .filter(x -> x.getType().equals(type))
            .collect(Collectors.toList());
}

}
```

The first thing to note about DesignTacoController is the set of annotations applied at the class level. The first, @Slf4j, is a Lombok-provided annotation that, at compilation time, will automatically generate an SLF4J (Simple Logging Facade for Java, https://www.slf4j.org/) Logger static property in the class. This modest annotation has the same effect as if you were to explicitly add the following lines within the class:

```
private static final org.slf4j.Logger log =
    org.slf4j.LoggerFactory.getLogger(DesignTacoController.class);
```

You'll make use of this Logger a little later.

The next annotation applied to DesignTacoController is @Controller. This annotation serves to identify this class as a controller and to mark it as a candidate for component scanning, so that Spring will discover it and automatically create an instance of DesignTacoController as a bean in the Spring application context.

DesignTacoController is also annotated with @RequestMapping. The @Request-Mapping annotation, when applied at the class level, specifies the kind of requests that this controller handles. In this case, it specifies that DesignTacoController will handle requests whose path begins with /design.

Finally, you see that DesignTacoController is annotated with @SessionAttributes ("tacoOrder"). This indicates that the TacoOrder object that is put into the model a little later in the class should be maintained in session. This is important because the creation of a taco is also the first step in creating an order, and the order we create will need to be carried in the session so that it can span multiple requests.

HANDLING A GET REQUEST

The class-level @RequestMapping specification is refined with the @GetMapping annotation that adorns the showDesignForm() method. @GetMapping, paired with the class-level @RequestMapping, specifies that when an HTTP GET request is received for /design, Spring MVC will call showDesignForm() to handle the request.

@GetMapping is just one member of a family of request-mapping annotations. Table 2.1 lists all of the request-mapping annotations available in Spring MVC.

Table 2.1   Spring MVC request-mapping annotations

Annotation	Description
@RequestMapping	General-purpose request handling
@GetMapping	Handles HTTP GET requests
@PostMapping	Handles HTTP POST requests
@PutMapping	Handles HTTP PUT requests
@DeleteMapping	Handles HTTP DELETE requests
@PatchMapping	Handles HTTP PATCH requests

When showDesignForm() handles a GET request for /design, it doesn't really do much. The main thing it does is return a String value of "taco", which is the logical name of the view that will be used to render the model to the browser. But before it does that, it also populates the given Model with an empty Taco object under a key whose name is "taco". This will enable the form to have a blank slate on which to create a taco masterpiece.

It would seem that a GET request to /design doesn't do much. But on the contrary, there's a bit more involved than what is found in the showDesignForm() method. You'll also notice a method named addIngredientsToModel() that is annotated with @ModelAttribute. This method will also be invoked when a request is handled and will construct a list of Ingredient objects to be put into the model. The list is hard-coded for now. When we get to chapter 3, you'll pull the list of available taco ingredients from a database.

Once the list of ingredients is ready, the next few lines of addIngredientsTo-Model() filters the list by ingredient type using a helper method named filterBy-Type(). A list of ingredient types is then added as an attribute to the Model object that will be passed into showDesignForm(). Model is an object that ferries data between a controller and whatever view is charged with rendering that data. Ultimately, data that's placed in Model attributes is copied into the servlet request attributes, where the view can find them and use them to render a page in the user's browser.

Following `addIngredientsToModel()` are two more methods that are also anno-tated with `@ModelAttribute`. These methods are much simpler and create only a new `TacoOrder` and `Taco` object to place into the model. The `TacoOrder` object, referred to earlier in the `@SessionAttributes` annotation, holds state for the order being built as the user creates tacos across multiple requests. The `Taco` object is placed into the model so that the view rendered in response to the GET request for /design will have a non-null object to display.

Your `DesignTacoController` is really starting to take shape. If you were to run the application now and point your browser at the /design path, the `DesignTaco-Controller`'s `showDesignForm()` and `addIngredientsToModel()` would be engaged, placing ingredients and an empty `Taco` into the model before passing the request on to the view. But because you haven't defined the view yet, the request would take a horrible turn, resulting in an HTTP 500 (Internal Server Error) error. To fix that, let's switch our attention to the view where the data will be decorated with HTML to be presented in the user's web browser.

2.1.3   *Designing the view*

After the controller is finished with its work, it's time for the view to get going. Spring offers several great options for defining views, including JavaServer Pages (JSP), Thymeleaf, FreeMarker, Mustache, and Groovy-based templates. For now, we'll use Thymeleaf, the choice we made in chapter 1 when starting the project. We'll consider a few of the other options in section 2.5.

We have already added Thymeleaf as a dependency in chapter 1. At run time, Spring Boot autoconfiguration sees that Thymeleaf is in the classpath and automati-cally creates the beans that support Thymeleaf views for Spring MVC.

View libraries such as Thymeleaf are designed to be decoupled from any particular web framework. As such, they're unaware of Spring's model abstraction and are unable to work with the data that the controller places in `Model`. But they can work with servlet request attributes. Therefore, before Spring hands the request over to a view, it copies the model data into request attributes that Thymeleaf and other view-templating options have ready access to.

Thymeleaf templates are just HTML with some additional element attributes that guide a template in rendering request data. For example, if there were a request attri-bute whose key is `"message"`, and you wanted it to be rendered into an HTML `<p>` tag by Thymeleaf, you'd write the following in your Thymeleaf template:

```
<p th:text="${message}">placeholder message</p>
```

When the template is rendered into HTML, the body of the `<p>` element will be replaced with the value of the servlet request attribute whose key is `"message"`. The `th:text` attribute is a Thymeleaf namespace attribute that performs the replace-ment. The `${}` operator tells it to use the value of a request attribute (`"message"`, in this case).

Thymeleaf also offers another attribute, `th:each`, that iterates over a collection of elements, rendering the HTML once for each item in the collection. This attribute will come in handy as you design your view to list taco ingredients from the model. For example, to render just the list of "wrap" ingredients, you can use the following snippet of HTML:

```
<h3>Designate your wrap:</h3>
<div th:each="ingredient : ${wrap}">
  <input th:field="*{ingredients}" type="checkbox"
         th:value="${ingredient.id}"/>
  <span th:text="${ingredient.name}">INGREDIENT</span><br/>
</div>
```

Here, you use the `th:each` attribute on the `<div>` tag to repeat rendering of the `<div>` once for each item in the collection found in the wrap request attribute. On each iteration, the ingredient item is bound to a Thymeleaf variable named `ingredient`.

Inside the `<div>` element are a check box `<input>` element and a `<span>` element to provide a label for the check box. The check box uses Thymeleaf's `th:value` to set the rendered `<input>` element's value attribute to the value found in the ingredient's id property. The `th:field` attribute ultimately sets the `<input>` element's name attribute and is used to remember whether or not the check box is checked. When we add validation later, this will ensure that the check box maintains its state should the form need to be redisplayed after a validation error. The `<span>` element uses `th:text` to replace the `"INGREDIENT"` placeholder text with the value of the ingredient's name property.

When rendered with actual model data, one iteration of that `<div>` loop might look like this:

```
<div>
  <input name="ingredients" type="checkbox" value="FLTO" />
  <span>Flour Tortilla</span><br/>
</div>
```

Ultimately, the preceding Thymeleaf snippet is just part of a larger HTML form through which your taco artist users will submit their tasty creations. The complete Thymeleaf template, including all ingredient types and the form, is shown in the following listing.

Listing 2.5 The complete design-a-taco page

```
<!DOCTYPE html>
<html xmlns="http://www.w3.org/1999/xhtml"
      xmlns:th="http://www.thymeleaf.org">
  <head>
    <title>Taco Cloud</title>
    <link rel="stylesheet" th:href="@{/styles.css}" />
  </head>
```

```
<body>
  <h1>Design your taco!</h1>
  <img th:src="@{/images/TacoCloud.png}"/>

  <form method="POST" th:object="${taco}">
  <div class="grid">
    <div class="ingredient-group" id="wraps">
    <h3>Designate your wrap:</h3>
    <div th:each="ingredient : ${wrap}">
      <input th:field="*{ingredients}" type="checkbox"
             th:value="${ingredient.id}"/>
      <span th:text="${ingredient.name}">INGREDIENT</span><br/>
    </div>
    </div>

    <div class="ingredient-group" id="proteins">
    <h3>Pick your protein:</h3>
    <div th:each="ingredient : ${protein}">
      <input th:field="*{ingredients}" type="checkbox"
             th:value="${ingredient.id}"/>
      <span th:text="${ingredient.name}">INGREDIENT</span><br/>
    </div>
    </div>

    <div class="ingredient-group" id="cheeses">
    <h3>Choose your cheese:</h3>
    <div th:each="ingredient : ${cheese}">
      <input th:field="*{ingredients}" type="checkbox"
             th:value="${ingredient.id}"/>
      <span th:text="${ingredient.name}">INGREDIENT</span><br/>
    </div>
    </div>

    <div class="ingredient-group" id="veggies">
    <h3>Determine your veggies:</h3>
    <div th:each="ingredient : ${veggies}">
      <input th:field="*{ingredients}" type="checkbox"
             th:value="${ingredient.id}"/>
      <span th:text="${ingredient.name}">INGREDIENT</span><br/>
    </div>
    </div>

    <div class="ingredient-group" id="sauces">
    <h3>Select your sauce:</h3>
    <div th:each="ingredient : ${sauce}">
      <input th:field="*{ingredients}" type="checkbox"
             th:value="${ingredient.id}"/>
      <span th:text="${ingredient.name}">INGREDIENT</span><br/>
    </div>
    </div>
    </div>

    <div>
```

```
        <h3>Name your taco creation:</h3>
        <input type="text" th:field="*{name}"/>
        <br/>

        <button>Submit Your Taco</button>
        </div>
      </form>
    </body>
</html>
```

As you can see, you repeat the `<div>` snippet for each of the types of ingredients, and you include a Submit button and field where the user can name their creation.

It's also worth noting that the complete template includes the Taco Cloud logo image and a `<link>` reference to a stylesheet.[2] In both cases, Thymeleaf's `@{}` operator is used to produce a context-relative path to the static artifacts that these tags are referencing. As you learned in chapter 1, static content in a Spring Boot application is served from the /static directory at the root of the classpath.

Now that your controller and view are complete, you can fire up the application to see the fruits of your labor. We have many ways to run a Spring Boot application. In chapter 1, I showed you how to run the application by clicking the Start button in the Spring Boot Dashboard. No matter how you fire up the Taco Cloud application, once it starts, point your browser to http://localhost:8080/design. You should see a page that looks something like figure 2.3.

It's looking good! A taco artist visiting your site is presented with a form containing a palette of taco ingredients from which they can create their masterpiece. But what happens when they click the Submit Your Taco button?

Your `DesignTacoController` isn't yet ready to accept taco creations. If the design form is submitted, the user will be presented with an error. (Specifically, it will be an HTTP 405 error: Request Method "POST" Not Supported.) Let's fix that by writing some more controller code that handles form submission.

2.2 *Processing form submission*

If you take another look at the `<form>` tag in your view, you can see that its `method` attribute is set to `POST`. Moreover, the `<form>` doesn't declare an `action` attribute. This means that when the form is submitted, the browser will gather all the data in the form and send it to the server in an HTTP `POST` request to the same path for which a `GET` request displayed the form—the /design path.

Therefore, you need a controller handler method on the receiving end of that `POST` request. You need to write a new handler method in `DesignTacoController` that handles a `POST` request for /design.

---

[2] The contents of the stylesheet aren't relevant to our discussion; it contains only styling to present the ingredients in two columns instead of one long list of ingredients.

Figure 2.3   The rendered taco design page

In listing 2.4, you used the @GetMapping annotation to specify that the showDesign-Form() method should handle HTTP GET requests for /design. Just like @GetMapping handles GET requests, you can use @PostMapping to handle POST requests. For handling taco design submissions, add the processTaco() method in the following listing to DesignTacoController.

```
@PostMapping
public String processTaco(Taco taco,
            @ModelAttribute TacoOrder tacoOrder) {
  tacoOrder.addTaco(taco);
  log.info("Processing taco: {}", taco);

  return "redirect:/orders/current";
}
```

As applied to the processTaco() method, @PostMapping coordinates with the class-level @RequestMapping to indicate that processTaco() should handle POST requests for /design. This is precisely what you need to process a taco artist's submitted creations.

When the form is submitted, the fields in the form are bound to properties of a Taco object (whose class is shown in the next listing) that's passed as a parameter into processTaco(). From there, the processTaco() method can do whatever it wants with the Taco object. In this case, it adds the Taco to the TacoOrder object passed as a parameter to the method and then logs it. The @ModelAttribute applied to the Taco-Order parameter indicates that it should use the TacoOrder object that was placed into the model via the @ModelAttribute-annotated order() method shown earlier in listing 2.4.

If you look back at the form in listing 2.5, you'll see several checkbox elements, all with the name ingredients, and a text input element named name. Those fields in the form correspond directly to the ingredients and name properties of the Taco class.

The name field on the form needs to capture only a simple textual value. Thus the name property of Taco is of type String. The ingredients check boxes also have textual values, but because zero or many of them may be selected, the ingredients property that they're bound to is a List<Ingredient> that will capture each of the chosen ingredients.

But wait. If the ingredients check boxes have textual (e.g., String) values, but the Taco object represents a list of ingredients as List<Ingredient>, then isn't there a mismatch? How can a textual list like ["FLTO", "GRBF", "LETC"] be bound to a list of Ingredient objects that are richer objects containing not only an ID but also a descriptive name and ingredient type?

That's where a converter comes in handy. A converter is any class that implements Spring's Converter interface and implements its convert() method to take one value and convert it to another. To convert a String to an Ingredient, we'll use the IngredientByIdConverter as follows.

```
package tacos.web;

import java.util.HashMap;
import java.util.Map;
```

```
import org.springframework.core.convert.converter.Converter;
import org.springframework.stereotype.Component;

import tacos.Ingredient;
import tacos.Ingredient.Type;

@Component
public class IngredientByIdConverter implements Converter<String, Ingredient> {

  private Map<String, Ingredient> ingredientMap = new HashMap<>();

  public IngredientByIdConverter() {
    ingredientMap.put("FLTO",
        new Ingredient("FLTO", "Flour Tortilla", Type.WRAP));
    ingredientMap.put("COTO",
        new Ingredient("COTO", "Corn Tortilla", Type.WRAP));
    ingredientMap.put("GRBF",
        new Ingredient("GRBF", "Ground Beef", Type.PROTEIN));
    ingredientMap.put("CARN",
        new Ingredient("CARN", "Carnitas", Type.PROTEIN));
    ingredientMap.put("TMTO",
        new Ingredient("TMTO", "Diced Tomatoes", Type.VEGGIES));
    ingredientMap.put("LETC",
        new Ingredient("LETC", "Lettuce", Type.VEGGIES));
    ingredientMap.put("CHED",
        new Ingredient("CHED", "Cheddar", Type.CHEESE));
    ingredientMap.put("JACK",
        new Ingredient("JACK", "Monterrey Jack", Type.CHEESE));
    ingredientMap.put("SLSA",
        new Ingredient("SLSA", "Salsa", Type.SAUCE));
    ingredientMap.put("SRCR",
        new Ingredient("SRCR", "Sour Cream", Type.SAUCE));
  }

  @Override
  public Ingredient convert(String id) {
    return ingredientMap.get(id);
  }

}
```

Because we don't yet have a database from which to pull `Ingredient` objects, the constructor of `IngredientByIdConverter` creates a `Map` keyed on a `String` that is the ingredient ID and whose values are `Ingredient` objects. In chapter 3, we'll adapt this converter to pull the ingredient data from a database instead of being hardcoded like this. The `convert()` method then simply takes a `String` that is the ingredient ID and uses it to look up the `Ingredient` from the map.

Notice that the `IngredientByIdConverter` is annotated with `@Component` to make it discoverable as a bean in the Spring application context. Spring Boot autoconfiguration will discover this, and any other `Converter` beans, and will automatically register them with Spring MVC to be used when the conversion of request parameters to bound properties is needed.

For now, the processTaco() method does nothing with the Taco object. In fact, it doesn't do much of anything at all. That's OK. In chapter 3, you'll add some persistence logic that will save the submitted Taco to a database.

Just as with the showDesignForm() method, processTaco() finishes by returning a String value. And just like showDesignForm(), the value returned indicates a view that will be shown to the user. But what's different is that the value returned from processTaco() is prefixed with "redirect:", indicating that this is a redirect view. More specifically, it indicates that after processTaco() completes, the user's browser should be redirected to the relative path /orders/current.

The idea is that after creating a taco, the user will be redirected to an order form from which they can place an order to have their taco creations delivered. But you don't yet have a controller that will handle a request for /orders/current.

Given what you now know about @Controller, @RequestMapping, and @Get-Mapping, you can easily create such a controller. It might look something like the following listing.

Listing 2.8 A controller to present a taco order form

```java
package tacos.web;
import org.springframework.stereotype.Controller;
import org.springframework.web.bind.annotation.GetMapping;
import org.springframework.web.bind.annotation.RequestMapping;
import org.springframework.web.bind.annotation.SessionAttributes;
import org.springframework.web.bind.support.SessionStatus;

import lombok.extern.slf4j.Slf4j;
import tacos.TacoOrder;

@Slf4j
@Controller
@RequestMapping("/orders")
@SessionAttributes("tacoOrder")
public class OrderController {

  @GetMapping("/current")
  public String orderForm() {
    return "orderForm";
  }

}
```

Once again, you use Lombok's @Slf4j annotation to create a free SLF4J Logger object at compile time. You'll use this Logger in a moment to log the details of the order that's submitted.

The class-level @RequestMapping specifies that any request-handling methods in this controller will handle requests whose path begins with /orders. When combined with the method-level @GetMapping, it specifies that the orderForm() method will handle HTTP GET requests for /orders/current.

As for the `orderForm()` method itself, it's extremely basic, only returning a logical view name of `orderForm`. Once you have a way to persist taco creations to a database in chapter 3, you'll revisit this method and modify it to populate the model with a list of `Taco` objects to be placed in the order.

The `orderForm` view is provided by a Thymeleaf template named orderForm.html, which is shown next.

Listing 2.9 A taco order form view

```html
<!DOCTYPE html>
<html xmlns="http://www.w3.org/1999/xhtml"
      xmlns:th="http://www.thymeleaf.org">
  <head>
    <title>Taco Cloud</title>
    <link rel="stylesheet" th:href="@{/styles.css}" />
  </head>

  <body>

    <form method="POST" th:action="@{/orders}" th:object="${tacoOrder}">
      <h1>Order your taco creations!</h1>

      <img th:src="@{/images/TacoCloud.png}"/>

      <h3>Your tacos in this order:</h3>
      <a th:href="@{/design}" id="another">Design another taco</a><br/>
      <ul>
        <li th:each="taco : ${tacoOrder.tacos}">
          <span th:text="${taco.name}">taco name</span></li>
      </ul>

      <h3>Deliver my taco masterpieces to...</h3>
      <label for="deliveryName">Name: </label>
      <input type="text" th:field="*{deliveryName}"/>
      <br/>

      <label for="deliveryStreet">Street address: </label>
      <input type="text" th:field="*{deliveryStreet}"/>
      <br/>

      <label for="deliveryCity">City: </label>
      <input type="text" th:field="*{deliveryCity}"/>
      <br/>

      <label for="deliveryState">State: </label>
      <input type="text" th:field="*{deliveryState}"/>
      <br/>

      <label for="deliveryZip">Zip code: </label>
      <input type="text" th:field="*{deliveryZip}"/>
      <br/>

      <h3>Here's how I'll pay...</h3>
      <label for="ccNumber">Credit Card #: </label>
```

```
        <input type="text" th:field="*{ccNumber}"/>
        <br/>

        <label for="ccExpiration">Expiration: </label>
        <input type="text" th:field="*{ccExpiration}"/>
        <br/>

        <label for="ccCVV">CVV: </label>
        <input type="text" th:field="*{ccCVV}"/>
        <br/>

        <input type="submit" value="Submit Order"/>
    </form>
  </body>
</html>
```

For the most part, the orderForm.html view is typical HTML/Thymeleaf content, with very little of note. It starts by listing the tacos that were added to the order. It uses Thymeleaf's th:each to cycle through the order's tacos property as it creates the list. Then it renders the order form.

But notice that the <form> tag here is different from the <form> tag used in listing 2.5 in that it also specifies a form action. Without an action specified, the form would submit an HTTP POST request back to the same URL that presented the form. But here, you specify that the form should be POSTed to /orders (using Thymeleaf's @{...} operator for a context-relative path).

Therefore, you're going to need to add another method to your OrderController class that handles POST requests for /orders. You won't have a way to persist orders until the next chapter, so you'll keep it simple here—something like what you see in the next listing.

Listing 2.10   Handling a taco order submission

```
@PostMapping
public String processOrder(TacoOrder order,
        SessionStatus sessionStatus) {
  log.info("Order submitted: {}", order);
  sessionStatus.setComplete();

  return "redirect:/";
}
```

When the processOrder() method is called to handle a submitted order, it's given a TacoOrder object whose properties are bound to the submitted form fields. Taco-Order, much like Taco, is a fairly straightforward class that carries order information.

In the case of this processOrder() method, the TacoOrder object is simply logged. We'll see how to persist it to a database in the next chapter. But before process-Order() is done, it also calls setComplete() on the SessionStatus object passed in as a parameter. The TacoOrder object was initially created and placed into the session when the user created their first taco. By calling `setComplete()`, we are ensuring that the session is cleaned up and ready for a new order the next time the user creates a taco.

Now that you've developed an `OrderController` and the order form view, you're ready to try it out. Open your browser to http://localhost:8080/design, select some ingredients for your taco, and click the Submit Your Taco button. You should see a form similar to what's shown in figure 2.4.

Figure 2.4   The taco order form

Fill in some fields in the form, and press the Submit Order button. As you do, keep an eye on the application logs to see your order information. When I tried it, the log entry looked something like this (reformatted to fit the width of this page):

```
Order submitted: TacoOrder(deliveryName=Craig Walls, deliveryStreet=1234 7th
Street, deliveryCity=Somewhere, deliveryState=Who knows?,
deliveryZip=zipzap, ccNumber=Who can guess?, ccExpiration=Some day,
ccCVV=See-vee-vee, tacos=[Taco(name=Awesome Sauce, ingredients=[
Ingredient(id=FLTO, name=Flour Tortilla, type=WRAP), Ingredient(id=GRBF,
name=Ground Beef, type=PROTEIN), Ingredient(id=CHED, name=Cheddar,
type=CHEESE), Ingredient(id=TMTO, name=Diced Tomatoes, type=VEGGIES),
Ingredient(id=SLSA, name=Salsa, type=SAUCE), Ingredient(id=SRCR,
name=Sour Cream, type=SAUCE)]), Taco(name=Quesoriffic, ingredients=
[Ingredient(id=FLTO, name=Flour Tortilla, type=WRAP), Ingredient(id=CHED,
name=Cheddar, type=CHEESE), Ingredient(id=JACK, name=Monterrey Jack,
type=CHEESE), Ingredient(id=TMTO, name=Diced Tomatoes, type=VEGGIES),
Ingredient(id=SRCR,name=Sour Cream, type=SAUCE)])])
```

It appears that the `processOrder()` method did its job, handling the form submission by logging details about the order. But if you look carefully at the log entry from my test order, you can see that it let a little bit of bad information get in. Most of the fields in the form contained data that couldn't possibly be correct. Let's add some validation to ensure that the data provided at least resembles the kind of information required.

2.3 Validating form input

When designing a new taco creation, what if the user selects no ingredients or fails to specify a name for their creation? When submitting the order, what if the user fails to fill in the required address fields? Or what if they enter a value into the credit card field that isn't even a valid credit card number?

As things stand now, nothing will stop the user from creating a taco without any ingredients or with an empty delivery address, or even submitting the lyrics to their favorite song as the credit card number. That's because you haven't yet specified how those fields should be validated.

One way to perform form validation is to litter the `processTaco()` and `process-Order()` methods with a bunch of `if/then` blocks, checking each and every field to ensure that it meets the appropriate validation rules. But that would be cumbersome and difficult to read and debug.

Fortunately, Spring supports the JavaBean Validation API (also known as JSR 303; https://jcp.org/en/jsr/detail?id=303). This makes it easy to declare validation rules as opposed to explicitly writing validation logic in your application code.

To apply validation in Spring MVC, you need to

- Add the Spring Validation starter to the build.
- Declare validation rules on the class that is to be validated: specifically, the Taco class.

- Specify that validation should be performed in the controller methods that require validation: specifically, the `DesignTacoController`'s `processTaco()` method and the `OrderController`'s `processOrder()` method.
- Modify the form views to display validation errors.

The Validation API offers several annotations that can be placed on properties of domain objects to declare validation rules. Hibernate's implementation of the Validation API adds even more validation annotations. Both can be added to a project by adding the Spring Validation starter to the build. The Validation check box under I/O in the Spring Boot Starter wizard will get the job done, but if you prefer manually editing your build, the following entry in the Maven pom.xml file will do the trick:

```
<dependency>
  <groupId>org.springframework.boot</groupId>
  <artifactId>spring-boot-starter-validation</artifactId>
</dependency>
```

Or if you're using Gradle, then this is the dependency you'll need:

```
implementation 'org.springframework.boot:spring-boot-starter-validation'
```

Is the validation starter required?

In earlier versions of Spring Boot, the Spring Validation starter was automatically included with the web starter. Starting with Spring Boot 2.3.0, you'll need to explicitly add it to your build if you intend to apply validation.

With the validation starter in place, let's see how you can apply a few annotations to validate a submitted `Taco` or `TacoOrder`.

2.3.1 *Declaring validation rules*

For the `Taco` class, you want to ensure that the `name` property isn't empty or `null` and that the list of selected ingredients has at least one item. The following listing shows an updated `Taco` class that uses `@NotNull` and `@Size` to declare those validation rules.

Listing 2.11 Adding validation to the `Taco` domain class

```
package tacos;
import java.util.List;
import javax.validation.constraints.NotNull;
import javax.validation.constraints.Size;
import lombok.Data;

@Data
public class Taco {

  @NotNull
  @Size(min=5, message="Name must be at least 5 characters long")
  private String name;
```

```
@NotNull
@Size(min=1, message="You must choose at least 1 ingredient")
private List<Ingredient> ingredients;

}
```

You'll notice that in addition to requiring that the `name` property isn't `null`, you declare that it should have a value that's at least five characters in length.

When it comes to declaring validation on submitted taco orders, you must apply annotations to the `TacoOrder` class. For the address properties, you want to be sure that the user doesn't leave any of the fields blank. For that, you'll use the `@NotBlank` annotation.

Validation of the payment fields, however, is a bit more exotic. You need to ensure not only that the `ccNumber` property isn't empty but also that it contains a value that could be a valid credit card number. The `ccExpiration` property must conform to a format of MM/YY (two-digit month and year), and the `ccCVV` property needs to be a three-digit number. To achieve this kind of validation, you need to use a few other Java-Bean Validation API annotations and borrow a validation annotation from the Hibernate Validator collection of annotations. The following listing shows the changes needed to validate the `TacoOrder` class.

Listing 2.12 Validating order fields

```
package tacos;
import javax.validation.constraints.Digits;
import javax.validation.constraints.NotBlank;
import javax.validation.constraints.Pattern;
import org.hibernate.validator.constraints.CreditCardNumber;
import java.util.List;
import java.util.ArrayList;
import lombok.Data;

@Data
public class TacoOrder {

  @NotBlank(message="Delivery name is required")
  private String deliveryName;

  @NotBlank(message="Street is required")
  private String deliveryStreet;

  @NotBlank(message="City is required")
  private String deliveryCity;

  @NotBlank(message="State is required")
  private String deliveryState;

  @NotBlank(message="Zip code is required")
  private String deliveryZip;
```

```
@CreditCardNumber(message="Not a valid credit card number")
private String ccNumber;

@Pattern(regexp="^(0[1-9]|1[0-2])([\\/])([2-9][0-9])$",
         message="Must be formatted MM/YY")
private String ccExpiration;

@Digits(integer=3, fraction=0, message="Invalid CVV")
private String ccCVV;

private List<Taco> tacos = new ArrayList<>();

public void addTaco(Taco taco) {
  tacos.add(taco);
}
}
```

As you can see, the ccNumber property is annotated with @CreditCardNumber. This annotation declares that the property's value must be a valid credit card number that passes the Luhn algorithm check (https://creditcardvalidator.org/articles/luhn-algorithm). This prevents user mistakes and deliberately bad data but doesn't guarantee that the credit card number is actually assigned to an account or that the account can be used for charging.

Unfortunately, there's no ready-made annotation for validating the MM/YY format of the ccExpiration property. I've applied the @Pattern annotation, providing it with a regular expression that ensures that the property value adheres to the desired format. If you're wondering how to decipher the regular expression, I encourage you to check out the many online regular expression guides, including http://www.regular-expressions.info/. Regular expression syntax is a dark art and certainly outside the scope of this book. Finally, we annotate the ccCVV property with @Digits to ensure that the value contains exactly three numeric digits.

All of the validation annotations include a message attribute that defines the message you'll display to the user if the information they enter doesn't meet the requirements of the declared validation rules.

2.3.2   *Performing validation at form binding*

Now that you've declared how a Taco and TacoOrder should be validated, we need to revisit each of the controllers, specifying that validation should be performed when the forms are POSTed to their respective handler methods.

To validate a submitted Taco, you need to add the JavaBean Validation API's @Valid annotation to the Taco argument of the DesignTacoController's process-Taco() method, as shown next.

Listing 2.13   Validating a POSTed Taco

```
import javax.validation.Valid;
import org.springframework.validation.Errors;

...

  @PostMapping
  public String processTaco(
        @Valid Taco taco, Errors errors,
        @ModelAttribute TacoOrder tacoOrder) {

    if (errors.hasErrors()) {
      return "design";
    }

    tacoOrder.addTaco(taco);
    log.info("Processing taco: {}", taco);

    return "redirect:/orders/current";
  }
```

The @Valid annotation tells Spring MVC to perform validation on the submitted Taco object after it's bound to the submitted form data and before the processTaco() method is called. If there are any validation errors, the details of those errors will be captured in an Errors object that's passed into processTaco(). The first few lines of processTaco() consult the Errors object, asking its hasErrors() method if there are any validation errors. If there are, the method concludes without processing the Taco and returns the "design" view name so that the form is redisplayed.

To perform validation on submitted TacoOrder objects, similar changes are also required in the processOrder() method of OrderController, as shown in the next code listing.

Listing 2.14   Validating a POSTed TacoOrder

```
@PostMapping
public String processOrder(@Valid TacoOrder order, Errors errors,
        SessionStatus sessionStatus) {
  if (errors.hasErrors()) {
    return "orderForm";
  }

  log.info("Order submitted: {}", order);
  sessionStatus.setComplete();

  return "redirect:/";
}
```

In both cases, the method will be allowed to process the submitted data if there are no validation errors. If there are validation errors, the request will be forwarded to the form view to give the user a chance to correct their mistakes.

But how will the user know what mistakes require correction? Unless you call out the errors on the form, the user will be left guessing about how to successfully submit the form.

2.3.3   *Displaying validation errors*

Thymeleaf offers convenient access to the Errors object via the fields property and with its th:errors attribute. For example, to display validation errors on the credit card number field, you can add a <span> element that uses these error references to the order form template, as follows.

Listing 2.15   Displaying validation errors

```
<label for="ccNumber">Credit Card #: </label>
    <input type="text" th:field="*{ccNumber}"/>
    <span class="validationError"
          th:if="${#fields.hasErrors('ccNumber')}"
          th:errors="*{ccNumber}">CC Num Error</span>
```

Aside from a class attribute that can be used to style the error so that it catches the user's attention, the <span> element uses a th:if attribute to decide whether to display the <span>. The fields property's hasErrors() method checks whether there are any errors in the ccNumber field. If so, the <span> will be rendered.

The th:errors attribute references the ccNumber field and, assuming errors exist for that field, it will replace the placeholder content of the <span> element with the validation message.

If you were to sprinkle similar <span> tags around the order form for the other fields, you might see a form that looks like figure 2.5 when you submit invalid information. The errors indicate that the name, city, and ZIP code fields have been left blank and that all of the payment fields fail to meet the validation criteria.

Now your Taco Cloud controllers not only display and capture input, but they also validate that the information meets some basic validation rules. Let's step back and reconsider the HomeController from chapter 1, looking at an alternative implementation.

2.4   *Working with view controllers*

Thus far, you've written three controllers for the Taco Cloud application. Although each controller serves a distinct purpose in the functionality of the application, they all pretty much adhere to the following programming model:

- They're all annotated with @Controller to indicate that they're controller classes that should be automatically discovered by Spring component scanning and instantiated as beans in the Spring application context.
- All but HomeController are annotated with @RequestMapping at the class level to define a baseline request pattern that the controller will handle.

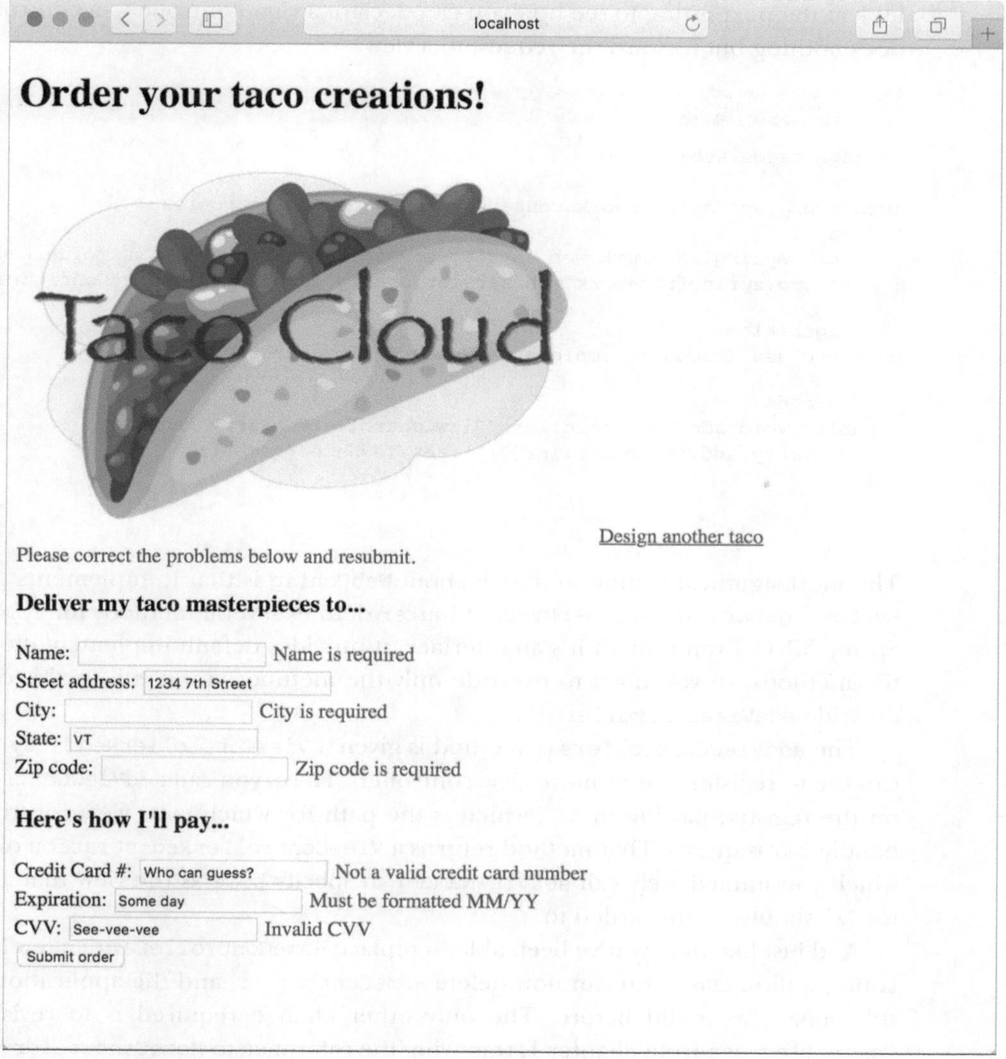

Figure 2.5 Validation errors displayed on the order form

- They all have one or more methods that are annotated with @GetMapping or @PostMapping to provide specifics on which methods should handle which kinds of requests.

Most of the controllers you'll write will follow that pattern. But when a controller is simple enough that it doesn't populate a model or process input—as is the case with your HomeController—there's another way that you can define the controller. Have a look at the next listing to see how you can declare a view controller—a controller that does nothing but forward the request to a view.

Listing 2.16   Declaring a view controller

```
package tacos.web;

import org.springframework.context.annotation.Configuration;
import
     org.springframework.web.servlet.config.annotation.ViewControllerRegistry;
import org.springframework.web.servlet.config.annotation.WebMvcConfigurer;

@Configuration
public class WebConfig implements WebMvcConfigurer {

  @Override
  public void addViewControllers(ViewControllerRegistry registry) {
    registry.addViewController("/").setViewName("home");
  }

}
```

The most significant thing to notice about WebConfig is that it implements the Web-MvcConfigurer interface. WebMvcConfigurer defines several methods for configuring Spring MVC. Even though it's an interface, it provides default implementations of all the methods, so you need to override only the methods you need. In this case, you override addViewControllers().

The addViewControllers() method is given a ViewControllerRegistry that you can use to register one or more view controllers. Here, you call addViewController() on the registry, passing in "/", which is the path for which your view controller will handle GET requests. That method returns a ViewControllerRegistration object, on which you immediately call setViewName() to specify home as the view that a request for "/" should be forwarded to.

And just like that, you've been able to replace HomeController with a few lines in a configuration class. You can now delete HomeController, and the application should still behave as it did before. The only other change required is to revisit Home-ControllerTest from chapter 1, removing the reference to HomeController from the @WebMvcTest annotation, so that the test class will compile without errors.

Here, you've created a new WebConfig configuration class to house the view controller declaration. But any configuration class can implement WebMvcConfigurer and override the addViewController method. For instance, you could have added the same view controller declaration to the bootstrap TacoCloudApplication class like this:

```
@SpringBootApplication
public class TacoCloudApplication implements WebMvcConfigurer {

  public static void main(String[] args) {
    SpringApplication.run(TacoCloudApplication.class, args);
  }
```

```
    @Override
    public void addViewControllers(ViewControllerRegistry registry) {
        registry.addViewController("/").setViewName("home");
    }

}
```

By extending an existing configuration class, you can avoid creating a new configuration class, keeping your project artifact count down. But I prefer creating a new configuration class for each kind of configuration (web, data, security, and so on), keeping the application bootstrap configuration clean and simple.

Speaking of view controllers—and more generically, the views that controllers forward requests to—so far you've been using Thymeleaf for all of your views. I like Thymeleaf a lot, but maybe you prefer a different template model for your application views. Let's have a look at Spring's many supported view options.

2.5 Choosing a view template library

For the most part, your choice of a view template library is a matter of personal taste. Spring is flexible and supports many common templating options. With only a few small exceptions, the template library you choose will itself have no idea that it's even working with Spring.[3]

Table 2.2 catalogs the template options supported by Spring Boot autoconfiguration.

Table 2.2 Supported template options

Template	Spring Boot starter dependency
FreeMarker	`spring-boot-starter-freemarker`
Groovy templates	`spring-boot-starter-groovy-templates`
JavaServer Pages (JSP)	None (provided by Tomcat or Jetty)
Mustache	`spring-boot-starter-mustache`
Thymeleaf	`spring-boot-starter-thymeleaf`

Generally speaking, you select the view template library you want, add it as a dependency in your build, and start writing templates in the /templates directory (under the src/main/resources directory in a Maven or Gradle project). Spring Boot detects your chosen template library and automatically configures the components required for it to serve views for your Spring MVC controllers.

You've already done this with Thymeleaf for the Taco Cloud application. In chapter 1, you selected the Thymeleaf check box when initializing the project. This resulted in Spring Boot's Thymeleaf starter being included in the pom.xml file. When

---

[3] One such exception is Thymeleaf's Spring Security dialect, which we'll talk about in chapter 5.

the application starts up, Spring Boot autoconfiguration detects the presence of Thymeleaf and automatically configures the Thymeleaf beans for you. All you had to do was start writing templates in /templates.

If you'd rather use a different template library, you simply select it at project initialization or edit your existing project build to include the newly chosen template library.

For example, let's say you wanted to use Mustache instead of Thymeleaf. No problem. Just visit the project pom.xml file and replace this

```
<dependency>
  <groupId>org.springframework.boot</groupId>
  <artifactId>spring-boot-starter-thymeleaf</artifactId>
</dependency>
```

with this:

```
<dependency>
  <groupId>org.springframework.boot</groupId>
  <artifactId>spring-boot-starter-mustache</artifactId>
</dependency>
```

Of course, you'd need to make sure that you write all the templates with Mustache syntax instead of Thymeleaf tags. The specifics of working with Mustache (or any of the template language choices) is well outside of the scope of this book, but to give you an idea of what to expect, here's a snippet from a Mustache template that will render one of the ingredient groups in the taco design form:

```
<h3>Designate your wrap:</h3>
{{#wrap}}
<div>
  <input name="ingredients" type="checkbox" value="{{id}}" />
  <span>{{name}}</span><br/>
</div>
{{/wrap}}
```

This is the Mustache equivalent of the Thymeleaf snippet in section 2.1.3. The {{#wrap}} block (which concludes with {{/wrap}}) iterates through a collection in the request attribute whose key is wrap and renders the embedded HTML for each item. The {{id}} and {{name}} tags reference the id and name properties of the item (which should be an Ingredient).

You'll notice in table 2.2 that JSP doesn't require any special dependency in the build. That's because the servlet container itself (Tomcat by default) implements the JSP specification, thus requiring no further dependencies.

But there's a gotcha if you choose to use JSP. As it turns out, Java servlet containers—including embedded Tomcat and Jetty containers—usually look for JSPs somewhere under /WEB-INF. But if you're building your application as an executable JAR file, there's no way to satisfy that requirement. Therefore, JSP is an option only if you're building your application as a WAR file and deploying it in a traditional servlet container. If you're building an executable JAR file, you must choose Thymeleaf, Free-Marker, or one of the other options in table 2.2.

2.5.1 Caching templates

By default, templates are parsed only once—when they're first used—and the results of that parse are cached for subsequent use. This is a great feature for production, because it prevents redundant template parsing on each request and thus improves performance.

That feature is not so awesome at development time, however. Let's say you fire up your application, hit the taco design page, and decide to make a few changes to it. When you refresh your web browser, you'll still be shown the original version. The only way you can see your changes is to restart the application, which is quite inconvenient.

Fortunately, we have a way to disable caching. All we need to do is set a template-appropriate caching property to `false`. Table 2.3 lists the caching properties for each of the supported template libraries.

Table 2.3 Properties to enable/disable template caching

Template	Cache-enable property
FreeMarker	`spring.freemarker.cache`
Groovy templates	`spring.groovy.template.cache`
Mustache	`spring.mustache.cache`
Thymeleaf	`spring.thymeleaf.cache`

By default, all of these properties are set to `true` to enable caching. You can disable caching for your chosen template engine by setting its cache property to `false`. For example, to disable Thymeleaf caching, add the following line in application.properties:

```
spring.thymeleaf.cache=false
```

The only catch is that you'll want to be sure to remove this line (or set it to `true`) before you deploy your application to production. One option is to set the property in a profile. (We'll talk about profiles in chapter 6.)

A much simpler option is to use Spring Boot's DevTools, as we opted to do in chapter 1. Among the many helpful bits of development-time help offered by DevTools, it will disable caching for all template libraries but will disable itself (and thus reenable template caching) when your application is deployed.

Summary

- Spring offers a powerful web framework called Spring MVC that can be used to develop the web frontend for a Spring application.
- Spring MVC is annotation-based, enabling the declaration of request-handling methods with annotations such as `@RequestMapping`, `@GetMapping`, and `@Post-Mapping`.
- Most request-handling methods conclude by returning the logical name of a view, such as a Thymeleaf template, to which the request (along with any model data) is forwarded.
- Spring MVC supports validation through the JavaBean Validation API and implementations of the Validation API such as Hibernate Validator.
- View controllers can be registered with `addViewController` in a `WebMvc-Configurer` class to handle HTTP `GET` requests for which no model data or processing is required.
- In addition to Thymeleaf, Spring supports a variety of view options, including FreeMarker, Groovy templates, and Mustache.

Working with data 3

This chapter covers

- Using Spring's `JdbcTemplate`
- Creating Spring Data JDBC repositories
- Declaring JPA repositories with Spring Data

Most applications offer more than just a pretty face. Although the user interface may provide interaction with an application, it's the data it presents and stores that separates applications from static websites.

In the Taco Cloud application, you need to be able to maintain information about ingredients, tacos, and orders. Without a database to store this information, the application wouldn't be able to progress much further than what you developed in chapter 2.

In this chapter, you're going to add data persistence to the Taco Cloud application. You'll start by using Spring support for JDBC (Java Database Connectivity) to eliminate boilerplate code. Then you'll rework the data repositories to work with JPA (Java Persistence API), eliminating even more code.

3.1   *Reading and writing data with JDBC*

For decades, relational databases and SQL have enjoyed their position as the leading choice for data persistence. Even though many alternative database types have emerged in recent years, the relational database is still a top choice for a general-purpose data store and will not likely be usurped from its position any time soon.

When it comes to working with relational data, Java developers have several options. The two most common choices are JDBC and JPA. Spring supports both with abstractions, making working with either JDBC or JPA easier than it would be without Spring. In this section, we'll focus on how Spring supports JDBC, and then we'll look at Spring support for JPA in section 3.3.

Spring JDBC support is rooted in the JdbcTemplate class. JdbcTemplate provides a means by which developers can perform SQL operations against a relational database without all the ceremony and boilerplate typically required when working with JDBC.

To gain an appreciation of what JdbcTemplate does, let's start by looking at an example of how to perform a simple query in Java without JdbcTemplate.

Listing 3.1   Querying a database without `JdbcTemplate`

```java
@Override
public Optional<Ingredient> findById(String id) {
  Connection connection = null;
  PreparedStatement statement = null;
  ResultSet resultSet = null;
  try {
    connection = dataSource.getConnection();
    statement = connection.prepareStatement(
        "select id, name, type from Ingredient where id=?");
    statement.setString(1, id);
    resultSet = statement.executeQuery();
    Ingredient ingredient = null;
    if(resultSet.next()) {
      ingredient = new Ingredient(
          resultSet.getString("id"),
          resultSet.getString("name"),
          Ingredient.Type.valueOf(resultSet.getString("type")));
    }
    return Optional.of(ingredient);
  } catch (SQLException e) {
    // ??? What should be done here ???
  } finally {
    if (resultSet != null) {
      try {
        resultSet.close();
      } catch (SQLException e) {}
    }
    if (statement != null) {
      try {
        statement.close();
      } catch (SQLException e) {}
    }
```

```
    if (connection != null) {
      try {
        connection.close();
      } catch (SQLException e) {}
    }
  }
  return Optional.empty();
}
```

I assure you that somewhere in listing 3.1 are a couple of lines that query the database for ingredients. But I'll bet you had a hard time spotting that query needle in the JDBC haystack. It's surrounded by code that creates a connection, creates a statement, and cleans up by closing the connection, statement, and result set.

To make matters worse, any number of things could go wrong when creating the connection or the statement, or when performing the query. This requires that you catch a SQLException, which may or may not be helpful in figuring out what went wrong or how to address the problem.

SQLException is a checked exception, which requires handling in a catch block. But the most common problems, such as failure to create a connection to the database or a mistyped query, can't possibly be addressed in a catch block and are likely to be rethrown for handling upstream. In contrast, consider the following method that uses Spring's JdbcTemplate.

Listing 3.2 Querying a database with `JdbcTemplate`

```java
private JdbcTemplate jdbcTemplate;

public Optional<Ingredient> findById(String id) {
  List<Ingredient> results = jdbcTemplate.query(
      "select id, name, type from Ingredient where id=?",
      this::mapRowToIngredient,
      id);
  return results.size() == 0 ?
        Optional.empty() :
        Optional.of(results.get(0));
}
private Ingredient mapRowToIngredient(ResultSet row, int rowNum)
    throws SQLException {
  return new Ingredient(
      row.getString("id"),
      row.getString("name"),
      Ingredient.Type.valueOf(row.getString("type")));
}
```

The code in listing 3.2 is clearly much simpler than the raw JDBC example in listing 3.1; there aren't any statements or connections being created. And, after the method is finished, there isn't any cleanup of those objects. Finally, there isn't any handling of exceptions that can't properly be handled in a catch block. What's left is code that's focused solely on performing a query (the call to JdbcTemplate's query()

method) and mapping the results to an `Ingredient` object (handled by the `mapRow-ToIngredient()` method).

The code in listing 3.2 is a snippet of what you need to do to use `JdbcTemplate` to persist and read data in the Taco Cloud application. Let's take the next steps necessary to outfit the application with JDBC persistence. We'll start by making a few tweaks to the domain objects.

3.1.1 *Adapting the domain for persistence*

When persisting objects to a database, it's generally a good idea to have one field that uniquely identifies the object. Your `Ingredient` class already has an `id` field, but you need to add `id` fields to both `Taco` and `TacoOrder` as well.

Moreover, it might be useful to know when a `Taco` is created and when a `Taco-Order` is placed. You'll also need to add a field to each object to capture the date and time that the objects are saved. The following listing shows the new `id` and `createdAt` fields needed in the `Taco` class.

> **Listing 3.3 Adding ID and timestamp fields to the `Taco` class**

```
@Data
public class Taco {

  private Long id;

  private Date createdAt = new Date();

  // ...

}
```

Because you use Lombok to automatically generate accessor methods at run time, there's no need to do anything more than declare the `id` and `createdAt` properties. They'll have appropriate getter and setter methods as needed at run time. Similar changes are required in the `TacoOrder` class, as shown here:

```
@Data
public class TacoOrder implements Serializable {

  private static final long serialVersionUID = 1L;

  private Long id;

  private Date placedAt;
  // ...

}
```

Again, Lombok automatically generates the accessor methods, so these are the only changes required in `TacoOrder`. If for some reason you choose not to use Lombok, you'll need to write these methods yourself.

Your domain classes are now ready for persistence. Let's see how to use `Jdbc-Template` to read and write them to a database.

3.1.2 *Working with JdbcTemplate*

Before you can start using `JdbcTemplate`, you need to add it to your project classpath. You can do this easily by adding Spring Boot's JDBC starter dependency to the build as follows:

```
<dependency>
  <groupId>org.springframework.boot</groupId>
  <artifactId>spring-boot-starter-jdbc</artifactId>
</dependency>
```

You're also going to need a database where your data will be stored. For development purposes, an embedded database will be just fine. I favor the H2 embedded database, so I've added the following dependency to the build:

```
<dependency>
  <groupId>com.h2database</groupId>
  <artifactId>h2</artifactId>
  <scope>runtime</scope>
</dependency>
```

By default, the database name is randomly generated. But that makes it hard to determine the database URL if, for some reason, you need to connect to the database using the H2 console (which Spring Boot DevTools enables at http://localhost:8080/h2-console). So, it's a good idea to pin down the database name by setting a couple of properties in application.properties, as shown next:

```
spring.datasource.generate-unique-name=false
spring.datasource.name=tacocloud
```

Or, if you prefer, rename application.properties to application.yml and add the properties in YAML format like so:

```
spring:
  datasource:
    generate-unique-name: false
    name: tacocloud
```

The choice between properties file format and YAML format is up to you. Spring Boot is happy to work with either. Given the structure and increased readability of YAML, we'll use YAML for configuration properties throughout the rest of the book.

By setting the `spring.datasource.generate-unique-name` property to `false`, we're telling Spring to not generate a unique random value for the database name. Instead, it should use the value set to the `spring.datasource.name` property. In this case, the database name will be `"tacocloud"`. Consequently, the database URL will be "jdbc:h2:mem:tacocloud", which you can specify in the JDBC URL for the H2 console connection.

Later, you'll see how to configure the application to use an external database. But for now, let's move on to writing a repository that fetches and saves Ingredient data.

DEFINING JDBC REPOSITORIES

Your Ingredient repository needs to perform the following operations:

- Query for all ingredients into a collection of Ingredient objects
- Query for a single Ingredient by its id
- Save an Ingredient object

The following IngredientRepository interface defines those three operations as method declarations:

```
package tacos.data;

import java.util.Optional;

import tacos.Ingredient;

public interface IngredientRepository {

  Iterable<Ingredient> findAll();

  Optional<Ingredient> findById(String id);

  Ingredient save(Ingredient ingredient);

}
```

Although the interface captures the essence of what you need an ingredient repository to do, you'll still need to write an implementation of IngredientRepository that uses JdbcTemplate to query the database. The code shown next is the first step in writing that implementation.

Listing 3.4   Beginning an ingredient repository with JdbcTemplate

```
package tacos.data;
import java.sql.ResultSet;
import java.sql.SQLException;

import org.springframework.jdbc.core.JdbcTemplate;
import org.springframework.stereotype.Repository;

import tacos.Ingredient;

@Repository
public class JdbcIngredientRepository implements IngredientRepository {

  private JdbcTemplate jdbcTemplate;
```

```
  public JdbcIngredientRepository(JdbcTemplate jdbcTemplate) {
    this.jdbcTemplate = jdbcTemplate;
  }

  // ...

}
```

As you can see, `JdbcIngredientRepository` is annotated with `@Repository`. This annotation is one of a handful of stereotype annotations that Spring defines, including `@Controller` and `@Component`. By annotating `JdbcIngredientRepository` with `@Repository`, you declare that it should be automatically discovered by Spring component scanning and instantiated as a bean in the Spring application context.

When Spring creates the `JdbcIngredientRepository` bean, it injects it with `Jdbc-Template`. That's because when there's only one constructor, Spring implicitly applies autowiring of dependencies through that constructor's parameters. If there is more than one constructor, or if you just want autowiring to be explicitly stated, then you can annotate the constructor with `@Autowired` as follows:

```
@Autowired
public JdbcIngredientRepository(JdbcTemplate jdbcTemplate) {
  this.jdbcTemplate = jdbcTemplate;
}
```

The constructor assigns `JdbcTemplate` to an instance variable that will be used in other methods to query and insert into the database. Speaking of those other methods, let's take a look at the implementations of `findAll()` and `findById()`, shown in the code sample.

Listing 3.5　Querying the database with `JdbcTemplate`

```
@Override
public Iterable<Ingredient> findAll() {
  return jdbcTemplate.query(
      "select id, name, type from Ingredient",
      this::mapRowToIngredient);
}

@Override
public Optional<Ingredient> findById(String id) {
  List<Ingredient> results = jdbcTemplate.query(
      "select id, name, type from Ingredient where id=?",
      this::mapRowToIngredient,
      id);
  return results.size() == 0 ?
          Optional.empty() :
          Optional.of(results.get(0));
}

private Ingredient mapRowToIngredient(ResultSet row, int rowNum)
    throws SQLException {
```

```
    return new Ingredient(
        row.getString("id"),
        row.getString("name"),
        Ingredient.Type.valueOf(row.getString("type")));
}
```

Both findAll() and findById() use JdbcTemplate in a similar way. The findAll() method, expecting to return a collection of objects, uses JdbcTemplate's query() method. The query() method accepts the SQL for the query as well as an implementation of Spring's RowMapper for the purpose of mapping each row in the result set to an object. query() also accepts as its final argument(s) a list of any parameters required in the query. But, in this case, there aren't any required parameters.

In contrast, the findById() method will need to include a where clause in its query to compare the value of the id column with the value of the id parameter passed into the method. Therefore, the call to query() includes, as its final parameter, the id parameter. When the query is performed, the ? will be replaced with this value.

As shown in listing 3.5, the RowMapper parameter for both findAll() and findById() is given as a method reference to the mapRowToIngredient() method. Java's method references and lambdas are convenient when working with JdbcTemplate as an alternative to an explicit RowMapper implementation. If for some reason you want or need an explicit RowMapper, then the following implementation of findById() shows how to do that:

```
@Override
public Ingredient findById(String id) {
  return jdbcTemplate.queryForObject(
      "select id, name, type from Ingredient where id=?",
      new RowMapper<Ingredient>() {
        public Ingredient mapRow(ResultSet rs, int rowNum)
            throws SQLException {
          return new Ingredient(
              rs.getString("id"),
              rs.getString("name"),
              Ingredient.Type.valueOf(rs.getString("type")));
        };
      }, id);
}
```

Reading data from a database is only part of the story. At some point, data must be written to the database so that it can be read. Let's see about implementing the save() method.

INSERTING A ROW

JdbcTemplate's update() method can be used for any query that writes or updates data in the database. And, as shown in the following listing, it can be used to insert data into the database.

Listing 3.6　Inserting data with `JdbcTemplate`

```
@Override
public Ingredient save(Ingredient ingredient) {
  jdbcTemplate.update(
    "insert into Ingredient (id, name, type) values (?, ?, ?)",
    ingredient.getId(),
    ingredient.getName(),
    ingredient.getType().toString());
  return ingredient;
}
```

Because it isn't necessary to map `ResultSet` data to an object, the `update()` method is much simpler than `query()`. It requires only a `String` containing the SQL to perform as well as values to assign to any query parameters. In this case, the query has three parameters, which correspond to the final three parameters of the `save()` method, providing the ingredient's ID, name, and type.

With `JdbcIngredientRepository` complete, you can now inject it into `Design-TacoController` and use it to provide a list of `Ingredient` objects instead of using hardcoded values (as you did in chapter 2). The changes to `DesignTacoController` are shown next.

Listing 3.7　Injecting and using a repository in the controller

```
@Controller
@RequestMapping("/design")
@SessionAttributes("tacoOrder")
public class DesignTacoController {

  private final IngredientRepository ingredientRepo;

  @Autowired
  public DesignTacoController(
      IngredientRepository ingredientRepo) {
    this.ingredientRepo = ingredientRepo;
  }

  @ModelAttribute
  public void addIngredientsToModel(Model model) {
    Iterable<Ingredient> ingredients = ingredientRepo.findAll();
    Type[] types = Ingredient.Type.values();
    for (Type type : types) {
      model.addAttribute(type.toString().toLowerCase(),
        filterByType(ingredients, type));
    }
  }

  // ...
}
```

The `addIngredientsToModel()` method uses the injected `IngredientRepository`'s `findAll()` method to fetch all ingredients from the database. It then filters them into distinct ingredient types before adding them to the model.

Now that we have an `IngredientRepository` from which to fetch `Ingredient` objects, we can also simplify the `IngredientByIdConverter` that we created in chapter 2, replacing its hardcoded `Map` of `Ingredient` objects with a simple call to the `IngredientRepository.findById()` method, as shown next.

Listing 3.8   Simplifying `IngredientByIdConverter`

```
package tacos.web;

import org.springframework.beans.factory.annotation.Autowired;
import org.springframework.core.convert.converter.Converter;
import org.springframework.stereotype.Component;

import tacos.Ingredient;
import tacos.data.IngredientRepository;

@Component
public class IngredientByIdConverter implements Converter<String, Ingredient> {

  private IngredientRepository ingredientRepo;

  @Autowired
  public IngredientByIdConverter(IngredientRepository ingredientRepo) {
    this.ingredientRepo = ingredientRepo;
  }

  @Override
  public Ingredient convert(String id) {
    return ingredientRepo.findById(id).orElse(null);
  }

}
```

You're almost ready to fire up the application and try out these changes. But before you can start reading data from the `Ingredient` table referenced in the queries, you should probably create that table and populate it with some ingredient data.

3.1.3   *Defining a schema and preloading data*

Aside from the `Ingredient` table, you're also going to need some tables that hold order and design information. Figure 3.1 illustrates the tables you'll need, as well as the relationships between those tables.

The tables in figure 3.1 serve the following purposes:

- *Taco_Order*—Holds essential order details
- *Taco*—Holds essential information about a taco design
- *Ingredient_Ref*—Contains one or more rows for each row in `Taco`, mapping the taco to the ingredients for that taco
- *Ingredient*—Holds ingredient information

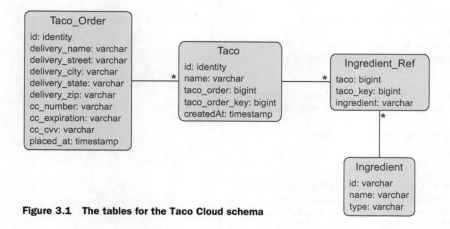

Figure 3.1   The tables for the Taco Cloud schema

In our application, a Taco can't exist outside of the context of a Taco_Order. Thus, Taco_Order and Taco are considered members of an aggregate where Taco_Order is the aggregate root. Ingredient objects, on the other hand, are sole members of their own aggregate and are referenced by Taco by way of Ingredient_Ref.

> **NOTE**   Aggregates and aggregate roots are core concepts of *domain-driven design*, a design approach that promotes the idea that the structure and language of software code should match the business domain. Although we're applying a little domain-driven design (DDD) in the Taco Cloud domain objects, there's much more to DDD than aggregates and aggregate roots. For more on this subject, read the seminal work on the subject, *Domain-Driven Design: Tackling Complexity in the Heart of Software* (https://www.dddcommunity .org/book/evans_2003/), by Eric Evans.

The next listing shows the SQL that creates the tables.

Listing 3.9   Defining the Taco Cloud schema

```
create table if not exists Taco_Order (
  id identity,
  delivery_Name varchar(50) not null,
  delivery_Street varchar(50) not null,
  delivery_City varchar(50) not null,
  delivery_State varchar(2) not null,
  delivery_Zip varchar(10) not null,
  cc_number varchar(16) not null,
  cc_expiration varchar(5) not null,
  cc_cvv varchar(3) not null,
  placed_at timestamp not null
);

create table if not exists Taco (
  id identity,
```

```
  name varchar(50) not null,
  taco_order bigint not null,
  taco_order_key bigint not null,
  created_at timestamp not null
);

create table if not exists Ingredient_Ref (
  ingredient varchar(4) not null,
  taco bigint not null,
  taco_key bigint not null
);


create table if not exists Ingredient (
  id varchar(4) not null,
  name varchar(25) not null,
  type varchar(10) not null
);


alter table Taco
    add foreign key (taco_order) references Taco_Order(id);
alter table Ingredient_Ref
    add foreign key (ingredient) references Ingredient(id);
```

The big question is where to put this schema definition. As it turns out, Spring Boot answers that question.

If there's a file named schema.sql in the root of the application's classpath, then the SQL in that file will be executed against the database when the application starts. Therefore, you should place the contents of listing 3.9 in your project as a file named schema.sql in the src/main/resources folder.

You also need to preload the database with some ingredient data. Fortunately, Spring Boot will also execute a file named data.sql from the root of the classpath when the application starts. Therefore, you can load the database with ingredient data using the insert statements in the next listing, placed in src/main/resources/data.sql.

Listing 3.10   Preloading the database with data.sql

```
delete from Ingredient_Ref;
delete from Taco;
delete from Taco_Order;

delete from Ingredient;
insert into Ingredient (id, name, type)
            values ('FLTO', 'Flour Tortilla', 'WRAP');
insert into Ingredient (id, name, type)
            values ('COTO', 'Corn Tortilla', 'WRAP');
insert into Ingredient (id, name, type)
            values ('GRBF', 'Ground Beef', 'PROTEIN');
insert into Ingredient (id, name, type)
            values ('CARN', 'Carnitas', 'PROTEIN');
```

```
insert into Ingredient (id, name, type)
              values ('TMTO', 'Diced Tomatoes', 'VEGGIES');
insert into Ingredient (id, name, type)
              values ('LETC', 'Lettuce', 'VEGGIES');
insert into Ingredient (id, name, type)
              values ('CHED', 'Cheddar', 'CHEESE');
insert into Ingredient (id, name, type)
              values ('JACK', 'Monterrey Jack', 'CHEESE');
insert into Ingredient (id, name, type)
              values ('SLSA', 'Salsa', 'SAUCE');
insert into Ingredient (id, name, type)
              values ('SRCR', 'Sour Cream', 'SAUCE');
```

Even though you've only developed a repository for ingredient data, you can fire up the Taco Cloud application at this point and visit the design page to see JdbcIngredient-Repository in action. Go ahead … give it a try. When you get back, you'll write the repositories for persisting Taco and TacoOrder data.

3.1.4 *Inserting data*

You've already had a glimpse into how to use JdbcTemplate to write data to the database. The save() method in JdbcIngredientRepository used the update() method of JdbcTemplate to save Ingredient objects to the database.

Although that was a good first example, it was perhaps a bit too simple. As you'll soon see, saving data can be more involved than what JdbcIngredientRepository needed.

In our design, TacoOrder and Taco are part of an aggregate in which TacoOrder is the aggregate root. In other words, Taco objects don't exist outside of the context of a TacoOrder. So, for now, we only need to define a repository to persist TacoOrder objects and, in turn, Taco objects along with them. Such a repository can be defined in a OrderRepository interface like this:

```
package tacos.data;

import java.util.Optional;

import tacos.TacoOrder;

public interface OrderRepository {

  TacoOrder save(TacoOrder order);

}
```

Seems simple enough, right? Not so quick. When you save a TacoOrder, you also must save the Taco objects that go with it. And when you save the Taco objects, you'll also need to save an object that represents the link between the Taco and each Ingredient that makes up the taco. The IngredientRef class defines that linking between Taco and Ingredient as follows:

```
package tacos;

import lombok.Data;

@Data
public class IngredientRef {

  private final String ingredient;

}
```

Suffice it to say that the save() method will be a bit more interesting than the corresponding method you created earlier for saving a humble Ingredient object.

Another thing that the save() method will need to do is determine what ID is assigned to the order once it has been saved. Per the schema, the id property on the Taco_Order table is an identity, meaning that the database will determine the value automatically. But if the database determines the value for you, then you will need to know what that value is so that it can be returned in the TacoOrder object returned from the save() method. Fortunately, Spring offers a helpful GeneratedKeyHolder type that can help with that. But it involves working with a prepared statement, as shown in the following implementation of the save() method:

```
package tacos.data;

import java.sql.Types;
import java.util.Arrays;
import java.util.Date;
import java.util.List;
import java.util.Optional;

import org.springframework.asm.Type;
import org.springframework.jdbc.core.JdbcOperations;
import org.springframework.jdbc.core.PreparedStatementCreator;
import org.springframework.jdbc.core.PreparedStatementCreatorFactory;
import org.springframework.jdbc.support.GeneratedKeyHolder;
import org.springframework.stereotype.Repository;
import org.springframework.transaction.annotation.Transactional;

import tacos.IngredientRef;
import tacos.Taco;
import tacos.TacoOrder;

@Repository
public class JdbcOrderRepository implements OrderRepository {

  private JdbcOperations jdbcOperations;

  public JdbcOrderRepository(JdbcOperations jdbcOperations) {
    this.jdbcOperations = jdbcOperations;
  }
```

```
@Override
@Transactional
public TacoOrder save(TacoOrder order) {
  PreparedStatementCreatorFactory pscf =
    new PreparedStatementCreatorFactory(
      "insert into Taco_Order "
      + "(delivery_name, delivery_street, delivery_city, "
      + "delivery_state, delivery_zip, cc_number, "
      + "cc_expiration, cc_cvv, placed_at) "
      + "values (?,?,?,?,?,?,?,?,?)",
      Types.VARCHAR, Types.VARCHAR, Types.VARCHAR,
      Types.VARCHAR, Types.VARCHAR, Types.VARCHAR,
      Types.VARCHAR, Types.VARCHAR, Types.TIMESTAMP
  );
  pscf.setReturnGeneratedKeys(true);

  order.setPlacedAt(new Date());
  PreparedStatementCreator psc =
      pscf.newPreparedStatementCreator(
          Arrays.asList(
              order.getDeliveryName(),
              order.getDeliveryStreet(),
              order.getDeliveryCity(),
              order.getDeliveryState(),
              order.getDeliveryZip(),
              order.getCcNumber(),
              order.getCcExpiration(),
              order.getCcCVV(),
              order.getPlacedAt()));

  GeneratedKeyHolder keyHolder = new GeneratedKeyHolder();
  jdbcOperations.update(psc, keyHolder);
  long orderId = keyHolder.getKey().longValue();
  order.setId(orderId);

  List<Taco> tacos = order.getTacos();
  int i=0;
  for (Taco taco : tacos) {
    saveTaco(orderId, i++, taco);
  }

  return order;
  }
}
```

There appears to be a lot going on in the save() method, but we can break it down into only a handful of significant steps. First, you create a PreparedStatement-CreatorFactory that describes the insert query along with the types of the query's input fields. Because you'll later need to fetch the saved order's ID, you also will need to call setReturnGeneratedKeys(true).

After defining the PreparedStatementCreatorFactory, you use it to create a PreparedStatementCreator, passing in the values from the TacoOrder object that will be persisted. The last field given to the PreparedStatementCreator is the date that the order is created, which you'll also need to set on the TacoOrder object itself so that the returned TacoOrder will have that information available.

Now that you have a PreparedStatementCreator in hand, you're ready to actually save the order data by calling the update() method on JdbcOperations, passing in the PreparedStatementCreator and a GeneratedKeyHolder. After the order data has been saved, the GeneratedKeyHolder will contain the value of the id field as assigned by the database and should be copied into the TacoOrder object's id property.

At this point, the order has been saved, but you need to also save the Taco objects associated with the order. You can do that by calling saveTaco() for each Taco in the order.

The saveTaco() method is quite similar to the save() method, as you can see here:

```
private long saveTaco(Long orderId, int orderKey, Taco taco) {
  taco.setCreatedAt(new Date());
  PreparedStatementCreatorFactory pscf =
          new PreparedStatementCreatorFactory(
      "insert into Taco "
      + "(name, created_at, taco_order, taco_order_key) "
      + "values (?, ?, ?, ?)",
      Types.VARCHAR, Types.TIMESTAMP, Type.LONG, Type.LONG
  );
  pscf.setReturnGeneratedKeys(true);

  PreparedStatementCreator psc =
      pscf.newPreparedStatementCreator(
          Arrays.asList(
              taco.getName(),
              taco.getCreatedAt(),
              orderId,
              orderKey));

  GeneratedKeyHolder keyHolder = new GeneratedKeyHolder();
  jdbcOperations.update(psc, keyHolder);
  long tacoId = keyHolder.getKey().longValue();
  taco.setId(tacoId);

  saveIngredientRefs(tacoId, taco.getIngredients());

  return tacoId;
}
```

Step by step, saveTaco() mirrors the structure of save(), albeit for Taco data instead of TacoOrder data. In the end, it makes a call to saveIngredientRefs() to create rows in the Ingredient_Ref table to link the Taco row to an Ingredient row. The save-IngredientRefs() method looks like this:

```
private void saveIngredientRefs(
    long tacoId, List<IngredientRef> ingredientRefs) {
```

```
    int key = 0;
    for (IngredientRef ingredientRef : ingredientRefs) {
      jdbcOperations.update(
          "insert into Ingredient_Ref (ingredient, taco, taco_key) "
          + "values (?, ?, ?)",
          ingredientRef.getIngredient(), tacoId, key++);
    }
  }
}
```

Thankfully, the saveIngredientRefs() method is much simpler. It cycles through a
list of Ingredient objects, saving each into the Ingredient_Ref table. It also has a local
key variable that is used as an index to ensure that the ordering of the ingredients
stays intact.

   All that's left to do with OrderRepository is to inject it into OrderController and
use it when saving an order. The following listing shows the changes necessary for
injecting the repository.

Listing 3.11   Injecting and using OrderRepository

```
package tacos.web;
import javax.validation.Valid;

import org.springframework.stereotype.Controller;
import org.springframework.validation.Errors;
import org.springframework.web.bind.annotation.GetMapping;
import org.springframework.web.bind.annotation.PostMapping;
import org.springframework.web.bind.annotation.RequestMapping;
import org.springframework.web.bind.annotation.SessionAttributes;
import org.springframework.web.bind.support.SessionStatus;

import tacos.TacoOrder;
import tacos.data.OrderRepository;

@Controller
@RequestMapping("/orders")
@SessionAttributes("tacoOrder")
public class OrderController {

  private OrderRepository orderRepo;

  public OrderController(OrderRepository orderRepo) {
    this.orderRepo = orderRepo;
  }

  // ...

  @PostMapping
  public String processOrder(@Valid TacoOrder order, Errors errors,
      SessionStatus sessionStatus) {
    if (errors.hasErrors()) {
      return "orderForm";
    }
```

```
    orderRepo.save(order);
    sessionStatus.setComplete();

    return "redirect:/";
  }

}
```

As you can see, the constructor takes an `OrderRepository` as a parameter and assigns it to an instance variable that it will use in the `processOrder()` method. Speaking of the `processOrder()` method, it has been changed to call the `save()` method on the `OrderRepository` instead of logging the `TacoOrder` object.

Spring's `JdbcTemplate` makes working with relational databases significantly simpler than with plain vanilla JDBC. But even with `JdbcTemplate`, some persistence tasks are still challenging, especially when persisting nested domain objects in an aggregate. If only there were a way to work with JDBC that was even simpler.

Let's have a look at Spring Data JDBC, which makes working with JDBC insanely easy—even when persisting aggregates.

3.2   *Working with Spring Data JDBC*

The Spring Data project is a rather large umbrella project comprising several subprojects, most of which are focused on data persistence with a variety of different database types. A few of the most popular Spring Data projects include these:

- *Spring Data JDBC*—JDBC persistence against a relational database
- *Spring Data JPA*—JPA persistence against a relational database
- *Spring Data MongoDB*—Persistence to a Mongo document database
- *Spring Data Neo4j*—Persistence to a Neo4j graph database
- *Spring Data Redis*—Persistence to a Redis key-value store
- *Spring Data Cassandra*—Persistence to a Cassandra column store database

One of the most interesting and useful features provided by Spring Data for all of these projects is the ability to automatically create repositories, based on a repository specification interface. Consequently, persistence with Spring Data projects has little or no persistence logic and involves writing only one or more repository interfaces.

Let's see how to apply Spring Data JDBC to our project to simplify data persistence with JDBC. First, you'll need to add Spring Data JDBC to the project build.

3.2.1   *Adding Spring Data JDBC to the build*

Spring Data JDBC is available as a starter dependency for Spring Boot apps. When added to the project's pom.xml file, the starter dependency looks like the following code snippet.

Listing 3.12   Adding the Spring Data JDBC dependency to the build

```
<dependency>
  <groupId>org.springframework.boot</groupId>
  <artifactId>spring-boot-starter-data-jdbc</artifactId>
</dependency>
```

You will no longer need the JDBC starter that gave us `JdbcTemplate`, so you can remove the starter that looks like this:

```
<dependency>
  <groupId>org.springframework.boot</groupId>
  <artifactId>spring-boot-starter-jdbc</artifactId>
</dependency>
```

You'll still need a database, however, so don't remove the H2 dependency.

3.2.2   *Defining repository interfaces*

Fortunately, we've already created `IngredientRepository` and `OrderRepository`, so much of the work in defining our repositories is already done. But we'll need to make a subtle change to them in order to use them with Spring Data JDBC.

Spring Data will automatically generate implementations for our repository interfaces at run time. But it will do that only for interfaces that extend one of the repository interfaces provided by Spring Data. At the very least, our repository interfaces will need to extend `Repository` so that Spring Data knows to create the implementation automatically. For example, here's how you might write `IngredientRepository` such that it extends `Repository`:

```
package tacos.data;
import java.util.Optional;
import org.springframework.data.repository.Repository;
import tacos.Ingredient;

public interface IngredientRepository
        extends Repository<Ingredient, String> {

  Iterable<Ingredient> findAll();

  Optional<Ingredient> findById(String id);

  Ingredient save(Ingredient ingredient);

}
```

As you can see, the `Repository` interface is parameterized. The first parameter is the type of the object to be persisted by this repository—in this case, `Ingredient`. The second parameter is the type of the persisted object's ID field. For `Ingredient`, that's `String`.

Although `IngredientRepository` will work as shown here by extending `Repository`, Spring Data also offers `CrudRepository` as a base interface for common operations, including the three methods we've defined in `IngredientRepository`. So, instead of extending `Repository`, it's often easier to extend `CrudRepository`, as shown next.

Listing 3.13   Defining a repository interface for persisting ingredients

```
package tacos.data;

import org.springframework.data.repository.CrudRepository;

import tacos.Ingredient;

public interface IngredientRepository
        extends CrudRepository<Ingredient, String> {

}
```

Similarly, our `OrderRepository` can extend `CrudRepository` as shown in the next listing.

Listing 3.14   Defining a repository interface for persisting taco orders

```
package tacos.data;

import org.springframework.data.repository.CrudRepository;

import tacos.TacoOrder;

public interface OrderRepository
        extends CrudRepository<TacoOrder, Long> {

}
```

In both cases, because `CrudRepository` already defines the methods you need, there's no need to explicitly define them in the `IngredientRepository` and `OrderRepository` interfaces.

And now you have your two repositories. You might be thinking that you need to write the implementations for both repositories, including the dozen methods defined in `CrudRepository`. But that's the good news about Spring Data—there's no need to write an implementation! When the application starts, Spring Data automatically generates an implementation on the fly. This means the repositories are ready to use from the get-go. Just inject them into the controllers and you're done.

What's more, because Spring Data automatically creates implementations of these interfaces at run time, you no longer need the explicit implementations in `Jdbc-IngredientRepository` and `JdbcOrderRepository`. You can delete those two classes and never look back!

3.2.3   *Annotating the domain for persistence*

The only other thing we'll need to do is annotate our domain classes so that Spring Data JDBC will know how to persist them. Generally speaking, this means annotating the identity properties with `@Id`—so that Spring Data will know which field represents the object's identity—and optionally annotating the class with `@Table`.

For example, the `TacoOrder` class might be annotated with `@Table` and `@Id` as shown in the following code.

Listing 3.15   Preparing the `Taco` class for persistence

```
package tacos;
import java.io.Serializable;
import java.util.ArrayList;
import java.util.Date;
import java.util.List;

import javax.validation.constraints.Digits;
import javax.validation.constraints.NotBlank;
import javax.validation.constraints.Pattern;

import org.hibernate.validator.constraints.CreditCardNumber;
import org.springframework.data.annotation.Id;
import org.springframework.data.relational.core.mapping.Table;

import lombok.Data;

@Data
@Table
public class TacoOrder implements Serializable {

  private static final long serialVersionUID = 1L;

  @Id
  private Long id;

  // ...

}
```

The `@Table` annotation is completely optional. By default, the object is mapped to a table based on the domain class name. In this case, `TacoOrder` is mapped to a table named "Taco_Order". If that's fine for you, then you can leave the `@Table` annotation off completely or use it without parameters. But if you'd prefer to map it to a different table name, then you can specify the table name as a parameter to `@Table` like this:

```
@Table("Taco_Cloud_Order")
public class TacoOrder {
  ...
}
```

As shown here, `TacoOrder` will be mapped to a table named "Taco_Cloud_Order".

As for the @Id annotation, it designates the id property as being the identity for a TacoOrder. All other properties in TacoOrder will be mapped automatically to columns based on their property names. For example, the deliveryName property will be automatically mapped to the column named delivery_name. But if you want to explicitly define the column name mapping, you could annotate the property with @Column like this:

```
@Column("customer_name")
@NotBlank(message="Delivery name is required")
private String deliveryName;
```

In this case, @Column is specifying that the deliveryName property will be mapped to the column whose name is customer_name.

You'll also need to apply @Table and @Id to the other domain classes. This includes @Ingredient.

Listing 3.16   Preparing the Ingredient class for persistence

```
package tacos;

import org.springframework.data.annotation.Id;
import org.springframework.data.domain.Persistable;
import org.springframework.data.relational.core.mapping.Table;

import lombok.AccessLevel;
import lombok.AllArgsConstructor;
import lombok.Data;
import lombok.NoArgsConstructor;

@Data
@Table
@AllArgsConstructor
@NoArgsConstructor(access=AccessLevel.PRIVATE, force=true)
public class Ingredient implements Persistable<String> {

  @Id
  private String id;

  // ...

}
```

...and Taco.

Listing 3.17   Preparing the Taco class for persistence

```
package tacos;
import java.util.ArrayList;
import java.util.Date;
import java.util.List;
```

```
import javax.validation.constraints.NotNull;
import javax.validation.constraints.Size;

import org.springframework.data.annotation.Id;
import org.springframework.data.relational.core.mapping.Table;

import lombok.Data;

@Data
@Table
public class Taco {

  @Id
  private Long id;

  // ...

}
```

As for `IngredientRef`, it will be mapped automatically to the table whose name is `"Ingredient_Ref"`, which is perfect for our application. You can annotate it with `@Table` if you want, but it's not necessary. And the `"Ingredient_Ref"` table has no identity column, so there is no need to annotate anything in `IngredientRef` with `@Id`.

With these small changes, not to mention the complete removal of the `Jdbc-IngredientRepository` and `JdbcOrderRepository` classes, you now have a lot less persistence code. Even so, the repository implementations that are generated at runtime by Spring Data still do everything that the repositories using `JdbcTemplate` did. In fact, they have potential for doing even more, because the two repository interfaces extend `CrudRepository`, which offers a dozen or so operations for creating, reading, updating, and deleting objects.

3.2.4 *Preloading data with CommandLineRunner*

When working with `JdbcTemplate`, we preloaded the `Ingredient` data at application startup using data.sql, which was executed against the database when the data source bean was created. That same approach will work with Spring Data JDBC. In fact, it will work with any persistence mechanism for which the backing database is a relational database. But let's see another way of populating a database at startup that offers a bit more flexibility.

Spring Boot offers two useful interfaces for executing logic when an application starts up: `CommandLineRunner` and `ApplicationRunner`. These two interfaces are quite similar. Both are functional interfaces that require that a single `run()` method be implemented. When the application starts up, any beans in the application context that implement `CommandLineRunner` or `ApplicationRunner` will have their `run()` methods invoked after the application context and all beans are wired up, but before anything else happens. This provides a convenient place for data to be loaded into the database.

Because both `CommandLineRunner` and `ApplicationRunner` are functional interfaces, they can easily be declared as beans in a configuration class using a `@Bean`-annotated method that returns a lambda function. For example, here's how you might create a data-loading `CommandLineRunner` bean:

```
@Bean
public CommandLineRunner dataLoader(IngredientRepository repo) {
  return args -> {
    repo.save(new Ingredient("FLTO", "Flour Tortilla", Type.WRAP));
    repo.save(new Ingredient("COTO", "Corn Tortilla", Type.WRAP));
    repo.save(new Ingredient("GRBF", "Ground Beef", Type.PROTEIN));
    repo.save(new Ingredient("CARN", "Carnitas", Type.PROTEIN));
    repo.save(new Ingredient("TMTO", "Diced Tomatoes", Type.VEGGIES));
    repo.save(new Ingredient("LETC", "Lettuce", Type.VEGGIES));
    repo.save(new Ingredient("CHED", "Cheddar", Type.CHEESE));
    repo.save(new Ingredient("JACK", "Monterrey Jack", Type.CHEESE));
    repo.save(new Ingredient("SLSA", "Salsa", Type.SAUCE));
    repo.save(new Ingredient("SRCR", "Sour Cream", Type.SAUCE));
  };
}
```

Here, the `IngredientRepository` is injected into the bean method and used within the lambda to create `Ingredient` objects. The `run()` method of `CommandLineRunner` accepts a single parameter that is a `String` vararg containing all of the command-line arguments for the running application. We don't need those to load ingredients into the database, so the `args` parameter is ignored.

Alternatively, we could have defined the data-loader bean as a lambda implementation of `ApplicationRunner` like this:

```
@Bean
public ApplicationRunner dataLoader(IngredientRepository repo) {
  return args -> {
    repo.save(new Ingredient("FLTO", "Flour Tortilla", Type.WRAP));
    repo.save(new Ingredient("COTO", "Corn Tortilla", Type.WRAP));
    repo.save(new Ingredient("GRBF", "Ground Beef", Type.PROTEIN));
    repo.save(new Ingredient("CARN", "Carnitas", Type.PROTEIN));
    repo.save(new Ingredient("TMTO", "Diced Tomatoes", Type.VEGGIES));
    repo.save(new Ingredient("LETC", "Lettuce", Type.VEGGIES));
    repo.save(new Ingredient("CHED", "Cheddar", Type.CHEESE));
    repo.save(new Ingredient("JACK", "Monterrey Jack", Type.CHEESE));
    repo.save(new Ingredient("SLSA", "Salsa", Type.SAUCE));
    repo.save(new Ingredient("SRCR", "Sour Cream", Type.SAUCE));
  };
}
```

The key difference between `CommandLineRunner` and `ApplicationRunner` is in the parameter passed to the respective `run()` methods. `CommandLineRunner` accepts a `String` vararg, which is a raw representation of arguments passed on the command line. But `ApplicationRunner` accepts an `ApplicationArguments` parameter that offers methods for accessing the arguments as parsed components of the command line.

For example, suppose that we want our application to accept a command line with arguments such as `"--version 1.2.3"` and need to consider that argument in our loader bean. If using a `CommandLineRunner`, we'd need to search the array for "–version" and then take the very next value from the array. But with `ApplicationRunner`, we can query the given `ApplicationArguments` for the "–version" argument like this:

```
public ApplicationRunner dataLoader(IngredientRepository repo) {
  return args -> {
    List<String> version = args.getOptionValues("version");
    ...
  };
}
```

The `getOptionValues()` method returns a `List<String>` to allow for the option argument to be specified multiple times.

In the case of either `CommandLineRunner` or `ApplicationRunner`, however, we don't need command-line arguments to load data. So the `args` parameter is ignored in our data-loader bean.

What's nice about using `CommandLineRunner` or `ApplicationRunner` to do an initial data load is that they are using the repositories to create the persisted objects instead of a SQL script. This means that they'll work equally well for relational databases and nonrelational databases. This will come in handy in the next chapter when we see how to use Spring Data to persist to nonrelational databases.

But before we do that, let's have a look at another Spring Data project for persisting data in relational databases: Spring Data JPA.

3.3 Persisting data with Spring Data JPA

Whereas Spring Data JDBC makes easy work of persisting data, the Java Persistence API (JPA) is another popular option for working with data in a relational database. Spring Data JPA offers an approach to persistence with JPA similar to what Spring Data JDBC gave us for JDBC.

To see how Spring Data works, you're going to start over, replacing the JDBC-based repositories from earlier in this chapter with repositories created by Spring Data JPA. But first, you need to add Spring Data JPA to the project build.

3.3.1 Adding Spring Data JPA to the project

Spring Data JPA is available to Spring Boot applications with the JPA starter. This starter dependency not only brings in Spring Data JPA but also transitively includes Hibernate as the JPA implementation, as shown here:

```
<dependency>
  <groupId>org.springframework.boot</groupId>
  <artifactId>spring-boot-starter-data-jpa</artifactId>
</dependency>
```

If you want to use a different JPA implementation, then you'll need to, at least, exclude the Hibernate dependency and include the JPA library of your choice. For example, to use EclipseLink instead of Hibernate, you'll need to alter the build as follows:

```
<dependency>
  <groupId>org.springframework.boot</groupId>
  <artifactId>spring-boot-starter-data-jpa</artifactId>
  <exclusions>
    <exclusion>
        <groupId>org.hibernate</groupId>
        <artifactId>hibernate-core</artifactId>
    </exclusion>
  </exclusions>
</dependency>
<dependency>
  <groupId>org.eclipse.persistence</groupId>
  <artifactId>org.eclipse.persistence.jpa</artifactId>
  <version>2.7.6</version>
</dependency>
```

Note that there may be other changes required, depending on your choice of JPA implementation. Consult the documentation of your chosen JPA implementation for details. Now let's revisit your domain objects and annotate them for JPA persistence.

3.3.2   *Annotating the domain as entities*

As you've already seen with Spring Data JDBC, Spring Data does some amazing things when it comes to creating repositories. But unfortunately, it doesn't help much when it comes to annotating your domain objects with JPA mapping annotations. You'll need to open up the `Ingredient`, `Taco`, and `TacoOrder` classes and throw in a few annotations. First up is the `Ingredient` class, shown next.

Listing 3.18   Annotating `Ingredient` for JPA persistence

```
package tacos;

import javax.persistence.Entity;
import javax.persistence.Id;

import lombok.AccessLevel;
import lombok.AllArgsConstructor;
import lombok.Data;
import lombok.NoArgsConstructor;

@Data
@Entity
@AllArgsConstructor
@NoArgsConstructor(access=AccessLevel.PRIVATE, force=true)
public class Ingredient {

  @Id
  private String id;
  private String name;
  private Type type;
```

```
public enum Type {
  WRAP, PROTEIN, VEGGIES, CHEESE, SAUCE
}

}
```

To declare this as a JPA entity, `Ingredient` must be annotated with `@Entity`. And its id property must be annotated with `@Id` to designate it as the property that will uniquely identify the entity in the database. Note that this `@Id` annotation is the JPA variety from the `javax.persistence` package, as opposed to the `@Id` provided by Spring Data in the `org.springframework.data.annotation` package.

Also note that we no longer need the `@Table` annotation or need to implement `Persistable`. Although we could still use `@Table` here, it is unnecessary when working with JPA and defaults to the name of the class (`"Ingredient"`, in this case). As for `Persistable`, it was only necessary with Spring Data JDBC to determine whether or not an entity was to be created new, or to update an existing entity; JPA sorts that out automatically.

In addition to the JPA-specific annotations, you'll also note that you've added a `@NoArgsConstructor` annotation at the class level. JPA requires that entities have a no-arguments constructor, so Lombok's `@NoArgsConstructor` does that for you. You don't want to be able to use it, though, so you make it `private` by setting the access attribute to `AccessLevel.PRIVATE`. And because you must set `final` properties, you also set the `force` attribute to `true`, which results in the Lombok-generated constructor setting them to a default value of `null`, `0`, or `false`, depending on the property type.

You also will add an `@AllArgsConstructor` to make it easy to create an `Ingredient` object with all properties initialized.

You also need a `@RequiredArgsConstructor`. The `@Data` annotation implicitly adds a required arguments constructor, but when a `@NoArgsConstructor` is used, that constructor is removed. An explicit `@RequiredArgsConstructor` ensures that you'll still have a required arguments constructor, in addition to the `private` no-arguments constructor.

Now let's move on to the `Taco` class and see how to annotate it as a JPA entity.

Listing 3.19 Annotating `Taco` as an entity

```
package tacos;
import java.util.ArrayList;
import java.util.Date;
import java.util.List;

import javax.persistence.Entity;
import javax.persistence.GeneratedValue;
import javax.persistence.GenerationType;
import javax.persistence.Id;
import javax.persistence.ManyToMany;
```

```
import javax.validation.constraints.NotNull;
import javax.validation.constraints.Size;

import lombok.Data;

@Data
@Entity
public class Taco {

  @Id
  @GeneratedValue(strategy = GenerationType.AUTO)
  private Long id;

  @NotNull
  @Size(min=5, message="Name must be at least 5 characters long")
  private String name;

  private Date createdAt = new Date();

  @Size(min=1, message="You must choose at least 1 ingredient")
  @ManyToMany()
  private List<Ingredient> ingredients = new ArrayList<>();

  public void addIngredient(Ingredient ingredient) {
    this.ingredients.add(ingredient);
  }

}
```

As with `Ingredient`, the `Taco` class is now annotated with `@Entity` and has its `id` property annotated with `@Id`. Because you're relying on the database to automatically generate the ID value, you also annotate the `id` property with `@GeneratedValue`, specifying a `strategy` of `AUTO`.

To declare the relationship between a `Taco` and its associated `Ingredient` list, you annotate ingredients with `@ManyToMany`. A `Taco` can have many `Ingredient` objects, and an `Ingredient` can be a part of many `Tacos`.

Finally, let's annotate the `TacoOrder` object as an entity. The next listing shows the new `TacoOrder` class.

> **Listing 3.20 Annotating `TacoOrder` as a JPA entity**

```
package tacos;
import java.io.Serializable;
import java.util.ArrayList;
import java.util.Date;
import java.util.List;

import javax.persistence.CascadeType;
import javax.persistence.Entity;
import javax.persistence.GeneratedValue;
import javax.persistence.GenerationType;
import javax.persistence.Id;
```

```
import javax.persistence.OneToMany;
import javax.validation.constraints.Digits;
import javax.validation.constraints.NotBlank;
import javax.validation.constraints.Pattern;

import org.hibernate.validator.constraints.CreditCardNumber;

import lombok.Data;

@Data
@Entity
public class TacoOrder implements Serializable {

  private static final long serialVersionUID = 1L;

  @Id
  @GeneratedValue(strategy = GenerationType.AUTO)
  private Long id;

  private Date placedAt = new Date();

  ...

  @OneToMany(cascade = CascadeType.ALL)
  private List<Taco> tacos = new ArrayList<>();

  public void addTaco(Taco taco) {
    tacos.add(taco);
  }

}
```

As you can see, the changes to `TacoOrder` closely mirror the changes to `Taco`. One significant thing worth noting is that the relationship to the list of `Taco` objects is annotated with `@OneToMany`, indicating that the tacos are all specific to this one order. Moreover, the `cascade` attribute is set to `CascadeType.ALL` so that if the order is deleted, its related tacos will also be deleted.

3.3.3 *Declaring JPA repositories*

When you created the `JdbcTemplate` versions of the repositories, you explicitly declared the methods you wanted the repository to provide. But with Spring Data JDBC, you were able to dismiss the explicit implementation classes and instead extend the `CrudRepository` interface. As it turns out, `CrudRepository` works equally well for Spring Data JPA. For example, here's the new `IngredientRepository` interface:

```
package tacos.data;

import org.springframework.data.repository.CrudRepository;

import tacos.Ingredient;
```

```
public interface IngredientRepository
        extends CrudRepository<Ingredient, String> {

}
```

In fact, the IngredientRepository interface we'll use with Spring Data JPA is identical to the one we defined for use with Spring Data JDBC. The CrudRepository interface is commonly used across many of Spring Data's projects, regardless of the underlying persistence mechanism. Similarly, you can define OrderRepository for the Spring Data JPA the same as it was for Spring Data JDBC, as follows:

```
package tacos.data;

import org.springframework.data.repository.CrudRepository;

import tacos.TacoOrder;

public interface OrderRepository
        extends CrudRepository<TacoOrder, Long> {

}
```

The methods provided by CrudRepository are great for general-purpose persistence of entities. But what if you have some requirements beyond basic persistence? Let's see how to customize the repositories to perform queries unique to your domain.

3.3.4   *Customizing repositories*

Imagine that in addition to the basic CRUD operations provided by CrudRepository, you also need to fetch all the orders delivered to a given ZIP code. As it turns out, this can easily be addressed by adding the following method declaration to Order-Repository:

```
List<TacoOrder> findByDeliveryZip(String deliveryZip);
```

When generating the repository implementation, Spring Data examines each method in the repository interface, parses the method name, and attempts to understand the method's purpose in the context of the persisted object (a TacoOrder, in this case). In essence, Spring Data defines a sort of miniature domain-specific language (DSL), where persistence details are expressed in repository method signatures.

Spring Data knows that this method is intended to find Orders, because you've parameterized CrudRepository with TacoOrder. The method name, findByDelivery-Zip(), makes it clear that this method should find all TacoOrder entities by matching their deliveryZip property with the value passed in as a parameter to the method.

The findByDeliveryZip() method is simple enough, but Spring Data can handle even more interesting method names as well. Repository methods are composed of a verb, an optional subject, the word By, and a predicate. In the case of findBy-DeliveryZip(), the verb is find and the predicate is DeliveryZip; the subject isn't specified and is implied to be a TacoOrder.

Let's consider another, more complex example. Suppose that you need to query for all orders delivered to a given ZIP code within a given date range. In that case, the following method, when added to OrderRepository, might prove useful:

```
List<TacoOrder> readOrdersByDeliveryZipAndPlacedAtBetween(
        String deliveryZip, Date startDate, Date endDate);
```

Figure 3.2 illustrates how Spring Data parses and understands the readOrdersByDeliveryZipAndPlacedAtBetween() method when generating the repository implementation. As you can see, the verb in readOrdersByDeliveryZipAndPlacedAtBetween() is read. Spring Data also understands find, read, and get as synonymous for fetching one or more entities. Alternatively, you can also use count as the verb if you want the method to return only an int with the count of matching entities.

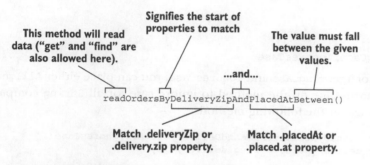

Figure 3.2   Spring Data parses repository method signatures to determine the query that should be performed.

Although the subject of the method is optional, here it says Orders. Spring Data ignores most words in a subject, so you could name the method readPuppiesBy… and it would still find TacoOrder entities, because that is the type that CrudRepository is parameterized with.

The predicate follows the word By in the method name and is the most interesting part of the method signature. In this case, the predicate refers to two TacoOrder properties: deliveryZip and placedAt. The deliveryZip property must be equal to the value passed into the first parameter of the method. The keyword Between indicates that the value of placedAt must fall between the values passed into the last two parameters of the method.

In addition to an implicit Equals operation and the Between operation, Spring Data method signatures can also include any of the following operators:

- IsAfter, After, IsGreaterThan, GreaterThan
- IsGreaterThanEqual, GreaterThanEqual
- IsBefore, Before, IsLessThan, LessThan
- IsLessThanEqual, LessThanEqual
- IsBetween, Between
- IsNull, Null
- IsNotNull, NotNull
- IsIn, In
- IsNotIn, NotIn
- IsStartingWith, StartingWith, StartsWith
- IsEndingWith, EndingWith, EndsWith
- IsContaining, Containing, Contains
- IsLike, Like
- IsNotLike, NotLike
- IsTrue, True
- IsFalse, False
- Is, Equals
- IsNot, Not
- IgnoringCase, IgnoresCase

As alternatives for `IgnoringCase` and `IgnoresCase`, you can place either `AllIgnoring-Case` or `AllIgnoresCase` on the method to ignore case for all `String` comparisons. For example, consider the following method:

```
List<TacoOrder> findByDeliveryNameAndDeliveryCityAllIgnoresCase(
        String deliveryName, String deliveryCity);
```

Finally, you can also place `OrderBy` at the end of the method name to sort the results by a specified column. For example, to order by the `deliveryName` property, use the following code:

```
List<TacoOrder> findByDeliveryCityOrderByDeliveryName(String city);
```

Although the naming convention can be useful for relatively simple queries, it doesn't take much imagination to see that method names could get out of hand for more complex queries. In that case, feel free to name the method anything you want and annotate it with `@Query` to explicitly specify the query to be performed when the method is called, as this example shows:

```
@Query("Order o where o.deliveryCity='Seattle'")
List<TacoOrder> readOrdersDeliveredInSeattle();
```

In this simple usage of `@Query`, you ask for all orders delivered in Seattle. But you can use `@Query` to perform virtually any JPA query you can dream up, even when it's difficult or impossible to achieve the query by following the naming convention.

Custom query methods also work with Spring Data JDBC but with the following key differences:

- All custom query methods require `@Query`. This is because, unlike JPA, there's no mapping metadata to help Spring Data JDBC automatically infer the query from the method name.
- All queries specified in `@Query` must be SQL queries, not JPA queries.

In the next chapter, we'll expand our use of Spring Data to work with nonrelational databases. When we do, you'll see that custom query methods work very similarly, although the query language used in `@Query` will be specific to the underlying database.

Summary

- Spring's `JdbcTemplate` greatly simplifies working with JDBC.
- `PreparedStatementCreator` and `KeyHolder` can be used together when you need to know the value of a database-generated ID.
- Spring Data JDBC and Spring Data JPA make working with relational data as easy as writing a repository interface.

Working with nonrelational data

They say that variety is the spice of life.

You probably have a favorite flavor of ice cream. It's that one flavor that you choose the most often because it satisfies that creamy craving more than any other. But most people, despite having a favorite flavor, try different flavors from time to time to mix things up.

Databases are like ice cream. For decades, the relational database has been the favorite flavor for storing data. But these days, we have more options available than ever before. So-called "NoSQL" databases (https://aws.amazon.com/nosql/) offer different concepts and structures in which data can be stored. And although the choice may still be somewhat based on taste, some databases are better suited for persisting different kinds of data than others.

Fortunately, Spring Data has you covered for many of the NoSQL databases, including MongoDB, Cassandra, Couchbase, Neo4j, Redis, and many more. And fortunately, the programming model is nearly identical, regardless of which database you choose.

There's not enough space in this chapter to cover all of the databases that Spring Data supports. But to give you a sample of Spring Data's other "flavors," we'll look at two popular NoSQL databases, Cassandra and MongoDB, and see how to create repositories to persist data to them. Let's start by looking at how to create Cassandra repositories with Spring Data.

4.1 Working with Cassandra repositories

Cassandra is a distributed, high-performance, always available, eventually consistent, partitioned-column-store, NoSQL database.

That's a mouthful of adjectives to describe a database, but each one accurately speaks to the power of working with Cassandra. To put it in simpler terms, Cassandra deals in rows of data written to tables, which are partitioned across one-to-many distributed nodes. No single node carries all the data, but any given row may be replicated across multiple nodes, thus eliminating any single point of failure.

Spring Data Cassandra provides automatic repository support for the Cassandra database that's quite similar to—and yet quite different from—what's offered by Spring Data JPA for relational databases. In addition, Spring Data Cassandra offers annotations for mapping application domain types to the backing database structures.

Before we explore Cassandra any further, it's important to understand that although Cassandra shares many concepts similar to relational databases like Oracle and SQL Server, Cassandra isn't a relational database and is in many ways quite a different beast. I'll explain the idiosyncrasies of Cassandra as they pertain to working with Spring Data. But I encourage you to read Cassandra's own documentation (http://cassandra.apache.org/doc/latest/) for a thorough understanding of what makes it tick.

Let's get started by enabling Spring Data Cassandra in the Taco Cloud project.

4.1.1 Enabling Spring Data Cassandra

To get started using Spring Data Cassandra, you'll need to add the Spring Boot starter dependency for nonreactive Spring Data Cassandra. There are actually two separate Spring Data Cassandra starter dependencies to choose from: one for reactive data persistence and one for standard, nonreactive persistence.

We'll talk more about writing reactive repositories later in chapter 15. For now, though, we'll use the nonreactive starter in our build as shown here:

```
<dependency>
  <groupId>org.springframework.boot</groupId>
  <artifactId>spring-boot-starter-data-cassandra</artifactId>
</dependency>
```

This dependency is also available from the Initializr by checking the Cassandra check box.

It's important to understand that this dependency is in lieu of the Spring Data JPA starter or Spring Data JDBC dependencies we used in the previous chapter. Instead of persisting Taco Cloud data to a relational database with JPA or JDBC, you'll be using Spring Data to persist data to a Cassandra database. Therefore, you'll want to remove the Spring Data JPA or Spring Data JDBC starter dependencies and any relational database dependencies (such as JDBC drivers or the H2 dependency) from the build.

The Spring Data Cassandra starter dependency brings a handful of dependencies to the project, specifically, the Spring Data Cassandra library. As a result of Spring Data Cassandra being in the runtime classpath, autoconfiguration for creating Cassandra repositories is triggered. This means you're able to begin writing Cassandra repositories with minimal explicit configuration.

Cassandra operates as a cluster of nodes that together act as a complete database system. If you don't already have a Cassandra cluster to work with, you can start a single-node cluster for development purposes using Docker like this:

```
$ docker network create cassandra-net
$ docker run --name my-cassandra \
         --network cassandra-net \
         -p 9042:9042 \
         -d cassandra:latest
```

This starts the single-node cluster and exposes the node's port (9042) on the host machine so that your application can access it.

You'll need to provide a small amount of configuration, though. At the very least, you'll need to configure the name of a keyspace within which your repositories will operate. To do that, you'll first need to create such a keyspace.

> **NOTE** In Cassandra, a *keyspace* is a grouping of tables in a Cassandra node. It's roughly analogous to how tables, views, and constraints are grouped in a relational database.

Although it's possible to configure Spring Data Cassandra to create the keyspace automatically, it's typically much easier to manually create it yourself (or to use an existing keyspace). Using the Cassandra CQL (Cassandra Query Language) shell, you can create a keyspace for the Taco Cloud application. You can start the CQL shell using Docker like this:

```
$ docker run -it --network cassandra-net --rm cassandra cqlsh my-cassandra
```

> **NOTE** If this command fails to start up the CQL shell with an error indicating "Unable to connect to any servers," wait a minute or two and try again. You need to be sure that the Cassandra cluster is fully started before the CQL shell can connect to it.

When the shell is ready, use the `create keyspace` command like this:

```
cqlsh> create keyspace tacocloud
   ... with replication={'class':'SimpleStrategy', 'replication_factor':1}
   ... and durable_writes=true;
```

Put simply, this will create a keyspace named tacocloud with simple replication and durable writes. By setting the replication factor to 1, you ask Cassandra to keep one copy of each row. The replication strategy determines how replication is handled. The SimpleStrategy replication strategy is fine for single data center use (and for demo code), but you might consider the NetworkTopologyStrategy if you have your Cassandra cluster spread across multiple data centers. I refer you to the Cassandra documentation for more details of how replication strategies work and alternative ways of creating keyspaces.

Now that you've created a keyspace, you need to configure the spring.data .cassandra.keyspace-name property to tell Spring Data Cassandra to use that keyspace, as shown next:

```
spring:
  data:
    cassandra:
      keyspace-name: taco_cloud
      schema-action: recreate
      local-datacenter: datacenter1
```

Here, you also set the spring.data.cassandra.schema-action to recreate. This setting is very useful for development purposes because it ensures that any tables and user-defined types will be dropped and recreated every time the application starts. The default value, none, takes no action against the schema and is useful in production settings where you'd rather not drop all tables whenever an application starts up.

Finally, the spring.data.cassandra.local-datacenter property identifies the name of the local data center for purposes of setting Cassandra's load-balancing policy. In a single-node setup, "datacenter1" is the value to use. For more information on Cassandra load-balancing policies and how to set the local data center, see the DataStax Cassandra driver's reference documentation (http://mng.bz/XrQM).

These are the only properties you'll need for working with a locally running Cassandra database. In addition to these two properties, however, you may wish to set others, depending on how you've configured your Cassandra cluster.

By default, Spring Data Cassandra assumes that Cassandra is running locally and listening on port 9042. If that's not the case, as in a production setting, you may want to set the spring.data.cassandra.contact-points and spring.data.cassandra .port properties as follows:

```
spring:
  data:
    cassandra:
      keyspace-name: tacocloud
      local-datacenter: datacenter1
      contact-points:
      - casshost-1.tacocloud.com
      - casshost-2.tacocloud.com
      - casshost-3.tacocloud.com
      port: 9043
```

Notice that the `spring.data.cassandra.contact-points` property is where you identify the hostname(s) of Cassandra. A contact point is the host where a Cassandra node is running. By default, it's set to `localhost`, but you can set it to a list of hostnames. It will try each contact point until it's able to connect to one. This is to ensure that there's no single point of failure in the Cassandra cluster and that the application will be able to connect with the cluster through one of the given contact points.

You may also need to specify a username and password for your Cassandra cluster. This can be done by setting the `spring.data.cassandra.username` and `spring.data` `.cassandra.password` properties, as shown next:

```
spring:
  data:
    cassandra:
      ...
      username: tacocloud
      password: s3cr3tP455w0rd
```

Here the `spring.data.cassandra.username` and `spring.data.cassandra.password` properties specify "tacocloud" and "s3cr3tP455w0rd" as the credentials needed to access the Cassandra cluster.

Now that Spring Data Cassandra is enabled and configured in your project, you're almost ready to map your domain types to Cassandra tables and write repositories. But first, let's step back and consider a few basic points of Cassandra data modeling.

4.1.2   *Understanding Cassandra data modeling*

As I mentioned, Cassandra is quite different from a relational database. Before you can start mapping your domain types to Cassandra tables, it's important to understand a few of the ways that Cassandra data modeling is different from how you might model your data for persistence in a relational database.

A few of the most important things to understand about Cassandra data modeling follow:

- Cassandra tables may have any number of columns, but not all rows will necessarily use all of those columns.
- Cassandra databases are split across multiple partitions. Any row in a given table may be managed by one or more partitions, but it's unlikely that all partitions will have all rows.
- A Cassandra table has two kinds of keys: partition keys and clustering keys. Hash operations are performed on each row's partition key to determine which partition(s) that row will be managed by. Clustering keys determine the order in which the rows are maintained within a partition (not necessarily the order in which they may appear in the results of a query). Refer to Cassandra documentation (http://mng.bz/yJ6E) for a more detailed explanation of data modeling in Cassandra, including partitions, clusters, and their respective keys.

- Cassandra is highly optimized for read operations. As such, it's common and desirable for tables to be highly denormalized and for data to be duplicated across multiple tables. (For example, customer information may be kept in a customer table as well as duplicated in a table containing orders placed by customers.)

Suffice it to say that adapting the Taco Cloud domain types to work with Cassandra won't be a matter of simply swapping out a few JPA annotations for Cassandra annotations. You'll have to rethink how you model the data.

4.1.3   *Mapping domain types for Cassandra persistence*

In chapter 3, you marked up your domain types (`Taco`, `Ingredient`, `TacoOrder`, and so on) with annotations provided by the JPA specification. These annotations mapped your domain types as entities to be persisted to a relational database. Although those annotations won't work for Cassandra persistence, Spring Data Cassandra provides its own set of mapping annotations for a similar purpose.

Let's start with the `Ingredient` class, because it's the simplest to map for Cassandra. The new Cassandra-ready `Ingredient` class looks like this:

```
package tacos;

import org.springframework.data.cassandra.core.mapping.PrimaryKey;
import org.springframework.data.cassandra.core.mapping.Table;

import lombok.AccessLevel;
import lombok.AllArgsConstructor;
import lombok.Data;
import lombok.NoArgsConstructor;
import lombok.RequiredArgsConstructor;

@Data
@AllArgsConstructor
@NoArgsConstructor(access=AccessLevel.PRIVATE, force=true)
@Table("ingredients")
public class Ingredient {

  @PrimaryKey
  private String id;
  private String name;
  private Type type;

  public enum Type {
    WRAP, PROTEIN, VEGGIES, CHEESE, SAUCE
  }

}
```

The `Ingredient` class seems to contradict everything I said about just swapping out a few annotations. Rather than annotating the class with `@Entity` as you did for JPA persistence, it's annotated with `@Table` to indicate that ingredients should be persisted to a table named `ingredients`. And rather than annotate the `id` property with `@Id`, this time it's annotated with `@PrimaryKey`. So far, it seems that you're only swapping out a few annotations.

But don't let the `Ingredient` mapping fool you. The `Ingredient` class is one of your simplest domain types. Things get more interesting when you map the `Taco` class for Cassandra persistence, as shown in the next listing.

Listing 4.1   Annotating the `Taco` class for Cassandra persistence

```java
package tacos;
import java.util.ArrayList;
import java.util.Date;
import java.util.List;
import java.util.UUID;

import javax.validation.constraints.NotNull;
import javax.validation.constraints.Size;

import org.springframework.data.cassandra.core.cql.Ordering;
import org.springframework.data.cassandra.core.cql.PrimaryKeyType;
import org.springframework.data.cassandra.core.mapping.Column;
import org.springframework.data.cassandra.core.mapping.PrimaryKeyColumn;
import org.springframework.data.cassandra.core.mapping.Table;

import com.datastax.oss.driver.api.core.uuid.Uuids;

import lombok.Data;

@Data
@Table("tacos")                                        Persists to the
public class Taco {                                    "tacos" table

  @PrimaryKeyColumn(type=PrimaryKeyType.PARTITIONED)   Defines the
  private UUID id = Uuids.timeBased();                 partition key

  @NotNull
  @Size(min = 5, message = "Name must be at least 5 characters long")
  private String name;
                                                       Defines the
  @PrimaryKeyColumn(type=PrimaryKeyType.CLUSTERED,     clustering key
                    ordering=Ordering.DESCENDING)
  private Date createdAt = new Date();

  @Size(min=1, message="You must choose at least 1 ingredient")   Maps the list to
  @Column("ingredients")                                          the "ingredients"
  private List<IngredientUDT> ingredients = new ArrayList<>();     column

  public void addIngredient(Ingredient ingredient) {
    this.ingredients.add(TacoUDRUtils.toIngredientUDT(ingredient));
  }
}
```

As you can see, mapping the Taco class is a bit more involved. As with Ingredient, the @Table annotation is used to identify tacos as the name of the table that tacos should be written to. But that's the only thing similar to Ingredient.

The id property is still your primary key, but it's only one of two primary key columns. More specifically, the id property is annotated with @PrimaryKeyColumn with a type of PrimaryKeyType.PARTITIONED. This specifies that the id property serves as the partition key, used to determine to which Cassandra partition(s) each row of taco data will be written.

You'll also notice that the id property is now a UUID instead of a Long. Although it's not required, properties that hold a generated ID value are commonly of type UUID. Moreover, the UUID is initialized with a time-based UUID value for new Taco objects (but which may be overridden when reading an existing Taco from the database).

A little further down, you see the createdAt property that's mapped as another primary key column. But in this case, the type attribute of @PrimaryKeyColumn is set to PrimaryKeyType.CLUSTERED, which designates the createdAt property as a clustering key. As mentioned earlier, clustering keys are used to determine the ordering of rows *within a partition*. More specifically, the ordering is set to descending order— therefore, within a given partition, newer rows appear first in the tacos table.

Finally, the ingredients property is now a List of IngredientUDT objects instead of a List of Ingredient objects. As you'll recall, Cassandra tables are highly denormalized and may contain data that's duplicated from other tables. Although the ingredient table will serve as the table of record for all available ingredients, the ingredients chosen for a taco will be duplicated in the ingredients column. Rather than simply reference one or more rows in the ingredients table, the ingredients property will contain full data for each chosen ingredient.

But why do you need to introduce a new IngredientUDT class? Why can't you just reuse the Ingredient class? Put simply, columns that contain collections of data, such as the ingredients column, must be collections of native types (integers, strings, and so on) or user-defined types.

In Cassandra, user-defined types enable you to declare table columns that are richer than simple native types. Often they're used as a denormalized analog for relational foreign keys. In contrast to foreign keys, which only hold a reference to a row in another table, columns with user-defined types actually carry data that may be copied from a row in another table. In the case of the ingredients column in the tacos table, it will contain a collection of data structures that define the ingredients themselves.

You can't use the Ingredient class as a user-defined type, because the @Table annotation has already mapped it as an entity for persistence in Cassandra. Therefore, you must create a new class to define how ingredients will be stored in the ingredients column of the taco table. IngredientUDT (where UDT means *user-defined type*) is the class for the job, as shown here:

```
package tacos;

import org.springframework.data.cassandra.core.mapping.UserDefinedType;

import lombok.AccessLevel;
import lombok.Data;
import lombok.NoArgsConstructor;
import lombok.RequiredArgsConstructor;

@Data
@RequiredArgsConstructor
@NoArgsConstructor(access = AccessLevel.PRIVATE, force = true)
@UserDefinedType("ingredient")
public class IngredientUDT {

  private final String name;

  private final Ingredient.Type type;

}
```

Although `IngredientUDT` looks a lot like `Ingredient`, its mapping requirements are much simpler. It's annotated with `@UserDefinedType` to identify it as a user-defined type in Cassandra. But otherwise, it's a simple class with a few properties.

You'll also note that the `IngredientUDT` class doesn't include an `id` property. Although it could include a copy of the `id` property from the source `Ingredient`, that's not necessary. In fact, the user-defined type may include any properties you wish—it doesn't need to be a one-to-one mapping with any table definition.

I realize that it might be difficult to visualize how data in a user-defined type relates to data that's persisted to a table. Figure 4.1 shows the data model for the entire Taco Cloud database, including user-defined types.

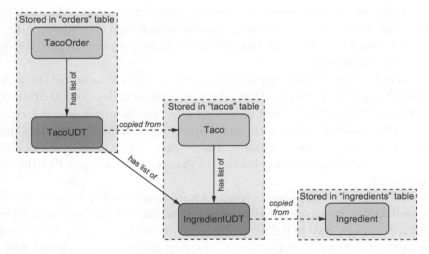

Figure 4.1   Instead of using foreign keys and joins, Cassandra tables are denormalized, with user-defined types containing data copied from related tables.

Specific to the user-defined type that you just created, notice how Taco has a list of IngredientUDT objects, which holds data copied from Ingredient objects. When a Taco is persisted, it's the Taco object and the list of IngredientUDT objects that's persisted to the tacos table. The list of IngredientUDT objects is persisted entirely within the ingredients column.

Another way of looking at this that might help you understand how user-defined types are used is to query the database for rows from the tacos table. Using CQL and the cqlsh tool that comes with Cassandra, you see the following results:

```
cqlsh:tacocloud> select id, name, createdAt, ingredients from tacos;

 id        | name       | createdat   | ingredients
-----------+------------+-------------+-----------------------------------------
 827390...| Carnivore  | 2018-04...  | [{name: 'Flour Tortilla', type: 'WRAP'},
                                        {name: 'Carnitas', type: 'PROTEIN'},
                                        {name: 'Sour Cream', type: 'SAUCE'},
                                        {name: 'Salsa', type: 'SAUCE'},
                                        {name: 'Cheddar', type: 'CHEESE'}]

(1 rows)
```

As you can see, the id, name, and createdat columns contain simple values. In that regard, they aren't much different than what you'd expect from a similar query against a relational database. But the ingredients column is a little different. Because it's defined as containing a collection of the user-defined ingredient type (defined by IngredientUDT), its value appears as a JSON array filled with JSON objects.

You likely noticed other user-defined types in figure 4.1. You'll certainly be creating some more as you continue mapping your domain to Cassandra tables, including some that will be used by the TacoOrder class. The next listing shows the TacoOrder class, modified for Cassandra persistence.

Listing 4.2 Mapping the `TacoOrder` class to a Cassandra `orders` table

```java
package tacos;
import java.io.Serializable;
import java.util.ArrayList;
import java.util.Date;
import java.util.List;
import java.util.UUID;

import javax.validation.constraints.Digits;
import javax.validation.constraints.NotBlank;
import javax.validation.constraints.Pattern;

import org.hibernate.validator.constraints.CreditCardNumber;
import org.springframework.data.cassandra.core.mapping.Column;
import org.springframework.data.cassandra.core.mapping.PrimaryKey;
import org.springframework.data.cassandra.core.mapping.Table;

import com.datastax.oss.driver.api.core.uuid.Uuids;
```

```
import lombok.Data;
                                        Maps to the
@Data                                   orders table
@Table("orders")            ◄────┘
public class TacoOrder implements Serializable {

  private static final long serialVersionUID = 1L;

  @PrimaryKey                              ◄────┐  Declares the
  private UUID id = Uuids.timeBased();          │  primary key

  private Date placedAt = new Date();

  // delivery and credit card properties omitted for brevity's sake

  @Column("tacos")                             ◄────┐  Maps a list to the
  private List<TacoUDT> tacos = new ArrayList<>();   │  tacos column

  public void addTaco(TacoUDT taco) {
    tacos.add(taco);
  }

}
```

Listing 4.2 purposefully omits many of the properties of `TacoOrder` that don't lend themselves to a discussion of Cassandra data modeling. What's left are a few properties and mappings, similar to how `Taco` was defined. `@Table` is used to map `TacoOrder` to the `orders` table, much as `@Table` has been used before. In this case, you're unconcerned with ordering, so the `id` property is simply annotated with `@PrimaryKey`, designating it as both a partition key and a clustering key with default ordering.

The `tacos` property is of some interest in that it's a `List<TacoUDT>` instead of a list of `Taco` objects. The relationship between `TacoOrder` and `Taco/TacoUDT` here is similar to the relationship between `Taco` and `Ingredient/IngredientUDT`. That is, rather than joining data from several rows in a separate table through foreign keys, the `orders` table will contain all of the pertinent taco data, optimizing the table for quick reads.

The `TacoUDT` class is quite similar to the `IngredientUDT` class, although it does include a collection that references another user-defined type, as follows:

```
package tacos;

import java.util.List;
import org.springframework.data.cassandra.core.mapping.UserDefinedType;
import lombok.Data;

@Data
@UserDefinedType("taco")
public class TacoUDT {

  private final String name;
  private final List<IngredientUDT> ingredients;

}
```

Although it would have been nice to reuse the same domain classes you created in chapter 3, or at most to swap out some JPA annotations for Cassandra annotations, the nature of Cassandra persistence is such that it requires you to rethink how your data is modeled. But now that you've mapped your domain, you're ready to write repositories.

4.1.4 Writing Cassandra repositories

As you saw in chapter 3, writing a repository with Spring Data involves simply declaring an interface that extends one of Spring Data's base repository interfaces and optionally declaring additional query methods for custom queries. As it turns out, writing Cassandra repositories isn't much different.

In fact, there's very little that you'll need to change in the repositories we've already written to make them work for Cassandra persistence. For example, consider the following `IngredientRepository` we created in chapter 3:

```
package tacos.data;

import org.springframework.data.repository.CrudRepository;

import tacos.Ingredient;

public interface IngredientRepository
        extends CrudRepository<Ingredient, String> {

}
```

By extending `CrudRepository` as shown here, `IngredientRepository` is ready to persist `Ingredient` objects whose ID property (or, in the case of Cassandra, the primary key property) is a `String`. That's perfect! No changes are needed for `Ingredient-Repository`.

The changes required for `OrderRepository` are only slightly more involved. Instead of a `Long` parameter, the ID parameter type specified when extending `Crud-Repository` will be changed to `UUID` as follows:

```
package tacos.data;

import java.util.UUID;

import org.springframework.data.repository.CrudRepository;

import tacos.TacoOrder;

public interface OrderRepository
        extends CrudRepository<TacoOrder, UUID> {

}
```

There's a lot of power in Cassandra, and when it's teamed up with Spring Data, you can wield that power in your Spring applications. But let's shift our attention to another database for which Spring Data repository support is available: MongoDB.

4.2   *Writing MongoDB repositories*

MongoDB is a another well-known NoSQL database. Whereas Cassandra is a column-store database, MongoDB is considered a document database. More specifically, MongoDB stores documents in BSON (Binary JSON) format, which can be queried for and retrieved in a way that's roughly similar to how you might query for data in any other database.

As with Cassandra, it's important to understand that MongoDB isn't a relational database. The way you manage your MongoDB server cluster, as well as how you model your data, requires a different mindset than when working with other kinds of databases.

That said, working with MongoDB and Spring Data isn't dramatically different from how you might use Spring Data for working with JPA or Cassandra. You'll annotate your domain classes with annotations that map the domain type to a document structure. And you'll write repository interfaces that very much follow the same programming model as those you've seen for JPA and Cassandra. Before you can do any of that, though, you must enable Spring Data MongoDB in your project.

4.2.1   *Enabling Spring Data MongoDB*

To get started with Spring Data MongoDB, you'll need to add the Spring Data MongoDB starter to the project build. As with Spring Data Cassandra, Spring Data MongoDB has two separate starters to choose from: one reactive and one nonreactive. We'll look at the reactive options for persistence in chapter 13. For now, add the following dependency to the build to work with the nonreactive MongoDB starter:

```
<dependency>
  <groupId>org.springframework.boot</groupId>
  <artifactId>
    spring-boot-starter-data-mongodb
  </artifactId>
</dependency>
```

This dependency is also available from the Spring Initializr by checking the MongoDB check box under NoSQL.

By adding the starter to the build, autoconfiguration will be triggered to enable Spring Data support for writing automatic repository interfaces, such as those you wrote for JPA in chapter 3 or for Cassandra earlier in this chapter.

By default, Spring Data MongoDB assumes that you have a MongoDB server running locally and listening on port 27017. If you have Docker installed on your machine, an easy way to get a MongoDB server running is with the following command line:

```
$ docker run -p 27017:27017 -d mongo:latest
```

But for convenience in testing or developing, you can choose to work with an embedded Mongo database instead. To do that, add the following Flapdoodle embedded MongoDB dependency to your build:

```
<dependency>
  <groupId>de.flapdoodle.embed</groupId>
  <artifactId>de.flapdoodle.embed.mongo</artifactId>
  <!-- <scope>test</scope> -->
</dependency>
```

The Flapdoodle embedded database affords you all of the same convenience of working with an in-memory Mongo database as you'd get with H2 when working with relational data. That is, you won't need to have a separate database running, but all data will be wiped clean when you restart the application.

Embedded databases are fine for development and testing, but once you take your application to production, you'll want to be sure you set a few properties to let Spring Data MongoDB know where and how your production Mongo database can be accessed, as shown next:

```
spring:
  data:
    mongodb:
      host: mongodb.tacocloud.com
      port: 27017
      username: tacocloud
      password: s3cr3tp455w0rd
      database: tacoclouddb
```

Not all of these properties are required, but they're available to help point Spring Data MongoDB in the right direction in the event that your Mongo database isn't running locally. Breaking it down, here's what each property configures:

- *spring.data.mongodb.host*—The hostname where Mongo is running (default: localhost)
- *spring.data.mongodb.port*—The port that the Mongo server is listening on (default: 27017)
- *spring.data.mongodb.username*—The username for accessing a secured Mongo database
- *spring.data.mongodb.password*—The password for accessing a secured Mongo database
- *spring.data.mongodb.database*—The database name (default: test)

Now that you have Spring Data MongoDB enabled in your project, you need to annotate your domain objects for persistence as documents in MongoDB.

4.2.2 *Mapping domain types to documents*

Spring Data MongoDB offers a handful of annotations that are useful for mapping domain types to document structures to be persisted in MongoDB. Although Spring Data MongoDB provides a half-dozen annotations for mapping, only the following four are useful for most common use cases:

- *@Id*—Designates a property as the document ID (from Spring Data Commons)
- *@Document*—Declares a domain type as a document to be persisted to MongoDB
- *@Field*—Specifies the field name (and, optionally, the order) for storing a property in the persisted document
- *@Transient*—Specifies that a property is not to be persisted

Of those three annotations, only the @Id and @Document annotations are strictly required. Unless you specify otherwise, properties that aren't annotated with @Field or @Transient will assume a field name equal to the property name.

Applying these annotations to the Ingredient class, you get the following:

```
package tacos;

import org.springframework.data.annotation.Id;
import org.springframework.data.mongodb.core.mapping.Document;

import lombok.AccessLevel;
import lombok.AllArgsConstructor;
import lombok.Data;
import lombok.NoArgsConstructor;

@Data
@Document
@AllArgsConstructor
@NoArgsConstructor(access=AccessLevel.PRIVATE, force=true)
public class Ingredient {

  @Id
  private String id;
  private String name;
  private Type type;

  public enum Type {
    WRAP, PROTEIN, VEGGIES, CHEESE, SAUCE
  }

}
```

As you can see, you place the @Document annotation at the class level to indicate that Ingredient is a document entity that can be written to and read from a Mongo database. By default, the collection name (the Mongo analog to a relational database table) is based on the class name, with the first letter lowercase. Because you haven't specified otherwise, Ingredient objects will be persisted to a collection named ingredient. But you can change that by setting the collection attribute of @Document as follows:

```
@Data
@AllArgsConstructor
@NoArgsConstructor(access=AccessLevel.PRIVATE, force=true)
@Document(collection="ingredients")
public class Ingredient {
  ...
}
```

You'll also notice that the id property has been annotated with @Id. This designates the property as being the ID of the persisted document. You can use @Id on any property whose type is Serializable, including String and Long. In this case, you're already using the String-defined id property as a natural identifier, so there's no need to change it to any other type.

So far, so good. But you'll recall from earlier in this chapter that Ingredient was the easy domain type to map for Cassandra. The other domain types, such as Taco, were a bit more challenging. Let's look at how you can map the Taco class to see what surprises it might hold.

MongoDB's approach to document persistence lends itself very well to the domain-driven-design way of applying persistence at the aggregate root level. Documents in MongoDB tend to be defined as aggregate roots, with members of the aggregate as subdocuments.

What that means for Taco Cloud is that because Taco is only ever persisted as a member of the TacoOrder-rooted aggregate, the Taco class doesn't need to be annotated as a @Document, nor does it need an @Id property. The Taco class can remain clean of any persistence annotations, as shown here:

```
package tacos;
import java.util.ArrayList;
import java.util.Date;
import java.util.List;

import javax.validation.constraints.NotNull;
import javax.validation.constraints.Size;

import lombok.Data;

@Data
public class Taco {

  @NotNull
  @Size(min=5, message="Name must be at least 5 characters long")
  private String name;

  private Date createdAt = new Date();

  @Size(min=1, message="You must choose at least 1 ingredient")
  private List<Ingredient> ingredients = new ArrayList<>();

  public void addIngredient(Ingredient ingredient) {
    this.ingredients.add(ingredient);
  }

}
```

The TacoOrder class, however, being the root of the aggregate, will need to be annotated with @Document and have an @Id property, as follows:

```
package tacos;
import java.io.Serializable;
import java.util.ArrayList;
import java.util.Date;
import java.util.List;

import javax.validation.constraints.Digits;
import javax.validation.constraints.NotBlank;
import javax.validation.constraints.Pattern;

import org.hibernate.validator.constraints.CreditCardNumber;
import org.springframework.data.annotation.Id;
import org.springframework.data.mongodb.core.mapping.Document;

import lombok.Data;

@Data
@Document
public class TacoOrder implements Serializable {

  private static final long serialVersionUID = 1L;

  @Id
  private String id;

  private Date placedAt = new Date();

  // other properties omitted for brevity's sake

  private List<Taco> tacos = new ArrayList<>();

  public void addTaco(Taco taco) {
    tacos.add(taco);
  }

}
```

For brevity's sake, I've snipped out the various delivery and credit card fields. But from what's left, it's clear that all you need is @Document and @Id, as with the other domain types.

Notice, however, that the id property has been changed to be a String (as opposed to a Long in the JPA version or a UUID in the Cassandra version). As I said earlier, @Id can be applied to any Serializable type. But if you choose to use a String property as the ID, you get the benefit of Mongo automatically assigning a value to it when it's saved (assuming that it's null). By choosing String, you get a database-managed ID assignment and needn't worry about setting that property manually.

Although there are some more-advanced and unusual use cases that require additional mapping, you'll find that for most cases, @Document and @Id, along with an occasional @Field or @Transient, are sufficient for MongoDB mapping. They certainly do the job for the Taco Cloud domain types.

All that's left is to write the repository interfaces.

4.2.3 *Writing MongoDB repository interfaces*

Spring Data MongoDB offers automatic repository support similar to what's provided by the Spring Data JPA and Spring Data Cassandra.

You'll start by defining a repository for persisting `Ingredient` objects as documents. As before, you can write `IngredientRepository` to extend `CrudRepository`, as shown here:

```
package tacos.data;

import org.springframework.data.repository.CrudRepository;

import tacos.Ingredient;

public interface IngredientRepository
        extends CrudRepository<Ingredient, String> {

}
```

Wait a minute! That looks *identical* to the `IngredientRepository` interface you wrote in section 4.1 for Cassandra! Indeed, it's the same interface, with no changes. This highlights one of the benefits of extending `CrudRepository`—it's more portable across various database types and works equally well for MongoDB as for Cassandra.

Moving on to the `OrderRepository` interface, you can see in the following snippet that it's quite straightforward:

```
package tacos.data;

import org.springframework.data.repository.CrudRepository;

import tacos.TacoOrder;

public interface OrderRepository
        extends CrudRepository<TacoOrder, String> {

}
```

Just like `IngredientRepository`, `OrderRepository` extends `CrudRepository` to gain the optimizations afforded in its `insert()` methods. Otherwise, there's nothing terribly special about this repository, compared to some of the other repositories you've defined thus far. Note, however, that the ID parameter when extending `CrudRepository` is now `String` instead of `Long` (as for JPA) or `UUID` (as for Cassandra). This reflects the change we made in `TacoOrder` to support automatic assignment of IDs.

In the end, working with Spring Data MongoDB isn't drastically different from the other Spring Data projects we've worked with. The domain types are annotated differently. But aside from the ID parameter specified when extending `CrudRepository`, the repository interfaces are nearly identical.

Summary

- Spring Data supports repositories for a variety of NoSQL databases, including Cassandra, MongoDB, Neo4j, and Redis.
- The programming model for creating repositories differs very little across different underlying databases.
- Working with nonrelational databases demands an understanding of how to model data appropriately for how the database ultimately stores the data.

Securing Spring

This chapter covers

- Autoconfiguring Spring Security
- Defining custom user storage
- Customizing the login page
- Securing against CSRF attacks
- Knowing your user

Have you ever noticed that most people in television sitcoms don't lock their doors? In the days of *Leave It to Beaver*, it wasn't so unusual for people to leave their doors unlocked. But it seems crazy that at a time when we're concerned with privacy and security, we see television characters enabling unhindered access to their apartments and homes.

Information is probably the most valuable item we now have; crooks are looking for ways to steal our data and identities by sneaking into unsecured applications. As software developers, we must take steps to protect the information that resides in our applications. Whether it's an email account protected with a username-password pair or a brokerage account protected with a trading PIN, security is a crucial aspect of most applications.

5.1   *Enabling Spring Security*

The very first step in securing your Spring application is to add the Spring Boot security starter dependency to your build. In the project's pom.xml file, add the following <dependency> entry:

```
<dependency>
    <groupId>org.springframework.boot</groupId>
    <artifactId>spring-boot-starter-security</artifactId>
</dependency>
```

If you're using Spring Tool Suite, this is even easier. Right-click on the pom.xml file and select Add Starters from the Spring context menu. In the starter dependencies dialog box, select the Spring Security entry under the Security category, as shown in figure 5.1.

Believe it or not, that dependency is the only thing that's required to secure an application. When the application starts, autoconfiguration will detect that Spring Security is in the classpath and will set up some basic security configuration.

If you want to try it out, fire up the application and try to visit the home page (or any page, for that matter). You'll be prompted for authentication with a rather plain login page that looks something like figure 5.2.

> **TIP**   Going incognito: You may find it useful to set your browser to private or incognito mode when manually testing security. This will ensure that you have a fresh session each time you open a private/incognito window. You'll have to sign in to the application each time, but you can be assured that any changes you've made in security are applied and that there aren't any remnants of an older session preventing you from seeing your changes.

To get past the login page, you'll need to provide a username and password. The username is *user*. As for the password, it's randomly generated and written to the application log file. The log entry will look something like this:

```
Using generated security password: 087cfc6a-027d-44bc-95d7-cbb3a798a1ea
```

Assuming you enter the username and password correctly, you'll be granted access to the application.

It seems that securing Spring applications is pretty easy work. With the Taco Cloud application secured, I suppose I could end this chapter now and move on to the next topic. But before we get ahead of ourselves, let's consider what kind of security autoconfiguration has provided.

By doing nothing more than adding the security starter to the project build, you get the following security features:

- All HTTP request paths require authentication.
- No specific roles or authorities are required.
- Authentication is prompted with a simple login page.
- There's only one user; the username is *user*.

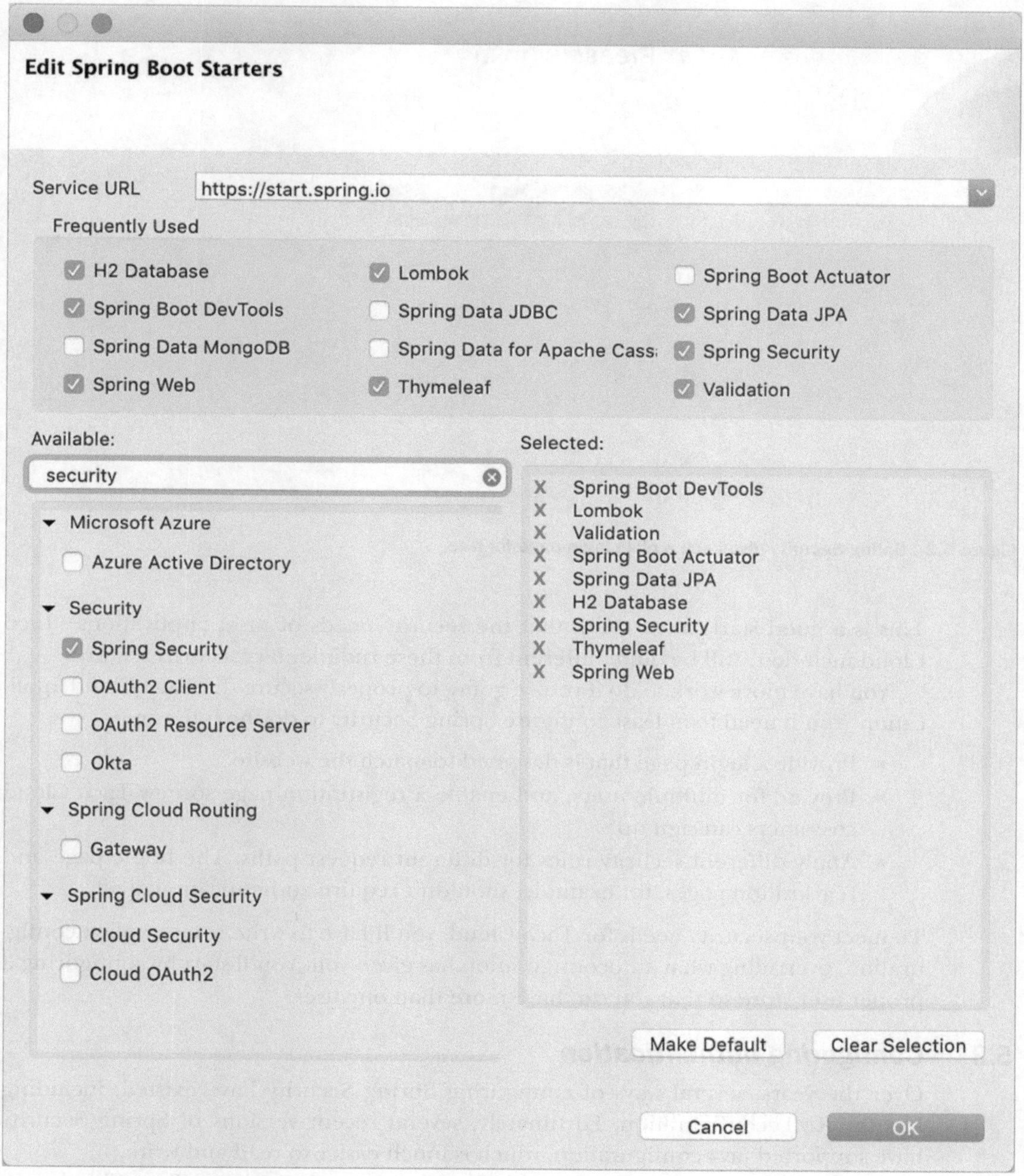

Figure 5.1 Adding the security starter with Spring Tool Suite

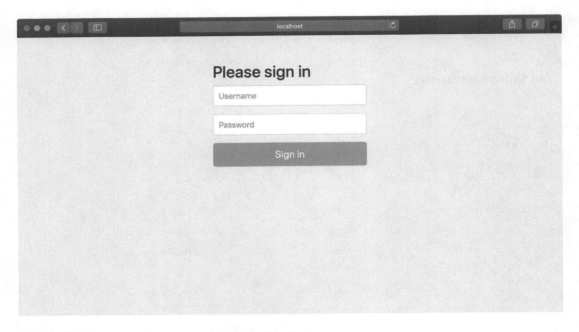

Figure 5.2   Spring Security gives you a plain login page for free.

This is a good start, but I think that the security needs of most applications (Taco Cloud included) will be quite different from these rudimentary security features.

You have more work to do if you're going to properly secure the Taco Cloud application. You'll need to at least configure Spring Security to do the following:

- Provide a login page that is designed to match the website.
- Provide for multiple users, and enable a registration page so new Taco Cloud customers can sign up.
- Apply different security rules for different request paths. The home page and registration pages, for example, shouldn't require authentication at all.

To meet your security needs for Taco Cloud, you'll have to write some explicit configuration, overriding what autoconfiguration has given you. You'll start by configuring a proper user store so that you can have more than one user.

5.2   *Configuring authentication*

Over the years, several ways of configuring Spring Security have existed, including lengthy XML configuration. Fortunately, several recent versions of Spring Security have supported Java configuration, which is much easier to read and write.

Before this chapter is finished, you'll have configured all of your Taco Cloud security needs in a Java configuration for Spring Security. But to get started, you'll ease into it by writing the configuration class shown in the following listing.

Listing 5.1 A barebones configuration class for Spring Security

```
package tacos.security;
import org.springframework.context.annotation.Bean;
import org.springframework.context.annotation.Configuration;
import org.springframework.security.crypto.bcrypt.BCryptPasswordEncoder;
import org.springframework.security.crypto.password.PasswordEncoder;

@Configuration
public class SecurityConfig {

  @Bean
  public PasswordEncoder passwordEncoder() {
    return new BCryptPasswordEncoder();
  }

}
```

What does this barebones security configuration do for you? Not much, actually. The main thing it does is declare a `PasswordEncoder` bean, which we'll use both when creating new users and when authenticating users at login. In this case, we're using `BCryptPasswordEncoder`, one of a handful of password encoders provided by Spring Security, including the following:

- *BCryptPasswordEncoder*—Applies bcrypt strong hashing encryption
- *NoOpPasswordEncoder*—Applies no encoding
- *Pbkdf2PasswordEncoder*—Applies PBKDF2 encryption
- *SCryptPasswordEncoder*—Applies Scrypt hashing encryption
- *StandardPasswordEncoder*—Applies SHA-256 hashing encryption

No matter which password encoder you use, it's important to understand that the password in the database is never decoded. Instead, the password that the user enters at login is encoded using the same algorithm, and it's then compared with the encoded password in the database. That comparison is performed in the `PasswordEncoder`'s `matches()` method.

Which password encoder should you use?

Not all password encoders are created equal. Ultimately, you'll need to weigh each password encoder's algorithm against your security goals and decide for yourself. But you should avoid a couple of password encoders for production applications.

`NoOpPasswordEncoder` applies no encryption whatsoever. Therefore, although it may be useful for testing, it is unsuitable for production use. And `StandardPassword-Encoder` is not considered secure enough for password encryption and has, in fact, been deprecated.

Instead, consider one of the other password encoders, any of which are more secure. We're going to use `BCryptPasswordEncoder` for the examples in this book.

In addition to the password encoder, we'll fill in this configuration class with more beans to define the specifics of security for our application. We'll start by configuring a user store that can handle more than one user.

To configure a user store for authentication purposes, you'll need to declare a `UserDetailsService` bean. The `UserDetailsService` interface is relatively simple, including only one method that must be implemented. Here's what `UserDetails-Service` looks like:

```
public interface UserDetailsService {

    UserDetails loadUserByUsername(String username) throws
      UsernameNotFoundException;

}
```

The `loadUserByUsername()` method accepts a username and uses it to look up a `UserDetails` object. If no user can be found for the given username, then it will throw a `UsernameNotFoundException`.

As it turns out, Spring Security offers several out-of-the-box implementations of `UserDetailsService`, including the following:

- An in-memory user store
- A JDBC user store
- An LDAP user store

Or, you can also create your own implementation to suit your application's specific security needs.

To get started, let's try out the in-memory implementation of `UserDetailsService`.

5.2.1 *In-memory user details service*

One place where user information can be kept is in memory. Suppose you have only a handful of users, none of which are likely to change. In that case, it may be simple enough to define those users as part of the security configuration.

The following bean method shows how to create an `InMemoryUserDetailsManager` (which implements `UserDetailsService`) with two users, "buzz" and "woody," for that purpose.

Listing 5.2 Declaring users in an in-memory user details service bean

```
@Bean
public UserDetailsService userDetailsService(PasswordEncoder encoder) {
  List<UserDetails> usersList = new ArrayList<>();
  usersList.add(new User(
      "buzz", encoder.encode("password"),
        Arrays.asList(new SimpleGrantedAuthority("ROLE_USER"))));
  usersList.add(new User(
      "woody", encoder.encode("password"),
        Arrays.asList(new SimpleGrantedAuthority("ROLE_USER"))));
  return new InMemoryUserDetailsManager(usersList);
}
```

Here, a list of Spring Security `User` objects are created, each with a username, password, and a list of one or more authorities. Then an `InMemoryUserDetailsManager` is created using that list.

If you try out the application now, you should be able to log in as either "woody" or "buzz," using *password* as the password.

The in-memory user details service is convenient for testing purposes or for very simple applications, but it doesn't allow for easy editing of users. If you need to add, remove, or change a user, you'll have to make the necessary changes and then rebuild and redeploy the application.

For the Taco Cloud application, you want customers to be able to register with the application and manage their own user accounts. That doesn't fit with the limitations of the in-memory user details service. So let's take a look at how to create our own implementation of `UserDetailsService` that allows for a user store database.

5.2.2 *Customizing user authentication*

In the previous chapter, you settled on using Spring Data JPA as your persistence option for all taco, ingredient, and order data. It would thus make sense to persist user data in the same way. If you do so, the data will ultimately reside in a relational database, so you could use JDBC authentication. But it'd be even better to leverage the Spring Data JPA repository used to store users.

First things first, though. Let's create the domain object and repository interface that represents and persists user information.

DEFINING THE USER DOMAIN AND PERSISTENCE

When Taco Cloud customers register with the application, they'll need to provide more than just a username and password. They'll also give you their full name, address, and phone number. This information can be used for a variety of purposes, including pre-populating the order form (not to mention potential marketing opportunities).

To capture all of that information, you'll create a `User` class, as follows.

Listing 5.3 Defining a user entity

```
package tacos;
import java.util.Arrays;
import java.util.Collection;
import javax.persistence.Entity;
import javax.persistence.GeneratedValue;
import javax.persistence.GenerationType;
import javax.persistence.Id;
import org.springframework.security.core.GrantedAuthority;
import org.springframework.security.core.authority.
                                        SimpleGrantedAuthority;
import org.springframework.security.core.userdetails.UserDetails;
import lombok.AccessLevel;
import lombok.Data;
import lombok.NoArgsConstructor;
import lombok.RequiredArgsConstructor;
```

```
@Entity
@Data
@NoArgsConstructor(access=AccessLevel.PRIVATE, force=true)
@RequiredArgsConstructor
public class User implements UserDetails {

  private static final long serialVersionUID = 1L;

  @Id
  @GeneratedValue(strategy=GenerationType.AUTO)
  private Long id;

  private final String username;
  private final String password;
  private final String fullname;
  private final String street;
  private final String city;
  private final String state;
  private final String zip;
  private final String phoneNumber;

  @Override
  public Collection<? extends GrantedAuthority> getAuthorities() {
    return Arrays.asList(new SimpleGrantedAuthority("ROLE_USER"));
  }

  @Override
  public boolean isAccountNonExpired() {
    return true;
  }

  @Override
  public boolean isAccountNonLocked() {
    return true;
  }

  @Override
  public boolean isCredentialsNonExpired() {
    return true;
  }

  @Override
  public boolean isEnabled() {
    return true;
  }

}
```

The first thing to notice about this User type is that it's not the same as the User class we used when creating the in-memory user details service. This one has more details about the user that we'll need to fulfill taco orders, including the user's address and contact information.

You've also probably noticed that the User class is a bit more involved than any of the other entities defined in chapter 3. In addition to defining a handful of properties, User also implements the UserDetails interface from Spring Security.

Implementations of UserDetails will provide some essential user information to the framework, such as what authorities are granted to the user and whether the user's account is enabled.

The getAuthorities() method should return a collection of authorities granted to the user. The various is* methods return a boolean to indicate whether the user's account is enabled, locked, or expired.

For your User entity, the getAuthorities() method simply returns a collection indicating that all users will have been granted ROLE_USER authority. And, at least for now, Taco Cloud has no need to disable users, so all of the is* methods return true to indicate that the users are active.

With the User entity defined, you can now define the repository interface as follows:

```
package tacos.data;
import org.springframework.data.repository.CrudRepository;
import tacos.User;

public interface UserRepository extends CrudRepository<User, Long> {

  User findByUsername(String username);

}
```

In addition to the CRUD operations provided by extending CrudRepository, User-Repository defines a findByUsername() method that you'll use in the user details service to look up a User by their username.

As you learned in chapter 3, Spring Data JPA automatically generates the implementation of this interface at run time. Therefore, you're now ready to write a custom user details service that uses this repository.

CREATING A USER DETAILS SERVICE

As you'll recall, the UserDetailsService interface defines only a single loadUserBy-Username() method. That means it is a functional interface and can be implemented as a lambda instead of as a full-blown implementation class. Because all we really need is for our custom UserDetailsService to delegate to the UserRepository, it can be simply declared as a bean using the following configuration method.

Listing 5.4 Defining a custom user details service bean

```
@Bean
public UserDetailsService userDetailsService(UserRepository userRepo) {
  return username -> {
    User user = userRepo.findByUsername(username);
    if (user != null) return user;

    throw new UsernameNotFoundException("User '" + username + "' not found");
  };
}
```

The `userDetailsService()` method is given a `UserRepository` as a parameter. To create the bean, it returns a lambda that takes a `username` parameter and uses it to call `findByUsername()` on the given `UserRepository`.

The `loadByUsername()` method has one simple rule: it must never return `null`. Therefore, if the call to `findByUsername()` returns `null`, the lambda will throw a `UsernameNotFoundException` (which is defined by Spring Security). Otherwise, the `User` that was found will be returned.

Now that you have a custom user details service that reads user information via a JPA repository, you just need a way to get users into the database in the first place. You need to create a registration page for Taco Cloud patrons to register with the application.

REGISTERING USERS

Although Spring Security handles many aspects of security, it really isn't directly involved in the process of user registration, so you're going to rely on a little bit of Spring MVC to handle that task. The `RegistrationController` class in the following listing presents and processes registration forms.

Listing 5.5   A user registration controller

```
package tacos.security;
import org.springframework.security.crypto.password.PasswordEncoder;
import org.springframework.stereotype.Controller;
import org.springframework.web.bind.annotation.GetMapping;
import org.springframework.web.bind.annotation.PostMapping;
import org.springframework.web.bind.annotation.RequestMapping;
import tacos.data.UserRepository;

@Controller
@RequestMapping("/register")
public class RegistrationController {

  private UserRepository userRepo;
  private PasswordEncoder passwordEncoder;

  public RegistrationController(
      UserRepository userRepo, PasswordEncoder passwordEncoder) {
    this.userRepo = userRepo;
    this.passwordEncoder = passwordEncoder;
  }

  @GetMapping
  public String registerForm() {
    return "registration";
  }

  @PostMapping
  public String processRegistration(RegistrationForm form) {
    userRepo.save(form.toUser(passwordEncoder));
    return "redirect:/login";
  }

}
```

Like any typical Spring MVC controller, `RegistrationController` is annotated with `@Controller` to designate it as a controller and to mark it for component scanning. It's also annotated with `@RequestMapping` such that it will handle requests whose path is /register.

More specifically, a GET request for /register will be handled by the `register-Form()` method, which simply returns a logical view name of `registration`. The following listing shows a Thymeleaf template that defines the `registration` view.

Listing 5.6 A Thymeleaf registration form view

```html
<!DOCTYPE html>
<html xmlns="http://www.w3.org/1999/xhtml"
      xmlns:th="http://www.thymeleaf.org">
  <head>
    <title>Taco Cloud</title>
  </head>

<body>
  <h1>Register</h1>

  <img th:src="@{/images/TacoCloud.png}"/>

  <form method="POST" th:action="@{/register}" id="registerForm">

      <label for="username">Username: </label>
      <input type="text" name="username"/><br/>

      <label for="password">Password: </label>
      <input type="password" name="password"/><br/>

      <label for="confirm">Confirm password: </label>
      <input type="password" name="confirm"/><br/>

      <label for="fullname">Full name: </label>
      <input type="text" name="fullname"/><br/>

      <label for="street">Street: </label>
      <input type="text" name="street"/><br/>

      <label for="city">City: </label>
      <input type="text" name="city"/><br/>

      <label for="state">State: </label>
      <input type="text" name="state"/><br/>

      <label for="zip">Zip: </label>
      <input type="text" name="zip"/><br/>

      <label for="phone">Phone: </label>
      <input type="text" name="phone"/><br/>

      <input type="submit" value="Register"/>
  </form>
```

```
    </body>
</html>
```

When the form is submitted, the processRegistration() method handles the HTTPS POST request. The form fields will be bound to a RegistrationForm object by Spring MVC and passed into the processRegistration() method for processing. RegistrationForm is defined in the following class:

```
package tacos.security;
import org.springframework.security.crypto.password.PasswordEncoder;
import lombok.Data;
import tacos.User;

@Data
public class RegistrationForm {

  private String username;
  private String password;
  private String fullname;
  private String street;
  private String city;
  private String state;
  private String zip;
  private String phone;

  public User toUser(PasswordEncoder passwordEncoder) {
    return new User(
        username, passwordEncoder.encode(password),
        fullname, street, city, state, zip, phone);
  }

}
```

For the most part, RegistrationForm is just a basic Lombok class with a handful of properties. But the toUser() method uses those properties to create a new User object, which is what processRegistration() will save, using the injected UserRepository.

You've no doubt noticed that RegistrationController is injected with a Password-Encoder. This is the exact same PasswordEncoder bean you declared earlier. When processing a form submission, RegistrationController passes it to the toUser() method, which uses it to encode the password before saving it to the database. In this way, the submitted password is written in an encoded form, and the user details service will be able to authenticate against that encoded password.

Now the Taco Cloud application has complete user registration and authentication support. But if you start it up at this point, you'll notice that you can't even get to the registration page without being prompted to log in. That's because, by default, all requests require authentication. Let's look at how web requests are intercepted and secured so you can fix this strange chicken-and-egg situation.

5.3   Securing web requests

The security requirements for Taco Cloud should require that a user be authenticated before designing tacos or placing orders. But the home page, login page, and registration page should be available to unauthenticated users.

To configure these security rules, we'll need to declare a `SecurityFilterChain` bean. The following `@Bean` method shows a minimal (but not useful) `SecurityFilter-Chain` bean declaration:

```
@Bean
public SecurityFilterChain filterChain(HttpSecurity http) throws Exception {
  return http.build();
}
```

The `filterChain()` method accepts an `HttpSecurity` object, which acts as a builder that can be used to configure how security is handled at the web level. Once security configuration is set up via the `HttpSecurity` object, a call to `build()` will create a `SecurityFilterChain` that is returned from the bean method.

The following are among the many things you can configure with `HttpSecurity`:

- Requiring that certain security conditions be met before allowing a request to be served
- Configuring a custom login page
- Enabling users to log out of the application
- Configuring cross-site request forgery protection

Intercepting requests to ensure that the user has proper authority is one of the most common things you'll configure `HttpSecurity` to do. Let's ensure that your Taco Cloud customers meet those requirements.

5.3.1   Securing requests

You need to ensure that requests for /design and /orders are available only to authenticated users; all other requests should be permitted for all users. The following configuration does exactly that:

```
@Bean
public SecurityFilterChain filterChain(HttpSecurity http) throws Exception {
  return http
    .authorizeRequests()
      .antMatchers("/design", "/orders").hasRole("USER")
      .antMatchers("/", "/**").permitAll()

    .and()
    .build();
}
```

The call to `authorizeRequests()` returns an object (`ExpressionUrlAuthorization-Configurer.ExpressionInterceptUrlRegistry`) on which you can specify URL paths and patterns and the security requirements for those paths. In this case, you specify the following two security rules:

- Requests for /design and /orders should be for users with a granted authority of ROLE_USER. Don't include the ROLE_ prefix on roles passed to hasRole(); it will be assumed by hasRole().
- All requests should be permitted to all users.

The order of these rules is important. Security rules declared first take precedence over those declared lower down. If you were to swap the order of those two security rules, all requests would have permitAll() applied to them; the rule for /design and /orders requests would have no effect.

The hasRole() and permitAll() methods are just a couple of the methods for declaring security requirements for request paths. Table 5.1 describes all the available methods.

Table 5.1   Configuration methods to define how a path is to be secured

Method	What it does
access(String)	Allows access if the given Spring Expression Language (SpEL) expression evaluates to true
anonymous()	Allows access to anonymous users
authenticated()	Allows access to authenticated users
denyAll()	Denies access unconditionally
fullyAuthenticated()	Allows access if the user is fully authenticated (not remembered)
hasAnyAuthority(String...)	Allows access if the user has any of the given authorities
hasAnyRole(String...)	Allows access if the user has any of the given roles
hasAuthority(String)	Allows access if the user has the given authority
hasIpAddress(String)	Allows access if the request comes from the given IP address
hasRole(String)	Allows access if the user has the given role
not()	Negates the effect of any of the other access methods
permitAll()	Allows access unconditionally
rememberMe()	Allows access for users who are authenticated via remember-me

Most of the methods in table 5.1 provide essential security rules for request handling, but they're self-limiting, enabling security rules only as defined by those methods. Alternatively, you can use the access() method to provide a SpEL expression to declare richer security rules. Spring Security extends SpEL to include several security-specific values and functions, as listed in table 5.2.

Table 5.2 Spring Security extensions to the Spring Expression Language

Security expression	What it evaluates to
`authentication`	The user's authentication object
`denyAll`	Always evaluates to `false`
`hasAnyAuthority(String… authorities)`	`true` if the user has been granted any of the given authorities
`hasAnyRole(String… roles)`	`true` if the user has any of the given roles
`hasAuthority(String authority)`	`true` if the user has been granted the specified authority
`hasPermission(Object target, Object permission)`	`true` if the user has access to the specified target object for the given permission
`hasPermission(Serializable targetId, String targetType, Object permission)`	`true` if the user has access to the object specified by `targetId` and the specified `targetType` for the given permission
`hasRole(String role)`	`true` if the user has the given role
`hasIpAddress(String ipAddress)`	`true` if the request comes from the given IP address
`isAnonymous()`	`true` if the user is anonymous
`isAuthenticated()`	`true` if the user is authenticated
`isFullyAuthenticated()`	`true` if the user is fully authenticated (not authenticated with remember-me)
`isRememberMe()`	`true` if the user is authenticated via `remember-me`
`permitAll`	Always evaluates to `true`
`principal`	The user's principal object

As you can see, most of the security expression extensions in table 5.2 correspond to similar methods in table 5.1. In fact, using the `access()` method along with the `hasRole()` and `permitAll` expressions, you can rewrite the `SecurityFilterChain` configuration as follows.

Listing 5.7 Using Spring expressions to define authorization rules

```
@Bean
public SecurityFilterChain filterChain(HttpSecurity http) throws Exception {
  return http
    .authorizeRequests()
      .antMatchers("/design", "/orders").access("hasRole('USER')")
      .antMatchers("/", "/**").access("permitAll()")

    .and()
    .build();
}
```

This may not seem like a big deal at first. After all, these expressions only mirror what you already did with method calls. But expressions can be much more flexible. For instance, suppose that (for some crazy reason) you wanted to allow only users with ROLE_USER authority to create new tacos on Tuesdays (for example, on Taco Tuesday); you could rewrite the expression as shown in this modified version of the Security-FilterChain bean method:

```
@Bean
public SecurityFilterChain filterChain(HttpSecurity http) throws Exception {
  return http
    .authorizeRequests()
      .antMatchers("/design", "/orders")
        .access("hasRole('USER') && " +
          "T(java.util.Calendar).getInstance().get("+
          "T(java.util.Calendar).DAY_OF_WEEK) == " +
          "T(java.util.Calendar).TUESDAY")
      .antMatchers("/", "/**").access("permitAll()")

    .and()
    .build();
}
```

With SpEL security constraints, the possibilities are virtually endless. I'll bet that you're already dreaming up interesting security constraints based on SpEL.

The authorization needs for the Taco Cloud application are met by the simple use of access() and the SpEL expressions. Now let's see about customizing the login page to fit the look of the Taco Cloud application.

5.3.2   *Creating a custom login page*

The default login page is much better than the clunky HTTP basic dialog box you started with, but it's still rather plain and doesn't quite fit with the look of the rest of the Taco Cloud application.

To replace the built-in login page, you first need to tell Spring Security what path your custom login page will be at. That can be done by calling formLogin() on the HttpSecurity object, as shown next:

```
@Bean
public SecurityFilterChain filterChain(HttpSecurity http) throws Exception {
  return http
    .authorizeRequests()
      .antMatchers("/design", "/orders").access("hasRole('USER')")
      .antMatchers("/", "/**").access("permitAll()")

    .and()
      .formLogin()
        .loginPage("/login")

    .and()
    .build();
}
```

Notice that before you call formLogin(), you bridge this section of configuration and the previous section with a call to and(). The and() method signifies that you're finished with the authorization configuration and are ready to apply some additional HTTP configuration. You'll use and() several times as you begin new sections of configuration.

After the bridge, you call formLogin() to start configuring your custom login form. The call to loginPage() after that designates the path where your custom login page will be provided. When Spring Security determines that the user is unauthenticated and needs to log in, it will redirect them to this path.

Now you need to provide a controller that handles requests at that path. Because your login page will be fairly simple—nothing but a view—it's easy enough to declare it as a view controller in WebConfig. The following addViewControllers() method sets up the login page view controller alongside the view controller that maps "/" to the home controller:

```
@Override
public void addViewControllers(ViewControllerRegistry registry) {
    registry.addViewController("/").setViewName("home");
    registry.addViewController("/login");
}
```

Finally, you need to define the login page view itself. Because you're using Thymeleaf as your template engine, the following Thymeleaf template should do fine:

```
<!DOCTYPE html>
<html xmlns="http://www.w3.org/1999/xhtml"
      xmlns:th="http://www.thymeleaf.org">
  <head>
    <title>Taco Cloud</title>
  </head>

  <body>
    <h1>Login</h1>
    <img th:src="@{/images/TacoCloud.png}"/>

    <div th:if="${error}">
      Unable to login. Check your username and password.
    </div>

    <p>New here? Click
        <a th:href="@{/register}">here</a> to register.</p>

    <form method="POST" th:action="@{/login}" id="loginForm">
      <label for="username">Username: </label>
      <input type="text" name="username" id="username" /><br/>

      <label for="password">Password: </label>
      <input type="password" name="password" id="password" /><br/>

      <input type="submit" value="Login"/>
    </form>
```

```
  </body>
</html>
```

The key things to note about this login page are the path it posts to and the names of the username and password fields. By default, Spring Security listens for login requests at /login and expects that the username and password fields be named username and password. This is configurable, however. For example, the following configuration customizes the path and field names:

```
.and()
  .formLogin()
    .loginPage("/login")
    .loginProcessingUrl("/authenticate")
    .usernameParameter("user")
    .passwordParameter("pwd")
```

Here, you specify that Spring Security should listen for requests to /authenticate to handle login submissions. Also, the username and password fields should now be named user and pwd.

By default, a successful login will take the user directly to the page that they were navigating to when Spring Security determined that they needed to log in. If the user were to directly navigate to the login page, a successful login would take them to the root path (for example, the home page). But you can change that by specifying a default success page, as shown next:

```
.and()
  .formLogin()
    .loginPage("/login")
    .defaultSuccessUrl("/design")
```

As configured here, if the user were to successfully log in after directly going to the login page, they would be directed to the /design page.

Optionally, you can force the user to the design page after login, even if they were navigating elsewhere prior to logging in, by passing true as a second parameter to defaultSuccessUrl as follows:

```
.and()
  .formLogin()
    .loginPage("/login")
    .defaultSuccessUrl("/design", true)
```

Signing in with a username and password is the most common way to authenticate in a web application. But let's have a look at another way to authenticate a user that uses someone else's login page.

5.3.3 *Enabling third-party authentication*

You may have seen links or buttons on your favorite website that say "Sign in with Facebook," "Log in with Twitter," or something similar. Rather than asking a user to enter their credentials on a login page specific to the website, they offer a way to sign in via another website like Facebook that they may already be logged into.

This type of authentication is based on OAuth2 or OpenID Connect (OIDC). Although OAuth2 is an authorization specification, and we'll talk more about how to use it to secure REST APIs in chapter 8, it can be also used to perform authentication via a third-party website. OpenID Connect is another security specification that is based on OAuth2 to formalize the interaction that takes place during a third-party authentication.

To employ this type of authentication in your Spring application, you'll need to add the OAuth2 client starter to the build as follows:

```
<dependency>
  <groupId>org.springframework.boot</groupId>
  <artifactId>spring-boot-starter-oauth2-client</artifactId>
</dependency>
```

Then, at the very least, you'll need to configure details about one or more OAuth2 or OpenID Connect servers that you want to be able to authenticate against. Spring Security supports sign-in with Facebook, Google, GitHub, and Okta out of the box, but you can configure other clients by specifying a few extra properties.

The general set of properties you'll need to set for your application to act as an OAuth2/OpenID Connect client follows:

```
spring:
  security:
    oauth2:
      client:
        registration:
          <oauth2 or openid provider name>:
            clientId: <client id>
            clientSecret: <client secret>
            scope: <comma-separated list of requested scopes>
```

For example, suppose that for Taco Cloud, we want users to be able to sign in using Facebook. The following configuration in application.yml will set up the OAuth2 client:

```
spring:
  security:
    oauth2:
      client:
        registration:
          facebook:
            clientId: <facebook client id>
            clientSecret: <facebook client secret>
            scope: email, public_profile
```

The client ID and secret are the credentials that identify your application to Facebook. You can obtain a client ID and secret by creating a new application entry at https://developers.facebook.com/. The scope property specifies the access that the application will be granted. In this case, the application will have access to the user's email address and the essential information from their public Facebook profile.

In a very simple application, this is all you will need. When the user attempts to access a page that requires authentication, their browser will redirect to Facebook. If they're not already logged in to Facebook, they'll be greeted with the Facebook sign-in page. After signing in to Facebook, they'll be asked to authorize your application and grant the requested scope. Finally, they'll be redirected back to your application, where they will have been authenticated.

If, however, you've customized security by declaring a SecurityFilterChain bean, then you'll need to enable OAuth2 login along with the rest of the security configuration as follows:

```
@Bean
public SecurityFilterChain filterChain(HttpSecurity http) throws Exception {
  return http
    .authorizeRequests()
      .mvcMatchers("/design", "/orders").hasRole("USER")
      .anyRequest().permitAll()

    .and()
      .formLogin()
        .loginPage("/login")

    .and()
      .oauth2Login()

  ...

    .and()
    .build();
}
```

You may also want to offer both a traditional username-password login and third-party login. In that case, you can specify the login page in the configuration like this:

```
.and()
  .oauth2Login()
    .loginPage("/login")
```

This will cause the application to always take the user to the application-provided login page where they may choose to log in with their username and password as usual. But you can also provide a link on that same login page that offers them the opportunity to log in with Facebook. Such a link could look like this in the login page's HTML template:

```
<a th:href="@{/oauth2/authorization/facebook}">Sign in with Facebook</a>
```

Now that you've dealt with logging in, let's flip to the other side of the authentication coin and see how you can enable a user to log out. Just as important as logging in to an application is logging out. To enable logout, you simply need to call `logout` on the `HttpSecurity` object as follows:

```
.and()
  .logout()
```

This sets up a security filter that intercepts POST requests to /logout. Therefore, to provide logout capability, you just need to add a logout form and button to the views in your application, as shown next:

```
<form method="POST" th:action="@{/logout}">
  <input type="submit" value="Logout"/>
</form>
```

When the user clicks the button, their session will be cleared, and they will be logged out of the application. By default, they'll be redirected to the login page where they can log in again. But if you'd rather they be sent to a different page, you can call `logoutSuccessUrl()` to specify a different post-logout landing page, as shown here:

```
.and()
  .logout()
    .logoutSuccessUrl("/")
```

In this case, users will be sent to the home page following logout.

5.3.4 *Preventing cross-site request forgery*

Cross-site request forgery (CSRF) is a common security attack. It involves subjecting a user to code on a maliciously designed web page that automatically (and usually secretly) submits a form to another application on behalf of a user who is often the victim of the attack. For example, a user may be presented with a form on an attacker's website that automatically posts to a URL on the user's banking website (which is presumably poorly designed and vulnerable to such an attack) to transfer money. The user may not even know that the attack happened until they notice money missing from their account.

To protect against such attacks, applications can generate a CSRF token upon displaying a form, place that token in a hidden field, and then stow it for later use on the server. When the form is submitted, the token is sent back to the server along with the rest of the form data. The request is then intercepted by the server and compared with the token that was originally generated. If the token matches, the request is allowed to proceed. Otherwise, the form must have been rendered by an evil website without knowledge of the token generated by the server.

Fortunately, Spring Security has built-in CSRF protection. Even more fortunate is that it's enabled by default and you don't need to explicitly configure it. You only need to make sure that any forms your application submits include a field named _csrf that contains the CSRF token.

Spring Security even makes that easy by placing the CSRF token in a request attribute with the name _csrf. Therefore, you could render the CSRF token in a hidden field with the following in a Thymeleaf template:

```
<input type="hidden" name="_csrf" th:value="${_csrf.token}"/>
```

If you're using Spring MVC's JSP tag library or Thymeleaf with the Spring Security dialect, you needn't even bother explicitly including a hidden field. The hidden field will be rendered automatically for you.

In Thymeleaf, you just need to make sure that one of the attributes of the <form> element is prefixed as a Thymeleaf attribute. That's usually not a concern, because it's quite common to let Thymeleaf render the path as context relative. For example, the th:action attribute shown next is all you need for Thymeleaf to render the hidden field for you:

```
<form method="POST" th:action="@{/login}" id="loginForm">
```

It's possible to disable CSRF support, but I'm hesitant to show you how. CSRF protection is important and easily handled in forms, so there's little reason to disable it. But if you insist on disabling it, you can do so by calling disable() like this:

```
.and()
  .csrf()
    .disable()
```

Again, I caution you not to disable CSRF protection, especially for production applications.

All of your web layer security is now configured for Taco Cloud. Among other things, you now have a custom login page and the ability to authenticate users against a JPA user repository. Now let's see how you can obtain information about the logged-in user.

5.4   *Applying method-level security*

Although it's easy to think about security at the web-request level, that's not always where security constraints are best applied. Sometimes it's better to verify that the user is authenticated and has been granted adequate authority at the point where the secured action will be performed.

For example, let's say that for administrative purposes, we have a service class that includes a method for clearing out all orders from the database. Using an injected OrderRepository, that method might look something like this:

```
public void deleteAllOrders() {
  orderRepository.deleteAll();
}
```

Now, suppose we have a controller that calls the `deleteAllOrders()` method as the result of a POST request, as shown here:

```
@Controller
@RequestMapping("/admin")
public class AdminController {

  private OrderAdminService adminService;

  public AdminController(OrderAdminService adminService) {
    this.adminService = adminService;
  }

  @PostMapping("/deleteOrders")
  public String deleteAllOrders() {
    adminService.deleteAllOrders();
    return "redirect:/admin";
  }

}
```

It'd be easy enough to tweak `SecurityConfig` as follows to ensure that only authorized users are allowed to perform that POST request:

```
.authorizeRequests()
  ...
  .antMatchers(HttpMethod.POST, "/admin/**")
        .access("hasRole('ADMIN')")
  ....
```

That's great and would prevent any unauthorized user from making a POST request to /admin/deleteOrders that would result in all orders disappearing from the database.

But suppose that some other controller method also calls `deleteAllOrders()`. You'd need to add more matchers to secure the requests for the other controllers that will need to be secured.

Instead, we can apply security directly on the `deleteAllOrders()` method like this:

```
@PreAuthorize("hasRole('ADMIN')")
public void deleteAllOrders() {
  orderRepository.deleteAll();
}
```

The `@PreAuthorize` annotation takes a SpEL expression, and, if the expression evaluates to `false`, the method will not be invoked. On the other hand, if the expression evaluates to `true`, then the method will be allowed. In this case, `@PreAuthorize` is checking that the user has the `ROLE_ADMIN` privilege. If so, then the method will be called and all orders will be deleted. Otherwise, it will be stopped in its tracks.

In the event that `@PreAuthorize` blocks the call, then Spring Security's `Access-DeniedException` will be thrown. This is an unchecked exception, so you don't need to catch it, unless you want to apply some custom behavior around the exception handling. If left uncaught, it will bubble up and eventually be caught by Spring Security's filters and handled accordingly, either with an HTTP 403 page or perhaps by redirecting to the login page if the user is unauthenticated.

For @PreAuthorize to work, you'll need to enable global method security. For that, you'll need to annotate the security configuration class with @EnableGlobalMethodSecurity as follows:

```
@Configuration
@EnableGlobalMethodSecurity
public class SecurityConfig extends WebSecurityConfigurerAdapter {
  ...
}
```

You'll find @PreAuthorize to be a useful annotation for most method-level security needs. But know that it has a slightly less useful after-invocation counterpart in @PostAuthorize. The @PostAuthorize annotation works almost the same as the @PreAuthorize annotation, except that its expression won't be evaluated until after the target method is invoked and returns. This allows the expression to consider the return value of the method in deciding whether to permit the method invocation.

For example, suppose we have a method that fetches an order by its ID. If you want to restrict it from being used except by admins or by the user who the order belongs to, you can use @PostAuthorize like this:

```
@PostAuthorize("hasRole('ADMIN') || " +
    "returnObject.user.username == authentication.name")
public TacoOrder getOrder(long id) {
  ...
}
```

In this case, the returnObject is the TacoOrder returned from the method. If its user property has a username that is equal to the authentication's name property, then it will be allowed. To know that, though, the method will need to be executed so that it can return the TacoOrder object for consideration.

But wait! How can you secure a method from being invoked if the condition for applying security relies on the return value from the method invocation? That chicken-and-egg riddle is solved by allowing the method to be invoked, then throwing an AccessDeniedException if the expression returns false.

5.5   *Knowing your user*

Often, it's not enough to simply know that the user has logged in and what permissions they have been granted. It's usually important to also know who they are, so that you can tailor their experience.

For example, in OrderController, when you initially create the TacoOrder object that's bound to the order form, it'd be nice if you could prepopulate the TacoOrder with the user's name and address, so they don't have to reenter it for each order. Perhaps even more important, when you save their order, you should associate the Taco-Order entity with the User that created the order.

To achieve the desired connection between an TacoOrder entity and a User entity, you need to add the following new property to the TacoOrder class:

```
@Data
@Entity
@Table(name="Taco_Order")
public class TacoOrder implements Serializable {

  ...

  @ManyToOne
  private User user;

  ...

}
```

The @ManyToOne annotation on this property indicates that an order belongs to a single user and, conversely, that a user may have many orders. (Because you're using Lombok, you won't need to explicitly define accessor methods for the property.)

In OrderController, the processOrder() method is responsible for saving an order. It will need to be modified to determine who the authenticated user is and to call setUser() on the TacoOrder object to connect the order with the user.

We have several ways to determine who the user is. A few of the most common ways follow:

- Inject a java.security.Principal object into the controller method.
- Inject an org.springframework.security.core.Authentication object into the controller method.
- Use org.springframework.security.core.context.SecurityContextHolder to get at the security context.
- Inject an @AuthenticationPrincipal annotated method parameter. (@AuthenticationPrincipal is from Spring Security's org.springframework.security.core.annotation package.)

For example, you could modify processOrder() to accept a java.security.Principal as a parameter. You could then use the principal name to look up the user from a UserRepository as follows:

```
@PostMapping
public String processOrder(@Valid TacoOrder order, Errors errors,
    SessionStatus sessionStatus,
    Principal principal) {

  ...
```

```
    User user = userRepository.findByUsername(
            principal.getName());

    order.setUser(user);

    ...

}
```

This works fine, but it litters code that's otherwise unrelated to security with security code. You can trim down some of the security-specific code by modifying process-Order() to accept an Authentication object as a parameter instead of a Principal, as shown next:

```
@PostMapping
public String processOrder(@Valid TacoOrder order, Errors errors,
    SessionStatus sessionStatus,
    Authentication authentication) {

  ...

  User user = (User) authentication.getPrincipal();
  order.setUser(user);

  ...

}
```

With the Authentication in hand, you can call getPrincipal() to get the principal object which, in this case, is a User. Note that getPrincipal() returns a java.util .Object, so you need to cast it to User.

Perhaps the cleanest solution of all, however, is to simply accept a User object in processOrder() but annotate it with @AuthenticationPrincipal so that it will be the authentication's principal, as follows:

```
@PostMapping
public String processOrder(@Valid TacoOrder order, Errors errors,
    SessionStatus sessionStatus,
    @AuthenticationPrincipal User user) {

  if (errors.hasErrors()) {
    return "orderForm";
  }

  order.setUser(user);

  orderRepo.save(order);
  sessionStatus.setComplete();

  return "redirect:/";
}
```

What's nice about @AuthenticationPrincipal is that it doesn't require a cast (as with Authentication), and it limits the security-specific code to the annotation itself. By the time you get the User object in processOrder(), it's ready to be used and assigned to the TacoOrder.

There's one other way of identifying who the authenticated user is, although it's a bit messy in the sense that it's very heavy with security-specific code. You can obtain an Authentication object from the security context and then request its principal like this:

```
Authentication authentication =
    SecurityContextHolder.getContext().getAuthentication();
User user = (User) authentication.getPrincipal();
```

Although this snippet is thick with security-specific code, it has one advantage over the other approaches described: it can be used anywhere in the application, not just in a controller's handler methods. This makes it suitable for use in lower levels of the code.

Summary

- Spring Security autoconfiguration is a great way to get started with security, but most applications will need to explicitly configure security to meet their unique security requirements.
- User details can be managed in user stores backed by relational databases, LDAP, or completely custom implementations.
- Spring Security automatically protects against CSRF attacks.
- Information about the authenticated user can be obtained via the Security-Context object (returned from SecurityContextHolder.getContext()) or injected into controllers using @AuthenticationPrincipal.

Working with configuration properties

6

This chapter covers

- Fine-tuning autoconfigured beans
- Applying configuration properties to application components
- Working with Spring profiles

Do you remember when the iPhone first came out? A small slab of metal and glass hardly fit the description of what the world had come to recognize as a phone. And yet, it pioneered the modern smartphone era, changing everything about how we communicate. Although touch phones are in many ways easier and more powerful than their predecessor, the flip phone, when the iPhone was first announced, it was hard to imagine how a device with a single button could be used to place calls.

In some ways, Spring Boot autoconfiguration is like this. Autoconfiguration greatly simplifies Spring application development. But after a decade of setting property values in Spring XML configuration and calling setter methods on bean instances, it's not immediately apparent how to set properties on beans for which there's no explicit configuration.

Fortunately, Spring Boot provides a way to set property values on application components with configuration properties. Configuration properties are nothing more than properties on @ConfigurationProperties-annotated beans in the Spring

140

application context. Spring will inject values from one of several property sources—including JVM system properties, command-line arguments, and environment variables—into the bean properties. We'll see how to use @ConfigurationProperties on our own beans in section 6.2. But Spring Boot itself provides several @Configuration-Properties-annotated beans that we'll configure first.

In this chapter, you're going to take a step back from implementing new features in the Taco Cloud application to explore configuration properties. What you take away will no doubt prove useful as you move forward in the chapters that follow. We'll start by seeing how to employ configuration properties to fine-tune what Spring Boot automatically configures.

6.1 *Fine-tuning autoconfiguration*

Before we dive in too deeply with configuration properties, it's important to establish the following different (but related) kinds of configurations in Spring:

- *Bean wiring*—Configuration that declares application components to be created as beans in the Spring application context and how they should be injected into each other
- *Property injection*—Configuration that sets values on beans in the Spring application context

In Spring's XML and Java configuration, these two types of configurations are often declared explicitly in the same place. In Java configuration, a @Bean-annotated method is likely to both instantiate a bean and then set values to its properties. For example, consider the following @Bean method that declares a DataSource for an embedded H2 database:

```
@Bean
public DataSource dataSource() {
  return new EmbeddedDatabaseBuilder()
      .setType(H2)
      .addScript("taco_schema.sql")
      .addScripts("user_data.sql", "ingredient_data.sql")
      .build();
}
```

Here the addScript() and addScripts() methods set some String properties with the name of SQL scripts that should be applied to the database once the data source is ready. Whereas this is how you might configure a DataSource bean if you aren't using Spring Boot, autoconfiguration makes this method completely unnecessary.

If the H2 dependency is available in the runtime classpath, then Spring Boot automatically creates in the Spring application context an appropriate DataSource bean, which applies the SQL scripts schema.sql and data.sql.

But what if you want to name the SQL scripts something else? Or what if you need to specify more than two SQL scripts? That's where configuration properties come in.

But before you can start using configuration properties, you need to understand where those properties come from.

6.1.1   *Understanding Spring's environment abstraction*

The Spring environment abstraction is a one-stop shop for any configurable property. It abstracts the origins of properties so that beans needing those properties can consume them from Spring itself. The Spring environment pulls from several property sources, including the following:

- JVM system properties
- Operating system environment variables
- Command-line arguments
- Application property configuration files

It then aggregates those properties into a single source from which Spring beans can be injected. Figure 6.1 illustrates how properties from property sources flow through the Spring environment abstraction to Spring beans.

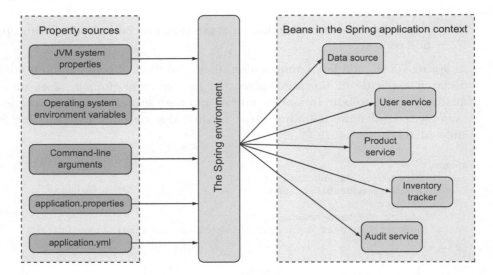

Figure 6.1   The Spring environment pulls properties from property sources and makes them available to beans in the application context.

The beans that are automatically configured by Spring Boot are all configurable by properties drawn from the Spring environment. As a simple example, suppose that you would like the application's underlying servlet container to listen for requests on some port other than the default port of 8080. To do that, specify a different port by setting the `server.port` property in src/main/resources/application.properties like this:

```
server.port=9090
```

Personally, I prefer using YAML when setting configuration properties. Therefore, instead of using application.properties, I might set the `server.port` value in src/main/resources/application.yml like this:

```
server:
  port: 9090
```

If you'd prefer to configure that property externally, you could also specify the port when starting the application using a command-line argument as follows:

```
$ java -jar tacocloud-0.0.5-SNAPSHOT.jar --server.port=9090
```

If you want the application to always start on a specific port, you could set it one time as an operating system environment variable, as shown next:

```
$ export SERVER_PORT=9090
```

Notice that when setting properties as environment variables, the naming style is slightly different to accommodate restrictions placed on environment variable names by the operating system. That's OK. Spring is able to sort it out and interpret `SERVER_PORT` as `server.port` with no problems.

As I said, we have several ways of setting configuration properties. In fact, you could use one of several hundred configuration properties to tweak and adjust how Spring beans behave. You've already seen a few: `server.port` in this chapter, as well as `spring.datasource.name` and `spring.thymeleaf.cache` in earlier chapters.

It's impossible to examine all of the available configuration properties in this chapter. Even so, let's take a look at a few of the most useful configuration properties you might commonly encounter. We'll start with a few properties that let you tweak the autoconfigured data source.

6.1.2 Configuring a data source

At this point, the Taco Cloud application is still unfinished, but you'll have several more chapters to take care of that before you're ready to deploy the application. As such, the embedded H2 database you're using as a data source is perfect for your needs—for now. But once you take the application into production, you'll probably want to consider a more permanent database solution.

Although you could explicitly configure your own `DataSource` bean, that's usually unnecessary. Instead, it's simpler to configure the URL and credentials for your database via configuration properties. For example, if you were to start using a MySQL database, you might add the following configuration properties to application.yml:

```
spring:
  datasource:
    url: jdbc:mysql://localhost/tacocloud
    username: tacouser
    password: tacopassword
```

Although you'll need to add the appropriate JDBC driver to the build, you won't usually need to specify the JDBC driver class—Spring Boot can figure it out from the structure of the database URL. But if there's a problem, you can try setting the `spring.datasource.driver-class-name` property like so:

```
spring:
  datasource:
    url: jdbc:mysql://localhost/tacocloud
    username: tacouser
    password: tacopassword
    driver-class-name: com.mysql.jdbc.Driver
```

Spring Boot uses this connection data when autoconfiguring the `DataSource` bean. The `DataSource` bean will be pooled using the HikariCP connection pool if it's available on the classpath. If not, Spring Boot looks for and uses one of the following other connection pool implementations on the classpath:

- Tomcat JDBC Connection Pool
- Apache Commons DBCP2

Although these are the only connection pool options available through autoconfiguration, you're always welcome to explicitly configure a `DataSource` bean to use whatever connection pool implementation you'd like.

Earlier in this chapter, we suggested that there might be a way to specify the database initialization scripts to run when the application starts. In that case, the `spring.sql.init.schema-locations` property proves useful, as shown here:

```
spring:
sql:
init:
schema-locations:
- order-schema.sql
- ingredient-schema.sql
- taco-schema.sql
- user-schema.sql
- ingredients.sql
```

Maybe explicit data source configuration isn't your style. Instead, perhaps you'd prefer to configure your data source in the Java Naming and Directory Interface (JNDI) (http://mng.bz/MvEo) and have Spring look it up from there. In that case, set up your data source by configuring `spring.datasource.jndi-name` as follows:

```
spring:
  datasource:
    jndi-name: java:/comp/env/jdbc/tacoCloudDS
```

If you set the `spring.datasource.jndi-name` property, the other data source connection properties (if set) are ignored.

6.1.3 Configuring the embedded server

You've already seen how to set the servlet container's port by setting `server.port`. What I didn't show you is what happens if `server.port` is set to 0, as shown here:

```
server:
  port: 0
```

Although you're explicitly setting `server.port` to 0, the server won't start on port 0. Instead, it'll start on a randomly chosen available port. This is useful when running automated integration tests to ensure that any concurrently running tests don't clash on a hardcoded port number.

But there's more to the underlying server than just a port. One of the most common things you'll need to do with the underlying container is to set it up to handle HTTPS requests. To do that, the first thing you must do is create a keystore using the JDK's `keytool` command-line utility, as shown next:

```
$ keytool -keystore mykeys.jks -genkey -alias tomcat -keyalg RSA
```

You'll be asked several questions about your name and organization, most of which are irrelevant. But when asked for a password, remember what you choose. For the sake of this example, I chose letmein as the password.

Next, you'll need to set a few properties to enable HTTPS in the embedded server. You could specify them all on the command line, but that would be terribly inconvenient. Instead, you'll probably set them in the application.properties or application.yml file. In application.yml, the properties might look like this:

```
server:
  port: 8443
  ssl:
    key-store: file:///path/to/mykeys.jks
    key-store-password: letmein
    key-password: letmein
```

Here the) `server.port` property is set to 8443, a common choice for development HTTPS servers. The `server.ssl.key-store` property should be set to the path where the keystore file is created. Here it's shown with a `file://` URL to load it from the filesystem, but if you package it within the application JAR file, you'll use a `class-path:` URL to reference it. And both the `server.ssl.key-store-password` and `server.ssl.key-password` properties are set to the password that was given when creating the keystore.

With these properties in place, your application should be listening for HTTPS requests on port 8443. Depending on which browser you're using, you may encounter a warning about the server not being able to verify its identity. This is nothing to worry about when serving from localhost during development.

6.1.4   *Configuring logging*

Most applications provide some form of logging. And even if your application doesn't log anything directly, the libraries that your application uses will certainly log their activity.

By default, Spring Boot configures logging via Logback (http://logback.qos.ch) to write to the console at an INFO level. You've probably already seen plenty of INFO-level entries in the application logs as you've run the application and other examples. But as a reminder, here's a logging sample showing the default log format (wrapped to fit within the page margins):

```
2021-07-29 17:24:24.187 INFO 52240 --- [nio-8080-exec-1]
  com.example.demo.Hello                    Here's a log entry.
2021-07-29 17:24:24.187 INFO 52240 --- [nio-8080-exec-1]
  com.example.demo.Hello                    Here's another log entry.
2021-07-29 17:24:24.187 INFO 52240 --- [nio-8080-exec-1]
  com.example.demo.Hello                    And here's one more.
```

For full control over the logging configuration, you can create a logback.xml file at the root of the classpath (in src/main/resources). Here's an example of a simple logback.xml file you might use:

```
<configuration>
  <appender name="STDOUT" class="ch.qos.logback.core.ConsoleAppender">
    <encoder>
      <pattern>
        %d{HH:mm:ss.SSS} [%thread] %-5level %logger{36} - %msg%n
      </pattern>
    </encoder>
  </appender>
  <logger name="root" level="INFO"/>
  <root level="INFO">
    <appender-ref ref="STDOUT" />
  </root>
</configuration>
```

With this new configuration, the same sample log entries from earlier might look like this (wrapped to fit in the page margins):

```
17:25:09.088 [http-nio-8080-exec-1] INFO   com.example.demo.Hello -
                                            Here's a log entry.
17:25:09.088 [http-nio-8080-exec-1] INFO   com.example.demo.Hello -
                                            Here's another log entry.
17:25:09.088 [http-nio-8080-exec-1] INFO   com.example.demo.Hello -
                                            And here's one more.
```

Aside from the pattern used for logging, this Logback configuration is more or less equivalent to the default you'll get if you have no logback.xml file. But by editing logback.xml, you can gain full control over your application's log files.

NOTE The specifics of what can go into logback.xml are outside the scope of this book. Refer to Logback's documentation for more information.

The most common changes you'll make to a logging configuration are to change the logging levels and perhaps to specify a file where the logs should be written. With Spring Boot configuration properties, you can make those changes without having to create a logback.xml file.

To set the logging levels, you create properties that are prefixed with `logging .level`, followed by the name of the logger for which you want to set the logging level. For instance, suppose you'd like to set the root logging level to WARN, but log Spring Security logs at a DEBUG level. The following entries in application.yml will take care of that for you:

```
logging:
  level:
    root: WARN
    org:
      springframework:
        security: DEBUG
```

Optionally, you can collapse the Spring Security package name to a single line for easier reading as follows:

```
logging:
  level:
    root: WARN
    org.springframework.security: DEBUG
```

Now suppose that you want to write the log entries to the file TacoCloud.log at /tmp/logs/. The `logging.file.path` and `logging.file.name` properties can help achieve that, as shown next:

```
logging:
  file:
    name: /tmp/logs/TacoCloud.log
  level:
    root: WARN
    org:
      springframework:
        security: DEBUG
```

Assuming that the application has write permissions to /tmp/logs/, the log entries will be written to /tmp/logs/TacoCloud.log. By default, the log files rotate once they reach 10 MB in size.

6.1.5   *Using special property values*

When setting properties, you aren't limited to declaring their values as hardcoded `String` and numeric values. Instead, you can derive their values from other configuration properties.

For example, suppose (for whatever reason) you want to set a property named `greeting.welcome` to echo the value of another property named `spring.application` `.name`. To achieve this, you could use the `${}` placeholder markers when setting `greeting.welcome` as follows:

```
greeting:
  welcome: ${spring.application.name}
```

You can even embed that placeholder amid other text, as shown here:

```
greeting:
  welcome: You are using ${spring.application.name}.
```

As you've seen, configuring Spring's own components with configuration properties makes it easy to inject values into those components' properties and to fine-tune auto-configuration. Configuration properties aren't exclusive to the beans that Spring creates. With a small amount of effort, you can take advantage of configuration properties in your own beans. Let's see how.

6.2   *Creating your own configuration properties*

As I mentioned earlier, configuration properties are nothing more than properties of beans that have been designated to accept configurations from Spring's environment abstraction. What I didn't mention is how those beans are designated to consume those configurations.

To support property injection of configuration properties, Spring Boot provides the `@ConfigurationProperties` annotation. When placed on any Spring bean, it specifies that the properties of that bean can be injected from properties in the Spring environment.

To demonstrate how `@ConfigurationProperties` works, suppose that you've added the following method to `OrderController` to list the authenticated user's past orders:

```
@GetMapping
public String ordersForUser(
    @AuthenticationPrincipal User user, Model model) {

  model.addAttribute("orders",
      orderRepo.findByUserOrderByPlacedAtDesc(user));

  return "orderList";
}
```

Along with that, you've also added the next necessary findByUserOrderByPlacedAt-Desc() method to OrderRepository:

```
List<Order> findByUserOrderByPlacedAtDesc(User user);
```

Notice that this repository method is named with a clause of OrderByPlacedAtDesc. The OrderBy portion specifies a property by which the results will be ordered—in this case, the placedAt property. The Desc at the end causes the ordering to be in descending order. Therefore, the list of orders returned will be sorted from most recent to least recent.

As written, this controller method may be useful after the user has placed a handful of orders, but it could become a bit unwieldy for the most avid of taco connoisseurs. A few orders displayed in the browser are useful; a never-ending list of hundreds of orders is just noise. Let's say that you want to limit the number of orders displayed to the most recent 20 orders. You can change ordersForUser() as follows:

```
@GetMapping
public String ordersForUser(
    @AuthenticationPrincipal User user, Model model) {

  Pageable pageable = PageRequest.of(0, 20);
  model.addAttribute("orders",
      orderRepo.findByUserOrderByPlacedAtDesc(user, pageable));

  return "orderList";
}
```

along with the corresponding changes to OrderRepository, shown next:

```
List<TacoOrder> findByUserOrderByPlacedAtDesc(
        User user, Pageable pageable);
```

Here you've changed the signature of the findByUserOrderByPlacedAtDesc() method to accept a Pageable as a parameter. Pageable is Spring Data's way of selecting some subset of the results by a page number and page size. In the ordersForUser() controller method, you constructed a PageRequest object that implemented Pageable to request the first page (page zero) with a page size of 20 to get up to 20 of the most recently placed orders for the user.

Although this works fantastically, it leaves me a bit uneasy that you've hardcoded the page size. What if you later decide that 20 is too many orders to list, and you decide to change it to 10? Because it's hardcoded, you'd have to rebuild and redeploy the application.

Rather than hardcode the page size, you can set it with a custom configuration property. First, you need to add a new property called pageSize to OrderController, and then annotate OrderController with @ConfigurationProperties as shown in the next listing.

Listing 6.1   Enabling configuration properties in `OrderController`

```
@Controller
@RequestMapping("/orders")
@SessionAttributes("order")
@ConfigurationProperties(prefix="taco.orders")
public class OrderController {

  private int pageSize = 20;

  public void setPageSize(int pageSize) {
    this.pageSize = pageSize;
  }


  ...
  @GetMapping
  public String ordersForUser(
      @AuthenticationPrincipal User user, Model model) {

    Pageable pageable = PageRequest.of(0, pageSize);
    model.addAttribute("orders",
        orderRepo.findByUserOrderByPlacedAtDesc(user, pageable));
    return "orderList";
  }

}
```

The most significant change made in listing 6.1 is the addition of the `@Configuration-Properties` annotation. Its prefix attribute is set to `taco.orders`, which means that when setting the `pageSize` property, you need to use a configuration property named `taco.orders.pageSize`.

The new `pageSize` property defaults to 20, but you can easily change it to any value you want by setting a `taco.orders.pageSize` property. For example, you could set this property in application.yml like this:

```
taco:
  orders:
    pageSize: 10
```

Or, if you need to make a quick change while in production, you can do so without having to rebuild and redeploy the application by setting the `taco.orders.pageSize` property as an environment variable as follows:

```
$ export TACO_ORDERS_PAGESIZE=10
```

Any means by which a configuration property can be set can be used to adjust the page size of the recent orders page. Next, we'll look at how to set configuration data in property holders.

6.2.1 *Defining configuration property holders*

There's nothing that says @ConfigurationProperties must be set on a controller or any other specific kind of bean. @ConfigurationProperties are in fact often placed on beans whose sole purpose in the application is to be holders of configuration data. This keeps configuration-specific details out of the controllers and other application classes. It also makes it easy to share common configuration properties among several beans that may make use of that information.

In the case of the pageSize property in OrderController, you could extract it to a separate class. The following listing uses the OrderProps class in such a way.

Listing 6.2   Extracting pageSize to a holder class

```
package tacos.web;
import org.springframework.boot.context.properties.
                                        ConfigurationProperties;
import org.springframework.stereotype.Component;
import lombok.Data;

@Component
@ConfigurationProperties(prefix="taco.orders")
@Data
public class OrderProps {

  private int pageSize = 20;

}
```

As you did with OrderController, the pageSize property defaults to 20, and Order-Props is annotated with @ConfigurationProperties to have a prefix of taco.orders. It's also annotated with @Component so that Spring component scanning will automatically discover it and create it as a bean in the Spring application context. This is important, because the next step is to inject the OrderProps bean into OrderController.

There's nothing particularly special about configuration property holders. They're beans that have their properties injected from the Spring environment. They can be injected into any other bean that needs those properties. For OrderController, this means removing the pageSize property from OrderController and instead injecting and using the OrderProps bean, as shown next:

```
private OrderProps props;

public OrderController(OrderRepository orderRepo,
        OrderProps props) {
  this.orderRepo = orderRepo;
  this.props = props;
}

  ...
```

```
@GetMapping
public String ordersForUser(
    @AuthenticationPrincipal User user, Model model) {

  Pageable pageable = PageRequest.of(0, props.getPageSize());
  model.addAttribute("orders",
      orderRepo.findByUserOrderByPlacedAtDesc(user, pageable));

  return "orderList";
}
```

Now OrderController is no longer responsible for handling its own configuration properties. This keeps the code in OrderController slightly neater and allows you to reuse the properties in OrderProps in any other bean that may need them. Moreover, you're collecting configuration properties that pertain to orders in one place: the OrderProps class. If you need to add, remove, rename, or otherwise change the properties therein, you need to apply those changes only in OrderProps. And for testing purposes, it's easy to set configuration properties directly on a test-specific OrderProps and give it to the controller prior to the test.

For example, let's pretend that you're using the pageSize property in several other beans when you decide it would be best to apply some validation to that property to limit its values to no less than 5 and no more than 25. Without a holder bean, you'd have to apply validation annotations to OrderController, the pageSize property, and all other classes using that property. But because you've extracted pageSize into OrderProps, you only must make the changes to OrderProps, as shown here:

```
package tacos.web;
import javax.validation.constraints.Max;
import javax.validation.constraints.Min;

import org.springframework.boot.context.properties.
                                     ConfigurationProperties;
import org.springframework.stereotype.Component;
import org.springframework.validation.annotation.Validated;

import lombok.Data;

@Component
@ConfigurationProperties(prefix="taco.orders")
@Data
@Validated
public class OrderProps {

  @Min(value=5, message="must be between 5 and 25")
  @Max(value=25, message="must be between 5 and 25")
  private int pageSize = 20;

}
```

Although you could as easily apply the @Validated, @Min, and @Max annotations to OrderController (and any other beans that can be injected with OrderProps), it would just clutter up `OrderController` that much more. With a configuration property holder bean, you've collected configuration property specifics in one place, leaving the classes that need those properties relatively clean.

6.2.2 *Declaring configuration property metadata*

Depending on your IDE, you may have noticed that the `taco.orders.pageSize` entry in application.yml (or application.properties) has a warning saying something like Unknown Property 'taco'. This warning appears because there's missing metadata concerning the configuration property you just created. Figure 6.2 shows what this looks like when I hover over the `taco` portion of the property in the Spring Tool Suite.

```
 6  taco:¶
 7    ⚠ Unknown property 'taco'
 8    ⤸ Create metadata for `taco`
 9                      Press 'F2' for focus
10  ¶
```

Figure 6.2 **A warning for missing configuration property metadata**

Configuration property metadata is completely optional and doesn't prevent configuration properties from working. But the metadata can be useful for providing some minimal documentation around the configuration properties, especially in the IDE. For example, when I hover over the `spring.security.user.password` property, I see what's shown in figure 6.3. Although the hover help you get is minimal, it can be enough to help understand what the property is used for and how to use it.

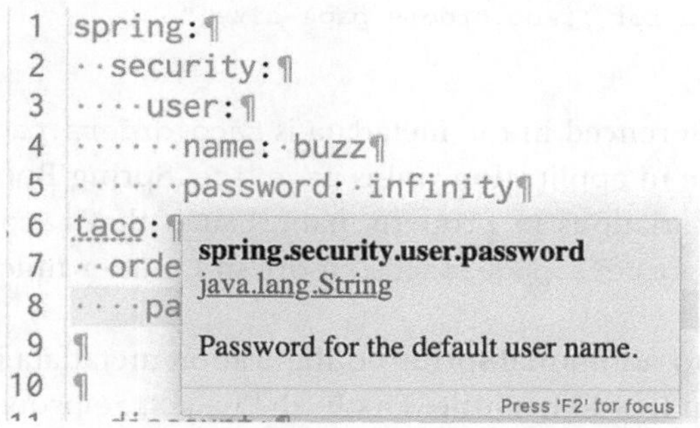

```
 1  spring:¶
 2  ··security:¶
 3  ····user:¶
 4  ······name:·buzz¶
 5  ······password:·infinity¶
 6  taco:¶
 7  ··orde
 8  ····pa
 9  ¶
10  ¶
11
```

spring.security.user.password
java.lang.String

Password for the default user name.
                      Press 'F2' for focus

Figure 6.3 **Hover documentation for configuration properties in the Spring Tool Suite**

To help those who might use the configuration properties that you define—which might even be you—it's generally a good idea to create some metadata around those properties. At least it gets rid of those annoying yellow warnings in the IDE.

To create metadata for your custom configuration properties, you'll need to create a file under the META-INF (e.g., in the project under src/main/resources/META-INF) named additional-spring-configuration-metadata.json.

QUICK-FIXING MISSING METADATA

If you're using the Spring Tool Suite, there's a quick-fix option for creating missing property metadata. Place your cursor on the line with the missing metadata warning and open the quick-fix pop-up with CMD-1 on Mac or Ctrl-1 on Windows and Linux (see figure 6.4).

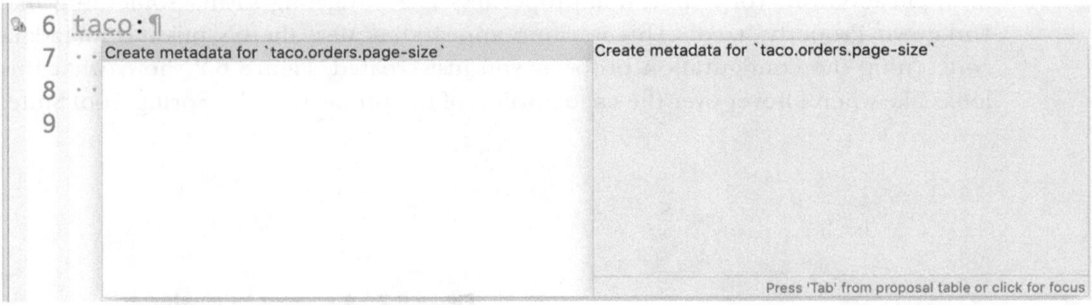

Figure 6.4   Creating configuration property metadata with the quick-fix pop-up in Spring Tool Suite

Then select the "Create Metadata for ..." option to add some metadata for the property. If it doesn't already exist, this quick fix will create a file in META-INF/additional-spring-configuration-metadata.json and fill it in with some metadata for the pageSize property, as shown in the next code:

```
{"properties": [{
  "name": "taco.orders.page-size",
  "type": "java.lang.String",
  "description": "A description for 'taco.orders.page-size'"
}]}
```

Notice that the property name referenced in the metadata is taco.orders.page-size, whereas the actual property name in application.yml is pageSize. Spring Boot's flexible property naming allows for variations in property names such that taco.orders.page-size is equivalent to taco.orders.pageSize, so it doesn't matter much which form you use.

The initial metadata written to additional-spring-configuration-metadata.json is a fine start, but you'll probably want to edit it a little. Firstly, the pageSize property isn't a java.lang.String, so you'll want to change it to java.lang.Integer. And the description property should be changed to be more descriptive of what pageSize is for. The following JSON code sample shows what the metadata might look like after a few edits:

```
{"properties": [{
  "name": "taco.orders.page-size",
  "type": "java.lang.Integer",
```

```
      "description": "Sets the maximum number of orders to display in a list."
}]}
```

With that metadata in place, the warnings should be gone. What's more, if you hover over the `taco.orders.pageSize` property, you'll see the description shown in figure 6.5.

```
6 taco:¶
7 ··orders:¶
8 ····pageSize:·10¶
9
```

taco.orders.page-size
java.lang.Integer

Sets the maximum number of orders to display in a list.

Press 'F2' for focus

Figure 6.5   Hover help for custom configuration properties

Also, as shown in figure 6.6, you get autocompletion help from the IDE, just like Spring-provided configuration properties.

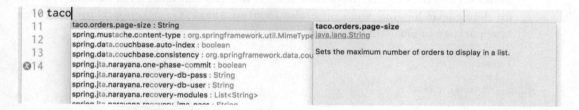

Figure 6.6   Configuration property metadata enables autocompletion of properties.

As you've seen, configuration properties are useful for tweaking both autoconfigured components as well as the details injected into your own application beans. But what if you need to configure different properties for different deployment environments? Let's take a look at how to use Spring profiles to set up environment-specific configurations.

6.3   Configuring with profiles

When applications are deployed to different runtime environments, usually some configuration details differ. The details of a database connection, for instance, are likely not the same in a development environment as in a quality assurance environment, and they are different still in a production environment. One way to configure properties uniquely in one environment over another is to use environment variables to specify configuration properties instead of defining them in application.properties and application.yml.

For instance, during development you can lean on the autoconfigured embedded H2 database. But in production, you can set database configuration properties as environment variables like this:

```
% export SPRING_DATASOURCE_URL=jdbc:mysql://localhost/tacocloud
% export SPRING_DATASOURCE_USERNAME=tacouser
% export SPRING_DATASOURCE_PASSWORD=tacopassword
```

Although this will work, it's somewhat cumbersome to specify more than one or two configuration properties as environment variables. Moreover, there's no good way to track changes to environment variables or to easily roll back changes if there's a mistake.

Instead, I prefer to take advantage of Spring profiles. Profiles are a type of conditional configuration where different beans, configuration classes, and configuration properties are applied or ignored based on what profiles are active at run time.

For instance, let's say that for development and debugging purposes, you want to use the embedded H2 database, and you want the logging levels for the Taco Cloud code to be set to DEBUG. But in production, you want to use an external MySQL database and set the logging levels to WARN. In the development situation, it's easy enough to not set any data source properties and get the autoconfigured H2 database. And as for debug-level logging, you can set the logging.level.tacos property for the tacos base package to DEBUG in application.yml as follows:

```
logging:
  level:
    tacos: DEBUG
```

This is precisely what you need for development purposes. But if you were to deploy this application in a production setting with no further changes to application.yml, you'd still have debug logging for the tacos package and an embedded H2 database. What you need is to define a profile with properties suited for production.

6.3.1   *Defining profile-specific properties*

One way to define profile-specific properties is to create yet another YAML or properties file containing only the properties for production. The name of the file should follow this convention: application-{profile name}.yml or application-{profile name}.properties. Then you can specify the configuration properties appropriate to that profile. For example, you could create a new file named application-prod.yml that contains the following properties:

```
spring:
  datasource:
    url: jdbc:mysql://localhost/tacocloud
    username: tacouser
    password: tacopassword
```

```
logging:
  level:
    tacos: WARN
```

Another way to specify profile-specific properties works only with YAML configuration. It involves placing profile-specific properties alongside nonprofiled properties in application.yml, separated by three hyphens and the `spring.profiles` property to name the profile. When applying the production properties to application.yml in this way, the entire application.yml would look like this:

```
logging:
  level:
    tacos: DEBUG

---
spring:
  profiles: prod

  datasource:
    url: jdbc:mysql://localhost/tacocloud
    username: tacouser
    password: tacopassword

logging:
  level:
    tacos: WARN
```

As you can see, this application.yml file is divided into two sections by a set of triple hyphens (`---`). The second section specifies a value for `spring.profiles`, indicating that the properties that follow apply to the prod profile. The first section, on the other hand, doesn't specify a value for `spring.profiles`. Therefore, its properties are common to all profiles or are defaults if the active profile doesn't otherwise have the properties set.

Regardless of which profiles are active when the application runs, the logging level for the `tacos` package will be set to DEBUG by the property set in the default profile. But if the profile named prod is active, then the `logging.level.tacos` property will be overridden with WARN. Likewise, if the prod profile is active, then the data source properties will be set to use the external MySQL database.

You can define properties for as many profiles as you need by creating additional YAML or properties files named with the pattern application-{profile name}.yml or application-{profile name}.properties. Or, if you prefer, type three more dashes in application.yml along with another `spring.profiles` property to specify the profile name. Then add all of the profile-specific properties you need. Although there's no benefit to either approach, you might find that putting all profile configurations in a single YAML file works best when the number of properties is small, whereas distinct files for each profile is better when you have a large number of properties.

6.3.2   *Activating profiles*

Setting profile-specific properties will do no good unless those profiles are active. But how can you make a profile active? All it takes to make a profile active is to include it in the list of profile names given to the `spring.profiles.active` property. For example, you could set it in application.yml like this:

```
spring:
  profiles:
    active:
    - prod
```

But that's perhaps the worst possible way to set an active profile. If you set the active profile in application.yml, then that profile becomes the default profile, and you achieve none of the benefits of using profiles to separate the production-specific properties from development properties. Instead, I recommend that you set the active profile(s) with environment variables. On the production environment, you would set `SPRING_PROFILES_ACTIVE` like this:

```
% export SPRING_PROFILES_ACTIVE=prod
```

From then on, any applications deployed to that machine will have the `prod` profile active, and the corresponding configuration properties would take precedence over the properties in the default profile.

If you're running the application as an executable JAR file, you might also set the active profile with a command-line argument like this:

```
% java -jar taco-cloud.jar --spring.profiles.active=prod
```

Note that the `spring.profiles.active` property name contains the plural word *profiles*. This means you can specify more than one active profile. Often, this is with a comma-separated list as when setting it with an environment variable, as shown here:

```
% export SPRING_PROFILES_ACTIVE=prod,audit,ha
```

But in YAML, you'd specify it as a list like this:

```
spring:
  profiles:
    active:
    - prod
    - audit
    - ha
```

It's also worth noting that if you deploy a Spring application to Cloud Foundry, a profile named `cloud` is automatically activated for you. If Cloud Foundry is your production environment, you'll want to be sure to specify production-specific properties under the `cloud` profile.

As it turns out, profiles aren't useful only for conditionally setting configuration properties in a Spring application. Let's see how to declare beans specific to an active profile.

6.3.3 Conditionally creating beans with profiles

Sometimes it's useful to provide a unique set of beans for different profiles. Normally, any bean declared in a Java configuration class is created, regardless of which profile is active. But suppose you need some beans to be created only if a certain profile is active. In that case, the `@Profile` annotation can designate beans as being applicable to only a given profile.

For instance, suppose you have a `CommandLineRunner` bean declared in `TacoCloudApplication` that's used to load the embedded database with ingredient data when the application starts. That's great for development but would be unnecessary (and undesirable) in a production application. To prevent the ingredient data from being loaded every time the application starts in a production deployment, you could annotate the `CommandLineRunner` bean method with `@Profile` like this:

```
@Bean
@Profile("dev")
public CommandLineRunner dataLoader(IngredientRepository repo,
        UserRepository userRepo, PasswordEncoder encoder) {

    ...

}
```

Or suppose that you need the `CommandLineRunner` created if either the `dev` profile or `qa` profile is active. In that case, you can list the profiles for which the bean should be created like so:

```
@Bean
@Profile({"dev", "qa"})
public CommandLineRunner dataLoader(IngredientRepository repo,
        UserRepository userRepo, PasswordEncoder encoder) {

    ...

}
```

Now the ingredient data will be loaded only if the `dev` or `qa` profiles are active. That would mean that you'd need to activate the `dev` profile when running the application in the development environment. It would be even more convenient if that `CommandLineRunner` bean were always created unless the `prod` profile is active. In that case, you can apply `@Profile` like this:

```
@Bean
@Profile("!prod")
```

```
public CommandLineRunner dataLoader(IngredientRepository repo,
      UserRepository userRepo, PasswordEncoder encoder) {

  ...

}
```

Here, the exclamation mark (!) negates the profile name. Effectively, it states that the CommandLineRunner bean will be created if the prod profile isn't active.

It's also possible to use @Profile on an entire @Configuration-annotated class. For example, suppose that you were to extract the CommandLineRunner bean into a separate configuration class named DevelopmentConfig. Then you could annotate DevelopmentConfig with @Profile as follows:

```
@Profile({"!prod", "!qa"})
@Configuration
public class DevelopmentConfig {

  @Bean
  public CommandLineRunner dataLoader(IngredientRepository repo,
        UserRepository userRepo, PasswordEncoder encoder) {

    ...

  }

}
```

Here, the CommandLineRunner bean (as well as any other beans defined in Development-Config) will be created only if neither the prod nor qa profile is active.

Summary

- We can annotate Spring beans with @ConfigurationProperties to enable injection of values from one of several property sources.
- Configuration properties can be set in command-line arguments, environment variables, JVM system properties, properties files, or YAML files, among other options.
- Use configuration properties to override autoconfiguration settings, including the ability to specify a data source URL and logging levels.
- Spring profiles can be used with property sources to conditionally set configuration properties based on the active profile(s).

Part 2

Integrated Spring

The chapters in part 2 cover topics that help integrate your Spring application with other applications.

Chapter 7 expands on the discussion of Spring MVC started in chapter 2 by looking at how to write REST APIs in Spring. We'll look at how to define REST endpoints in Spring MVC, automatically generate repository-based REST endpoints with Spring Data REST, and consume REST APIs. Chapter 8 looks at how to secure an API using Spring Security's support for OAuth 2 as well as how to obtain authorization in client code that can access OAuth 2–secured APIs. In chapter 9, we'll look at using asynchronous communication to enable a Spring application to both send and receive messages using the Java Message Service (JMS), RabbitMQ, and Kafka. And finally, chapter 10 discusses declarative application integration using the Spring Integration project. We'll cover processing data in real time, defining integration flows, and integrating with external systems like emails and filesystems.

Creating REST services 7

"The web browser is dead. What now?"

Several years ago, I heard someone suggest that the web browser was nearing legacy status and that something else would take over. But how could this be? What could possibly dethrone the near-ubiquitous web browser? How would we consume the growing number of sites and online services if not with a web browser? Surely these were the ramblings of a madman!

Fast-forward to the present day, and it's clear that the web browser hasn't gone away. But it no longer reigns as the primary means of accessing the internet. Mobile devices, tablets, smart watches, and voice-based devices are now commonplace. And even many browser-based applications are actually running JavaScript applications rather than letting the browser be a dumb terminal for server-rendered content.

With such a vast selection of client-side options, many applications have adopted a common design where the user interface is pushed closer to the client and the server exposes an API through which all kinds of clients can interact with the back-end functionality.

In this chapter, you're going to use Spring to provide a REST API for the Taco Cloud application. You'll use what you learned about Spring MVC in chapter 2 to create RESTful endpoints with Spring MVC controllers. You'll also automatically expose REST endpoints for the Spring Data repositories you defined in chapters 3 and 4. Finally, we'll look at ways to test and secure those endpoints.

But first, you'll start by writing a few new Spring MVC controllers that expose back-end functionality with REST endpoints to be consumed by a rich web frontend.

7.1 *Writing RESTful controllers*

In a nutshell, REST APIs aren't much different from websites. Both involve responding to HTTP requests. But the key difference is that instead of responding to those requests with HTML, as websites do, REST APIs typically respond with a data-oriented format such as JSON or XML.

In chapter 2 you used `@GetMapping` and `@PostMapping` annotations to fetch and post data to the server. Those same annotations will still come in handy as you define your REST API. In addition, Spring MVC supports a handful of other annotations for various types of HTTP requests, as listed in table 7.1.

Table 7.1   Spring MVC's HTTP request-handling annotations

Annotation	HTTP method	Typical use[a]
`@GetMapping`	HTTP GET requests	Reading resource data
`@PostMapping`	HTTP POST requests	Creating a resource
`@PutMapping`	HTTP PUT requests	Updating a resource
`@PatchMapping`	HTTP PATCH requests	Updating a resource
`@DeleteMapping`	HTTP DELETE requests	Deleting a resource
`@RequestMapping`	General-purpose request handling; HTTP `method` specified in the method attribute	

a. Mapping HTTP methods to create, read, update, and delete (CRUD) operations isn't a perfect match, but in practice, that's how they're often used and how you'll use them in Taco Cloud.

To see these annotations in action, you'll start by creating a simple REST endpoint that fetches a few of the most recently created tacos.

7.1.1 *Retrieving data from the server*

One thing that we'd like the Taco Cloud application to be able to do is allow taco fanatics to design their own taco creations and share them with their follow taco lovers. One way to do that is to display a list of the most recently created tacos on the website.

In support of that feature, we need to create an endpoint that handles GET requests for /api/tacos which include a "recent" parameter and responds with a list of recently designed tacos. You'll create a new controller to handle such a request. The next listing shows the controller for the job.

Listing 7.1   A RESTful controller for taco design API requests

```
package tacos.web.api;

import org.springframework.data.domain.PageRequest;
import org.springframework.data.domain.Sort;
import org.springframework.web.bind.annotation.CrossOrigin;
import org.springframework.web.bind.annotation.GetMapping;
import org.springframework.web.bind.annotation.RequestMapping;
import org.springframework.web.bind.annotation.RestController;

import tacos.Taco;
import tacos.data.TacoRepository;

@RestController
@RequestMapping(path="/api/tacos",              ◁──  Handles requests
                produces="application/json")          for /api/tacos
@CrossOrigin(origins="http://tacocloud:8080")   ◁──┐ Allows cross-origin
public class TacoController {                        │ requests
  private TacoRepository tacoRepo;

  public TacoController(TacoRepository tacoRepo) {
    this.tacoRepo = tacoRepo;
  }

  @GetMapping(params="recent")                  ◁──┐ Fetches and returns
  public Iterable<Taco> recentTacos() {              │ recent taco designs
    PageRequest page = PageRequest.of(
            0, 12, Sort.by("createdAt").descending());
    return tacoRepo.findAll(page).getContent();
  }
}
```

You may be thinking that this controller's name sounds somewhat familiar. In chapter 2 you created a similarly named `DesignTacoController` that handled similar types of requests. But where that controller was for producing an HTML result in the Taco Cloud application, this new `TacoController` is a REST controller, as indicated by the `@RestController` annotation.

The `@RestController` annotation serves two purposes. First, it's a stereotype annotation like `@Controller` and `@Service` that marks a class for discovery by component scanning. But most relevant to the discussion of REST, the `@RestController` annotation tells Spring that all handler methods in the controller should have their return value written directly to the body of the response, rather than being carried in the model to a view for rendering.

Alternatively, you could have annotated `TacoController` with `@Controller`, just like any Spring MVC controller. But then you'd need to also annotate all of the handler methods with @ResponseBody to achieve the same result. Yet another option would be to return a ResponseEntity object, which we'll discuss in a moment.

The @RequestMapping annotation at the class level works with the @GetMapping annotation on the recentTacos() method to specify that the recentTacos() method is responsible for handling GET requests for /api/tacos?recent.

You'll notice that the @RequestMapping annotation also sets a produces attribute. This specifies that any of the handler methods in TacoController will handle requests only if the client sends a request with an Accept header that includes "application/json", indicating that the client can handle responses only in JSON format. This use of produces limits your API to only producing JSON results, and it allows for another controller (perhaps the TacoController from chapter 2) to handle requests with the same paths, so long as those requests don't require JSON output.

Even though setting produces to "application/json" limits your API to being JSON-based (which is fine for your needs), you're welcome to set produces to an array of String for multiple content types. For example, to allow for XML output, you could add "text/xml" to the produces attribute as follows:

```
@RequestMapping(path="/api/tacos",
                produces={"application/json", "text/xml"})
```

The other thing you may have noticed in listing 7.1 is that the class is annotated with @CrossOrigin. It's common for a JavaScript-based user interface, such as those written in a framework like Angular or ReactJS, to be served from a separate host and/or port from the API (at least for now), and the web browser will prevent your client from consuming the API. This restriction can be overcome by including CORS (cross-origin resource sharing) headers in the server responses. Spring makes it easy to apply CORS with the @CrossOrigin annotation.

As applied here, @CrossOrigin allows clients from localhost, port 8080, to access the API. The origins attribute accepts an array, however, so you can also specify multiple values, as shown next:

```
@RestController
@RequestMapping(path="/api/tacos",
                produces="application/json")
@CrossOrigin(origins={"http://tacocloud:8080", "http://tacocloud.com"})
public class TacoController {
   ...
}
```

The logic within the recentTacos() method is fairly straightforward. It constructs a PageRequest object that specifies that you want only the first (0th) page of 12 results, sorted in descending order by the taco's creation date. In short, you want a dozen of the most recently created taco designs. The PageRequest is passed into the call to the findAll() method of TacoRepository, and the content of that page of results is returned to the client (which, as you saw in listing 7.1, will be used as model data to display to the user).

You now have the start of a Taco Cloud API for your client. For development testing purposes, you may also want to use command-line utilities like `curl` or HTTPie (https://httpie.org/) to poke about the API. For example, the following command line shows how you might fetch recently created tacos with `curl`:

```
$ curl localhost:8080/api/tacos?recent
```

Or like this, if you prefer HTTPie:

```
$ http :8080/api/tacos?recent
```

Initially, the database will be empty, so the results from these requests will likewise be empty. We'll see in a moment how to handle `POST` requests that save tacos. But in the meantime, you could add an `CommandLineRunner` bean to preload the database with some test data. The following `CommandLineRunner` bean method shows how you might preload a few ingredients and a few tacos:

```java
@Bean
public CommandLineRunner dataLoader(
    IngredientRepository repo,
    UserRepository userRepo,
    PasswordEncoder encoder,
    TacoRepository tacoRepo) {
  return args -> {
    Ingredient flourTortilla = new Ingredient(
        "FLTO", "Flour Tortilla", Type.WRAP);
    Ingredient cornTortilla = new Ingredient(
        "COTO", "Corn Tortilla", Type.WRAP);
    Ingredient groundBeef = new Ingredient(
        "GRBF", "Ground Beef", Type.PROTEIN);
    Ingredient carnitas = new Ingredient(
        "CARN", "Carnitas", Type.PROTEIN);
    Ingredient tomatoes = new Ingredient(
        "TMTO", "Diced Tomatoes", Type.VEGGIES);
    Ingredient lettuce = new Ingredient(
        "LETC", "Lettuce", Type.VEGGIES);
    Ingredient cheddar = new Ingredient(
        "CHED", "Cheddar", Type.CHEESE);
    Ingredient jack = new Ingredient(
        "JACK", "Monterrey Jack", Type.CHEESE);
    Ingredient salsa = new Ingredient(
        "SLSA", "Salsa", Type.SAUCE);
    Ingredient sourCream = new Ingredient(
        "SRCR", "Sour Cream", Type.SAUCE);
    repo.save(flourTortilla);
    repo.save(cornTortilla);
    repo.save(groundBeef);
    repo.save(carnitas);
    repo.save(tomatoes);
```

```
        repo.save(lettuce);
        repo.save(cheddar);
        repo.save(jack);
        repo.save(salsa);
        repo.save(sourCream);

        Taco taco1 = new Taco();
        taco1.setName("Carnivore");
        taco1.setIngredients(Arrays.asList(
                flourTortilla, groundBeef, carnitas,
                sourCream, salsa, cheddar));
        tacoRepo.save(taco1);

        Taco taco2 = new Taco();
        taco2.setName("Bovine Bounty");
        taco2.setIngredients(Arrays.asList(
                cornTortilla, groundBeef, cheddar,
                jack, sourCream));
        tacoRepo.save(taco2);

        Taco taco3 = new Taco();
        taco3.setName("Veg-Out");
        taco3.setIngredients(Arrays.asList(
                flourTortilla, cornTortilla, tomatoes,
                lettuce, salsa));
        tacoRepo.save(taco3);
    };
}
```

Now if you try to use curl or HTTPie to make a request to the recent tacos endpoint, you'll get a response something like this (response formatted for readability):

```
$ curl localhost:8080/api/tacos?recent
[
  {
    "id": 4,
    "name": "Veg-Out",
    "createdAt": "2021-08-02T00:47:09.624+00:00",
    "ingredients": [
      { "id": "FLTO", "name": "Flour Tortilla", "type": "WRAP" },
      { "id": "COTO", "name": "Corn Tortilla", "type": "WRAP" },
      { "id": "TMTO", "name": "Diced Tomatoes", "type": "VEGGIES" },
      { "id": "LETC", "name": "Lettuce", "type": "VEGGIES" },
      { "id": "SLSA", "name": "Salsa", "type": "SAUCE" }
    ]
  },
  {
    "id": 3,
    "name": "Bovine Bounty",
    "createdAt": "2021-08-02T00:47:09.621+00:00",
    "ingredients": [
      { "id": "COTO", "name": "Corn Tortilla", "type": "WRAP" },
      { "id": "GRBF", "name": "Ground Beef", "type": "PROTEIN" },
      { "id": "CHED", "name": "Cheddar", "type": "CHEESE" },
```

```
      { "id": "JACK", "name": "Monterrey Jack", "type": "CHEESE" },
      { "id": "SRCR", "name": "Sour Cream", "type": "SAUCE" }
    ]
  },
  {
    "id": 2,
    "name": "Carnivore",
    "createdAt": "2021-08-02T00:47:09.520+00:00",
    "ingredients": [
      { "id": "FLTO", "name": "Flour Tortilla", "type": "WRAP" },
      { "id": "GRBF", "name": "Ground Beef", "type": "PROTEIN" },
      { "id": "CARN", "name": "Carnitas", "type": "PROTEIN" },
      { "id": "SRCR", "name": "Sour Cream", "type": "SAUCE" },
      { "id": "SLSA", "name": "Salsa", "type": "SAUCE" },
      { "id": "CHED", "name": "Cheddar", "type": "CHEESE" }
    ]
  }
]
```

Now let's say that you want to offer an endpoint that fetches a single taco by its ID. By using a placeholder variable in the handler method's path and accepting a path variable, you can capture the ID and use it to look up the Taco object through the repository as follows:

```
@GetMapping("/{id}")
public Optional<Taco> tacoById(@PathVariable("id") Long id) {
  return tacoRepo.findById(id);
}
```

Because the controller's base path is /api/tacos, this controller method handles GET requests for /api/tacos/{id}, where the {id} portion of the path is a placeholder. The actual value in the request is given to the id parameter, which is mapped to the {id} placeholder by @PathVariable.

Inside of tacoById(), the id parameter is passed to the repository's findById() method to fetch the Taco. The repository's findById() method returns an Optional <Taco>, because it is possible that there may not be a taco that matches the given ID. The Optional<Taco> is simply returned from the controller method.

Spring then takes the Optional<Taco> and calls its get() method to produce the response. If the ID doesn't match any known tacos, the response body will contain "null" and the response's HTTP status code will be 200 (OK). The client is handed a response it can't use, but the status code indicates everything is fine. A better approach would be to return a response with an HTTP 404 (NOT FOUND) status.

As it's currently written, there's no easy way to return a 404 status code from taco-ById(). But if you make a few small tweaks, you can set the status code appropriately, as shown here:

```
@GetMapping("/{id}")
public ResponseEntity<Taco> tacoById(@PathVariable("id") Long id) {
  Optional<Taco> optTaco = tacoRepo.findById(id);
```

```
if (optTaco.isPresent()) {
    return new ResponseEntity<>(optTaco.get(), HttpStatus.OK);
}
return new ResponseEntity<>(null, HttpStatus.NOT_FOUND);
}
```

Now, instead of returning a `Taco` object, `tacoById()` returns a `ResponseEntity<Taco>`. If the taco is found, you wrap the `Taco` object in a `ResponseEntity` with an HTTP status of OK (which is what the behavior was before). But if the taco isn't found, you wrap a `null` in a `ResponseEntity` along with an HTTP status of NOT FOUND to indicate that the client is trying to fetch a taco that doesn't exist.

Defining an endpoint that returns information is only the start. What if your API needs to receive data from the client? Let's see how you can write controller methods that handle input on the requests.

7.1.2 *Sending data to the server*

So far your API is able to return up to a dozen of the most recently created tacos. But how do those tacos get created in the first place?

Although you could use a `CommandLineRunner` bean to preload the database with some test taco data, ultimately taco data will come from users when they craft their taco creations. Therefore, we'll need to write a method in `TacoController` that handles requests containing taco designs and save them to the database. By adding the following `postTaco()` method to `TacoController`, you enable the controller to do exactly that:

```
@PostMapping(consumes="application/json")
@ResponseStatus(HttpStatus.CREATED)
public Taco postTaco(@RequestBody Taco taco) {
    return tacoRepo.save(taco);
}
```

Because `postTaco()` will handle an HTTP POST request, it's annotated with `@Post-Mapping` instead of `@GetMapping`. You're not specifying a `path` attribute here, so the `postTaco()` method will handle requests for /api/tacos as specified in the class-level `@RequestMapping` on `TacoController`.

You do set the `consumes` attribute, however. The `consumes` attribute is to request input what `produces` is to request output. Here you use `consumes` to say that the method will only handle requests whose `Content-type` matches `application/json`.

The method's `Taco` parameter is annotated with `@RequestBody` to indicate that the body of the request should be converted to a `Taco` object and bound to the parameter. This annotation is important—without it, Spring MVC would assume that you want request parameters (either query parameters or form parameters) to be bound to the `Taco` object. But the `@RequestBody` annotation ensures that JSON in the request body is bound to the `Taco` object instead.

Once postTaco() has received the Taco object, it passes it to the save() method on the TacoRepository.

You may have also noticed that I've annotated the postTaco() method with @ResponseStatus(HttpStatus.CREATED). Under normal circumstances (when no exceptions are thrown), all responses will have an HTTP status code of 200 (OK), indicating that the request was successful. Although an HTTP 200 response is always welcome, it's not always descriptive enough. In the case of a POST request, an HTTP status of 201 (CREATED) is more descriptive. It tells the client that not only was the request successful but a resource was created as a result. It's always a good idea to use @ResponseStatus where appropriate to communicate the most descriptive and accurate HTTP status code to the client.

Although you've used @PostMapping to create a new Taco resource, POST requests can also be used to update resources. Even so, POST requests are typically used for resource creation, and PUT and PATCH requests are used to update resources. Let's see how you can update data using @PutMapping and @PatchMapping.

7.1.3 Updating data on the server

Before you write any controller code for handling HTTP PUT or PATCH commands, you should take a moment to consider the elephant in the room: why are there two different HTTP methods for updating resources?

Although it's true that PUT is often used to update resource data, it's actually the semantic opposite of GET. Whereas GET requests are for transferring data from the server to the client, PUT requests are for sending data from the client to the server.

In that sense, PUT is really intended to perform a wholesale *replacement* operation rather than an update operation. In contrast, the purpose of HTTP PATCH is to perform a patch or partial update of resource data.

For example, suppose you want to be able to change the address on an order. One way we could achieve this through the REST API is with a PUT request handled like this:

```
@PutMapping(path="/{orderId}", consumes="application/json")
public TacoOrder putOrder(
                    @PathVariable("orderId") Long orderId,
                    @RequestBody TacoOrder order) {
  order.setId(orderId);
  return repo.save(order);
}
```

This could work, but it would require that the client submit the complete order data in the PUT request. Semantically, PUT means "put this data at this URL," essentially replacing any data that's already there. If any of the order's properties are omitted, that property's value would be overwritten with null. Even the tacos in the order would need to be set along with the order data or else they'd be removed from the order.

If PUT does a wholesale replacement of the resource data, then how should you handle requests to do just a partial update? That's what HTTP PATCH requests and

Spring's @PatchMapping are good for. Here's how you might write a controller method to handle a PATCH request for an order:

```
@PatchMapping(path="/{orderId}", consumes="application/json")
public TacoOrder patchOrder(@PathVariable("orderId") Long orderId,
                            @RequestBody TacoOrder patch) {

  TacoOrder order = repo.findById(orderId).get();
  if (patch.getDeliveryName() != null) {
    order.setDeliveryName(patch.getDeliveryName());
  }
  if (patch.getDeliveryStreet() != null) {
    order.setDeliveryStreet(patch.getDeliveryStreet());
  }
  if (patch.getDeliveryCity() != null) {
    order.setDeliveryCity(patch.getDeliveryCity());
  }
  if (patch.getDeliveryState() != null) {
    order.setDeliveryState(patch.getDeliveryState());
  }
  if (patch.getDeliveryZip() != null) {
    order.setDeliveryZip(patch.getDeliveryZip());
  }
  if (patch.getCcNumber() != null) {
    order.setCcNumber(patch.getCcNumber());
  }
  if (patch.getCcExpiration() != null) {
    order.setCcExpiration(patch.getCcExpiration());
  }
  if (patch.getCcCVV() != null) {
    order.setCcCVV(patch.getCcCVV());
  }
  return repo.save(order);
}
```

The first thing to note here is that the patchOrder() method is annotated with @PatchMapping instead of @PutMapping, indicating that it should handle HTTP PATCH requests instead of PUT requests.

But the one thing you've no doubt noticed is that the patchOrder() method is a bit more involved than the putOrder() method. That's because Spring MVC's mapping annotations, including @PatchMapping and @PutMapping, specify only what kinds of requests a method should handle. These annotations don't dictate how the request will be handled. Even though PATCH semantically implies a partial update, it's up to you to write code in the handler method that actually performs such an update.

In the case of the putOrder() method, you accepted the complete data for an order and saved it, adhering to the semantics of HTTP PUT. But in order for patch-Mapping() to adhere to the semantics of HTTP PATCH, the body of the method requires more intelligence. Instead of completely replacing the order with the new data sent in, it inspects each field of the incoming TacoOrder object and applies any non-null values to the existing order. This approach allows the client to send only the properties that should be changed and enables the server to retain existing data for any properties not specified by the client.

> **There's more than one way to PATCH**
>
> The patching approach applied in the `patchOrder()` method has the following limitations:
>
> - If `null` values are meant to specify no change, how can the client indicate that a field should be set to `null`?
> - There's no way of removing or adding a subset of items from a collection. If the client wants to add or remove an entry from a collection, it must send the complete altered collection.
>
> There's really no hard-and-fast rule about how `PATCH` requests should be handled or what the incoming data should look like. Rather than sending the actual domain data, a client could send a patch-specific description of the changes to be applied. Of course, the request handler would have to be written to handle patch instructions instead of the domain data.

In both `@PutMapping` and `@PatchMapping`, notice that the request path references the resource that's to be changed. This is the same way paths are handled by `@GetMapping`-annotated methods.

You've now seen how to fetch and post resources with `@GetMapping` and `@Post-Mapping`. And you've seen two different ways of updating a resource with `@PutMapping` and `@PatchMapping`. All that's left is handling requests to delete a resource.

7.1.4 *Deleting data from the server*

Sometimes data simply isn't needed anymore. In those cases, a client should be able to request that a resource be removed with an HTTP DELETE request.

Spring MVC's `@DeleteMapping` comes in handy for declaring methods that handle DELETE requests. For example, let's say you want your API to allow for an order resource to be deleted. The following controller method should do the trick:

```
@DeleteMapping("/{orderId}")
@ResponseStatus(HttpStatus.NO_CONTENT)
public void deleteOrder(@PathVariable("orderId") Long orderId) {
  try {
    repo.deleteById(orderId);
  } catch (EmptyResultDataAccessException e) {}
}
```

By this point, the idea of another mapping annotation should be old hat to you. You've already seen `@GetMapping`, `@PostMapping`, `@PutMapping`, and `@PatchMapping`—each specifying that a method should handle requests for their corresponding HTTP methods. It will probably come as no surprise to you that `@DeleteMapping` is used to specify that the deleteOrder() method is responsible for handling DELETE requests for /orders/{orderId}.

The code within the method is what does the actual work of deleting an order. In this case, it takes the order ID, provided as a path variable in the URL, and passes it to the repository's deleteById() method. If the order exists when that method is called, it will be deleted. If the order doesn't exist, an EmptyResultDataAccessException will be thrown.

I've chosen to catch the EmptyResultDataAccessException and do nothing with it. My thinking here is that if you try to delete a resource that doesn't exist, the outcome is the same as if it did exist prior to deletion—that is, the resource will be nonexistent. Whether it existed before is irrelevant. Alternatively, I could've written deleteOrder() to return a ResponseEntity, setting the body to null and the HTTP status code to NOT FOUND.

The only other thing to take note of in the deleteOrder() method is that it's annotated with @ResponseStatus to ensure that the response's HTTP status is 204 (NO CONTENT). There's no need to communicate any resource data back to the client for a resource that no longer exists, so responses to DELETE requests typically have no body and, therefore, should communicate an HTTP status code to let the client know not to expect any content.

Your Taco Cloud API is starting to take shape. Now a client can be written to consume this API, presenting ingredients, accepting orders, and displaying recently created tacos. We'll talk about writing REST client code a little later in 7.3. But for now, let's see another way to create REST API endpoints: automatically based on Spring Data repositories.

7.2   *Enabling data-backed services*

As you saw in chapter 3, Spring Data performs a special kind of magic by automatically creating repository implementations based on interfaces you define in your code. But Spring Data has another trick up its sleeve that can help you define APIs for your application.

Spring Data REST is another member of the Spring Data family that automatically creates REST APIs for repositories created by Spring Data. By doing little more than adding Spring Data REST to your build, you get an API with operations for each repository interface you've defined.

To start using Spring Data REST, add the following dependency to your build:

```
<dependency>
  <groupId>org.springframework.boot</groupId>
  <artifactId>spring-boot-starter-data-rest</artifactId>
</dependency>
```

Believe it or not, that's all that's required to expose a REST API in a project that's already using Spring Data for automatic repositories. By simply having the Spring Data REST starter in the build, the application gets autoconfiguration that enables automatic creation of a REST API for any repositories that were created by Spring Data (including Spring Data JPA, Spring Data Mongo, and so on).

The REST endpoints that Spring Data REST creates are at least as good as (and possibly even better than) the ones you've created yourself. So at this point, feel free to do a little demolition work and remove any `@RestController`-annotated classes you've created up to this point before moving on.

To try out the endpoints provided by Spring Data REST, you can fire up the application and start poking at some of the URLs. Based on the set of repositories you've already defined for Taco Cloud, you should be able to perform GET requests for tacos, ingredients, orders, and users.

For example, you can get a list of all ingredients by making a GET request for /ingredients. Using `curl`, you might get something that looks like this (abridged to show only the first ingredient):

```
$ curl localhost:8080/ingredients
{
  "_embedded" : {
    "ingredients" : [ {
      "name" : "Flour Tortilla",
      "type" : "WRAP",
      "_links" : {
        "self" : {
          "href" : "http://localhost:8080/ingredients/FLTO"
        },
        "ingredient" : {
          "href" : "http://localhost:8080/ingredients/FLTO"
        }
      }
    },
    ...
    ]
  },
  "_links" : {
    "self" : {
      "href" : "http://localhost:8080/ingredients"
    },
    "profile" : {
      "href" : "http://localhost:8080/profile/ingredients"
    }
  }
}
```

Wow! By doing nothing more than adding a dependency to your build, you're not only getting an endpoint for ingredients, but the resources that come back also contain hyperlinks! These hyperlinks are implementations of Hypermedia as the Engine of Application State, or HATEOAS for short. A client consuming this API could (optionally) use these hyperlinks as a guide for navigating the API and performing the next request.

The Spring HATEOAS project (https://spring.io/projects/spring-hateoas) provides general support for adding hypermedia links in your Spring MVC controller responses. But Spring Data REST automatically adds these links in the responses to its generated APIs.

To HATEOAS or not to HATEOAS?

The general idea of HATEOAS is that it enables a client to navigate an API in much the same way that a human may navigate a website: by following links. Rather than encode API details in a client and having the client construct URLs for every request, the client can select a link, by name, from the list of hyperlinks and use it to make their next request. In this way, the client doesn't need to be coded to know the structure of an API and can instead use the API itself as a roadmap through the API.

On the other hand, the hyperlinks do add a small amount of extra data in the payload and add some complexity requiring that the client know how to navigate using those hyperlinks. For this reason, API developers often forego the use of HATEOAS, and client developers often simply ignore the hyperlinks if there are any in an API.

Other than the free hyperlinks you get from Spring Data REST responses, we'll ignore HATEOAS and focus on simple, nonhypermedia APIs.

Pretending to be a client of this API, you can also use `curl` to follow the `self` link for the flour tortilla entry as follows:

```
$ curl http://localhost:8080/ingredients/FLTO
{
  "name" : "Flour Tortilla",
  "type" : "WRAP",
  "_links" : {
    "self" : {
      "href" : "http://localhost:8080/ingredients/FLTO"
    },
    "ingredient" : {
      "href" : "http://localhost:8080/ingredients/FLTO"
    }
  }
}
```

To avoid getting too distracted, we won't waste much more time in this book digging into each and every endpoint and option that Spring Data REST has created. But you should know that it also supports POST, PUT, and DELETE methods for the endpoints it creates. That's right: you can POST to /ingredients to create a new ingredient and DELETE /ingredients/FLTO to remove flour tortillas from the menu.

One thing you might want to do is set a base path for the API so that its endpoints are distinct and don't collide with any controllers you write. To adjust the base path for the API, set the `spring.data.rest.base-path` property as shown next:

```
spring:
  data:
    rest:
      base-path: /data-api
```

This sets the base path for Spring Data REST endpoints to /data-api. Although you can set the base path to anything you'd like, the choice of /data-api ensures that endpoints exposed by Spring Data REST don't collide with any other controllers, including those whose path begins with "/api" that we created earlier in this chapter. Consequently, the ingredients endpoint is now /data-api/ingredients. Now give this new base path a spin by requesting a list of tacos as follows:

```
$ curl http://localhost:8080/data-api/tacos
{
  "timestamp": "2018-02-11T16:22:12.381+0000",
  "status": 404,
  "error": "Not Found",
  "message": "No message available",
  "path": "/api/tacos"
}
```

Oh dear! That didn't work quite as expected. You have an Ingredient entity and an IngredientRepository interface, which Spring Data REST exposed with a /data-api/ingredients endpoint. So if you have a Taco entity and a TacoRepository interface, why doesn't Spring Data REST give you a /data-api/tacos endpoint?

7.2.1 *Adjusting resource paths and relation names*

Actually, Spring Data REST does give you an endpoint for working with tacos. But as clever as Spring Data REST can be, it shows itself to be a tiny bit less awesome in how it exposes the tacos endpoint.

When creating endpoints for Spring Data repositories, Spring Data REST tries to pluralize the associated entity class. For the Ingredient entity, the endpoint is /data-api/ingredients. For the TacoOrder entity, it's /data-api/orders. So far, so good.

But sometimes, such as with "taco," it trips up on a word and the pluralized version isn't quite right. As it turns out, Spring Data REST pluralized "taco" as "tacoes," so to make a request for tacos, you must play along and request /data-api/tacoes, as shown here:

```
$ curl localhost:8080/data-api/tacoes
{
  "_embedded" : {
    "tacoes" : [ {
      "name" : "Carnivore",
      "createdAt" : "2018-02-11T17:01:32.999+0000",
      "_links" : {
        "self" : {
          "href" : "http://localhost:8080/data-api/tacoes/2"
        },
```

```
      "taco" : {
        "href" : "http://localhost:8080/data-api/tacoes/2"
      },
      "ingredients" : {
        "href" : "http://localhost:8080/data-api/tacoes/2/ingredients"
      }
    }
  }]
},
"page" : {
  "size" : 20,
  "totalElements" : 3,
  "totalPages" : 1,
  "number" : 0
}
}
```

You may be wondering how I knew that "taco" would be mispluralized as "tacoes." As it turns out, Spring Data REST also exposes a home resource that lists links for all exposed endpoints. Just make a GET request to the API base path to get the goods as follows:

```
$ curl localhost:8080/api
{
  "_links" : {
    "orders" : {
      "href" : "http://localhost:8080/data-api/orders"
    },
    "ingredients" : {
      "href" : "http://localhost:8080/data-api/ingredients"
    },
    "tacoes" : {
      "href" : "http://localhost:8080/data-api/tacoes{?page,size,sort}",
      "templated" : true
    },
    "users" : {
      "href" : "http://localhost:8080/data-api/users"
    },
    "profile" : {
      "href" : "http://localhost:8080/data-api/profile"
    }
  }
}
```

As you can see, the home resource shows the links for all of your entities. Everything looks good, except for the tacoes link, where both the relation name and the URL have that odd pluralization of "taco."

The good news is that you don't have to accept this little quirk of Spring Data REST. By adding the following simple annotation to the Taco class, you can tweak both the relation name and that path:

```
@Data
@Entity
```

```
@RestResource(rel="tacos", path="tacos")
public class Taco {
  ...
}
```

The `@RestResource` annotation lets you give the entity any relation name and path you want. In this case, you're setting them both to `"tacos"`. Now when you request the home resource, you see the `tacos` link with correct pluralization, as shown next:

```
"tacos" : {
  "href" : "http://localhost:8080/data-api/tacos{?page,size,sort}",
  "templated" : true
},
```

This also sorts out the path for the endpoint so that you can issue requests against /data-api/tacos to work with taco resources.

Speaking of sorting things out, let's look at how you can sort the results from Spring Data REST endpoints.

7.2.2 Paging and sorting

You may have noticed that the links in the home resource all offer optional `page`, `size`, and `sort` parameters. By default, requests to a collection resource such as /data-api/tacos will return up to 20 items per page from the first page. But you can adjust the page size and the page displayed by specifying the `page` and `size` parameters in your request.

For example, to request the first page of tacos where the page size is 5, you can issue the following GET request (using `curl`):

```
$ curl "localhost:8080/data-api/tacos?size=5"
```

Assuming there are more than five tacos to be seen, you can request the second page of tacos by adding the `page` parameter as follows:

```
$ curl "localhost:8080/data-api/tacos?size=5&page=1"
```

Notice that the `page` parameter is zero-based, which means that asking for page 1 is actually asking for the second page. (You'll also note that many command-line shells trip up over the ampersand in the request, which is why I quoted the whole URL in the preceding `curl` command.)

The `sort` parameter lets you sort the resulting list by any property of the entity. For example, you need a way to fetch the 12 most recently created tacos for the UI to display. You can do that by specifying the following mix of paging and sorting parameters:

```
$ curl "localhost:8080/data-api/tacos?sort=createdAt,desc&page=0&size=12"
```

Here the `sort` parameter specifies that you should sort by the `createdDate` property and that it should be sorted in descending order (so that the newest tacos are first). The `page` and `size` parameters specify that you should see the first page of 12 tacos.

This is precisely what the UI needs to show the most recently created tacos. It's approximately the same as the /api/tacos?recent endpoint you defined in Taco-Controller earlier in this chapter.

Now let's switch gears and see how to write client code to consume the API endpoints we've created.

7.3   *Consuming REST services*

Have you ever gone to a movie and, as the movie starts, discovered that you were the only person in the theater? It certainly is a wonderful experience to have what is essentially a private viewing of a movie. You can pick whatever seat you want, talk back to the characters onscreen, and maybe even open your phone and tweet about it without anyone getting angry for disrupting their movie-watching experience. And the best part is that nobody else is there ruining the movie for you, either!

This hasn't happened to me often. But when it has, I have wondered what would have happened if I hadn't shown up. Would they still have shown the film? Would the hero still have saved the day? Would the theater staff still have cleaned the theater after the movie was over?

A movie without an audience is kind of like an API without a client. It's ready to accept and provide data, but if the API is never invoked, is it really an API? Like Schrödinger's cat, we can't know if the API is active or returning HTTP 404 responses until we issue a request to it.

It's not uncommon for Spring applications to both provide an API and make requests to another application's API. In fact, this is becoming prevalent in the world of microservices. Therefore, it's worthwhile to spend a moment looking at how to use Spring to interact with REST APIs.

A Spring application can consume a REST API with the following:

- *RestTemplate*—A straightforward, synchronous REST client provided by the core Spring Framework.
- *Traverson*—A wrapper around Spring's RestTemplate, provided by Spring HATEOAS, to enable a hyperlink-aware, synchronous REST client. Inspired from a JavaScript library of the same name.
- *WebClient*—A reactive, asynchronous REST client.

For now, we'll focus on creating clients with RestTemplate. I'll defer discussion of WebClient until we cover Spring's reactive web framework in chapter 12. And if you're interested in writing hyperlink-aware clients, check out the Traverson documentation at http://mng.bz/aZno.

There's a lot that goes into interacting with a REST resource from the client's perspective—mostly tedium and boilerplate. Working with low-level HTTP libraries, the client needs to create a client instance and a request object, execute the request, interpret the response, map the response to domain objects, and handle any exceptions that may be thrown along the way. And all of this boilerplate is repeated, regardless of what HTTP request is sent.

To avoid such boilerplate code, Spring provides `RestTemplate`. Just as `Jdbc-Template` handles the ugly parts of working with JDBC, `RestTemplate` frees you from dealing with the tedium of consuming REST resources.

`RestTemplate` provides 41 methods for interacting with REST resources. Rather than examine all of the methods that it offers, it's easier to consider only a dozen unique operations, each overloaded to equal the complete set of 41 methods. The 12 operations are described in table 7.2.

Table 7.2 `RestTemplate` defines 12 unique operations, each of which is overloaded, providing a total of 41 methods.

Method	Description
delete (…)	Performs an HTTP DELETE request on a resource at a specified URL
exchange (…)	Executes a specified HTTP method against a URL, returning a `Response-Entity` containing an object mapped from the response body
execute (…)	Executes a specified HTTP method against a URL, returning an object mapped from the response body
getForEntity (…)	Sends an HTTP GET request, returning a `ResponseEntity` containing an object mapped from the response body
getForObject (…)	Sends an HTTP GET request, returning an object mapped from a response body
headForHeaders (…)	Sends an HTTP HEAD request, returning the HTTP headers for the specified resource URL
optionsForAllow (…)	Sends an HTTP OPTIONS request, returning the `Allow` header for the specified URL
patchForObject (…)	Sends an HTTP PATCH request, returning the resulting object mapped from the response body
postForEntity (…)	POSTs data to a URL, returning a `ResponseEntity` containing an object mapped from the response body
postForLocation (…)	POSTs data to a URL, returning the URL of the newly created resource
postForObject (…)	POSTs data to a URL, returning an object mapped from the response body
put (…)	PUTs resource data to the specified URL

With the exception of TRACE, `RestTemplate` has at least one method for each of the standard HTTP methods. In addition, `execute()` and `exchange()` provide lower-level, general-purpose methods for sending requests with any HTTP method.

Most of the methods in table 7.2 are overloaded into the following three method forms:

- One accepts a `String` URL specification with URL parameters specified in a variable argument list.

- One accepts a `String` URL specification with URL parameters specified in a `Map<String,String>`.
- One accepts a `java.net.URI` as the URL specification, with no support for parameterized URLs.

Once you get to know the 12 operations provided by `RestTemplate` and how each of the variant forms works, you'll be well on your way to writing resource-consuming REST clients.

To use `RestTemplate`, you'll either need to create an instance at the point you need it, as follows:

```
RestTemplate rest = new RestTemplate();
```

or you can declare it as a bean and inject it where you need it, as shown next:

```
@Bean
public RestTemplate restTemplate() {
  return new RestTemplate();
}
```

Let's survey `RestTemplate`'s operations by looking at those that support the four primary HTTP methods: GET, PUT, DELETE, and POST. We'll start with `getForObject()` and `getForEntity()`—the GET methods.

7.3.1 GETting resources

Suppose that you want to fetch an ingredient from the Taco Cloud API. For that, you can use `RestTemplate`'s `getForObject()` to fetch the ingredient. For example, the following code uses `RestTemplate` to fetch an `Ingredient` object by its ID:

```
public Ingredient getIngredientById(String ingredientId) {
  return rest.getForObject("http://localhost:8080/ingredients/{id}",
                        Ingredient.class, ingredientId);
}
```

Here you're using the `getForObject()` variant that accepts a `String` URL and uses a variable list for URL variables. The `ingredientId` parameter passed into `getForObject()` is used to fill in the `{id}` placeholder in the given URL. Although there's only one URL variable in this example, it's important to know that the variable parameters are assigned to the placeholders in the order that they're given.

The second parameter to `getForObject()` is the type that the response should be bound to. In this case, the response data (that's likely in JSON format) should be deserialized into an `Ingredient` object that will be returned.

Alternatively, you can use a `Map` to specify the URL variables, as shown next:

```
public Ingredient getIngredientById(String ingredientId) {
  Map<String, String> urlVariables = new HashMap<>();
  urlVariables.put("id", ingredientId);
```

```
    return rest.getForObject("http://localhost:8080/ingredients/{id}",
        Ingredient.class, urlVariables);
}
```

In this case, the value of ingredientId is mapped to a key of id. When the request is made, the {id} placeholder is replaced by the map entry whose key is id.

Using a URI parameter is a bit more involved, requiring that you construct a URI object before calling getForObject(). Otherwise, it's similar to both of the other variants, as shown here:

```
public Ingredient getIngredientById(String ingredientId) {
  Map<String, String> urlVariables = new HashMap<>();
  urlVariables.put("id", ingredientId);
  URI url = UriComponentsBuilder
            .fromHttpUrl("http://localhost:8080/ingredients/{id}")
            .build(urlVariables);
  return rest.getForObject(url, Ingredient.class);
}
```

Here the URI object is defined from a String specification, and its placeholders filled in from entries in a Map, much like the previous variant of getForObject(). The get-ForObject() method is a no-nonsense way of fetching a resource. But if the client needs more than the payload body, you may want to consider using getForEntity().

getForEntity() works in much the same way as getForObject(), but instead of returning a domain object that represents the response's payload, it returns a ResponseEntity object that wraps that domain object. The ResponseEntity gives access to additional response details, such as the response headers.

For example, suppose that in addition to the ingredient data, you want to inspect the Date header from the response. With getForEntity() that becomes straightforward, as shown in the following code:

```
public Ingredient getIngredientById(String ingredientId) {
  ResponseEntity<Ingredient> responseEntity =
      rest.getForEntity("http://localhost:8080/ingredients/{id}",
          Ingredient.class, ingredientId);
  log.info("Fetched time: {}",
          responseEntity.getHeaders().getDate());
  return responseEntity.getBody();
}
```

The getForEntity() method is overloaded with the same parameters as get-ForObject(), so you can provide the URL variables as a variable list parameter or call getForEntity() with a URI object.

7.3.2 PUTting resources

For sending HTTP PUT requests, RestTemplate offers the put() method. All three overloaded variants of put() accept an Object that is to be serialized and sent to the given URL. As for the URL itself, it can be specified as a URI object or as a String. And like `getForObject()` and `getForEntity()`, the URL variables can be provided as either a variable argument list or as a `Map`.

Suppose that you want to replace an ingredient resource with the data from a new `Ingredient` object. The following code should do the trick:

```
public void updateIngredient(Ingredient ingredient) {
  rest.put("http://localhost:8080/ingredients/{id}",
      ingredient, ingredient.getId());
}
```

Here the URL is given as a `String` and has a placeholder that's substituted by the given `Ingredient` object's id property. The data to be sent is the `Ingredient` object itself. The `put()` method returns `void`, so there's nothing you need to do to handle a return value.

7.3.3   *DELETEing resources*

Suppose that Taco Cloud no longer offers an ingredient and wants it completely removed as an option. To make that happen, you can call the `delete()` method from `RestTemplate` as follows:

```
public void deleteIngredient(Ingredient ingredient) {
  rest.delete("http://localhost:8080/ingredients/{id}",
      ingredient.getId());
}
```

In this example, only the URL (specified as a `String`) and a URL variable value are given to `delete()`. But as with the other `RestTemplate` methods, the URL could be specified as a `URI` object or the URL parameters given as a `Map`.

7.3.4   *POSTing resource data*

Now let's say that you add a new ingredient to the Taco Cloud menu. An HTTP `POST` request to the …/ingredients endpoint with ingredient data in the request body will make that happen. `RestTemplate` has three ways of sending a `POST` request, each of which has the same overloaded variants for specifying the URL. If you wanted to receive the newly created `Ingredient` resource after the `POST` request, you'd use `postForObject()` like this:

```
public Ingredient createIngredient(Ingredient ingredient) {
  return rest.postForObject("http://localhost:8080/ingredients",
      ingredient, Ingredient.class);
}
```

This variant of the `postForObject()` method takes a `String` URL specification, the object to be posted to the server, and the domain type that the response body should be bound to. Although you aren't taking advantage of it in this case, a fourth parameter could be a `Map` of the URL variable value or a variable list of parameters to substitute into the URL.

If your client has more need for the location of the newly created resource, then you can call postForLocation() instead, as shown here:

```
public java.net.URI createIngredient(Ingredient ingredient) {
  return rest.postForLocation("http://localhost:8080/ingredients",
      ingredient);
}
```

Notice that postForLocation() works much like postForObject(), with the exception that it returns a URI of the newly created resource instead of the resource object itself. The URI returned is derived from the response's Location header. In the off chance that you need both the location and response payload, you can call post-ForEntity() like so:

```
public Ingredient createIngredient(Ingredient ingredient) {
  ResponseEntity<Ingredient> responseEntity =
          rest.postForEntity("http://localhost:8080/ingredients",
                             ingredient,
                             Ingredient.class);
  log.info("New resource created at {}",
          responseEntity.getHeaders().getLocation());
  return responseEntity.getBody();
}
```

Although the methods of RestTemplate differ in their purpose, they're quite similar in how they're used. This makes it easy to become proficient with RestTemplate and use it in your client code.

Summary

- REST endpoints can be created with Spring MVC, with controllers that follow the same programming model as browser-targeted controllers.
- Controller handler methods can either be annotated with @ResponseBody or return ResponseEntity objects to bypass the model and view and write data directly to the response body.
- The @RestController annotation simplifies REST controllers, eliminating the need to use @ResponseBody on handler methods.
- Spring Data repositories can automatically be exposed as REST APIs using Spring Data REST.

Securing REST

This chapter covers

- Securing APIs with OAuth 2
- Creating an authorization server
- Adding a resource server to an API
- Consuming OAuth 2–secured APIs

Have you ever taken advantage of valet parking? It's a simple concept: you hand your car keys to a valet near the entrance of a store, hotel, theater, or restaurant, and they deal with the hassle of finding a parking space for you. And then they return your car to you when you ask for it. Maybe it's because I've seen *Ferris Bueller's Day Off* too many times, but I'm always reluctant to hand my car keys to a stranger and hope that they take good care of my vehicle for me.

Nonetheless, valet parking involves granting trust to someone to take care of your car. Many newer cars provide a "valet key," a special key that can be used only to open the car doors and start the engine. This way the amount of trust that you are granting is limited in scope. The valet cannot open the glove compartment or the trunk with the valet key.

In a distributed application, trust is critical between software systems. Even in a simple situation where a client application consumes a backend API, it's important that the client is trusted and anyone else attempting to use that same API is blocked out. And, like the valet, the amount of trust you grant to a client should be limited to only the functions necessary for the client to do its job.

Securing a REST API is different from securing a browser-based web application. In this chapter, we're going to look at OAuth 2, an authorization specification created specifically for API security. In doing so, we'll look at Spring Security's support for OAuth 2. But first, let's set the stage by seeing how OAuth 2 works.

8.1 Introducing OAuth 2

Suppose that we want to create a new back-office application for managing the Taco Cloud application. More specifically, let's say that we want this new application to be able to manage the ingredients available on the main Taco Cloud website.

Before we start writing code for the administrative application, we'll need to add a handful of new endpoints to the Taco Cloud API to support ingredient management. The REST controller in the following listing offers three endpoints for listing, adding, and deleting ingredients.

Listing 8.1   A controller to manage available ingredients

```
package tacos.web.api;

import org.springframework.beans.factory.annotation.Autowired;
import org.springframework.http.HttpStatus;
import org.springframework.web.bind.annotation.CrossOrigin;
import org.springframework.web.bind.annotation.DeleteMapping;
import org.springframework.web.bind.annotation.GetMapping;
import org.springframework.web.bind.annotation.PathVariable;
import org.springframework.web.bind.annotation.PostMapping;
import org.springframework.web.bind.annotation.RequestBody;
import org.springframework.web.bind.annotation.RequestMapping;
import org.springframework.web.bind.annotation.ResponseStatus;
import org.springframework.web.bind.annotation.RestController;

import tacos.Ingredient;
import tacos.data.IngredientRepository;

@RestController
@RequestMapping(path="/api/ingredients", produces="application/json")
@CrossOrigin(origins="http://localhost:8080")
public class IngredientController {

  private IngredientRepository repo;

  @Autowired
  public IngredientController(IngredientRepository repo) {
    this.repo = repo;
  }

  @GetMapping
  public Iterable<Ingredient> allIngredients() {
```

```
    return repo.findAll();
  }

  @PostMapping
  @ResponseStatus(HttpStatus.CREATED)
  public Ingredient saveIngredient(@RequestBody Ingredient ingredient) {
    return repo.save(ingredient);
  }

  @DeleteMapping("/{id}")
  @ResponseStatus(HttpStatus.NO_CONTENT)
  public void deleteIngredient(@PathVariable("id") String ingredientId) {
    repo.deleteById(ingredientId);
  }

}
```

Great! Now all we need to do is get started on the administrative application, calling those endpoints on the main Taco Cloud application as needed to add and delete ingredients.

But wait—there's no security around that API yet. If our backend application can make HTTP requests to add and delete ingredients, so can anyone else. Even using the curl command-line client, someone could add a new ingredient like this:

```
$ curl localhost:8080/ingredients \
  -H"Content-type: application/json" \
  -d'{"id":"FISH","name":"Stinky Fish", "type":"PROTEIN"}'
```

They could even use curl to delete existing ingredients[1] as follows:

```
$ curl localhost:8080/ingredients/GRBF -X DELETE
```

This API is part of the main application and available to the world; in fact, the GET endpoint is used by the user interface of the main application in home.html. Therefore, it's clear that we'll need to secure at least the POST and DELETE endpoints.

One option is to use HTTP Basic authentication to secure the /ingredients endpoints. This could be done by adding @PreAuthorize to the handler methods like this:

```
@PostMapping
@PreAuthorize("#{hasRole('ADMIN')}")
public Ingredient saveIngredient(@RequestBody Ingredient ingredient) {
  return repo.save(ingredient);
}

@DeleteMapping("/{id}")
@PreAuthorize("#{hasRole('ADMIN')}")
public void deleteIngredient(@PathVariable("id") String ingredientId) {
```

---

[1] Depending on the database and schema in play, integrity constraints may prevent a deletion from happening if an ingredient is already part of an existing taco. But it still may be possible to delete an ingredient if the database schema allows it.

```
        repo.deleteById(ingredientId);
}
```

Or, the endpoints could be secured in the security configuration like this:

```
@Override
protected void configure(HttpSecurity http) throws Exception {
  http
    .authorizeRequests()
      .antMatchers(HttpMethod.POST, "/ingredients").hasRole("ADMIN")
      .antMatchers(HttpMethod.DELETE, "/ingredients/**").hasRole("ADMIN")

      ...
}
```

Whether or not to use the "ROLE_" prefix

Authorities in Spring Security can take several forms, including roles, permissions, and (as we'll see later) OAuth2 scopes. Roles, specifically, are a specialized form of authority that are prefixed with `"ROLE_"`.

When working with methods or SpEL expressions that deal directly with roles, such as `hasRole()`, the `"ROLE_"` prefix is inferred. Thus, a call to `hasRole("ADMIN")` is internally checking for an authority whose name is `"ROLE_ADMIN"`. You do not need to explicitly use the `"ROLE_"` prefix when calling these methods and functions (and, in fact, doing so will result in a double `"ROLE_"` prefix).

Other Spring Security methods and functions that deal with authority more generically can also be used to check for roles. But in those cases, you must explicitly add the `"ROLE_"` prefix. For example, if you chose to use `hasAuthority()` instead of `hasRole()`, you'd need to pass in `"ROLE_ADMIN"` instead of `"ADMIN"`.

Either way, the ability to submit POST or DELETE requests to /ingredients will require that the submitter also provide credentials that have `"ROLE_ADMIN"` authority. For example, using `curl`, the credentials can be specified with the `-u` parameter, as shown here:

```
$ curl localhost:8080/ingredients \
  -H"Content-type: application/json" \
  -d'{"id":"FISH","name":"Stinky Fish", "type":"PROTEIN"}' \
  -u admin:l3tm31n
```

Although HTTP Basic will lock down the API, it is rather . . . um . . . basic. It requires that the client and the API share common knowledge of the user credentials, possibly duplicating information. Moreover, although HTTP Basic credentials are Base64-encoded in the header of the request, if a hacker were to somehow intercept the request, the credentials could easily be obtained, decoded, and used for evil purposes. If that were to happen, the password would need to be changed, thus requiring an update and reauthentication in all clients.

What if instead of requiring that the admin user identify themselves on every request, the API just asks for some token that proves that they are authorized to access the resources? This would be roughly like a ticket to a sporting event. To enter the game, the person at the turnstiles doesn't need to know who you are; they just need to know that you have a valid ticket. If so, then you are allowed access.

That's roughly how OAuth 2 authorization works. Clients request an access token—analogous to a valet key—from an authorization server, with the express permission of a user. That token allows them to interact with an API on behalf of the user who authorized the client. At any point, the token could expire or be revoked, without requiring that the user's password be changed. In such cases, the client would just need to request a new access token to be able to continue acting on the user's behalf. This flow is illustrated in figure 8.1.

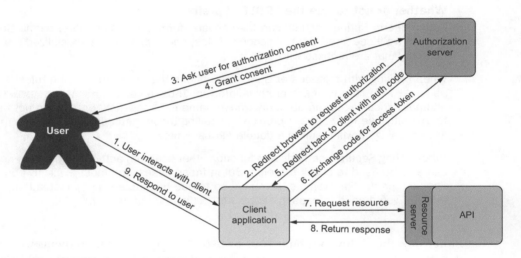

Figure 8.1   The OAuth 2 authorization code flow

OAuth 2 is a very rich security specification that offers a lot of ways to use it. The flow described in figure 8.1 is called *authorization code grant*. Other flows supported by the OAuth 2 specification include these:

- *Implicit grant*—Like authorization code grant, implicit grant redirects the user's browser to the authorization server to get user consent. But when redirecting back, rather than provide an authorization code in the request, the access token is granted implicitly in the request. Although originally designed for JavaScript clients running in a browser, this flow is not generally recommended anymore, and authorization code grant is preferred.
- *User credentials (or password) grant*—In this flow, no redirect takes place, and there may not even be a web browser involved. Instead, the client application obtains the

user's credentials and exchanges them directly for an access token. This flow seems suitable for clients that are not browser based, but modern applications often favor asking the user to go to a website in their browser and perform authorization code grant to avoid having to handle the user's credentials.

- *Client credentials grant*—This flow is like user credentials grant, except that instead of exchanging a user's credentials for an access token, the client exchanges its own credentials for an access token. However, the token granted is limited in scope to performing non-user-focused operations and can't be used to act on behalf of a user.

For our purposes, we're going to focus on the authorization code grant flow to obtain a JSON Web Token (JWT) access token. This will involve creating a handful of applications that work together, including the following:

- *The authorization server*—An authorization server's job is to obtain permission from a user on behalf of a client application. If the user grants permission, then the authorization server gives an access token to the client application that it can use to gain authenticated access to an API.
- *The resource server*—A resource server is just another name for an API that is secured by OAuth 2. Although the resource server is part of the API itself, for the sake of discussion, the two are often treated as two distinct concepts. The resource server restricts access to its resources unless the request provides a valid access token with the necessary permission scope. For our purposes, the Taco Cloud API we started in chapter 7 will serve as our resource server, once we add a bit of security configuration to it.
- *The client application*—The client application is an application that wants to consume an API but needs permission to do so. We'll build a simple administrative application for Taco Cloud to be able to add new ingredients.
- *The user*—This is the human who uses the client application and grants the application permission to access the resource server's API on their behalf.

In the authorization code grant flow, a series of browser redirects between the client application and the authorization server occurs as the client obtains an access token. It starts with the client redirecting the user's browser to the authorization server, asking for specific permissions (or "scope"). The authorization server then asks the user to log in and consent to the requested permissions. After the user has granted consent, the authorization server redirects the browser back to the client with a code that the client can then exchange for an access token. Once the client has the access token, it can then be used to interact with the resource server API by passing it in the "Authorization" header of every request.

Although we're going to restrict our focus on a specific use of OAuth 2, you are encouraged to dig deeper into the subject by reading the OAuth 2 specification (https://oauth.net/2/) or reading any one of the following books on the subject:

- *OAuth 2 in Action*: https://www.manning.com/books/oauth-2-in-action
- *Microservices Security in Action*: https://www.manning.com/books/microservices-security-in-action
- *API Security in Action*: https://www.manning.com/books/api-security-in-action

You might also want to have a look at a liveProject called "Protecting User Data with Spring Security and OAuth2" (http://mng.bz/4KdD).

For several years, a project called Spring Security for OAuth provided support for both OAuth 1.0a and OAuth 2. It was separate from Spring Security but developed by the same team. In recent years, however, the Spring Security team has absorbed the client and resource server components into Spring Security itself.

As for the authorization server, it was decided that it not be included in Spring Security. Instead, developers are encouraged to use authorization servers from various vendors such as Okta, Google, and others. But, due to demand from the developer community, the Spring Security team started a Spring Authorization Server project.[2] This project is labeled as "experimental" and is intended to eventually be community driven, but it serves as a great way to get started with OAuth 2 without signing up for one of those other authorization server implementations.

Throughout the rest of this chapter, we're going to see how to use OAuth 2 using Spring Security. Along the way, we'll create two new projects, an authorization server project and a client project, and we'll modify our existing Taco Cloud project such that its API acts as a resource server. We'll start by creating an authorization server using the Spring Authorization Server project.

8.2   *Creating an authorization server*

An authorization server's job is primarily to issue an access token on behalf of a user. As mentioned earlier, we have several authorization server implementations to choose from, but we're going to use Spring Authorization Server for our project. Spring Authorization Server is experimental and doesn't implement all of the OAuth 2 grant types, but it does implement the authorization code grant and client credentials grant.

The authorization server is a distinct application from any application that provides the API and is also distinct from the client. Therefore, to get started with Spring Authorization Server, you'll want to create a new Spring Boot project, choosing (at least) the web and security starters. For our authorization server, users will be stored in a relational database using JPA, so be sure to add the JPA starter and H2 dependencies as well. And, if you're using Lombok to handle getters, setters, constructors, and whatnot, then be sure to include it as well.

Spring Authorization Server isn't (yet) available as a dependency from the Initializr. So once your project has been created, you'll need to manually add the Spring

---

[2] See http://mng.bz/QqGR.

Authorization Server dependency to your build. For example, here's the Maven dependency you'll need to include in your pom.xml file:

```
<dependency>
    <groupId>org.springframework.security.experimental</groupId>
    <artifactId>spring-security-oauth2-authorization-server</artifactId>
    <version>0.1.2</version>
</dependency>
```

Next, because we'll be running this all on our development machines (at least for now), you'll want to make sure that there's not a port conflict between the main Taco Cloud application and the authorization server. Adding the following entry to the project's application.yml file will make the authorization server available on port 9000:

```
server:
  port: 9000
```

Now let's dive into the essential security configuration that will be used by the authorization server. The next code listing shows a very simple Spring Security configuration class that enables form-based login and requires that all requests be authenticated.

Listing 8.2 Essential security configuration for form-based login

```
package tacos.authorization;
import org.springframework.context.annotation.Bean;
import org.springframework.security.config.annotation.web.builders.
        HttpSecurity;
import org.springframework.security.config.annotation.web.configuration.
        EnableWebSecurity;
import org.springframework.security.core.userdetails.UserDetailsService;
import org.springframework.security.crypto.bcrypt.BCryptPasswordEncoder;
import org.springframework.security.crypto.password.PasswordEncoder;
import org.springframework.security.web.SecurityFilterChain;

import tacos.authorization.users.UserRepository;

@EnableWebSecurity
public class SecurityConfig {

    @Bean
    SecurityFilterChain defaultSecurityFilterChain(HttpSecurity http)
            throws Exception {
        return http
            .authorizeRequests(authorizeRequests ->
                authorizeRequests.anyRequest().authenticated()
            )

            .formLogin()

            .and().build();
    }
```

```
  @Bean
  UserDetailsService userDetailsService(UserRepository userRepo) {
    return username -> userRepo.findByUsername(username);
  }

  @Bean
  public PasswordEncoder passwordEncoder() {
    return new BCryptPasswordEncoder();
  }
}
```

Notice that the `UserDetailsService` bean works with a `TacoUserRepository` to look up users by their username. To get on with configuring the authorization server itself, we'll skip over the specifics of `TacoUserRepository`, but suffice it to say that it looks a lot like some of the Spring Data–based repositories we've created since chapter 3.

The only thing worth noting about the `TacoUserRepository` is that (for convenience in testing) you could use it in a `CommandLineRunner` bean to prepopulate the database with a couple of test users as follows:

```
@Bean
public ApplicationRunner dataLoader(
        UserRepository repo, PasswordEncoder encoder) {
  return args -> {
    repo.save(
        new User("habuma", encoder.encode("password"), "ROLE_ADMIN"));
    repo.save(
        new User("tacochef", encoder.encode("password"), "ROLE_ADMIN"));
  };
}
```

Now we can start applying configuration to enable an authorization server. The first step in configuring an authorization server is to create a new configuration class that imports some common configuration for an authorization server. The following code for `AuthorizationServerConfig` is a good start:

```
@Configuration(proxyBeanMethods = false)
public class AuthorizationServerConfig {

  @Bean
  @Order(Ordered.HIGHEST_PRECEDENCE)
  public SecurityFilterChain
    authorizationServerSecurityFilterChain(HttpSecurity http) throws
    Exception {
  OAuth2AuthorizationServerConfiguration
      .applyDefaultSecurity(http);
  return http
      .formLogin(Customizer.withDefaults())
      .build();
  }
```

```
...

}
```

The authorizationServerSecurityFilterChain() bean method defines a Security-FilterChain that sets up some default behavior for the OAuth 2 authorization server and a default form login page. The @Order annotation is given Ordered.HIGHEST_PRECEDENCE to ensure that if for some reason there are other beans of this type declared, this one takes precedence over the others.

For the most part, this is a boilerplate configuration. If you want, feel free to dive in a little deeper and customize the configuration. For now, we're just going to go with the defaults.

One component that isn't boilerplate, and thus not provided by OAuth2-AuthorizationServerConfiguration, is the client repository. A client repository is analogous to a user details service or user repository, except that instead of maintaining details about users, it maintains details about clients that might be asking for authorization on behalf of users. It is defined by the RegisteredClientRepository interface (provided by Spring Security), which looks like this:

```
interface RegisteredClientRepository {

    @Nullable
    RegisteredClient findById(String id);

    @Nullable
    RegisteredClient findByClientId(String clientId);

}
```

In a production setting, you might write a custom implementation of Registered-ClientRepository to retrieve client details from a database or from some other source. But out of the box, Spring Authorization Server offers an in-memory implementation that is perfect for demonstration and testing purposes. You're encouraged to implement RegisteredClientRepository however you see fit. But for our purposes, we'll use the in-memory implementation to register a single client with the authorization server. Add the following bean method to AuthorizationServerConfig:

```
@Bean
public RegisteredClientRepository registeredClientRepository(
        PasswordEncoder passwordEncoder) {
  RegisteredClient registeredClient =
    RegisteredClient.withId(UUID.randomUUID().toString())
      .clientId("taco-admin-client")
      .clientSecret(passwordEncoder.encode("secret"))
      .clientAuthenticationMethod(
              ClientAuthenticationMethod.CLIENT_SECRET_BASIC)
      .authorizationGrantType(AuthorizationGrantType.AUTHORIZATION_CODE)
      .authorizationGrantType(AuthorizationGrantType.REFRESH_TOKEN)
```

```
    .redirectUri(
        "http://127.0.0.1:9090/login/oauth2/code/taco-admin-client")
    .scope("writeIngredients")
    .scope("deleteIngredients")
    .scope(OidcScopes.OPENID)
    .clientSettings(
        clientSettings -> clientSettings.requireUserConsent(true))
    .build();
return new InMemoryRegisteredClientRepository(registeredClient);
}
```

As you can see, there are a lot of details that go into a `RegisteredClient`. But going from top to bottom, here's how our client is defined:

- *ID*—A random, unique identifier.
- *Client ID*—Analogous to a username, but instead of a user, it is a client. In this case, `"taco-admin-client"`.
- *Client secret*—Analogous to a password for the client. Here we're using the word `"secret"` for the client secret.
- *Authorization grant type*—The OAuth 2 grant types that this client will support. In this case, we're enabling authorization code and refresh token grants.
- *Redirect URL*—One or more registered URLs that the authorization server can redirect to after authorization has been granted. This adds another level of security, preventing some arbitrary application from receiving an authorization code that it could exchange for a token.
- *Scope*—One or more OAuth 2 scopes that this client is allowed to ask for. Here we are setting three scopes: `"writeIngredients"`, `"deleteIngredients"`, and the constant `OidcScopes.OPENID`, which resolves to `"openid"`. The `"openid"` scope will be necessary later when we use the authorization server as a single-sign-on solution for the Taco Cloud admin application.
- *Client settings*—This is a lambda that allows us to customize the client settings. In this case, we're requiring explicit user consent before granting the requested scope. Without this, the scope would be implicitly granted after the user logs in.

Finally, because our authorization server will be producing JWT tokens, the tokens will need to include a signature created using a JSON Web Key (JWK)[3] as the signing key. Therefore, we'll need a few beans to produce a JWK. Add the following bean method (and private helper methods) to `AuthorizationServerConfig` to handle that for us:

```
@Bean
  public JWKSource<SecurityContext> jwkSource()
          throws NoSuchAlgorithmException {
```

---

[3] See https://datatracker.ietf.org/doc/html/rfc7517.

```
    RSAKey rsaKey = generateRsa();
    JWKSet jwkSet = new JWKSet(rsaKey);
    return (jwkSelector, securityContext) -> jwkSelector.select(jwkSet);
}

private static RSAKey generateRsa() throws NoSuchAlgorithmException {
  KeyPair keyPair = generateRsaKey();
  RSAPublicKey publicKey = (RSAPublicKey) keyPair.getPublic();
  RSAPrivateKey privateKey = (RSAPrivateKey) keyPair.getPrivate();
  return new RSAKey.Builder(publicKey)
      .privateKey(privateKey)
      .keyID(UUID.randomUUID().toString())
      .build();
}

private static KeyPair generateRsaKey() throws NoSuchAlgorithmException {
    KeyPairGenerator keyPairGenerator =
    KeyPairGenerator.getInstance("RSA");
    keyPairGenerator.initialize(2048);
    return keyPairGenerator.generateKeyPair();
}

@Bean
public JwtDecoder jwtDecoder(JWKSource<SecurityContext> jwkSource) {
  return OAuth2AuthorizationServerConfiguration.jwtDecoder(jwkSource);
}
```

There appears to be a lot going on here. But to summarize, the JWKSource creates RSA 2048-bit key pairs that will be used to sign the token. The token will be signed using the private key. The resource server can then verify that the token received in a request is valid by obtaining the public key from the authorization server. We'll talk more about that when we create the resource server.

All of the pieces of our authorization server are now in place. All that's left to do is start it up and try it out. Build and run the application, and you should have an authorization server listening on port 9000.

Because we don't have a client yet, you can pretend to be a client using your web browser and the curl command-line tool. Start by pointing your web browser at http://localhost:9000/oauth2/authorize?response_type=code&client_id=tacoadmin-client&redirect_uri=http://127.0.0.1:9090/login/oauth2/code/taco-admin-client&scope=write Ingredients+deleteIngredients.[4] You should see a login page that looks like figure 8.2.

---

[4] Notice that this and all URLs in this chapter are using "http://" URLs. This makes local development and testing easy. But in a production setting, you should always use "https://" URLs for increased security.

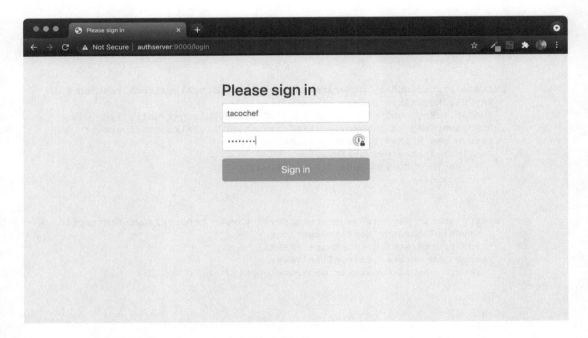

Figure 8.2   The authorization server login page

After logging in (with "tacochef" and "password," or some username-password combination in the database under `TacoUserRepository`), you'll be asked to consent to the requested scopes on a page that looks like figure 8.3.

After granting consent, the browser will be redirected back to the client URL. We don't have a client yet, so there's probably nothing there and you'll receive an error. But that's OK—we're pretending to be the client, so we'll obtain the authorization code from the URL ourselves.

Look in the browser's address bar, and you'll see that the URL has a `code` parameter. Copy the entire value of that parameter, and use it in the following `curl` command line in place of `$code`:

```
$ curl localhost:9000/oauth2/token \
   -H"Content-type: application/x-www-form-urlencoded" \
   -d"grant_type=authorization_code" \
   -d"redirect_uri=http://127.0.0.1:9090/login/oauth2/code/taco-admin-
   client" \
   -d"code=$code" \
   -u taco-admin-client:secret
```

Here we're exchanging the authorization code we received for an access token. The payload body is in "application/x-www-form-urlencoded" format and sends the grant type (`"authorization_code"`), the redirect URI (for additional security), and the

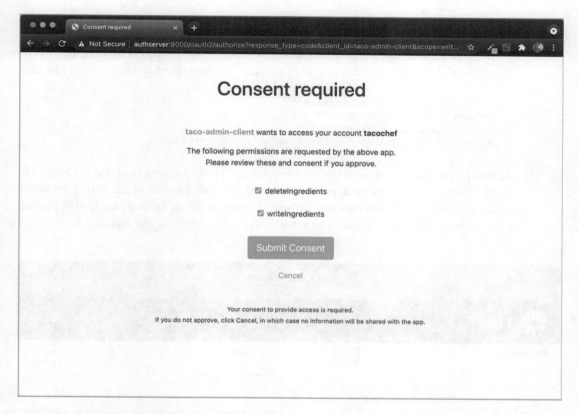

Figure 8.3 The authorization server consent page

authorization code itself. If all goes well, then you'll receive a JSON response that (when formatted) looks like this:

```
{
  "access_token":"eyJraWQ...",
  "refresh_token":"HOzHA5s...",
  "scope":"deleteIngredients writeIngredients",
  "token_type":"Bearer",
  "expires_in":"299"
}
```

The `"access_token"` property contains the access token that a client can use to make requests to the API. In reality, it is much longer than shown here. Likewise, the `"refresh_token"` has been abbreviated here to save space. But the access token can now be sent on requests to the resource server to gain access to resources requiring either the `"writeIngredients"` or `"deleteIngredients"` scope. The access token will expire in 299 seconds (or just less than 5 minutes), so we'll have to move quickly if we're going to use it. But if it expires, then we can use the refresh token to obtain a new access token without going through the authorization flow all over again.

So, how can we use the access token? Presumably, we'll send it in a request to the Taco Cloud API as part of the `"Authorization"` header—perhaps something like this:

```
$ curl localhost:8080/ingredients \
  -H"Content-type: application/json" \
  -H"Authorization: Bearer eyJraWQ..." \
  -d'{"id":"FISH","name":"Stinky Fish", "type":"PROTEIN"}'
```

At this point, the token achieves nothing for us. That's because our Taco Cloud API hasn't been enabled to be a resource server yet. But in lieu of an actual resource server and client API, we can still inspect the access token by copying it and pasting into the form at https://jwt.io. The result will look something like figure 8.4.

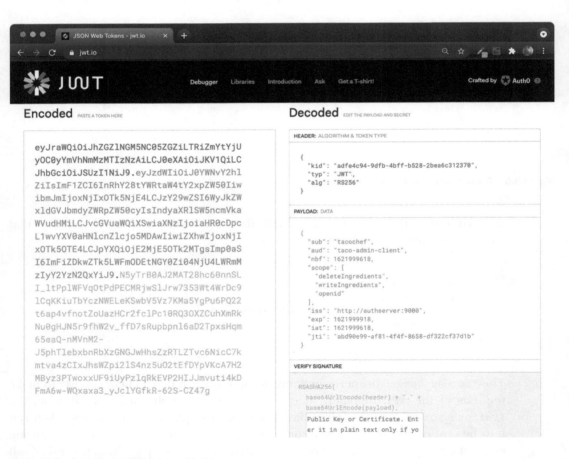

Figure 8.4   Decoding a JWT token at jwt.io

As you can see, the token is decoded into three parts: the header, the payload, and the signature. A closer look at the payload shows that this token was issued on behalf of the user named tacochef and the token has the `"writeIngredients"` and `"delete-Ingredients"` scopes. Just what we asked for!

After about 5 minutes, the access token will expire. You can still inspect it in the debugger at https://jwti.io, but if it were given in a real request to an API, it would be rejected. But you can request a new access token without going through the authorization code grant flow again. All you need to do is make a new request to the authorization server using the `"refresh_token"` grant and passing the refresh token as the value of the `"refresh_token"` parameter. Using curl, such a request will look like this:

```
$ curl localhost:9000/oauth2/token \
    -H"Content-type: application/x-www-form-urlencoded" \
    -d"grant_type=refresh_token&refresh_token=HOzHA5s..." \
    -u taco-admin-client:secret
```

The response to this request will be the same as the response from the request that exchanged the authorization code for an access token initially, only with a fresh new access token.

Although it's fun to paste access tokens into https://jwt.io, the real power and purpose of the access token is to gain access to an API. So let's see how to enable a resource server on the Taco Cloud API.

8.3 Securing an API with a resource server

The resource server is actually just a filter that sits in front of an API, ensuring that requests for resources that require authorization include a valid access token with the required scope. Spring Security provides an OAuth2 resource server implementation that you can add to an existing API by adding the following dependency to the build for the project build as follows:

```
<dependency>
    <groupId>org.springframework.boot</groupId>
    <artifactId>spring-boot-starter-oauth2-resource-server</artifactId>
</dependency>
```

You can also add the resource server dependency by selecting the "OAuth2 Resource Server" dependency from the Initializr when creating a project.

With the dependency in place, the next step is to declare that POST requests to /ingredients require the `"writeIngredients"` scope and that DELETE requests to /ingredients require the `"deleteIngredients"` scope. The following excerpt from the project's SecurityConfig class shows how to do that:

```
@Override
  protected void configure(HttpSecurity http) throws Exception {
    http
      .authorizeRequests()
      ...
```

```
        .antMatchers(HttpMethod.POST, "/api/ingredients")
            .hasAuthority("SCOPE_writeIngredients")
    .antMatchers(HttpMethod.DELETE, "/api//ingredients")
            .hasAuthority("SCOPE_deleteIngredients")
    ...
}
```

For each of the endpoints, the .hasAuthority() method is called to specify the required scope. Notice that the scopes are prefixed with "SCOPE_" to indicate that they should be matched against OAuth 2 scopes in the access token given on the request to those resources.

In that same configuration class, we'll also need to enable the resource server, as shown next:

```
@Override
protected void configure(HttpSecurity http) throws Exception {
  http
    ...
    .and()
      .oauth2ResourceServer(oauth2 -> oauth2.jwt())
  ...
}
```

The oauth2ResourceServer() method here is given a lambda with which to configure the resource server. Here, it simply enables JWT tokens (as opposed to opaque tokens) so that the resource server can inspect the contents of the token to find what security claims it includes. Specifically, it will look to see that the token includes the "writeIngredients" and/or "deleteIngredients" scope for the two endpoints we've secured.

It won't trust the token at face value, though. To be confident that the token was created by a trusted authorization server on behalf of a user, it will verify the token's signature using the public key that matches the private key that was used to create the token's signature. We'll need to configure the resource server to know where to obtain the public key, though. The following property will specify the JWK set URL on the authorization server from which the resource server will fetch the public key:

```
spring:
  security:
    oauth2:
      resourceserver:
        jwt:
          jwk-set-uri: http://localhost:9000/oauth2/jwks
```

And now our resource server is ready! Build the Taco Cloud application and start it up. Then you can try it out using curl like this:

```
$ curl localhost:8080/ingredients \
        -H"Content-type: application/json" \
        -d'{"id":"CRKT", "name":"Legless Crickets", "type":"PROTEIN"}'
```

The request should fail with an HTTP 401 response code. That's because we've configured the endpoint to require the "writeIngredients" scope for that endpoint, and we've not provided a valid access token with that scope on the request.

To make a successful request and add a new ingredient item, you'll need to obtain an access token using the flow we used in the previous section, making sure that we request the "writeIngredients" and "deleteIngredients" scopes when directing the browser to the authorization server. Then, provide the access token in the "Authorization" header using curl like this (substituting "$token" for the actual access token):

```
$ curl localhost:8080/ingredients \
    -H"Content-type: application/json" \
    -d'{"id":"SHMP", "name":"Coconut Shrimp", "type":"PROTEIN"}' \
    -H"Authorization: Bearer $token"
```

This time the new ingredient should be created. You can verify that by using curl or your chosen HTTP client to perform a GET request to the /ingredients endpoint as follows:

```
$ curl localhost:8080/ingredients
[
    {
        "id": "FLTO",
        "name": "Flour Tortilla",
        "type": "WRAP"
    },

    ...

    {
        "id": "SHMP",
        "name": "Coconut Shrimp",
        "type": "PROTEIN"
    }
]
```

Coconut Shrimp is now included at the end of the list of all of the ingredients returned from the /ingredients endpoint. Success!

Recall that the access token expires after 5 minutes. If you let the token expire, requests will start returning HTTP 401 responses again. But you can get a new access token by making a request to the authorization server using the refresh token that you got along with the access token (substituting the actual refresh token for "$refreshToken"), as shown here:

```
$ curl localhost:9000/oauth2/token \
    -H"Content-type: application/x-www-form-urlencoded" \
    -d"grant_type=refresh_token&refresh_token=$refreshToken" \
    -u taco-admin-client:secret
```

With a newly created access token, you can keep on creating new ingredients to your heart's content.

Now that we've secured the /ingredients endpoint, it's probably a good idea to apply the same techniques to secure other potentially sensitive endpoints in our API. The /orders endpoint, for example, should probably not be open for any kind of request, even HTTP GET requests, because it would allow a hacker to easily grab customer information. I'll leave it up to you to secure the /orders endpoint and the rest of the API as you see fit.

Administering the Taco Cloud application using curl works great for tinkering and getting to know how OAuth 2 tokens play a part in allowing access to a resource. But ultimately we want a real client application that can be used to manage ingredients. Let's now turn our attention to creating an OAuth-enabled client that will obtain access tokens and make requests to the API.

8.4   *Developing the client*

In the OAuth 2 authorization dance, the client application's role is to obtain an access token and make requests to the resource server on behalf of the user. Because we're using OAuth 2's authorization code flow, that means that when the client application determines that the user has not yet been authenticated, it should redirect the user's browser to the authorization server to get consent from the user. Then, when the authorization server redirects control back to the client, the client must exchange the authorization code it receives for the access token.

First things first: the client will need Spring Security's OAuth 2 client support in its classpath. The following starter dependency makes that happen:

```
<dependency>
  <groupId>org.springframework.boot</groupId>
  <artifactId>spring-boot-starter-oauth2-client</artifactId>
</dependency>
```

Not only does this give the application OAuth 2 client capabilities that we'll exploit in a moment, but it also transitively brings in Spring Security itself. This enables us to write some security configuration for the application. The following SecurityFilter-Chain bean sets up Spring Security so that all requests require authentication:

```
@Bean
SecurityFilterChain defaultSecurityFilterChain(HttpSecurity http) throws
    Exception {
  http
    .authorizeRequests(
        authorizeRequests -> authorizeRequests.anyRequest().authenticated()
    )
    .oauth2Login(
      oauth2Login ->
      oauth2Login.loginPage("/oauth2/authorization/taco-admin-client"))
    .oauth2Client(withDefaults());
  return http.build();
}
```

What's more, this `SecurityFilterChain` bean also enables the client-side bits of OAuth 2. Specifically, it sets up a login page at the path /oauth2/authorization/taco-admin-client. But this is no ordinary login page that takes a username and password. Instead, it accepts an authorization code, exchanges it for an access token, and uses the access token to determine the identity of the user. Put another way, this is the path that the authorization server will redirect to after the user has granted permission.

We also need to configure details about the authorization server and our application's OAuth 2 client details. That is done in configuration properties, such as in the following application.yml file, which configures a client named `taco-admin-client`:

```
spring:
  security:
    oauth2:
      client:
        registration:
          taco-admin-client:
            provider: tacocloud
            client-id: taco-admin-client
            client-secret: secret
            authorization-grant-type: authorization_code
            redirect-uri:
              ➥ "http://127.0.0.1:9090/login/oauth2/code/{registrationId}"
            scope: writeIngredients,deleteIngredients,openid
```

This registers a client with the Spring Security OAuth 2 client named `taco-admin-client`. The registration details include the client's credentials (`client-id` and `client-secret`), the grant type (`authorization-grant-type`), the scopes being requested (`scope`), and the redirect URI (`redirect-uri`). Notice that the value given to `redirect-uri` has a placeholder that references the client's registration ID, which is `taco-admin-client`. Consequently, the redirect URI is set to http://127.0.0.1:9090/login/oauth2/code/taco-admin-client, which has the same path that we configured as the OAuth 2 login earlier.

But what about the authorization server itself? Where do we tell the client that it should redirect the user's browser? That's what the `provider` property does, albeit indirectly. The `provider` property is set to `tacocloud`, which is a reference to a separate set of configuration that describes the `tacocloud` provider's authorization server. That provider configuration is configured in the same application.yml file like this:

```
spring:
  security:
    oauth2:
      client:
...
        provider:
          tacocloud:
            issuer-uri: http://authserver:9000
```

The only property required for a provider configuration is `issuer-uri`. This property identifies the base URI for the authorization server. In this case, it refers to a server host whose name is `authserver`. Assuming that you are running these examples locally, this is just another alias for `localhost`. On most Unix-based operating systems, this can be added in your /etc/hosts file with the following line:

```
127.0.0.1 authserver
```

Refer to documentation for your operating system for details on how to create custom host entries if /etc/hosts isn't what works on your machine.

Building on the base URL, Spring Security's OAuth 2 client will assume reasonable defaults for the authorization URL, token URL, and other authorization server specifics. But, if for some reason the authorization server you're working with differs from those default values, you can explicitly configure authorization details like this:

```yaml
spring:
  security:
    oauth2:
      client:
        provider:
          tacocloud:
            issuer-uri: http://authserver:9000
            authorization-uri: http://authserver:9000/oauth2/authorize
            token-uri: http://authserver:9000/oauth2/token
            jwk-set-uri: http://authserver:9000/oauth2/jwks
            user-info-uri: http://authserver:9000/userinfo
            user-name-attribute: sub
```

We've seen most of these URIs, such as the authorization, token, and JWK Set URIs already. The `user-info-uri` property is new, however. This URI is used by the client to obtain essential user information, most notably the user's username. A request to that URI should return a JSON response that includes the property specified in `user-name-attribute` to identify the user. Note, however, when using Spring Authorization Server, you do not need to create the endpoint for that URI; Spring Authorization Server will expose the user-info endpoint automatically.

Now all of the pieces are in place for the application to authenticate and obtain an access token from the authorization server. Without doing anything more, you could fire up the application, make a request to any URL on that application, and be redirected to the authorization server for authorization. When the authorization server redirects back, then the inner workings of Spring Security's OAuth 2 client library will exchange the code it receives in the redirect for an access token. Now, how can we use that token?

Let's suppose that we have a service bean that interacts with the Taco Cloud API using `RestTemplate`. The following `RestIngredientService` implementation shows such a class that offers two methods: one for fetching a list of ingredients and another for saving a new ingredient:

```java
package tacos;

import java.util.Arrays;
import org.springframework.web.client.RestTemplate;
```

```
public class RestIngredientService implements IngredientService {

  private RestTemplate restTemplate;

  public RestIngredientService() {
    this.restTemplate = new RestTemplate();
  }

  @Override
  public Iterable<Ingredient> findAll() {
    return Arrays.asList(restTemplate.getForObject(
            "http://localhost:8080/api/ingredients",
            Ingredient[].class));
  }

  @Override
  public Ingredient addIngredient(Ingredient ingredient) {
    return restTemplate.postForObject(
        "http://localhost:8080/api/ingredients",
        ingredient,
        Ingredient.class);
  }

}
```

The HTTP GET request for the /ingredients endpoint isn't secured, so the findAll()
method should work fine, as long as the Taco Cloud API is listening on localhost,
port 8080. But the addIngredient() method is likely to fail with an HTTP 401
response because we've secured POST requests to /ingredients to require "write-
Ingredients" scope. The only way around that is to submit an access token with
"writeIngredients" scope in the request's Authorization header.

Fortunately, Spring Security's OAuth 2 client should have the access token handy
after completing the authorization code flow. All we need to do is make sure that the
access token ends up in the request. To do that, let's change the constructor to attach
a request interceptor to the RestTemplate it creates as follows:

```
public RestIngredientService(String accessToken) {
    this.restTemplate = new RestTemplate();
    if (accessToken != null) {
      this.restTemplate
        .getInterceptors()
        .add(getBearerTokenInterceptor(accessToken));
    }
  }
  private ClientHttpRequestInterceptor
          getBearerTokenInterceptor(String accessToken) {
    ClientHttpRequestInterceptor interceptor =
          new ClientHttpRequestInterceptor() {
      @Override
      public ClientHttpResponse intercept(
            HttpRequest request, byte[] bytes,
            ClientHttpRequestExecution execution) throws IOException {
```

```
        request.getHeaders().add("Authorization", "Bearer " + accessToken);
        return execution.execute(request, bytes);
      }
    };

    return interceptor;
}
```

The constructor now takes a `String` parameter that is the access token. Using this token, it attaches a client request interceptor that adds the `Authorization` header to every request made by the `RestTemplate` such that the header's value is `"Bearer"` followed by the token value. In the interest of keeping the constructor tidy, the client interceptor is created in a separate `private` helper method.

Only one question remains: where does the access token come from? The following bean method is where the magic happens:

```
@Bean
@RequestScope
public IngredientService ingredientService(
             OAuth2AuthorizedClientService clientService) {
  Authentication authentication =
          SecurityContextHolder.getContext().getAuthentication();

  String accessToken = null;

  if (authentication.getClass()
          .isAssignableFrom(OAuth2AuthenticationToken.class)) {
    OAuth2AuthenticationToken oauthToken =
            (OAuth2AuthenticationToken) authentication;
    String clientRegistrationId =
            oauthToken.getAuthorizedClientRegistrationId();
    if (clientRegistrationId.equals("taco-admin-client")) {
      OAuth2AuthorizedClient client =
          clientService.loadAuthorizedClient(
              clientRegistrationId, oauthToken.getName());
      accessToken = client.getAccessToken().getTokenValue();
    }
  }
  return new RestIngredientService(accessToken);
}
```

To start, notice that the bean is declared to be request-scoped using the `@Request-Scope` annotation. This means that a new instance of the bean will be created on every request. The bean must be request-scoped because it needs to pull the authentication from the `SecurityContext`, which is populated on every request by one of Spring Security's filters; there is no `SecurityContext` at application startup time when default-scoped beans are created.

Before returning a `RestIngredientService` instance, the bean method checks to see that the authentication is, in fact, implemented as `OAuth2AuthenticationToken`. If so, then that means it will have the token. It then verifies that the authentication token is for the client named `taco-admin-client`. If so, then it extracts the token from the authorized client and passes it through the constructor for `RestIngredientService`. With that token in hand, `RestIngredientService` will have no trouble making requests to the Taco Cloud API's endpoints on behalf of the user who authorized the application.

Summary

- OAuth 2 security is a common way to secure APIs that is more robust than simple HTTP Basic authentication.
- An authorization server issues access tokens for a client to act on behalf of a user when making requests to an API (or on its own behalf in the case of client token flow).
- A resource server sits in front of an API to verify that valid, nonexpired tokens are presented with the scope necessary to access API resources.
- Spring Authorization Server is an experimental project that implements an OAuth 2 authorization server.
- Spring Security provides support for creating a resource server, as well as creating clients that obtain access tokens from the authorization server and pass those tokens when making requests through the resource server.

Sending messages
asynchronously

It's 4:55 p.m. on Friday. You're minutes away from starting a much-anticipated vacation. You have just enough time to drive to the airport and catch your flight. But before you pack up and head out, you need to be sure your boss and colleagues know the status of the work you've been doing so that on Monday they can pick up where you left off. Unfortunately, some of your colleagues have already skipped out for the weekend, and your boss is tied up in a meeting. What do you do?

The most practical way to communicate your status and still catch your plane is to send a quick email to your boss and your colleagues, detailing your progress and promising to send a postcard. You don't know where they are or when they'll read the email, but you do know they'll eventually return to their desks and read it. Meanwhile, you're on your way to the airport.

Synchronous communication, which is what we've seen with REST, has its place. But it's not the only style of interapplication communication available to developers. *Asynchronous* messaging is a way of indirectly sending messages from one application to another without waiting for a response. This indirection affords looser coupling and greater scalability between the communicating applications.

In this chapter, we're going to use asynchronous messaging to send orders from the Taco Cloud website to a separate application in the Taco Cloud kitchens where the tacos will be prepared. We'll consider three options that Spring offers for asynchronous messaging: the Java Message Service (JMS), RabbitMQ and Advanced Message Queueing Protocol (AMQP), and Apache Kafka. In addition to the basic sending and receiving of messages, we'll look at Spring's support for message-driven POJOs: a way to receive messages that resembles Enterprise JavaBeans' message-driven beans (MDBs).

9.1 Sending messages with JMS

JMS is a Java standard that defines a common API for working with message brokers. First introduced in 2001, JMS has been the go-to approach for asynchronous messaging in Java for a very long time. Before JMS, each message broker had a proprietary API, making an application's messaging code less portable between brokers. But with JMS, all compliant implementations can be worked with via a common interface in much the same way that JDBC has given relational database operations a common interface.

Spring supports JMS through a template-based abstraction known as JmsTemplate. Using JmsTemplate, it's easy to send messages across queues and topics from the producer side and to receive those messages on the consumer side. Spring also supports the notion of message-driven POJOs: simple Java objects that react to messages arriving on a queue or topic in an asynchronous fashion.

We're going to explore Spring's JMS support, including JmsTemplate and message-driven POJOs. Our focus will be on Spring's support for messaging with JMS, but if you want to know more about JMS, then have a look at *ActiveMQ in Action* by Bruce Snyder, Dejan Bosanac, and Rob Davies (Manning, 2011).

Before you can send and receive messages, you need a message broker that's ready to relay those messages between producers and consumers. Let's kick off our exploration of Spring JMS by setting up a message broker in Spring.

9.1.1 Setting up JMS

Before you can use JMS, you must add a JMS client to your project's build. With Spring Boot, that couldn't be any easier. All you need to do is add a starter dependency to the build. First, though, you must decide whether you're going to use Apache ActiveMQ, or the newer Apache ActiveMQ Artemis broker.

If you're using ActiveMQ, you'll need to add the following dependency to your project's pom.xml file:

```
<dependency>
  <groupId>org.springframework.boot</groupId>
  <artifactId>spring-boot-starter-activemq</artifactId>
</dependency>
```

If ActiveMQ Artemis is the choice, the starter dependency should look like this:

```
<dependency>
  <groupId>org.springframework.boot</groupId>
  <artifactId>spring-boot-starter-artemis</artifactId>
</dependency>
```

When using the Spring Initializr (or your IDE's frontend for the Initializr), you can also select either of these options as starter dependencies for your project. They are listed as "Spring for Apache ActiveMQ 5" and "Spring for Apache ActiveMQ Artemis," as shown in the screenshot in figure 9.1 from https://start.spring.io.

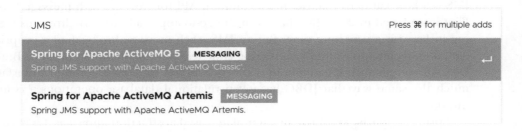

Figure 9.1   ActiveMQ and Artemis choices available in the Spring Initializr

Artemis is a next-generation reimplementation of ActiveMQ, effectively making ActiveMQ a legacy option. Therefore, for Taco Cloud you're going to choose Artemis. But the choice ultimately has little impact on how you'll write the code that sends and receives messages. The only significant differences will be in how you configure Spring to create connections to the broker.

> **RUNNING AN ARTEMIS BROKER**   You'll need an Artemis broker running to be able to run the code presented in this chapter. If you don't already have an Artemis instance running, you can follow the instructions from the Artemis documentation at http://mng.bz/Xr81.

By default, Spring assumes that your Artemis broker is listening on localhost at port 61616. That's fine for development purposes, but once you're ready to send your application into production, you'll need to set a few properties that tell Spring how to access the broker. The properties you'll find most useful are listed in table 9.1.

Table 9.1 Properties for configuring the location and credentials of an Artemis broker

Property	Description
`spring.artemis.host`	The broker's host
`spring.artemis.port`	The broker's port
`spring.artemis.user`	The user for accessing the broker (optional)
`spring.artemis.password`	The password for accessing the broker (optional)

For example, consider the following entry from an application.yml file that might be used in a nondevelopment setting:

```
spring:
  artemis:
    host: artemis.tacocloud.com
    port: 61617
    user: tacoweb
    password: 13tm31n
```

This sets up Spring to create broker connections to an Artemis broker listening at artemis.tacocloud.com, port 61617. It also sets the credentials for the application that will be interacting with that broker. The credentials are optional, but they're recommended for production deployments.

If you were to use ActiveMQ instead of Artemis, you'd need to use the ActiveMQ-specific properties listed in table 9.2.

Table 9.2 Properties for configuring the location and credentials of an ActiveMQ broker

Property	Description
`spring.activemq.broker-url`	The URL of the broker
`spring.activemq.user`	The user for accessing the broker (optional)
`spring.activemq.password`	The password for accessing the broker (optional)
`spring.activemq.in-memory`	Whether to start an in-memory broker (default: `true`)

Notice that instead of offering separate properties for the broker's hostname and port, an ActiveMQ broker's address is specified with a single property, `spring.activemq.broker-url`. The URL should be a tcp:// URL, as shown in the following YAML snippet:

```
spring:
  activemq:
    broker-url: tcp://activemq.tacocloud.com
    user: tacoweb
    password: 13tm31n
```

Whether you choose Artemis or ActiveMQ, you shouldn't need to configure these properties for development when the broker is running locally.

If you're using ActiveMQ, you will, however, need to set the `spring.activemq.in-memory` property to `false` to prevent Spring from starting an in-memory broker. An in-memory broker may seem useful, but it's helpful only when you'll be consuming messages from the same application that publishes them (which has limited usefulness).

Instead of using an embedded broker, you'll want to install and start an Artemis (or ActiveMQ) broker before moving on. Rather than repeat the installation instructions here, I refer you to the broker documentation for details:

- *Artemis*—http://mng.bz/yJOo
- *ActiveMQ*—http://mng.bz/MveD

With the JMS starter in your build and a broker waiting to ferry messages from one application to another, you're ready to start sending messages.

9.1.2 *Sending messages with JmsTemplate*

With a JMS starter dependency (either Artemis or ActiveMQ) in your build, Spring Boot will autoconfigure a `JmsTemplate` (among other things) that you can inject and use to send and receive messages.

`JmsTemplate` is the centerpiece of Spring's JMS integration support. Much like Spring's other template-oriented components, `JmsTemplate` eliminates a lot of boiler-plate code that would otherwise be required to work with JMS. Without `JmsTemplate`, you'd need to write code to create a connection and session with the message broker and more code to deal with any exceptions that might be thrown in the course of sending a message. `JmsTemplate` focuses on what you really want to do: send a message.

`JmsTemplate` has several methods that are useful for sending messages, including the following:

```
// Send raw messages
void send(MessageCreator messageCreator) throws JmsException;
void send(Destination destination, MessageCreator messageCreator)
                                            throws JmsException;
void send(String destinationName, MessageCreator messageCreator)
                                            throws JmsException;
// Send messages converted from objects
void convertAndSend(Object message) throws JmsException;
void convertAndSend(Destination destination, Object message)
                                            throws JmsException;
void convertAndSend(String destinationName, Object message)
                                            throws JmsException;

// Send messages converted from objects with post-processing
void convertAndSend(Object message,
            MessagePostProcessor postProcessor) throws JmsException;
void convertAndSend(Destination destination, Object message,
            MessagePostProcessor postProcessor) throws JmsException;
void convertAndSend(String destinationName, Object message,
            MessagePostProcessor postProcessor) throws JmsException;
```

As you can see, there are really only two methods, `send()` and `convertAndSend()`, each overridden to support different parameters. And if you look closer, you'll notice that the various forms of `convertAndSend()` can be broken into two subcategories. In trying to understand what all of these methods do, consider the following breakdown:

- Three `send()` methods require a `MessageCreator` to manufacture a `Message` object.
- Three `convertAndSend()` methods accept an `Object` and automatically convert that `Object` into a `Message` behind the scenes.
- Three `convertAndSend()` methods automatically convert an `Object` to a `Message` but also accept a `MessagePostProcessor` to allow for customization of the `Message` before it's sent.

Moreover, each of these three method categories is composed of three overriding methods that are distinguished by how the JMS destination (queue or topic) is specified, as follows:

- One method accepts no destination parameter and sends the message to a default destination.
- One method accepts a `Destination` object that specifies the destination for the message.
- One method accepts a `String` that specifies the destination for the message by name.

Putting these methods to work, consider `JmsOrderMessagingService` in the next listing, which uses the most basic form of the `send()` method.

Listing 9.1   Sending an order with `.send()` to a default destination

```
package tacos.messaging;
import javax.jms.JMSException;
import javax.jms.Message;
import javax.jms.Session;

import org.springframework.beans.factory.annotation.Autowired;
import org.springframework.jms.core.JmsTemplate;
import org.springframework.jms.core.MessageCreator;
import org.springframework.stereotype.Service;

@Service
public class JmsOrderMessagingService implements OrderMessagingService {
  private JmsTemplate jms;

  @Autowired
  public JmsOrderMessagingService(JmsTemplate jms) {
    this.jms = jms;
  }

  @Override
  public void sendOrder(TacoOrder order) {
```

```
      jms.send(new MessageCreator() {
            @Override
            public Message createMessage(Session session)
                                       throws JMSException {
              return session.createObjectMessage(order);
            }
          }
        );
      }
    }
```

The `sendOrder()` method calls `jms.send()`, passing in an anonymous inner-class implementation of `MessageCreator`. That implementation overrides `createMessage()` to create a new object message from the given `TacoOrder` object.

Because the JMS-specific `JmsOrderMessagingService` implements the more generic `OrderMessagingService` interface, we can put this service to work by injecting it into the `OrderApiController` and calling `sendOrder()` when an order is created, as shown here:

```
@RestController
@RequestMapping(path="/api/orders",
                produces="application/json")
@CrossOrigin(origins="http://localhost:8080")
public class OrderApiController {

  private OrderRepository repo;
  private OrderMessagingService messageService;

  public OrderApiController(
          OrderRepository repo,
          OrderMessagingService messageService) {
    this.repo = repo;
    this.messageService = messageService;
  }

  @PostMapping(consumes="application/json")
  @ResponseStatus(HttpStatus.CREATED)
  public TacoOrder postOrder(@RequestBody TacoOrder order) {
    messageService.sendOrder(order);
    return repo.save(order);
  }

  ...

}
```

Now when you create an order through the Taco Cloud website, a message should be sent to the broker for routing to another application that will receive the order. We don't yet have anything to receive that message, though. Even so, you can use the Artemis console to view the contents of the queue. See the Artemis documentation at http://mng.bz/aZx9 for details on how to do this.

I'm not sure about you, but I think the code in listing 9.1, although straightforward, is a bit clumsy. The ceremony involved in declaring an anonymous inner class complicates an otherwise simple method call. Recognizing that `MessageCreator` is a functional interface, you can tidy up the `sendOrder()` method a bit with a lambda, as shown next:

```java
@Override
public void sendOrder(TacoOrder order) {
  jms.send(session -> session.createObjectMessage(order));
}
```

But notice that the call to `jms.send()` doesn't specify a destination. For this to work, you must also specify a default destination name with the `spring.jms.template` `.default-destination` property. For example, you could set the property in your application.yml file like this:

```yaml
spring:
  jms:
    template:
      default-destination: tacocloud.order.queue
```

In many cases, using a default destination is the easiest choice. It lets you specify the destination name once, allowing the code to be concerned only with sending messages, without regard for where they're being sent. But if you ever need to send a message to a destination other than the default destination, you'll need to specify that destination as a parameter to `send()`.

One way of doing that is by passing a `Destination` object as the first parameter to `send()`. The easiest way to do this is to declare a `Destination` bean and then inject it into the bean that performs messaging. For example, the following bean declares the Taco Cloud order queue `Destination`:

```java
@Bean
public Destination orderQueue() {
  return new ActiveMQQueue("tacocloud.order.queue");
}
```

This bean method can be added to any configuration class in the application that will be sending or receiving messages via JMS. For the sake of organization, it's best to add it to a configuration class designated for messaging configuration, such as `Messaging-Config`.

It's important to note that the `ActiveMQQueue` used here is actually from Artemis (from the `org.apache.activemq.artemis.jms.client` package). If you're using ActiveMQ (not Artemis), there's also a class named `ActiveMQQueue` (from the `org.apache.activemq.command` package).

If this `Destination` bean is injected into `JmsOrderMessagingService`, you can use it to specify the destination when calling `send()` as follows:

```
    private Destination orderQueue;

    @Autowired
    public JmsOrderMessagingService(JmsTemplate jms,
                             Destination orderQueue) {
      this.jms = jms;
      this.orderQueue = orderQueue;
    }

    ...

    @Override
    public void sendOrder(TacoOrder order) {
      jms.send(
          orderQueue,
          session -> session.createObjectMessage(order));
    }
```

Specifying the destination with a Destination object like this affords you the opportunity to configure the Destination with more than just the destination name. But in practice, you'll almost never specify anything more than the destination name. It's often easier to just send the name as the first parameter to send(), as shown here:

```
    @Override
    public void sendOrder(TacoOrder order) {
      jms.send(
          "tacocloud.order.queue",
          session -> session.createObjectMessage(order));
    }
```

Although the send() method isn't particularly difficult to use (especially when the MessageCreator is given as a lambda), a sliver of complexity is added by requiring that you provide a MessageCreator. Wouldn't it be simpler if you needed to specify only the object that's to be sent (and optionally the destination)? That describes succinctly how convertAndSend() works. Let's take a look.

CONVERTING MESSAGES BEFORE SENDING

The JmsTemplatesconvertAndSend() method simplifies message publication by eliminating the need to provide a MessageCreator. Instead, you pass the object that's to be sent directly to convertAndSend(), and the object will be converted into a Message before being sent.

For example, the following reimplementation of sendOrder() uses convertAndSend() to send a TacoOrder to a named destination:

```
    @Override
    public void sendOrder(TacoOrder order) {
      jms.convertAndSend("tacocloud.order.queue", order);
    }
```

Just like the send() method, convertAndSend() will accept either a Destination or String value to specify the destination, or you can leave out the destination altogether to send the message to the default destination.

Whichever form of convertAndSend() you choose, the TacoOrder passed into convertAndSend() is converted into a Message before it's sent. Under the covers, this is achieved with an implementation of MessageConverter that does the dirty work of converting application domain objects to Message objects.

CONFIGURING A MESSAGE CONVERTER

MessageConverter is a Spring-defined interface that has only the following two methods to be implemented:

```
public interface MessageConverter {
  Message toMessage(Object object, Session session)
                throws JMSException, MessageConversionException;
  Object fromMessage(Message message)
}
```

Although this interface is simple enough to implement, you often won't need to create a custom implementation. Spring already offers a handful of implementations, such as those described in table 9.3.

Table 9.3 Spring message converters for common conversion tasks (all in the org.springframework.jms.support.converter package)

Message converter	What it does
MappingJackson2MessageConverter	Uses the Jackson 2 JSON library to convert messages to and from JSON
MarshallingMessageConverter	Uses JAXB to convert messages to and from XML
MessagingMessageConverter	Converts a Message from the messaging abstraction to and from a Message using an underlying MessageConverter for the payload and a JmsHeaderMapper to map the JMS headers to and from standard message headers
SimpleMessageConverter	Converts a String to and from a TextMessage, byte arrays to and from a BytesMessage, a Map to and from a MapMessage, and a Serializable to and from an ObjectMessage

SimpleMessageConverter is the default, but it requires that the object being sent implement Serializable. This may be a good idea, but you may prefer to use one of the other message converters, such as MappingJackson2MessageConverter, to avoid that restriction.

To apply a different message converter, all you must do is declare an instance of the chosen converter as a bean. For example, the following bean declaration will enable MappingJackson2MessageConverter to be used instead of SimpleMessageConverter:

```
@Bean
public MappingJackson2MessageConverter messageConverter() {
  MappingJackson2MessageConverter messageConverter =
                    new MappingJackson2MessageConverter();
  messageConverter.setTypeIdPropertyName("_typeId");
  return messageConverter;
}
```

This bean method can be placed in any configuration class in the application that sends and receives messages with JMS, including alongside the `Destination` bean in `MessagingConfig`.

Notice that you called `setTypeIdPropertyName()` on the `MappingJackson2-MessageConverter` before returning it. This is very important, because it enables the receiver to know what type to convert an incoming message to. By default, it will contain the fully qualified classname of the type being converted. But this method is somewhat inflexible, requiring that the receiver also have the same type, with the same fully qualified classname.

To allow for more flexibility, you can map a synthetic type name to the actual type by calling `setTypeIdMappings()` on the message converter. For example, the following change to the message converter bean method maps a synthetic `TacoOrder` type ID to the `TacoOrder` class:

```
@Bean
public MappingJackson2MessageConverter messageConverter() {
  MappingJackson2MessageConverter messageConverter =
                      new MappingJackson2MessageConverter();
  messageConverter.setTypeIdPropertyName("_typeId");

  Map<String, Class<?>> typeIdMappings = new HashMap<String, Class<?>>();
  typeIdMappings.put("order", TacoOrder.class);
  messageConverter.setTypeIdMappings(typeIdMappings);

  return messageConverter;
}
```

Instead of the fully qualified classname being sent in the message's _typeId property, the value `TacoOrder` will be sent. In the receiving application, a similar message converter will have been configured, mapping `TacoOrder` to its own understanding of what an order is. That implementation of an order may be in a different package, have a different name, and even have a subset of the sender's `TacoOrder` properties.

POSTPROCESSING MESSAGES

Let's suppose that in addition to its lucrative web business, Taco Cloud has decided to open a few brick-and-mortar taco joints. Given that any of their restaurants could also be a fulfillment center for the web business, they need a way to communicate the source of an order to the kitchens at the restaurants. This will enable the kitchen staff to employ a different process for store orders than for web orders.

It would be reasonable to add a new `source` property to the `TacoOrder` object to carry this information, populating it with `WEB` for orders placed online and with `STORE` for orders placed in the stores. But that would require a change to both the website's `TacoOrder` class and the kitchen application's `TacoOrder` class when, in reality, it's information that's required only for the taco preparers.

An easier solution would be to add a custom header to the message to carry the order's source. If you were using the `send()` method to send the taco orders, this could easily be accomplished by calling `setStringProperty()` on the `Message` object as follows:

```
jms.send("tacocloud.order.queue",
    session -> {
        Message message = session.createObjectMessage(order);
        message.setStringProperty("X_ORDER_SOURCE", "WEB");
    });
```

The problem here is that you aren't using `send()`. By choosing to use `convertAndSend()`, the `Message` object is created under the covers, and you don't have access to it.

Fortunately, you have a way to tweak a `Message` created under the covers before it's sent. By passing in a `MessagePostProcessor` as the final parameter to `convertAndSend()`, you can do whatever you want with the `Message` after it has been created. The following code still uses `convertAndSend()`, but it also uses a `MessagePostProcessor` to add the `X_ORDER_SOURCE` header before the message is sent:

```
jms.convertAndSend("tacocloud.order.queue", order, new MessagePostProcessor()
    {
  @Override
  public Message postProcessMessage(Message message) throws JMSException {
    message.setStringProperty("X_ORDER_SOURCE", "WEB");
    return message;
  }
});
```

You may have noticed that `MessagePostProcessor` is a functional interface. This means that you can simplify it a bit by replacing the anonymous inner class with a lambda as shown here:

```
jms.convertAndSend("tacocloud.order.queue", order,
    message -> {
      message.setStringProperty("X_ORDER_SOURCE", "WEB");
      return message;
    });
```

Although you need this particular `MessagePostProcessor` for only this one call to `convertAndSend()`, you may find yourself using the same `MessagePostProcessor` for several different calls to `convertAndSend()`. In those cases, perhaps a method reference, shown next, is a better choice than a lambda, avoiding unnecessary code duplication:

```
@GetMapping("/convertAndSend/order")
public String convertAndSendOrder() {
  TacoOrder order = buildOrder();
  jms.convertAndSend("tacocloud.order.queue", order,
      this::addOrderSource);
  return "Convert and sent order";
}

private Message addOrderSource(Message message) throws JMSException {
  message.setStringProperty("X_ORDER_SOURCE", "WEB");
  return message;
}
```

You've now seen several ways of sending messages. But it does no good to send a message if nobody ever receives it. Let's look at how you can receive messages with Spring JMS.

9.1.3 Receiving JMS messages

When it comes to consuming messages, you have the choice of a *pull model*, where your code requests a message and waits until one arrives, or a *push model*, in which messages are handed to your code as they become available.

JmsTemplate offers several methods for receiving messages, but all of them use a pull model. You call one of those methods to request a message, and the thread is blocked until a message is available (which could be immediately or it might take a while).

On the other hand, you also have the option of using a push model, wherein you define a message listener that's invoked any time a message is available.

Both options are suitable for a variety of use cases. It's generally accepted that the push model is the best choice, because it doesn't block a thread. But in some use cases, a listener could be overburdened if messages arrive too quickly. The pull model enables a consumer to declare that they're ready to process a new message.

Let's look at both ways of receiving messages. We'll start with the pull model offered by JmsTemplate.

RECEIVING WITH JMSTEMPLATE

JmsTemplate offers several methods for pulling methods from the broker, including the following:

```
Message receive() throws JmsException;
Message receive(Destination destination) throws JmsException;
Message receive(String destinationName) throws JmsException;

Object receiveAndConvert() throws JmsException;
Object receiveAndConvert(Destination destination) throws JmsException;
Object receiveAndConvert(String destinationName) throws JmsException;
```

As you can see, these six methods mirror the send() and convertAndSend() methods from JmsTemplate. The receive() methods receive a raw Message, whereas the receiveAndConvert() methods use a configured message converter to convert messages into domain types. And for each of these, you can specify either a Destination or a String containing the destination name, or you can pull a message from the default destination.

To see these in action, you'll write some code that pulls an TacoOrder from the tacocloud.order.queue destination. The following listing shows OrderReceiver, a service component that receives order data using JmsTemplate.receive().

Listing 9.2 Pulling orders from a queue

```java
package tacos.kitchen.messaging.jms;
import javax.jms.Message;
import org.springframework.beans.factory.annotation.Autowired;
import org.springframework.jms.core.JmsTemplate;
import org.springframework.jms.support.converter.MessageConverter;
import org.springframework.stereotype.Component;

@Component
public class JmsOrderReceiver implements OrderReceiver {
  private JmsTemplate jms;
  private MessageConverter converter;

  @Autowired
  public JmsOrderReceiver(JmsTemplate jms, MessageConverter converter) {
    this.jms = jms;
    this.converter = converter;
  }
  public TacoOrder receiveOrder() {
    Message message = jms.receive("tacocloud.order.queue");
    return (TacoOrder) converter.fromMessage(message);
  }
}
```

Here you've used a String to specify the destination from which to pull an order. The receive() method returns an unconverted Message. But what you really need is the TacoOrder that's inside of the Message, so the very next thing that happens is that you use an injected message converter to convert the message. The type ID property in the message will guide the converter in converting it to a TacoOrder, but it's returned as an Object that requires casting before you can return it.

Receiving a raw Message object might be useful in some cases where you need to inspect the message's properties and headers. But often you need only the payload. Converting that payload to a domain type is a two-step process and requires that the message converter be injected into the component. When you care only about the message's payload, receiveAndConvert() is a lot simpler. The next listing shows how JmsOrderReceiver could be reworked to use receiveAndConvert() instead of receive().

Listing 9.3   Receiving an already-converted `TacoOrder` object

```java
package tacos.kitchen.messaging.jms;

import org.springframework.jms.core.JmsTemplate;
import org.springframework.stereotype.Component;
import tacos.TacoOrder;
import tacos.kitchen.OrderReceiver;

@Component
public class JmsOrderReceiver implements OrderReceiver {

  private JmsTemplate jms;

  public JmsOrderReceiver(JmsTemplate jms) {
    this.jms = jms;
  }

  @Override
  public TacoOrder receiveOrder() {
    return (TacoOrder) jms.receiveAndConvert("tacocloud.order.queue");
  }

}
```

This new version of `JmsOrderReceiver` has a `receiveOrder()` method that has been reduced to only one line. Plus, you no longer need to inject a `MessageConverter`, because all of the message conversion will be done behind the scenes in `receiveAnd-Convert()`.

Before moving on, let's consider how `receiveOrder()` might be used in the Taco Cloud kitchen application. A food preparer at one of Taco Cloud's kitchens might push a button or take some action to indicate that they're ready to start building tacos. At that point, `receiveOrder()` would be invoked and the call to `receive()` or `receiveAndConvert()` would block. Nothing else would happen until an order message is ready. Once an order arrives, it will be returned from `receiveOrder()`, and its information will be used to display the details of the order for the food preparer to get to work. This seems like a natural choice for a pull model.

Now let's see how a push model works by declaring a JMS listener.

DECLARING MESSAGE LISTENERS

Unlike the pull model, where an explicit call to `receive()` or `receiveAndConvert()` was required to receive a message, a message listener is a passive component that's idle until a message arrives.

To create a message listener that reacts to JMS messages, you simply annotate a method in a component with `@JmsListener`. The next listing shows a new `Order-Listener` component that listens passively for messages, rather than actively requesting them.

Listing 9.4 An `OrderListener` component that listens for orders

```
package tacos.kitchen.messaging.jms.listener;

import org.springframework.beans.factory.annotation.Autowired;
import org.springframework.context.annotation.Profile;
import org.springframework.jms.annotation.JmsListener;
import org.springframework.stereotype.Component;

import tacos.TacoOrder;
import tacos.kitchen.KitchenUI;

@Profile("jms-listener")
@Component
public class OrderListener {

  private KitchenUI ui;

  @Autowired
  public OrderListener(KitchenUI ui) {
    this.ui = ui;
  }

  @JmsListener(destination = "tacocloud.order.queue")
  public void receiveOrder(TacoOrder order) {
    ui.displayOrder(order);
  }

}
```

The `receiveOrder()` method is annotated with `JmsListener` to "listen" for messages on the `tacocloud.order.queue` destination. It doesn't deal with `JmsTemplate`, nor is it explicitly invoked by your application code. Instead, framework code within Spring waits for messages to arrive on the specified destination, and when they arrive, the `receiveOrder()` method is invoked automatically with the message's `TacoOrder` payload as a parameter.

In many ways, the `@JmsListener` annotation is like one of Spring MVC's request mapping annotations, such as `@GetMapping` or `@PostMapping`. In Spring MVC, methods annotated with one of the request mapping methods react to requests to a specified path. Similarly, methods that are annotated with `@JmsListener` react to messages that arrive in a destination.

Message listeners are often touted as the best choice because they don't block and are able to handle multiple messages quickly. In the context of the Taco Cloud application, however, perhaps they aren't the best choice. The food preparers are a significant bottleneck in the system and may not be able to prepare tacos as quickly as orders come in. A food preparer may have half-fulfilled an order when a new order is displayed on the screen. The kitchen user interface would need to buffer the orders as they arrive to avoid overburdening the kitchen staff.

That's not to say that message listeners are bad. On the contrary, they're a perfect fit when messages can be handled quickly. But when the message handlers need to be able to ask for more messages on their own timing, the pull model offered by Jms-Template seems more fitting.

Because JMS is defined by a standard Java specification and supported by many message broker implementations, it's a common choice for messaging in Java. But JMS has a few shortcomings, not the least of which is that as a Java specification, its use is limited to Java applications. Newer messaging options such as RabbitMQ and Kafka address these shortcomings and are available for other languages and platforms beyond the JVM. Let's set JMS aside and see how you could have implemented your taco order messaging with RabbitMQ.

9.2   *Working with RabbitMQ and AMQP*

As arguably the most prominent implementation of AMQP, RabbitMQ offers a more advanced message-routing strategy than JMS. Whereas JMS messages are addressed with the name of a destination from which the receiver will retrieve them, AMQP messages are addressed with the name of an exchange and a routing key, which are decoupled from the queue to which the receiver is listening. This relationship between an exchange and queues is illustrated in figure 9.2.

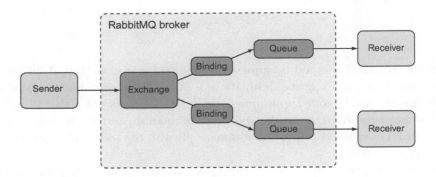

Figure 9.2   Messages sent to a RabbitMQ exchange are routed to one or more queues, based on routing keys and bindings.

When a message arrives at the RabbitMQ broker, it goes to the exchange for which it was addressed. The exchange is responsible for routing it to one or more queues, depending on the type of exchange, the binding between the exchange and queues, and the value of the message's routing key.

There are several different kinds of exchanges, including the following:

- *Default*—A special exchange that's automatically created by the broker. It routes messages to queues whose name is the same as the message's routing key. All queues will automatically be bound to the default exchange.

- *Direct*—Routes messages to a queue whose binding key is the same as the message's routing key.
- *Topic*—Routes a message to one or more queues where the binding key (which may contain wildcards) matches the message's routing key.
- *Fanout*—Routes messages to all bound queues without regard for binding keys or routing keys.
- *Headers*—Similar to a topic exchange, except that routing is based on message header values rather than routing keys.
- *Dead letter*—A catchall for any messages that are undeliverable (meaning they don't match any defined exchange-to-queue binding).

The simplest forms of exchanges are default and fanout—these roughly correspond to a JMS queue and topic. But the other exchanges allow you to define more flexible routing schemes.

The most important thing to understand is that messages are sent to exchanges with routing keys and they're consumed from queues. How they get from an exchange to a queue depends on the binding definitions and what best suits your use cases.

Which exchange type you use and how you define the bindings from exchanges to queues has little bearing on how messages are sent and received in your Spring applications. Therefore, we'll focus on how to write code that sends and receives messages with Rabbit.

> **NOTE** For a more detailed discussion on how best to bind queues to exchanges, see *RabbitMQ in Depth* by Gavin Roy (Manning, 2017) or *RabbitMQ in Action* by Alvaro Videla and Jason J. W. Williams (Manning, 2012).

9.2.1 Adding RabbitMQ to Spring

Before you can start sending and receiving RabbitMQ messages with Spring, you'll need to add Spring Boot's AMQP starter dependency to your build in place of the Artemis or ActiveMQ starter you added in the previous section, as shown here:

```
<dependency>
    <groupId>org.springframework.boot</groupId>
    <artifactId>spring-boot-starter-amqp</artifactId>
</dependency>
```

Adding the AMQP starter to your build will trigger autoconfiguration that will create an AMQP connection factory and `RabbitTemplate` beans, as well as other supporting components. Simply adding this dependency is all you need to do to start sending and receiving messages from a RabbitMQ broker with Spring. But there are a handful of useful properties you'll want to know about, listed in table 9.4.

For development purposes, you'll probably have a RabbitMQ broker that doesn't require authentication running on your local machine, listening on port 5672. These properties likely won't get much use while you're still in development, but they'll no doubt prove useful when your applications move into production.

Table 9.4 Properties for configuring the location and credentials of a RabbitMQ broker

Property	Description
`spring.rabbitmq.addresses`	A comma-separated list of RabbitMQ broker addresses
`spring.rabbitmq.host`	The broker's host (defaults to localhost)
`spring.rabbitmq.port`	The broker's port (defaults to 5672)
`spring.rabbitmq.username`	The username for accessing the broker (optional)
`spring.rabbitmq.password`	The password for accessing the broker (optional)

RUNNING A RABBITMQ BROKER   If you don't already have a RabbitMQ broker to work with, you have several options for running RabbitMQ on your local machine. See the official RabbitMQ documentation at https://www.rabbitmq.com/download.html for the latest instructions for running RabbitMQ.

For example, suppose that as you move into production, your RabbitMQ broker is on a server named rabbit.tacocloud.com, listening on port 5673, and requiring credentials. In that case, the following configuration in your application.yml file will set those properties when the `prod` profile is active:

```
spring:
  profiles: prod
  rabbitmq:
    host: rabbit.tacocloud.com
    port: 5673
    username: tacoweb
    password: l3tm31n
```

Now that RabbitMQ is configured in your application, it's time to start sending messages with `RabbitTemplate`.

9.2.2 *Sending messages with RabbitTemplate*

At the core of Spring's support for RabbitMQ messaging is `RabbitTemplate`. `RabbitTemplate` is similar to `JmsTemplate` and offers a similar set of methods. As you'll see, however, some subtle differences align with the unique way that RabbitMQ works.

With regard to sending messages with `RabbitTemplate`, the `send()` and `convertAndSend()` methods parallel the same-named methods from `JmsTemplate`. But unlike the `JmsTemplate` methods, which route messages only to a given queue or topic, `RabbitTemplate` methods send messages in terms of exchanges and routing keys. Here are a few of the most relevant methods for sending messages with `RabbitTemplate`:[1]

```
// Send raw messages
void send(Message message) throws AmqpException;
void send(String routingKey, Message message) throws AmqpException;
```

---

[1] These methods are defined by `AmqpTemplate`, an interface implemented by `RabbitTemplate`.

```
void send(String exchange, String routingKey, Message message)
                            throws AmqpException;

// Send messages converted from objects
void convertAndSend(Object message) throws AmqpException;
void convertAndSend(String routingKey, Object message)
                            throws AmqpException;
void convertAndSend(String exchange, String routingKey,
                    Object message) throws AmqpException;

// Send messages converted from objects with post-processing
void convertAndSend(Object message, MessagePostProcessor mPP)
                            throws AmqpException;
void convertAndSend(String routingKey, Object message,
                    MessagePostProcessor messagePostProcessor)
                    throws AmqpException;
void convertAndSend(String exchange, String routingKey,
                    Object message,
                    MessagePostProcessor messagePostProcessor)
                    throws AmqpException;
```

As you can see, these methods follow a pattern similar to their twins in `JmsTemplate`. The first three `send()` methods all send a raw `Message` object. The next three `convertAndSend()` methods accept an object that will be converted to a `Message` behind the scenes before being sent. The final three `convertAndSend()` methods are like the previous three, but they accept a `MessagePostProcessor` that can be used to manipulate the `Message` object before it's sent to the broker.

These methods differ from their `JmsTemplate` counterparts in that they accept `String` values to specify an exchange and routing key, rather than a destination name (or `Destination` object). The methods that don't take an exchange will have their messages sent to the default exchange. Likewise, the methods that don't take a routing key will have their messages routed with a default routing key.

Let's put `RabbitTemplate` to work sending taco orders. One way you can do that is by using the `send()` method, as shown in listing 9.5. But before you can call `send()`, you'll need to convert a `TacoOrder` object to a `Message`. That could be a tedious job, if not for the fact that `RabbitTemplate` makes its message converter readily available with a `getMessageConverter()` method.

> **Listing 9.5   Sending a message with `RabbitTemplate.send()`**

```
package tacos.messaging;
import org.springframework.amqp.core.Message;
import org.springframework.amqp.core.MessageProperties;
import org.springframework.amqp.rabbit.core.RabbitTemplate;
import
   org.springframework.amqp.support.converter.MessageConverter;
import org.springframework.beans.factory.annotation.Autowired;
import org.springframework.stereotype.Service;
import tacos.Order;
```

```
@Service
public class RabbitOrderMessagingService
        implements OrderMessagingService {
  private RabbitTemplate rabbit;

  @Autowired
  public RabbitOrderMessagingService(RabbitTemplate rabbit) {
    this.rabbit = rabbit;
  }

  public void sendOrder(TacoOrder order) {
    MessageConverter converter = rabbit.getMessageConverter();
    MessageProperties props = new MessageProperties();
    Message message = converter.toMessage(order, props);
    rabbit.send("tacocloud.order", message);
  }
}
```

You'll notice that `RabbitOrderMessagingService` implements `OrderMessaging-Service`, just like `JmsOrderMessagingService`. This means that it can be injected into `OrderApiController` the same way to send order messages when an order is placed. Because we don't yet have anything to receive those messages, though, you can use the RabbitMQ browser-based management console. See https://www.rabbitmq.com/management.html for details on how to enable and use the RabbitMQ console.

Once you have a `MessageConverter` in hand, it's simple work to convert a Taco-Order to a `Message`. You must supply any message properties with a `MessageProperties`, but if you don't need to set any such properties, a default instance of `Message-Properties` is fine. Then, all that's left is to call `send()`, passing in the exchange and routing key (both of which are optional) along with the message. In this example, you're specifying only the routing key—`tacocloud.order`—along with the message, so the default exchange will be used.

Speaking of default exchanges, the default exchange name is `""` (an empty `String`), which corresponds to the default exchange that's automatically created by the RabbitMQ broker. Likewise, the default routing key is `""` (whose routing is dependent upon the exchange and bindings in question). You can override these defaults by setting the `spring.rabbitmq.template.exchange` and `spring.rabbitmq.template.routing-key` properties as follows:

```
spring:
  rabbitmq:
    template:
      exchange: tacocloud.order
      routing-key: kitchens.central
```

In this case, all messages sent without specifying an exchange will automatically be sent to the exchange whose name is `tacocloud.order`. If the routing key is also unspecified in the call to `send()` or `convertAndSend()`, the messages will have a routing key of `kitchens.central`.

Creating a `Message` object from the message converter is easy enough, but it's even easier to use `convertAndSend()` to let `RabbitTemplate` handle all of the conversion work for you, as shown next:

```
public void sendOrder(TacoOrder order) {
  rabbit.convertAndSend("tacocloud.order", order);
}
```

CONFIGURING A MESSAGE CONVERTER

By default, message conversion is performed with `SimpleMessageConverter`, which is able to convert simple types (like `String`) and `Serializable` objects to `Message` objects. But Spring offers several message converters for `RabbitTemplate`, including the following:

- *Jackson2JsonMessageConverter*—Converts objects to and from JSON using the Jackson 2 JSON processor
- *MarshallingMessageConverter*—Converts using a Spring `Marshaller` and `Unmarshaller`
- *SerializerMessageConverter*—Converts `String` and native objects of any kind using Spring's `Serializer` and `Deserializer` abstractions
- *SimpleMessageConverter*—Converts `String`, byte arrays, and `Serializable` types
- *ContentTypeDelegatingMessageConverter*—Delegates to another `Message-Converter` based on the `contentType` header
- *MessagingMessageConverter*—Delegates to an underlying `MessageConverter` for the message conversion and to an `AmqpHeaderConverter` for the headers

If you need to change the message converter, just configure a bean of type `Message-Converter`. For example, for JSON-based message conversion, you can configure a `Jackson2JsonMessageConverter` like this:

```
@Bean
public Jackson2JsonMessageConverter messageConverter() {
  return new Jackson2JsonMessageConverter();
}
```

Spring Boot autoconfiguration will discover this bean and inject it into `Rabbit-Template` in place of the default message converter.

SETTING MESSAGE PROPERTIES

As with JMS, you may need to set some headers in the messages you send. For example, let's say you need to send an `X_ORDER_SOURCE` for all orders submitted through the Taco Cloud website. When creating your own `Message` objects, you can set the header through the `MessageProperties` instance you give to the message converter. Revisiting the `sendOrder()` method from listing 9.5, you only need one additional line of code to set the header, as shown next:

```
public void sendOrder(TacoOrder order) {
  MessageConverter converter = rabbit.getMessageConverter();
  MessageProperties props = new MessageProperties();
  props.setHeader("X_ORDER_SOURCE", "WEB");
  Message message = converter.toMessage(order, props);
  rabbit.send("tacocloud.order", message);
}
```

When using `convertAndSend()`, however, you don't have quick access to the `Message-Properties` object. A `MessagePostProcessor` can help you with that, though, as shown here:

```
public void sendOrder(TacoOrder order) {
    rabbit.convertAndSend("tacocloud.order.queue", order,
        new MessagePostProcessor() {
          @Override
          public Message postProcessMessage(Message message)
              throws AmqpException {
            MessageProperties props = message.getMessageProperties();
            props.setHeader("X_ORDER_SOURCE", "WEB");
            return message;
          }
        });
}
```

Here you supply `convertAndSend()` with an anonymous inner-class implementation of `MessagePostProcessor`. In the `postProcessMessage()` method, you pull the `MessageProperties` from the `Message` and then call `setHeader()` to set the `X_ORDER_SOURCE` header.

Now that you've seen how to send messages with `RabbitTemplate`, let's switch our focus over to the code that receives messages from a RabbitMQ queue.

9.2.3   *Receiving messages from RabbitMQ*

You've seen that sending messages with `RabbitTemplate` doesn't differ much from sending messages with `JmsTemplate`. And as it turns out, receiving messages from a RabbitMQ queue isn't very different than from JMS.

As with JMS, you have the following two choices:

- Pulling messages from a queue with `RabbitTemplate`
- Having messages pushed to a `@RabbitListener`-annotated method

Let's start by looking at the pull-based `RabbitTemplate.receive()` method.

RECEIVING MESSAGES WITH RABBITTEMPLATE

`RabbitTemplate` comes with several methods for pulling messages from a queue. A few of the most useful ones are listed here:

```
// Receive messages
Message receive() throws AmqpException;
Message receive(String queueName) throws AmqpException;
```

```
Message receive(long timeoutMillis) throws AmqpException;
Message receive(String queueName, long timeoutMillis) throws AmqpException;

// Receive objects converted from messages
Object receiveAndConvert() throws AmqpException;
Object receiveAndConvert(String queueName) throws AmqpException;
Object receiveAndConvert(long timeoutMillis) throws AmqpException;
Object receiveAndConvert(String queueName, long timeoutMillis)
                                                 throws AmqpException;

// Receive type-safe objects converted from messages
<T> T receiveAndConvert(ParameterizedTypeReference<T> type)
                                                 throws AmqpException;
<T> T receiveAndConvert(
    String queueName, ParameterizedTypeReference<T> type)
                                                 throws AmqpException;
<T> T receiveAndConvert(
    long timeoutMillis, ParameterizedTypeReference<T> type)
                                                 throws AmqpException;
<T> T receiveAndConvert(String queueName, long timeoutMillis,
    ParameterizedTypeReference<T> type)
                                                 throws AmqpException;
```

These methods are the mirror images of the send() and convertAndSend() methods described earlier. Whereas send() is used to send raw Message objects, receive() receives raw Message objects from a queue. Likewise, receiveAndConvert() receives messages and uses a message converter to convert them into domain objects before returning them.

But a few obvious differences occur in the method signatures. First, none of these methods take an exchange or routing key as a parameter. That's because exchanges and routing keys are used to route messages to queues, but once the messages are in the queue, their next destination is the consumer who pulls them off the queue. Consuming applications needn't concern themselves with exchanges or routing keys. A queue is the only thing the consuming applications need to know about.

You'll also notice that many of the methods accept a long parameter to indicate a time-out for receiving the messages. By default, the receive time-out is 0 milliseconds. That is, a call to receive() will return immediately, potentially with a null value if no messages are available. This is a marked difference from how the receive() methods behave in JmsTemplate. By passing in a time-out value, you can have the receive() and receive-AndConvert() methods block until a message arrives or until the time-out expires. But even with a non-zero time-out, your code will need to be ready to deal with a null return.

Let's see how you can put this in action. The next listing shows a new Rabbit-based implementation of OrderReceiver that uses RabbitTemplate to receive orders.

Listing 9.6   Pulling orders from RabbitMQ with RabbitTemplate

```
package tacos.kitchen.messaging.rabbit;
import org.springframework.amqp.core.Message;
import org.springframework.amqp.rabbit.core.RabbitTemplate;
```

```
import org.springframework.amqp.support.converter.MessageConverter;
import org.springframework.beans.factory.annotation.Autowired;
import org.springframework.stereotype.Component;

@Component
public class RabbitOrderReceiver {
  private RabbitTemplate rabbit;
  private MessageConverter converter;

  @Autowired
  public RabbitOrderReceiver(RabbitTemplate rabbit) {
    this.rabbit = rabbit;
    this.converter = rabbit.getMessageConverter();
  }

  public TacoOrder receiveOrder() {
    Message message = rabbit.receive("tacocloud.order");
    return message != null
           ? (TacoOrder) converter.fromMessage(message)
           : null;
  }
}
```

The receiveOrder() method is where all of the action takes place. It makes a call to the receive() method on the injected RabbitTemplate to pull an order from the tacocloud.order queue. It provides no time-out value, so you can assume only that the call returns immediately with either a Message or null. If a Message is returned, you use the MessageConverter from the RabbitTemplate to convert the Message to a TacoOrder. On the other hand, if receive() returns null, you'll return a null.

Depending on the use case, you may be able to tolerate a small delay. In the Taco Cloud kitchen's overhead display, for example, you can possibly wait a while if no orders are available. Let's say you decide to wait up to 30 seconds before giving up. Then the receiveOrder() method can be changed to pass a 30,000 millisecond delay to receive() as follows:

```
public TacoOrder receiveOrder() {
  Message message = rabbit.receive("tacocloud.order.queue", 30000);
  return message != null
        ? (TacoOrder) converter.fromMessage(message)
        : null;
}
```

If you're like me, seeing a hardcoded number like that gives you a bit of discomfort. You might be thinking that it'd be a good idea to create a @ConfigurationProperties-annotated class so you could configure that time-out with a Spring Boot configuration property. I'd agree with you, if it weren't for the fact that Spring Boot already offers such a configuration property. If you want to set the time-out via configuration, simply remove the time-out value in the call to receive() and set it in your configuration with the spring.rabbitmq.template.receive-timeout property like so:

```
spring:
  rabbitmq:
    template:
      receive-timeout: 30000
```

Back in the receiveOrder() method, notice that you had to use the message converter from RabbitTemplate to convert the incoming Message object to a TacoOrder object. But if the RabbitTemplate is carrying a message converter around, why can't it do the conversion for you? That's precisely what the receiveAndConvert() method is for. Using receiveAndConvert(), you can rewrite receiveOrder() like this:

```
public TacoOrder receiveOrder() {
  return (TacoOrder) rabbit.receiveAndConvert("tacocloud.order.queue");
}
```

That's a lot simpler, isn't it? The only troubling thing I see is the cast from Object to TacoOrder. There's an alternative to casting, though. Instead, you can pass a ParameterizedTypeReference to receiveAndConvert() to receive a TacoOrder object directly as follows:

```
public TacoOrder receiveOrder() {
  return rabbit.receiveAndConvert("tacocloud.order.queue",
            new ParameterizedTypeReference<Order>() {});
}
```

It's debatable whether that's better than casting, but it is a more type-safe approach than casting. The only requirement to using a ParameterizedTypeReference with receiveAndConvert() is that the message converter must be an implementation of SmartMessageConverter; Jackson2JsonMessageConverter is the only out-of-the-box implementation to choose from.

The pull model offered by JmsTemplate fits a lot of use cases, but often it's better to have code that listens for messages and that's invoked when messages arrive. Let's see how you can write message-driven beans that respond to RabbitMQ messages.

HANDLING RABBITMQ MESSAGES WITH LISTENERS

For message-driven RabbitMQ beans, Spring offers RabbitListener, the RabbitMQ counterpart to JmsListener. To specify that a method should be invoked when a message arrives in a RabbitMQ queue, annotate a bean's method with @RabbitListener.

For example, the following listing shows a RabbitMQ implementation of Order-Receiver that's annotated to listen for order messages rather than to poll for them with RabbitTemplate.

> Listing 9.7 Declaring a method as a RabbitMQ message listener

```
package tacos.kitchen.messaging.rabbit.listener;

import org.springframework.amqp.rabbit.annotation.RabbitListener;
import org.springframework.beans.factory.annotation.Autowired;
import org.springframework.stereotype.Component;
```

```
import tacos.TacoOrder;
import tacos.kitchen.KitchenUI;

@Component
public class OrderListener {

  private KitchenUI ui;

  @Autowired
  public OrderListener(KitchenUI ui) {
    this.ui = ui;
  }

  @RabbitListener(queues = "tacocloud.order.queue")
  public void receiveOrder(TacoOrder order) {
    ui.displayOrder(order);
  }

}
```

You'll no doubt notice that this looks remarkably like the code from listing 9.4. Indeed, the only thing that changed was the listener annotation—from @JmsListener to @RabbitListener. As wonderful as @RabbitListener is, this near duplication of code leaves me with little to say about @RabbitListener that I haven't already said about @JmsListener. They're both great for writing code that responds to messages that are pushed to them from their respective brokers—a JMS broker for @JmsListener and a RabbitMQ broker for @RabbitListener.

Although you may sense a lack of enthusiasm about @RabbitListener in that previous paragraph, be certain that isn't my intent. In truth, the fact that @RabbitListener works much like @JmsListener is actually quite exciting! It means you don't need to learn a completely different programming model when working with RabbitMQ vs. Artemis or ActiveMQ. The same excitement holds true for the similarities between RabbitTemplate and JmsTemplate.

Let's hold on to that excitement as we wrap up this chapter by looking at one more messaging option supported by Spring: Apache Kafka.

9.3   *Messaging with Kafka*

Apache is the newest messaging option we're examining in this chapter. At a glance, Kafka is a message broker just like ActiveMQ, Artemis, or Rabbit. But Kafka has a few unique tricks up its sleeves.

Kafka is designed to run in a cluster, affording great scalability. And by partitioning its topics across all instances in the cluster, it's very resilient. Whereas RabbitMQ deals primarily with queues in exchanges, Kafka utilizes topics only to offer pub/sub messaging.

Kafka topics are replicated across all brokers in the cluster. Each node in the cluster acts as a leader for one or more topics, being responsible for that topic's data and replicating it to the other nodes in the cluster.

Going a step further, each topic can be split into multiple partitions. In that case, each node in the cluster is the leader for one or more partitions of a topic, but not for the entire topic. Responsibility for the topic is split across all nodes. Figure 9.3 illustrates how this works.

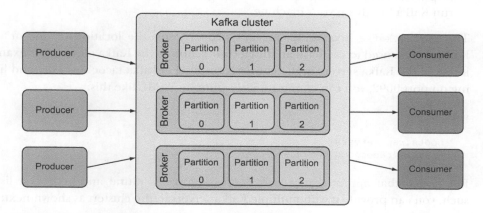

Figure 9.3 A Kafka cluster is composed of multiple brokers, each acting as a leader for partitions of the topics.

Due to Kafka's unique architecture, I encourage you to read more about it in *Kafka in Action* by Dylan Scott, Viktor Gamov, and Dave Klein (Manning, 2021). For our purposes, we'll focus on how to send messages to and receive them from Kafka with Spring.

9.3.1 Setting up Spring for Kafka messaging

To start using Kafka for messaging, you'll need to add the appropriate dependencies to your build. Unlike the JMS and RabbitMQ options, however, there isn't a Spring Boot starter for Kafka. Have no fear, though; you'll only need one dependency, shown next:

```
<dependency>
        <groupId>org.springframework.kafka</groupId>
        <artifactId>spring-kafka</artifactId>
    </dependency>
```

This one dependency brings everything you need for Kafka to the project. What's more, its presence will trigger Spring Boot autoconfiguration for Kafka that will, among other things, arrange for a `KafkaTemplate` in the Spring application context. All you need to do is inject the `KafkaTemplate` and go to work sending and receiving messages.

Before you start sending and receiving messages, however, you should be aware of a few properties that will come in handy when working with Kafka. Specifically, `Kafka-Template` defaults to work with a Kafka broker on localhost, listening on port 9092.

It's fine to start up a Kafka broker locally while developing an application, but when it's time to go to production, you'll need to configure a different host and port.

> **INSTALLING A KAFKA CLUSTER**   You'll need a Kafka cluster available if you want to run the examples presented in this chapter. The Kafka documentation at https://kafka.apache.org/quickstart is a great place to start to learn how to run Kafka locally on your machine.

The `spring.kafka.bootstrap-servers` property sets the location of one or more Kafka servers used to establish an initial connection to the Kafka cluster. For example, if one of the Kafka servers in the cluster is running at kafka.tacocloud.com and listening on port 9092, you can configure its location in YAML like this:

```
spring:
  kafka:
    bootstrap-servers:
    - kafka.tacocloud.com:9092
```

But notice that `spring.kafka.bootstrap-servers` is plural and accepts a list. As such, you can provide it with multiple Kafka servers in the cluster, as shown next:

```
spring:
  kafka:
    bootstrap-servers:
    - kafka.tacocloud.com:9092
    - kafka.tacocloud.com:9093
    - kafka.tacocloud.com:9094
```

These configurations are for Kafka bootstrap servers on a host named kafka.taco-cloud.com. If you're running your Kafka cluster locally (which is likely during development), then you'll want to use localhost instead, shown next:

```
spring:
  kafka:
    bootstrap-servers:
    - localhost:9092
```

With Kafka set up in your project, you're ready to send and receive messages. You'll start by sending `TacoOrder` objects to Kafka using `KafkaTemplate`.

9.3.2   *Sending messages with KafkaTemplate*

In many ways, `KafkaTemplate` is similar to its JMS and RabbitMQ counterparts. At the same time, however, it's very different. This becomes apparent as we consider its methods for sending messages, as shown here:

```
ListenableFuture<SendResult<K, V>> send(String topic, V data);
ListenableFuture<SendResult<K, V>> send(String topic, K key, V data);
ListenableFuture<SendResult<K, V>> send(String topic,
                        Integer partition, K key, V data);
```

```
ListenableFuture<SendResult<K, V>> send(String topic,
                    Integer partition, Long timestamp, K key, V data);
ListenableFuture<SendResult<K, V>> send(ProducerRecord<K, V> record);
ListenableFuture<SendResult<K, V>> send(Message<?> message);

ListenableFuture<SendResult<K, V>> sendDefault(V data);
ListenableFuture<SendResult<K, V>> sendDefault(K key, V data);
ListenableFuture<SendResult<K, V>> sendDefault(Integer partition,
                                                K key, V data);
ListenableFuture<SendResult<K, V>> sendDefault(Integer partition,
                                    Long timestamp, K key, V data);
```

The first thing you may have noticed is that there are no convertAndSend() methods. That's because KafkaTemplate is typed with generics and is able to deal with domain types directly when sending messages. In a way, all of the send() methods are doing the job of convertAndSend().

You may also have noticed that there are several parameters to send() and send-Default() that are quite different from what you used with JMS and Rabbit. When sending messages in Kafka, you can specify the following parameters to guide how the message is sent as follows:

- The topic to which to send the message (required for send())
- A partition to which to write the topic (optional)
- A key to send on the record (optional)
- A timestamp (optional; defaults to System.currentTimeMillis())
- The payload (required)

The topic and payload are the two most important parameters. Partitions and keys have little effect on how you use KafkaTemplate, aside from being extra information provided as parameters to send() and sendDefault(). For our purposes, we're going to focus on sending the message payload to a given topic and not worry ourselves with partitions and keys.

For the send() method, you can also choose to send a ProducerRecord, which is little more than a type that captures all of the preceding parameters in a single object. You can also send a Message object, but doing so would require you to convert your domain objects into a Message. Generally, it's easier to use one of the other methods rather than to create and send a ProducerRecord or Message object.

Using the KafkaTemplate and its send() method, you can write a Kafka-based implementation of OrderMessagingService. The following listing shows what such an implementation might look like.

Listing 9.8 Sending orders with KafkaTemplate

```
package tacos.messaging;

import org.springframework.beans.factory.annotation.Autowired;
import org.springframework.kafka.core.KafkaTemplate;
import org.springframework.stereotype.Service;
import tacos.TacoOrder;
```

```
@Service
public class KafkaOrderMessagingService
                                implements OrderMessagingService {

  private KafkaTemplate<String, TacoOrder> kafkaTemplate;

  @Autowired
  public KafkaOrderMessagingService(
          KafkaTemplate<String, TacoOrder> kafkaTemplate) {
    this.kafkaTemplate = kafkaTemplate;
  }

  @Override
  public void sendOrder(TacoOrder order) {
    kafkaTemplate.send("tacocloud.orders.topic", order);
  }

}
```

In this new implementation of OrderMessagingService, the sendOrder() method uses the send() method of the injected KafkaTemplate to send a TacoOrder to the topic named tacocloud.orders.topic. Except for the word "Kafka" scattered throughout the code, this isn't much different than the code you wrote for JMS and Rabbit. And, just like those other implementations of OrderMessagingService, it can be injected into OrderApiController and used to send orders through Kafka when orders are placed via the /api/orders endpoint.

Until we create a Kafka implementation of the message receiver, you'll need a console to view what was sent. There are several management consoles available for Kafka, including Offset Explorer (https://www.kafkatool.com/) and Confluent's Apache Kafka UI (http://mng.bz/g1P8).

If you set a default topic, you can simplify the sendOrder() method slightly. First, set your default topic to tacocloud.orders.topic by setting the spring.kafka .template.default-topic property as follows:

```
spring:
  kafka:
    bootstrap-servers:
    - localhost:9092
    template:
      default-topic: tacocloud.orders.topic
```

Then, in the sendOrder() method, you can call sendDefault() instead of send() and not specify the topic name, as shown here:

```
@Override
public void sendOrder(TacoOrder order) {
  kafkaTemplate.sendDefault(order);
}
```

Now that your message-sending code has been written, let's turn our attention to writing code that will receive those messages from Kafka.

9.3.3 Writing Kafka listeners

Aside from the unique method signatures for send() and sendDefault(), Kafka-Template differs from JmsTemplate and RabbitTemplate in that it doesn't offer any methods for receiving messages. That means the only way to consume messages from a Kafka topic using Spring is to write a message listener.

For Kafka, message listeners are defined as methods that are annotated with @KafkaListener. The @KafkaListener annotation is roughly analogous to @Jms-Listener and @RabbitListener and is used in much the same way. The next listing shows what your listener-based order receiver might look like if written for Kafka.

Listing 9.9 Receiving orders with @KafkaListener

```
package tacos.kitchen.messaging.kafka.listener;
import org.springframework.beans.factory.annotation.Autowired;
import org.springframework.kafka.annotation.KafkaListener;
import org.springframework.stereotype.Component;
import tacos.Order;
import tacos.kitchen.KitchenUI;

@Component
public class OrderListener {

  private KitchenUI ui;

  @Autowired
  public OrderListener(KitchenUI ui) {
    this.ui = ui;
  }

  @KafkaListener(topics="tacocloud.orders.topic")
  public void handle(TacoOrder order) {
    ui.displayOrder(order);
  }

}
```

The handle() method is annotated with @KafkaListener to indicate that it should be invoked when a message arrives in the topic named tacocloud.orders.topic. As it's written in listing 9.9, only a TacoOrder (the payload) is given to handle(). But if you need additional metadata from the message, it can also accept a ConsumerRecord or Message object.

For example, the following implementation of handle() accepts a Consumer-Record so that you can log the partition and timestamp of the message:

```
@KafkaListener(topics="tacocloud.orders.topic")
public void handle(
        TacoOrder order, ConsumerRecord<String, TacoOrder> record) {
  log.info("Received from partition {} with timestamp {}",
      record.partition(), record.timestamp());
```

```
  ui.displayOrder(order);
}
```

Similarly, you could ask for a Message instead of a ConsumerRecord and achieve the same thing, as shown here:

```
@KafkaListener(topics="tacocloud.orders.topic")
public void handle(Order order, Message<Order> message) {
  MessageHeaders headers = message.getHeaders();
  log.info("Received from partition {} with timestamp {}",
      headers.get(KafkaHeaders.RECEIVED_PARTITION_ID),
      headers.get(KafkaHeaders.RECEIVED_TIMESTAMP));
  ui.displayOrder(order);
}
```

It's worth noting that the message payload is also available via ConsumerRecord.value() or Message.getPayload(). This means that you could ask for the TacoOrder through those objects instead of asking for it directly as a parameter to handle().

Summary

- Asynchronous messaging provides a layer of indirection between communicating applications, which allows for looser coupling and greater scalability.
- Spring supports asynchronous messaging with JMS, RabbitMQ, or Apache Kafka.
- Applications can use template-based clients (JmsTemplate, RabbitTemplate, or KafkaTemplate) to send messages via a message broker.
- Receiving applications can consume messages in a pull-based model using the same template-based clients.
- Messages can also be pushed to consumers by applying message listener annotations (@JmsListener, @RabbitListener, or @KafkaListener) to bean methods.

Integrating Spring

10

One of the most frustrating things I encounter as I travel is being on a long flight and having a poor or nonexistent in-flight internet connection. I like to use my air time to get some work done, including writing many of the pages of this book. If there's no network connection, I'm at a disadvantage if I need to fetch a library or look up a Javadoc, and I'm not able to get much work done. I've learned to pack a book to read for those occasions.

Just as we need to connect to the internet to be productive, many applications must connect to external systems to perform their work. An application may need to read or send emails, interact with an external API, or react to data being written to a database. And, as data is ingested from or written to these external systems, the application may need to process data in some way to translate it to or from the application's own domain.

243

In this chapter, you'll see how to employ common integration patterns with Spring Integration. Spring Integration is a ready-to-use implementation of many of the integration patterns that are catalogued in *Enterprise Integration Patterns* by Gregor Hohpe and Bobby Woolf (Addison-Wesley, 2003). Each pattern is implemented as a component through which messages ferry data in a pipeline. Using Spring configuration, you can assemble these components into a pipeline through which data flows. Let's get started by defining a simple integration flow that introduces many of the features and characteristics of working with Spring Integration.

10.1   *Declaring a simple integration flow*

Generally speaking, Spring Integration enables the creation of integration flows through which an application can receive or send data to some resource external to the application itself. One such resource that an application may integrate with is the filesystem. Therefore, among Spring Integration's many components are channel adapters for reading and writing files.

To get your feet wet with Spring Integration, you're going to create an integration flow that writes data to the filesystem. To get started, you need to add Spring Integration to your project build. For Maven, the necessary dependencies follow:

```
<dependency>
    <groupId>org.springframework.boot</groupId>
    <artifactId>spring-boot-starter-integration</artifactId>
</dependency>
<dependency>
    <groupId>org.springframework.integration</groupId>
    <artifactId>spring-integration-file</artifactId>
</dependency>
```

The first dependency is the Spring Boot starter for Spring Integration. This dependency is essential to developing a Spring Integration flow, regardless of what the flow may integrate with. Like all Spring Boot starter dependencies, it's available as a check box in the Initializr[1] form.

The second dependency is for Spring Integration's file endpoint module. This module is one of over two dozen endpoint modules used to integrate with external systems. We'll talk more about the endpoint modules in section 10.2.9. But, for now, know that the file endpoint module offers the ability to ingest files from the filesystem into an integration flow and/or to write data from a flow to the filesystem.

Next you need to create a way for the application to send data into an integration flow so that it can be written to a file. To do that, you'll create a gateway interface, such as the one shown next.

---

[1]   See https://start.spring.io/.

Listing 10.1 Message gateway interface to transform method invocations into messages

```
package sia6;

import org.springframework.integration.annotation.MessagingGateway;
import org.springframework.integration.file.FileHeaders;
import org.springframework.messaging.handler.annotation.Header;

@MessagingGateway(defaultRequestChannel="textInChannel")       ⟵  Declares a
public interface FileWriterGateway {                               message gateway

    void writeToFile(
        @Header(FileHeaders.FILENAME) String filename,         ⟵  Writes to
        String data);                                              a file

}
```

Although it's a simple Java interface, there's a lot to be said about `FileWriterGateway`. The first thing you'll notice is that it's annotated with `@MessagingGateway`. This annotation tells Spring Integration to generate an implementation of this interface at run time—similar to how Spring Data automatically generates implementations of repository interfaces. Other parts of the code will use this interface when they need to write a file.

The `defaultRequestChannel` attribute of `@MessagingGateway` indicates that any messages resulting from a call to the interface methods should be sent to the given message channel. In this case, you state that any messages that result from a call to `writeToFile()` should be sent to the channel whose name is `textInChannel`.

As for the `writeToFile()` method, it accepts a filename as a `String`, and another `String` that will contain the text should be written to a file. What's notable about this method signature is that the `filename` parameter is annotated with `@Header`. In this case, the `@Header` annotation indicates that the value passed to `filename` should be placed in a message header (specified as `FileHeaders.FILENAME`, which is a constant in the `FileHeaders` class that is equal to the value `"file_name"`) rather than in the message payload. The `data` parameter value, on the other hand, is carried in the message payload.

Now that you've created a message gateway, you need to configure the integration flow. Although the Spring Integration starter dependency that you added to your build enables essential autoconfiguration for Spring Integration, it's still up to you to write additional configurations to define flows that meet the needs of the application. Three configuration options for declaring integration flows follow:

- XML configuration
- Java configuration
- Java configuration with a DSL

We'll take a look at all three of these configuration styles for Spring Integration, starting with the old-timer, XML configuration.

10.1.1 *Defining integration flows with XML*

Although I've avoided using XML configuration in this book, Spring Integration has a long history of integration flows defined in XML. Therefore, I think it's worthwhile for me to show at least one example of an XML-defined integration flow. The following listing shows how to configure your sample flow in XML.

Listing 10.2　Defining an integration flow with Spring XML configuration

```xml
<?xml version="1.0" encoding="UTF-8"?><beans
    xmlns="http://www.springframework.org/schema/beans"
  xmlns:xsi="http://www.w3.org/2001/XMLSchema-instance"
  xmlns:int="http://www.springframework.org/schema/integration"
  xmlns:int-file="http://www.springframework.org/schema/integration/file"
  xsi:schemaLocation="http://www.springframework.org/schema/beans
    http://www.springframework.org/schema/beans/spring-beans.xsd
    http://www.springframework.org/schema/integration
    http://www.springframework.org/schema/integration/spring-integration.xsd
    http://www.springframework.org/schema/integration/file
    http://www.springframework.org/schema/integration/file/spring-
    integration-file.xsd">

    <int:channel id="textInChannel" />          ⟵┐ Declares
                                                  │ textInChannel
    <int:transformer id="upperCase"
        input-channel="textInChannel"
        output-channel="fileWriterChannel"         ┐ Transforms
        expression="payload.toUpperCase()" />   ⟵─┘ the text

                                                     ┐ Declares
    <int:channel id="fileWriterChannel" />   ⟵──────┤ fileWriterChannel

    <int-file:outbound-channel-adapter id="writer"
        channel="fileWriterChannel"
        directory="/tmp/sia6/files"               ┐ Writes the
        mode="APPEND"                             │ text to a file
        append-new-line="true" />         ⟵──────┘

</beans>
```

Breaking down the XML in listing 10.2, we get the following:

- You configured a channel named `textInChannel`. You'll recognize this as the same channel that's set as the request channel for `FileWriterGateway`. When the `writeToFile()` method is called on `FileWriterGateway`, the resulting message is published to this channel.
- You configured a transformer that receives messages from `textInChannel`. It uses a Spring Expression Language (SpEL) expression to call `toUpperCase()` on the message payload. The result of the uppercase operation is then published to `fileWriterChannel`.
- You configured the channel named `fileWriterChannel`. This channel serves as the conduit that connects the transformer with the outbound channel adapter.

- Finally, you configured an outbound channel adapter using the `int-file` namespace. This XML namespace is provided by Spring Integration's file module to write files. As you configured it, it receives messages from `fileWriter-Channel` and writes the message payload to a file whose name is specified in the message's `"file_name"` header in the `directory` specified in the directory attribute. If the file already exists, the file will be appended with a newline rather than be overwritten.

This flow is illustrated in figure 10.1 using graphical elements styled after those in *Enterprise Integration Patterns*.

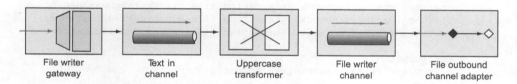

Figure 10.1   The file writer integration flow

| File writer gateway | Text in channel | Uppercase transformer | File writer channel | File outbound channel adapter |

The flow comprises five components: a gateway, two channels, a transformer, and a channel adapter. These are just a few of the components that can be assembled into an integration flow. We'll explore these components and others supported by Spring Integration in section 10.2.

If you want to use XML configuration in a Spring Boot application, you'll need to import the XML as a resource into the Spring application. The easiest way to do this is to use Spring's `@ImportResource` annotation, shown in the next code sample, on one of your application's Java configuration classes:

```
@Configuration
@ImportResource("classpath:/filewriter-config.xml")
public class FileWriterIntegrationConfig { ... }
```

Although XML-based configuration has served Spring Integration well, most developers have grown wary of using XML. (And, as I said, I'm avoiding XML configuration in this book.) Let's set aside those angle brackets and turn our attention to Spring Integration's Java configuration style.

10.1.2 *Configuring integration flows in Java*

Most modern Spring applications have eschewed XML configuration in favor of Java configuration. In fact, in Spring Boot applications, Java configuration is a natural style to complement autoconfiguration. Therefore, if you're adding an integration flow to a Spring Boot application, it makes perfect sense to define the flow in Java.

As a sample of how to write an integration flow with Java configuration, take a look at the next listing. This shows the same file-writing integration flow as before, but this time it's written in Java.

Listing 10.3   Using Java configuration to define an integration flow

```
package sia6;

import java.io.File;
import org.springframework.context.annotation.Bean;
import org.springframework.context.annotation.Configuration;
import org.springframework.integration.annotation.ServiceActivator;
import org.springframework.integration.annotation.Transformer;
import org.springframework.integration.file.FileWritingMessageHandler;
import org.springframework.integration.file.support.FileExistsMode;
import org.springframework.integration.transformer.GenericTransformer;


@Configuration
public class FileWriterIntegrationConfig {

  @Bean
  @Transformer(inputChannel="textInChannel",              ◄─┐ Declares a
              outputChannel="fileWriterChannel")             │ transformer
  public GenericTransformer<String, String> upperCaseTransformer() {
    return text -> text.toUpperCase();
  }

  @Bean
  @ServiceActivator(inputChannel="fileWriterChannel")     ──┐ Declares a
  public FileWritingMessageHandler fileWriter() {         ◄─┘ file writer
    FileWritingMessageHandler handler =
        new FileWritingMessageHandler(new File("/tmp/sia6/files"));
    handler.setExpectReply(false);
    handler.setFileExistsMode(FileExistsMode.APPEND);
    handler.setAppendNewLine(true);
    return handler;
  }

}
```

With Java configuration, you declare two beans: a transformer and a file-writing message handler. The transformer is a GenericTransformer. Because GenericTransformer is a functional interface, you're able to provide its implementation as a lambda that calls toUpperCase() on the message text. The transformer bean is annotated with @Transformer, designating it as a transformer in the integration flow that receives messages on a channel named textInChannel and writes messages to the channel named fileWriterChannel.

As for the file-writing bean, it's annotated with @ServiceActivator to indicate that it'll accept messages from fileWriterChannel and hand those messages over to the service defined by an instance of FileWritingMessageHandler. FileWritingMessage-Handler is a message handler that writes a message payload to a file in a specified directory using a filename specified in the message's "file_name" header. As with the XML example, FileWritingMessageHandler is configured to append to the file with a newline.

One thing unique about the configuration of the FileWritingMessageHandler bean is that there's a call to setExpectReply(false) to indicate that the service activator shouldn't expect a reply channel (a channel through which a value may be returned to upstream components in the flow). If you don't call setExpectReply (false), the file-writing bean defaults to true, and, although the pipeline still functions as expected, you'll see a few errors logged stating that no reply channel was configured.

You'll also notice that you didn't need to explicitly declare the channels. The textInChannel and fileWriterChannel will be created automatically if no beans with those names exist. But if you want more control over how the channels are configured, you can explicitly construct them as beans like this:

```
@Bean
public MessageChannel textInChannel() {
  return new DirectChannel();
}
...
@Bean
public MessageChannel fileWriterChannel() {
  return new DirectChannel();
}
```

The Java configuration option is arguably easier to read—and slightly briefer—and is certainly consistent with the Java-only configuration I'm shooting for in this book. But it can be made even more streamlined with Spring Integration's Java DSL (domain-specific language) configuration style.

10.1.3 *Using Spring Integration's DSL configuration*

Let's take one more stab at defining the file-writing integration flow. This time, you'll still define it in Java, but you'll use Spring Integration's Java DSL. Rather than declare an individual bean for each component in the flow, you'll declare a single bean that defines the entire flow.

Listing 10.4 Providing a fluent API for designing integration flows

```
package sia6;

import java.io.File;
import org.springframework.context.annotation.Bean;
import org.springframework.context.annotation.Configuration;
import org.springframework.integration.dsl.IntegrationFlow;
import org.springframework.integration.dsl.IntegrationFlows;
import org.springframework.integration.dsl.MessageChannels;
import org.springframework.integration.file.dsl.Files;
import org.springframework.integration.file.support.FileExistsMode;
```

```
@Configuration
public class FileWriterIntegrationConfig {

  @Bean
  public IntegrationFlow fileWriterFlow() {                    Inbound
    return IntegrationFlows                                    channel
        .from(MessageChannels.direct("textInChannel"))    ◄──
        .<String, String>transform(t -> t.toUpperCase())  ◄──  Declares a
        .handle(Files                                     ◄──  transformer
            .outboundAdapter(new File("/tmp/sia6/files"))
            .fileExistsMode(FileExistsMode.APPEND)             Handles
            .appendNewLine(true))                              writing to a file
        .get();
  }

}
```

This new configuration is as terse as it can possibly be, capturing the entire flow in a single bean method. The `IntegrationFlows` class initiates the builder API, from which you can declare the flow.

In listing 10.4, you start by receiving messages from the channel named `textIn-Channel`, which then go to a transformer that uppercases the message payload. After the transformer, messages are handled by an outbound channel adapter created from the `Files` type provided in Spring Integration's file module. Finally, a call to `get()` builds the `IntegrationFlow` to be returned. In short, this single bean method defines the same integration flow as the XML and Java configuration examples.

You'll notice that, as with the Java configuration example, you don't need to explicitly declare channel beans. Although you reference `textInChannel`, it's automatically created by Spring Integration because there's no existing channel bean with that name. But you can explicitly declare the channel bean if you want.

As for the channel that connects the transformer to the outbound channel adapter, you don't even reference it by name. If there's a need to explicitly configure the channel, you can reference it by name in the flow definition with a call to `channel()` as follows:

```
@Bean
public IntegrationFlow fileWriterFlow() {
  return IntegrationFlows
      .from(MessageChannels.direct("textInChannel"))
      .<String, String>transform(t -> t.toUpperCase())
      .channel(MessageChannels.direct("FileWriterChannel"))
      .handle(Files
          .outboundAdapter(new File("/tmp/sia6/files"))
          .fileExistsMode(FileExistsMode.APPEND)
          .appendNewLine(true))
      .get();
}
```

One thing to keep in mind when working with Spring Integration's Java DSL (as with any fluent API) is that you must employ whitespace shrewdly to maintain readability. In the example given here, I've been careful to indent lines to indicate blocks of related code. For even longer, more complex flows, you may even consider extracting portions of the flow into separate methods or subflows for better readability.

Now that you've seen a simple flow defined using three different configuration styles, let's step back and take a look at Spring Integration's big picture.

10.2 Surveying the Spring Integration landscape

Spring Integration covers a lot of ground with a multitude of integration scenarios. Trying to include all of it in a single chapter would be like trying to fit an elephant in an envelope. Instead of a comprehensive treatment of Spring Integration, I'll present a photograph of the Spring Integration elephant to give you some idea of how it works. Then you'll create one more integration flow that adds functionality to the Taco Cloud application.

An integration flow is composed of one or more of the following components. Before you write any more code, we'll take a brief look at the role each of these components plays in an integration flow:

- *Channel*—Passes messages from one element to another
- *Filter*—Conditionally allows messages to pass through the flow based on some criteria
- *Transformer*—Changes message values and/or converts message payloads from one type to another
- *Router*—Directs messages to one of several channels, typically based on message headers
- *Splitter*—Splits incoming messages into two or more messages, each sent to different channels
- *Aggregator*—The opposite of a splitter; combines multiple messages coming in from separate channels into a single message
- *Service activator*—Hands a message off to some Java method for processing, and then publishes the return value on an output channel
- *Channel adapter*—Connects a channel to some external system or transport; can either accept input or write to the external system
- *Gateway*—Passes data into an integration flow via an interface

You've already seen a few of these components in play when you defined the file-writing integration flow. The `FileWriterGateway` interface was the gateway through which an application submitted text to be written to a file. You also defined a transformer to convert the given text to uppercase; then you declared a service gateway that performed the task of writing the text to a file. And the flow had two channels, `textInChannel` and `fileWriterChannel`, that connected the other components with each other. Now, a quick tour of the integration flow components, as promised.

10.2.1 *Message channels*

Message channels are the means by which messages move through an integration pipeline, as shown in figure 10.2. They're the pipes that connect all the other parts of Spring Integration plumbing together.

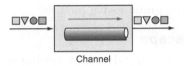

Channel

Figure 10.2   Message channels are conduits through which data flows between other components in an integration flow.

Spring Integration provides several channel implementations, including the following:

- *PublishSubscribeChannel*—Messages published into a `PublishSubscribe-Channel` are passed on to one or more consumers. If multiple consumers exist, all of them receive the message.
- *QueueChannel*—Messages published into a `QueueChannel` are stored in a queue until pulled by a consumer in a first in, first out (FIFO) fashion. If multiple consumers exist, only one of them receives the message.
- *PriorityChannel*—Like `QueueChannel` but, rather than FIFO behavior, messages are pulled by consumers based on the message `priority` header.
- *RendezvousChannel*—Like `QueueChannel` except that the sender blocks the channel until a consumer receives the message, effectively synchronizing the sender with the consumer.
- *DirectChannel*—Like `PublishSubscribeChannel`, but sends a message to a single consumer by invoking the consumer in the same thread as the sender. This allows for transactions to span across the channel.
- *ExecutorChannel*—Similar to `DirectChannel`, but the message dispatch occurs via a `TaskExecutor`, taking place in a thread separate from the sender. This channel type doesn't support transactions that span the channel.
- *FluxMessageChannel*—A Reactive Streams Publisher message channel based on Project Reactor's `Flux`. (We'll talk more about Reactive Streams, Reactor, and `Flux` in chapter 11.)

In both the Java configuration and Java DSL styles, input channels are automatically created, with `DirectChannel` as the default. But if you want to use a different channel implementation, you'll need to explicitly declare the channel as a bean and reference it in the integration flow. For example, to declare a `PublishSubscribeChannel`, you'd declare the following `@Bean` method:

```
@Bean
public MessageChannel orderChannel() {
  return new PublishSubscribeChannel();
}
```

Then you'd reference this channel by name in the integration flow definition. For example, if the channel were being consumed by a service activator bean, you'd reference it in the inputChannel attribute of @ServiceActivator like so:

```
@ServiceActivator(inputChannel="orderChannel")
```

Or, if you're using the Java DSL configuration style, you'd reference it with a call to channel() as follows:

```
@Bean
public IntegrationFlow orderFlow() {
  return IntegrationFlows
      ...
      .channel("orderChannel")
      ...
      .get();
}
```

It's important to note that if you're using QueueChannel, the consumers must be configured with a poller. For instance, suppose that you've declared a QueueChannel bean like this:

```
@Bean
public MessageChannel orderChannel() {
  return new QueueChannel();
}
```

You'd need to make sure that the consumer is configured to poll the channel for messages. In the case of a service activator, the @ServiceActivator annotation might look like this:

```
@ServiceActivator(inputChannel="orderChannel",
                  poller=@Poller(fixedRate="1000"))
```

In this example, the service activator polls from the channel named orderChannel every 1 second (or 1,000 ms).

10.2.2 Filters

You can place filters in the midst of an integration pipeline to allow or disallow messages from proceeding to the next step in the flow, as shown in figure 10.3.

Filter

Figure 10.3 Filters based on some criteria allow or disallow messages from proceeding in the pipeline.

For example, suppose that messages containing integer values are published through a channel named numberChannel, but you want only even numbers to pass on to the channel named evenNumberChannel. In that case, you could declare a filter with the @Filter annotation like this:

```
@Filter(inputChannel="numberChannel",
        outputChannel="evenNumberChannel")
public boolean evenNumberFilter(Integer number) {
  return number % 2 == 0;
}
```

Alternatively, if you're using the Java DSL configuration style to define your integration flow, you could make a call to filter() like this:

```
@Bean
public IntegrationFlow evenNumberFlow(AtomicInteger integerSource) {
  return IntegrationFlows
      ...
      .<Integer>filter((p) -> p % 2 == 0)
      ...
      .get();
}
```

In this case, you use a lambda to implement the filter. But, in truth, the filter() method accepts a GenericSelector as an argument. This means that you can implement the GenericSelector interface instead, should your filtering needs be too involved for a simple lambda.

10.2.3 *Transformers*

Transformers perform some operation on messages, typically resulting in a different message and, possibly, with a different payload type (see figure 10.4). The transformation can be something simple, such as performing mathematic operations on a number or manipulating a String value. Or the transformation can be more complex, such as using a String value representing an ISBN to look up and return details of the corresponding book.

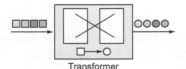

Transformer

Figure 10.4 Transformers morph messages as they flow through an integration flow.

For example, suppose that integer values are being published on a channel named numberChannel, and you want to convert those numbers to a String containing the Roman numeral equivalent. In that case, you can declare a bean of type Generic-Transformer and annotate it with @Transformer as follows:

```
@Bean
@Transformer(inputChannel="numberChannel",
             outputChannel="romanNumberChannel")
public GenericTransformer<Integer, String> romanNumTransformer() {
  return RomanNumbers::toRoman;
}
```

The @Transformer annotation designates this bean as a transformer bean that receives Integer values from the channel named numberChannel and uses a static method named toRoman() to do the conversion. (The toRoman() method is statically defined in a class named RomanNumbers and referenced here with a method reference.) The result is published to the channel named romanNumberChannel.

In the Java DSL configuration style, it's even easier with a call to transform(), passing in the method reference to the toRoman() method as follows:

```
@Bean
public IntegrationFlow transformerFlow() {
  return IntegrationFlows
      ...
      .transform(RomanNumbers::toRoman)
      ...
      .get();
}
```

Although you've used a method reference in both of the transformer code samples, know that the transformer can also be specified as a lambda. Or, if the transformer is complex enough to warrant a separate Java class, you can inject it as a bean into the flow configuration and pass the reference to the transform() method like so:

```
@Bean
public RomanNumberTransformer romanNumberTransformer() {
  return new RomanNumberTransformer();
}
```

```
@Bean
public IntegrationFlow transformerFlow(
                   RomanNumberTransformer romanNumberTransformer) {
  return IntegrationFlows
      ...
      .transform(romanNumberTransformer)
      ...
      .get();
}
```

Here, you declare a bean of type RomanNumberTransformer, which itself is an implementation of Spring Integration's Transformer or GenericTransformer interfaces. The bean is injected into the transformerFlow() method and passed to the transform() method when defining the integration flow.

10.2.4 *Routers*

Routers, based on some routing criteria, allow for branching in an integration flow, directing messages to different channels (see figure 10.5).

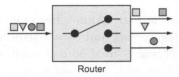

Figure 10.5   Routers direct messages to different channels, based on some criteria applied to the messages.

For example, suppose that you have a channel named `numberChannel` through which integer values flow. And let's say that you want to direct all messages with even numbers to a channel named `evenChannel`, whereas messages with odd numbers are routed to a channel named `oddChannel`. To create such a routing in your integration flow, you can declare a bean of type `AbstractMessageRouter` and annotate the bean with `@Router`, as shown next:

```
@Bean
@Router(inputChannel="numberChannel")
public AbstractMessageRouter evenOddRouter() {
  return new AbstractMessageRouter() {
    @Override
    protected Collection<MessageChannel>
            determineTargetChannels(Message<?> message) {
      Integer number = (Integer) message.getPayload();
      if (number % 2 == 0) {
        return Collections.singleton(evenChannel());
      }
      return Collections.singleton(oddChannel());
    }
  };
}

@Bean
public MessageChannel evenChannel() {
  return new DirectChannel();
}

@Bean
public MessageChannel oddChannel() {
  return new DirectChannel();
}
```

The `AbstractMessageRouter` bean declared here accepts messages from an input channel named `numberChannel`. The implementation, defined as an anonymous inner class, examines the message payload, and, if it's an even number, returns the channel named `evenChannel` (declared as a bean after the router bean). Otherwise,

the number in the channel payload must be odd, in which case, the channel named
oddChannel is returned (also declared in a bean declaration method).

In Java DSL form, routers are declared by calling route() in the course of a flow
definition, as shown here:

```java
@Bean
public IntegrationFlow numberRoutingFlow(AtomicInteger source) {
  return IntegrationFlows
    ...
    .<Integer, String>route(n -> n%2==0 ? "EVEN":"ODD", mapping -> mapping
      .subFlowMapping("EVEN", sf -> sf
        .<Integer, Integer>transform(n -> n * 10)
        .handle((i,h) -> { ... })
        )
      .subFlowMapping("ODD", sf -> sf
        .transform(RomanNumbers::toRoman)
        .handle((i,h) -> { ... })
        )
      )
    .get();
}
```

Although it's still possible to declare an AbstractMessageRouter and pass it into
route(), this example uses a lambda to determine whether a message payload is odd or
even. If it's even, then a String value of EVEN is returned. If it's odd, then ODD is returned.
These values are then used to determine which submapping will handle the message.

10.2.5 *Splitters*

At times in an integration flow, it can be useful to split a message into multiple messages to be handled independently. Splitters, as illustrated in figure 10.6, will split and
handle those messages for you.

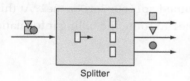

Splitter

**Figure 10.6 Splitters break down messages
into two or more separate messages that can
be handled by separate subflows.**

Splitters are useful in many circumstances, but you might use a splitter for the following two essential use cases:

- *A message payload contains a collection of items of the same type that you'd like to process
  as individual message payloads.* For example, a message carrying a list of products
  might be split into multiple messages with payloads of one product each.
- *A message payload carries information that, although related, can be split into two or
  more messages of different types.* For example, a purchase order might carry delivery,

billing, and line-item information. The delivery details might be processed by one subflow, billing by another, and line items in yet another. In this use case, the splitter is typically followed by a router that routes messages by payload type to ensure that the data is handled by the right subflow.

When splitting a message payload into two or more messages of different types, it's usually sufficient to define a POJO that extracts the individual pieces of the incoming payload and returns them as elements of a collection.

For example, suppose that you want to split a message carrying a purchase order into two messages: one carrying the billing information and another carrying a list of line items. The following `OrderSplitter` will do the job:

```
public class OrderSplitter {
  public Collection<Object> splitOrderIntoParts(PurchaseOrder po) {
    ArrayList<Object> parts = new ArrayList<>();
    parts.add(po.getBillingInfo());
    parts.add(po.getLineItems());
    return parts;
  }
}
```

You can then declare an `OrderSplitter` bean as part of the integration flow by annotating it with `@Splitter` like this:

```
@Bean
@Splitter(inputChannel="poChannel",
          outputChannel="splitOrderChannel")
public OrderSplitter orderSplitter() {
  return new OrderSplitter();
}
```

Here, purchase orders arrive on the channel named `poChannel` and are split by `OrderSplitter`. Then, each item in the returned collection is published as a separate message in the integration flow to a channel named `splitOrderChannel`. At this point in the flow, you can declare a `PayloadTypeRouter` to route the billing information and the line items to their own subflow as follows:

```
@Bean
@Router(inputChannel="splitOrderChannel")
public MessageRouter splitOrderRouter() {
  PayloadTypeRouter router = new PayloadTypeRouter();
  router.setChannelMapping(
      BillingInfo.class.getName(), "billingInfoChannel");
  router.setChannelMapping(
      List.class.getName(), "lineItemsChannel");
  return router;
}
```

As its name implies, `PayloadTypeRouter` routes messages to different channels based on their payload type. As configured here, messages whose payload is of type `BillingInfo` are routed to a channel named `billingInfoChannel` for further processing. As for the line items, they're in a `java.util.List` collection; therefore, you map payloads of type `List` to be routed to a channel named `lineItemsChannel`.

As things stand, the flow splits into two subflows: one through which `BillingInfo` objects flow and another through which a `List<LineItem>` flows. But what if you want to break it down further such that instead of dealing with a `List` of `LineItem` objects, you process each `LineItem` separately? All you need to do to split the line-item list into multiple messages, one for each line item, is write a method (not a bean) that's annotated with `@Splitter` and returns a collection of `LineItem` objects, perhaps something like this:

```
@Splitter(inputChannel="lineItemsChannel", outputChannel="lineItemChannel")
public List<LineItem> lineItemSplitter(List<LineItem> lineItems) {
  return lineItems;
}
```

When a message carrying a payload of `List<LineItem>` arrives in the channel named `lineItemsChannel`, it passes into the `lineItemSplitter()` method. Per the rules of a splitter, the method must return a collection of the items to be split. In this case, you already have a collection of `LineItem` objects, so you just return the collection directly. As a result, each `LineItem` in the collection is published in a message of its own to the channel named `lineItemChannel`.

If you'd rather use the Java DSL to declare the same splitter/router configuration, you can do so with calls to `split()` and `route()` as shown here:

```
return IntegrationFlows
    ...
    .split(orderSplitter())
    .<Object, String> route(
        p -> {
          if (p.getClass().isAssignableFrom(BillingInfo.class)) {
            return "BILLING_INFO";
          } else {
            return "LINE_ITEMS";
          }
        }, mapping -> mapping
          .subFlowMapping("BILLING_INFO", sf -> sf
            .<BillingInfo> handle((billingInfo, h) -> {
              ...
            }))
          .subFlowMapping("LINE_ITEMS", sf -> sf
            .split()
            .<LineItem> handle((lineItem, h) -> {
              ...
            }))

    )
  .get();
```

The DSL form of the flow definition is certainly terser, if not arguably a bit more difficult to follow. We could clean this up a bit by extracting the lambdas to methods. For example, we could use the following three methods to replace the lambdas used in the flow definition:

```
private String route(Object p) {
  return p.getClass().isAssignableFrom(BillingInfo.class)
      ? "BILLING_INFO"
      : "LINE_ITEMS";
}

private BillingInfo handleBillingInfo(
        BillingInfo billingInfo, MessageHeaders h) {
  // ...
}

private LineItem handleLineItems(
        LineItem lineItem, MessageHeaders h) {
  // ...
}
```

Then, we could rewrite the integration flow with method references like this:

```
return IntegrationFlows
  ...
    .split()
    .route(
      this::route,
      mapping -> mapping
        .subFlowMapping("BILLING_INFO", sf -> sf
          .<BillingInfo> handle(this::handleBillingInfo))
        .subFlowMapping("LINE_ITEMS", sf -> sf
          .split()
          .<LineItem> handle(this::handleLineItems)));
```

Either way, this uses the same `OrderSplitter` to split the order as the Java configuration example. After the order is split, it's routed by its type to two separate subflows.

10.2.6 *Service activators*

Service activators receive messages from an input channel and send those messages to an implementation of `MessageHandler`, as shown in figure 10.7.

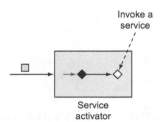

Invoke a
service

Service
activator

Figure 10.7   Service activators invoke some service by way of a `MessageHandler` on receipt of a message.

Spring Integration offers several `MessageHandler` implementations out of the box (even `PayloadTypeRouter` is an implementation of `MessageHandler`), but you'll often need to provide some custom implementation to act as a service activator. As an example, the following code shows how to declare a `MessageHandler` bean, configured to be a service activator:

```
@Bean
@ServiceActivator(inputChannel="someChannel")
public MessageHandler sysoutHandler() {
  return message -> {
    System.out.println("Message payload:  " + message.getPayload());
  };
}
```

The bean is annotated with `@ServiceActivator` to designate it as a service activator that handles messages from the channel named `someChannel`. As for the `Message-Handler` itself, it's implemented via a lambda. Although it's a simple `MessageHandler`, when given a `Message`, it emits its payload to the standard output stream.

Alternatively, you could declare a service activator that processes the data in the incoming message before returning a new payload, as shown in the next code snippet. In that case, the bean should be a `GenericHandler` rather than a `MessageHandler`.

```
@Bean
@ServiceActivator(inputChannel="orderChannel",
                  outputChannel="completeChannel")
public GenericHandler<EmailOrder> orderHandler(
                        OrderRepository orderRepo) {
  return (payload, headers) -> {
    return orderRepo.save(payload);
  };
}
```

In this case, the service activator is a `GenericHandler` that expects messages with a payload of type `EmailOrder`. When the order arrives, it's saved via a repository; the resulting saved `EmailOrder` is returned to be sent to the output channel whose name is `completeChannel`.

You may notice that a `GenericHandler` is given not only the payload but also the message headers (even if the example doesn't use those headers in any way). If you prefer, you can also use service activators in the Java DSL configuration style by passing a `MessageHandler` or `GenericHandler` to `handle()` in the flow definition as follows:

```
public IntegrationFlow someFlow() {
  return IntegrationFlows
    ...
      .handle(msg -> {
        System.out.println("Message payload:  " + msg.getPayload());
      })
      .get();
}
```

In this case, the `MessageHandler` is given as a lambda, but you could also provide it as a method reference or even as an instance of a class that implements the `Message-Handler` interface. If you give it a lambda or method reference, be aware that it accepts a message as a parameter.

Similarly, `handle()` can be written to accept a `GenericHandler` if the service activator isn't intended to be the end of the flow. Applying the order-saving service activator from before, you could configure the flow with the Java DSL like this:

```
public IntegrationFlow orderFlow(OrderRepository orderRepo) {
  return IntegrationFlows
    ...
      .<EmailOrder>handle((payload, headers) -> {
         return orderRepo.save(payload);
      })
    ...
      .get();
}
```

When working with a `GenericHandler`, the lambda or method reference accepts the message payload and headers as parameters. Also, if you choose to use `Generic-Handler` at the end of a flow, you'll need to return `null`, or else you'll get errors indicating that there's no output channel specified.

10.2.7 *Gateways*

Gateways are the means by which an application can submit data into an integration flow and, optionally, receive a response that's the result of the flow. Implemented by Spring Integration, gateways are realized as interfaces that the application can call to send messages to the integration flow (see figure 10.8).

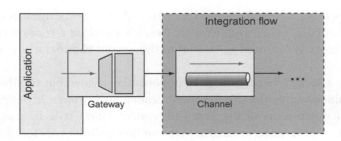

Figure 10.8   Service gateways are interfaces through which an application can submit messages to an integration flow.

You've already seen an example of a message gateway with `FileWriterGateway`. `File-WriterGateway` was a one-way gateway with a method accepting a `String` to write to a file, returning `void`. It's just about as easy to write a two-way gateway. When writing the gateway interface, be sure that the method returns some value to publish into the integration flow.

As an example, imagine a gateway that fronts a simple integration flow that accepts a `String` and translates the given `String` to all uppercase. The gateway interface might look something like this:

```
package sia6;
import org.springframework.integration.annotation.MessagingGateway;
import org.springframework.stereotype.Component;

@Component
@MessagingGateway(defaultRequestChannel="inChannel",
                  defaultReplyChannel="outChannel")
public interface UpperCaseGateway {
  String uppercase(String in);
}
```

What's amazing about this interface is that it's not necessary to implement it. Spring Integration automatically provides an implementation at run time that sends and receives data through the specified channels.

When uppercase() is called, the given `String` is published to the integration flow into the channel named inChannel. Regardless of how the flow is defined or what it does, when data arrives in the channel named outChannel, it's returned from the uppercase() method.

As for the uppercase integration flow, it's a simplistic integration flow with only a single step to transform the `String` to uppercase. Here, it's expressed in the Java DSL configuration:

```
@Bean
public IntegrationFlow uppercaseFlow() {
  return IntegrationFlows
    .from("inChannel")
    .<String, String> transform(s -> s.toUpperCase())
    .channel("outChannel")
    .get();
}
```

As defined here, the flow starts with data coming into the channel named inChannel. The message payload is then transformed by the transformer, which is defined here as a lambda expression, to perform an uppercase operation. The resulting message is then published to the channel named outChannel, which is what you've declared as the reply channel for the UpperCaseGateway interface.

10.2.8 Channel adapters

Channel adapters represent the entry and exit points of an integration flow. Data enters an integration flow by way of an inbound channel adapter and exits an integration flow by way of an outbound channel adapter. This is illustrated in figure 10.9.

Inbound channel adapters can take many forms, depending on the source of the data they introduce into the flow. For example, you might declare an inbound channel

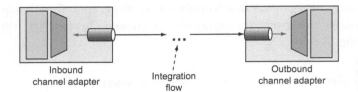

Inbound
channel adapter

Integration
flow

Outbound
channel adapter

**Figure 10.9   Channel adapters
are the entry and exit points of
an integration flow.**

adapter that introduces incrementing numbers from an `AtomicInteger`[2] into the flow. Using Java configuration, it might look like this:

```
@Bean
@InboundChannelAdapter(
    poller=@Poller(fixedRate="1000"), channel="numberChannel")
public MessageSource<Integer> numberSource(AtomicInteger source) {
  return () -> {
    return new GenericMessage<>(source.getAndIncrement());
  };
}
```

This `@Bean` method declares an inbound channel adapter bean which, per the `@InboundChannelAdapter` annotation, submits a number from the injected `Atomic-Integer` to the channel named `numberChannel` every 1 second (or 1,000 ms).

Whereas `@InboundChannelAdapter` indicates an inbound channel adapter when using Java configuration, the `from()` method is how it's done when using the Java DSL to define the integration flow. The following snippet of a flow definition shows a similar inbound channel adapter as defined in the Java DSL:

```
@Bean
public IntegrationFlow someFlow(AtomicInteger integerSource) {
  return IntegrationFlows
      .from(integerSource, "getAndIncrement",
          c -> c.poller(Pollers.fixedRate(1000)))
    ...
      .get();
}
```

Often, channel adapters are provided by one of Spring Integration's many endpoint modules. Suppose, for example, that you need an inbound channel adapter that monitors a specified directory and submits any files that are written to that directory as messages to a channel named `file-channel`. The following Java configuration uses `FileReadingMessageSource` from Spring Integration's file endpoint module to achieve that:

---

[2] `AtomicInteger` is useful for incrementing a counter in a multithreaded situation, such as the one here where multiple messages may arrive on the channel simultaneously.

```
@Bean
@InboundChannelAdapter(channel="file-channel",
                                      poller=@Poller(fixedDelay="1000"))
public MessageSource<File> fileReadingMessageSource() {
  FileReadingMessageSource sourceReader = new FileReadingMessageSource();
  sourceReader.setDirectory(new File(INPUT_DIR));
  sourceReader.setFilter(new SimplePatternFileListFilter(FILE_PATTERN));
  return sourceReader;
}
```

When writing the equivalent file-reading inbound channel adapter in the Java DSL, the `inboundAdapter()` method from the `Files` class achieves the same thing. As shown next, an outbound channel adapter is the end of the line for the integration flow, handing off the final message to the application or to some other system:

```
@Bean
public IntegrationFlow fileReaderFlow() {
  return IntegrationFlows
      .from(Files.inboundAdapter(new File(INPUT_DIR))
          .patternFilter(FILE_PATTERN))
      .get();
}
```

Service activators, implemented as message handlers, often serve the purpose of an outbound channel adapter, especially when data needs to be handed off to the application itself. We've already discussed service activators, so there's no point in repeating that discussion.

It's worth noting, however, that Spring Integration endpoint modules provide useful message handlers for several common use cases. You saw an example of such an outbound channel adapter, `FileWritingMessageHandler`, in listing 10.3. Speaking of Spring Integration endpoint modules, let's take a quick look at what ready-to-use integration endpoint modules are available.

10.2.9 *Endpoint modules*

It's great that Spring Integration lets you create your own channel adapters. But what's even better is that Spring Integration provides more than two dozen endpoint modules containing channel adapters—both inbound and outbound—for integration with a variety of common external systems, including those listed in table 10.1.

Table 10.1 Spring Integration provides more than two dozen endpoint modules for integration with external systems.

Module	Dependency artifact ID (Group ID: `org.springframework.integration`)
AMQP	`spring-integration-amqp`
Application events	`spring-integration-event`
Atom and RSS	`spring-integration-feed`

Table 10.1　Spring Integration provides more than two dozen endpoint modules for integration with external systems. *(continued)*

Module	Dependency artifact ID (Group ID: `org.springframework.integration`)
Email	`spring-integration-mail`
Filesystem	`spring-integration-file`
FTP/FTPS	`spring-integration-ftp`
GemFire	`spring-integration-gemfire`
HTTP	`spring-integration-http`
JDBC	`spring-integration-jdbc`
JMS	`spring-integration-jms`
JMX	`spring-integration-jmx`
JPA	`spring-integration-jpa`
Kafka	`spring-integration-kafka`
MongoDB	`spring-integration-mongodb`
MQTT	`spring-integration-mqtt`
R2DBC	`spring-integration-r2dbc`
Redis	`spring-integration-redis`
RMI	`spring-integration-rmi`
RSocket	`spring-integration-rsocket`
SFTP	`spring-integration-sftp`
STOMP	`spring-integration-stomp`
Stream	`spring-integration-stream`
Syslog	`spring-integration-syslog`
TCP/UDP	`spring-integration-ip`
WebFlux	`spring-integration-webflux`
Web Services	`spring-integration-ws`
WebSocket	`spring-integration-websocket`
XMPP	`spring-integration-xmpp`
ZeroMQ	`spring-integration-zeromq`
ZooKeeper	`spring-integration-zookeeper`

One thing that's clear from looking at table 10.1 is that Spring Integration provides an extensive set of components to meet many integration needs. Most applications will never need even a fraction of what Spring Integration offers. But it's good to know that Spring Integration has you covered if you need any of these components.

What's more, it would be impossible to cover all the channel adapters afforded by the modules listed in table 10.1 in the space of this chapter. You've already seen examples that use the filesystem module to write to the filesystem. And you're soon going to use the email module to read emails.

Each of the endpoint modules offers channel adapters that can be either declared as beans when using Java configuration or referenced via static methods when using Java DSL configuration. I encourage you to explore any of the other endpoint modules that interest you most. You'll find that they're fairly consistent in how they're used. But for now, let's turn our attention to the email endpoint module to see how you might use it in the Taco Cloud application.

10.3 Creating an email integration flow

You've decided that Taco Cloud should enable its customers to submit their taco designs and place orders by email. You send out flyers and place takeout ads in newspapers inviting everyone to send in their taco orders by email. It's a tremendous success! Unfortunately, it's a bit too successful. There are so many emails coming in that you have to hire temporary help to do nothing more than read all the emails and submit order details into the ordering system.

In this section, you'll implement an integration flow that polls the Taco Cloud inbox for taco order emails, parses the emails for order details, and submits the orders to Taco Cloud for handling. In short, the integration flow you're going to need will use an inbound channel adapter from the email endpoint module to ingest emails from the Taco Cloud inbox into the integration flow.

The next step in the integration flow will parse the emails into order objects that are handed off to another handler to submit orders to Taco Cloud's REST API, where they'll be processed the same as any order. To start with, let's define a simple configuration properties class to capture the specifics of how to handle Taco Cloud emails, as shown here:

```java
package tacos.email;

import org.springframework.boot.context.properties.ConfigurationProperties;
import org.springframework.stereotype.Component;
import lombok.Data;

@Data
@ConfigurationProperties(prefix="tacocloud.email")
@Component
public class EmailProperties {

  private String username;
  private String password;
  private String host;
  private String mailbox;
  private long pollRate = 30000;
```

```
public String getImapUrl() {
    return String.format("imaps://%s:%s@%s/%s",
        this.username, this.password, this.host, this.mailbox);
}

}
```

As you can see, `EmailProperties` captures properties that are used to produce an IMAP URL. The flow uses this URL to connect to the Taco Cloud email server and poll for emails. Among the properties captured are the email user's username and password, as well as the hostname of the IMAP server, the mailbox to poll, and the rate at which the mailbox is polled (which defaults to every 30 seconds).

The `EmailProperties` class is annotated at the class level with `@Configuration-Properties` with a `prefix` attribute set to `tacocloud.email`. This means that you can configure the details of consuming an email in the application.yml file like this:

```
tacocloud:
  email:
    host: imap.tacocloud.com
    mailbox: INBOX
    username: taco-in-flow
    password: 1L0v3T4c0s
    poll-rate: 10000
```

Of course, the email server configuration shown here is fictional. You'll need to tweak it to match the email server details that you'll be using.

Also, you may get an "unknown property" warning in your IDE. That's because the IDE is looking for metadata it needs to understand what those properties mean. The warnings won't break the actual code, and you can ignore them if you want. Or you can make them go away by adding the following dependency to your build (also available as a Spring Initializr option called "Spring Configuration Processor"):

```
<dependency>
  <groupId>org.springframework.boot</groupId>
  <artifactId>spring-boot-configuration-processor</artifactId>
  <optional>true</optional>
</dependency>
```

This dependency includes support for automatically generating metadata for custom configuration properties such as the ones we're using to configure the email server details.

Now let's use `EmailProperties` to configure the integration flow. The flow you're aiming to create will look a little like figure 10.10.

You have the following two options when defining this flow:

- *Define it within the Taco Cloud application itself.* At the end of the flow, a service activator will call into the repositories you've defined to create the taco order.
- *Define it as a separate application.* At the end of the flow, a service activator will send a POST request to the Taco Cloud API to submit the taco order.

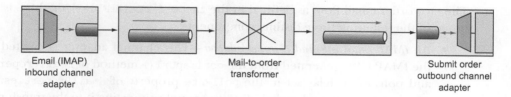

Figure 10.10 An integration flow to accept taco orders by email

Whichever you choose has little bearing on the flow itself, aside from how the service activator is implemented. But because you're going to need some types that represent tacos, orders, and ingredients, which are subtly different from those you've already defined in the main Taco Cloud application, you'll proceed by defining the integration flow in a separate application to avoid any confusion with the existing domain types.

You also have the choice of defining the flow using either XML configuration, Java configuration, or the Java DSL. I rather like the elegance of the Java DSL, so that's what you'll use. Feel free to write the flow using one of the other configuration styles if you're interested in a little extra challenge. For now, let's take a look at the Java DSL configuration for the taco order email flow as shown next.

Listing 10.5 Defining an integration flow to accept emails and submit them as orders

```java
package tacos.email;

import org.springframework.context.annotation.Bean;
import org.springframework.context.annotation.Configuration;
import org.springframework.integration.dsl.IntegrationFlow;
import org.springframework.integration.dsl.IntegrationFlows;
import org.springframework.integration.dsl.Pollers;
import org.springframework.integration.mail.dsl.Mail;

@Configuration
public class TacoOrderEmailIntegrationConfig {

  @Bean
  public IntegrationFlow tacoOrderEmailFlow(
      EmailProperties emailProps,
      EmailToOrderTransformer emailToOrderTransformer,
      OrderSubmitMessageHandler orderSubmitHandler) {

    return IntegrationFlows
        .from(Mail.imapInboundAdapter(emailProps.getImapUrl()),
            e -> e.poller(
                Pollers.fixedDelay(emailProps.getPollRate()))))
        .transform(emailToOrderTransformer)
        .handle(orderSubmitHandler)
        .get();
  }

}
```

The taco order email flow, as defined in the `tacoOrderEmailFlow()` method, is composed of the following three distinct components:

- *An IMAP email inbound channel adapter*—This channel adapter is created with the IMAP URL generated from the `getImapUrl()` method of `EmailProperties` and polls on a delay set in the `pollRate` property of `EmailProperties`. The emails coming in are handed off to a channel connecting it to the transformer.
- *A transformer that transforms an email into an order object*—The transformer is implemented in `EmailToOrderTransformer`, which is injected into the `tacoOrderEmailFlow()` method. The orders resulting from the transformation are handed off to the final component through another channel.
- *A handler (acting as an outbound channel adapter)*—The handler accepts an order object and submits it to Taco Cloud's REST API.

The call to `Mail.imapInboundAdapter()` is made possible by including the `Email` endpoint module as a dependency in your project build. The Maven dependency looks like this:

```
<dependency>
  <groupId>org.springframework.integration</groupId>
  <artifactId>spring-integration-mail</artifactId>
</dependency>
```

The `EmailToOrderTransformer` class is an implementation of Spring Integration's `Transformer` interface, by way of extending `AbstractMailMessageTransformer` (shown in the following listing).

Listing 10.6   Converting incoming emails to taco orders using an integration transformer

```
package tacos.email;

import java.io.IOException;
import java.util.ArrayList;
import java.util.List;
import javax.mail.Message;
import javax.mail.MessagingException;
import javax.mail.internet.InternetAddress;
import org.apache.commons.text.similarity.LevenshteinDistance;
import org.slf4j.Logger;
import org.slf4j.LoggerFactory;
import org.springframework.integration.mail.transformer
                                        .AbstractMailMessageTransformer;
import org.springframework.integration.support

      .AbstractIntegrationMessageBuilder;
import org.springframework.integration.support.MessageBuilder;
import org.springframework.stereotype.Component;

@Component
public class EmailToOrderTransformer
    extends AbstractMailMessageTransformer<EmailOrder> {
```

```java
private static Logger log =
        LoggerFactory.getLogger(EmailToOrderTransformer.class);

private static final String SUBJECT_KEYWORDS = "TACO ORDER";

@Override
protected AbstractIntegrationMessageBuilder<EmailOrder>
            doTransform(Message mailMessage) throws Exception {
  EmailOrder tacoOrder = processPayload(mailMessage);
  return MessageBuilder.withPayload(tacoOrder);
}

private EmailOrder processPayload(Message mailMessage) {
  try {
    String subject = mailMessage.getSubject();
    if (subject.toUpperCase().contains(SUBJECT_KEYWORDS)) {
      String email =
            ((InternetAddress) mailMessage.getFrom()[0]).getAddress();
      String content = mailMessage.getContent().toString();
      return parseEmailToOrder(email, content);
    }
  } catch (MessagingException e) {
    log.error("MessagingException: {}", e);
  } catch (IOException e) {
    log.error("IOException: {}", e);
  }
  return null;
}

private EmailOrder parseEmailToOrder(String email, String content) {
  EmailOrder order = new EmailOrder(email);
  String[] lines = content.split("\\r?\\n");
  for (String line : lines) {
    if (line.trim().length() > 0 && line.contains(":")) {
      String[] lineSplit = line.split(":");
      String tacoName = lineSplit[0].trim();
      String ingredients = lineSplit[1].trim();
      String[] ingredientsSplit = ingredients.split(",");
      List<String> ingredientCodes = new ArrayList<>();
      for (String ingredientName : ingredientsSplit) {
        String code = lookupIngredientCode(ingredientName.trim());
        if (code != null) {
          ingredientCodes.add(code);
        }
      }

      Taco taco = new Taco(tacoName);
      taco.setIngredients(ingredientCodes);
      order.addTaco(taco);
    }
  }
  return order;
}

private String lookupIngredientCode(String ingredientName) {
  for (Ingredient ingredient : ALL_INGREDIENTS) {
```

```
        String ucIngredientName = ingredientName.toUpperCase();
        if (LevenshteinDistance.getDefaultInstance()
                    .apply(ucIngredientName, ingredient.getName()) < 3 ||
            ucIngredientName.contains(ingredient.getName()) ||
            ingredient.getName().contains(ucIngredientName)) {
          return ingredient.getCode();
        }
      }
    }
    return null;
  }

  private static Ingredient[] ALL_INGREDIENTS = new Ingredient[] {
      new Ingredient("FLTO", "FLOUR TORTILLA"),
      new Ingredient("COTO", "CORN TORTILLA"),
      new Ingredient("GRBF", "GROUND BEEF"),
      new Ingredient("CARN", "CARNITAS"),
      new Ingredient("TMTO", "TOMATOES"),
      new Ingredient("LETC", "LETTUCE"),
      new Ingredient("CHED", "CHEDDAR"),
      new Ingredient("JACK", "MONTERREY JACK"),
      new Ingredient("SLSA", "SALSA"),
      new Ingredient("SRCR", "SOUR CREAM")
  };
}
```

AbstractMailMessageTransformer is a convenient base class for handling messages whose payload is an email. It takes care of extracting the email information from the incoming message into a Message object that's passed into the doTransform() method.

In the doTransform() method, you pass the Message to a private method named processPayload() to parse the email into an EmailOrder object. Although similar, the EmailOrder object in question isn't the same as the TacoOrder object used in the main Taco Cloud application; it's slightly simpler, as shown next:

```
package tacos.email;
import java.util.ArrayList;
import java.util.List;
import lombok.Data;

@Data
public class EmailOrder {

  private final String email;
  private List<Taco> tacos = new ArrayList<>();

  public void addTaco(Taco taco) {
    tacos.add(taco);
  }

}
```

Rather than carry the customer's entire delivery and billing information, this Email-Order class carries only the customer's email, obtained from the incoming email.

Parsing emails into taco orders is a nontrivial task. In fact, even a naive implementation involves several dozen lines of code. And those several dozen lines of code do nothing to further the discussion of Spring Integration and how to implement a transformer. Therefore, to save space, I'm leaving out the details of the processPayload() method.

The last thing that EmailToOrderTransformer does is return a MessageBuilder with a payload containing the EmailOrder object. The message that's produced by the MessageBuilder is sent to the final component in the integration flow: a message handler that posts the order to Taco Cloud's API. The OrderSubmitMessageHandler, as shown in the next listing, implements Spring Integration's GenericHandler to handle messages with an EmailOrder payload.

Listing 10.7   Posting orders to the Taco Cloud API via a message handler

```
package tacos.email;

import org.springframework.integration.handler.GenericHandler;
import org.springframework.messaging.MessageHeaders;
import org.springframework.stereotype.Component;
import org.springframework.web.client.RestTemplate;

@Component
public class OrderSubmitMessageHandler
        implements GenericHandler<EmailOrder> {

  private RestTemplate rest;
  private ApiProperties apiProps;

  public OrderSubmitMessageHandler(ApiProperties apiProps, RestTemplate rest) {
    this.apiProps = apiProps;
    this.rest = rest;
  }

  @Override
  public Object handle(EmailOrder order, MessageHeaders headers) {
    rest.postForObject(apiProps.getUrl(), order, String.class);
    return null;
  }
}
```

To satisfy the requirements of the GenericHandler interface, OrderSubmitMessage-Handler overrides the handle() method. This method receives the incoming Email-Order object and uses an injected RestTemplate to submit the EmailOrder via a POST request to the URL captured in an injected ApiProperties object. Finally, the handle() method returns null to indicate that this handler marks the end of the flow.

ApiProperties is used to avoid hardcoding the URL in the call to postFor-Object(). It's a configuration properties file that looks like this:

```
package tacos.email;

import org.springframework.boot.context.properties.ConfigurationProperties;
import org.springframework.stereotype.Component;
import lombok.Data;

@Data
@ConfigurationProperties(prefix = "tacocloud.api")
@Component
public class ApiProperties {
  private String url;
}
```

And in application.yml, the URL for the Taco Cloud API might be configured like this:

```
tacocloud:
  api:
    url: http://localhost:8080/orders/fromEmail
```

To make RestTemplate available in the project so that it can be injected into Order-SubmitMessageHandler, you need to add the Spring Boot web starter to the project build like so:

```
<dependency>
  <groupId>org.springframework.boot</groupId>
  <artifactId>spring-boot-starter-web</artifactId>
</dependency>
```

Although this makes RestTemplate available in the classpath, it also triggers autoconfiguration for Spring MVC. As a standalone Spring Integration flow, the application doesn't need Spring MVC or even the embedded Tomcat that autoconfiguration provides. Therefore, you should disable Spring MVC autoconfiguration with the following entry in application.yml:

```
spring:
  main:
    web-application-type: none
```

The spring.main.web-application-type property can be set to either servlet, reactive, or none. When Spring MVC is in the classpath, autoconfiguration sets its value to servlet. But here you override it to none so that Spring MVC and Tomcat won't be autoconfigured. (We'll talk more about what it means for an application to be a reactive web application in chapter 12.)

Summary

- Spring Integration enables the definition of flows through which data can be processed as it enters or leaves an application.
- Integration flows can be defined in XML, Java, or using a succinct Java DSL configuration style.
- Message gateways and channel adapters act as entry and exit points of an integration flow.
- Messages can be transformed, split, aggregated, routed, and processed by service activators in the course of a flow.
- Message channels connect the components of an integration flow.

Part 3

Reactive Spring

In part 3, we'll explore the support for reactive programming in Spring. Chapter 11 discusses the essentials of reactive programming with Project Reactor, the reactive programming library that underpins Spring's reactive features. We'll then look at some of Reactor's most useful reactive operations. In chapter 12, we'll revisit REST API development, introducing Spring WebFlux, a web framework that borrows much from Spring MVC while offering a new reactive model for web development. Chapter 13 takes a look at writing reactive data persistence with Spring Data to read and write data to Cassandra and Mongo databases. Chapter 14 rounds out part 3 by looking at RSocket, a communication protocol that enables a reactive alternative to HTTP.

Introducing Reactor

This chapter covers

- Understanding reactive programming
- Project Reactor
- Operating on data reactively

Have you ever held a subscription for a newspaper or a magazine? The internet has certainly taken a bite out of the subscriber base of traditional publications, but there was a time when a newspaper subscription was one of the best ways to keep up with the events of the day. You could count on a fresh delivery of current events every morning, to read during breakfast or on the way to work.

Now suppose that if, after paying for your subscription, several days go by and no papers have been delivered. A few more days go by, and you call the newspaper sales office to ask why you haven't yet received your daily paper. Imagine your surprise if they explain, "You paid for a full year of newspapers. The year hasn't completed yet. You'll certainly receive them all once the full year of newspapers is ready."

Thankfully, that's not at all how subscriptions work. Newspapers have a certain timeliness to them. They're delivered as quickly as possible after publication so that they can be read while their content is still fresh. Moreover, as you're reading the latest issue, newspaper reporters are writing new stories for future editions, and the presses are fired up producing the next edition—all in parallel.

As we develop application code, we can write two styles of code—imperative and reactive, which are described as follows:

- *Imperative* code is a lot like that absurd hypothetical newspaper subscription. It's a serial set of tasks, each running one at a time, each after the previous task. Data is processed in bulk and can't be handed over to the next task until the previous task has completed its work on the bulk of data.
- *Reactive* code is a lot like a real newspaper subscription. A set of tasks is defined to process data, but those tasks can run in parallel. Each task can process subsets of the data, handing it off to the next task in line while it continues to work on another subset of the data.

In this chapter, we're going to step away from the Taco Cloud application temporarily to explore Project Reactor (https://projectreactor.io/). Reactor is a library for reactive programming that's part of the Spring family of projects. And because it serves as the foundation of Spring's support for reactive programming, it's important that you understand Reactor before we look at building reactive controllers and repositories with Spring. Before we start working with Reactor, though, let's quickly examine the essentials of reactive programming.

11.1 *Understanding reactive programming*

Reactive programming is a paradigm that's an alternative to imperative programming. This alternative exists because reactive programming addresses a limitation in imperative programming. By understanding these limitations, you can better grasp the benefits of the reactive model.

> **NOTE**   Reactive programming isn't a silver bullet. In no way should you infer from this chapter or any other discussion of reactive programming that imperative programming is evil and that reactive programming is your savior. Like anything you learn as a developer, reactive programming is a perfect fit in some use cases, and it's ill-fitted in others. An ounce of pragmatism is advised.

If you're like me and many developers, you cut your programming teeth with imperative programming. There's a good chance that most (or all) of the code you write today is still imperative in nature. Imperative programming is intuitive enough that young students are learning it with ease in their school's STEM programs, and it's powerful enough that it makes up the bulk of code that drives the largest enterprises.

The idea is simple: you write code as a list of instructions to be followed, one at a time, in the order that they're encountered. A task is performed and the program waits for it to complete before moving on to the next task. At each step along the way, the data that's to be processed must be fully available so that it can be processed as a whole.

This is fine . . . until it isn't. While a task is being performed—and especially if it's an I/O task, such as writing data to a database or fetching data from a remote server—the thread that invoked that task is blocked, unable to do anything else until the task completes. To put it bluntly, blocked threads are wasteful.

Most programming languages, including Java, support concurrent programming. It's fairly easy to fire up another thread in Java and send it on its way to perform some work while the invoking thread carries on with something else. But although it's easy to create threads, those threads are likely to end up blocked themselves. Managing concurrency in multiple threads is challenging. More threads mean more complexity.

In contrast, reactive programming is functional and declarative in nature. Rather than describe a set of steps that are to be performed sequentially, reactive programming involves describing a pipeline or stream through which data flows. Rather than requiring the data to be available and processed as a whole, a reactive stream processes data as it becomes available. In fact, the incoming data may be endless (a constant stream of a location's real-time temperature data, for instance).

> **NOTE** If you're new to functional programming in Java, you may want to have a look at *Functional Programming in Java* by Pierre-Yves Saumont (Manning, 2017), or *Grokking Functional Programming* by Michał Płachta (Manning, 2021).

To apply a real-world analogy, consider imperative programming as a water balloon and reactive programming as a garden hose. Both are suitable ways to surprise and soak an unsuspecting friend on a hot summer day. But they differ in their execution style as follows:

- A water balloon carries its payload all at once, soaking its intended target at the moment of impact. The water balloon has a finite capacity, however, and if you wish to soak more people (or the same person to a greater extent), your only choice is to scale up by increasing the number of water balloons.
- A garden hose carries its payload as a stream of water that flows from the spigot to the nozzle. The garden hose's capacity may be finite at any given point in time, but it's unlimited over the course of a water battle. As long as water is entering the hose from the spigot, it will continue to flow through the hose and spray out of the nozzle. The same garden hose is easily scalable to soak as many friends as you wish.

There's nothing inherently wrong with water balloons (or imperative programming), but the person holding the garden hose (or applying reactive programming) has an advantage in regard to scalability and performance.

11.1.1 Defining Reactive Streams

Reactive Streams is an initiative started in late 2013 by engineers from Netflix, Lightbend, and Pivotal (the company behind Spring). Reactive Streams aims to provide a standard for asynchronous stream processing with nonblocking backpressure.

We've already touched on the asynchronous trait of reactive programming; it's what enables us to perform tasks in parallel to achieve greater scalability. Backpressure is a means by which consumers of data can avoid being overwhelmed by an overly fast data source, by establishing limits on how much they're willing to handle.

Java streams vs. Reactive Streams

There's a lot of similarity between Java streams and Reactive Streams. To start with, they both have the word *streams* in their names. They also both provide a functional API for working with data. In fact, as you'll see later when we look at Reactor, they even share many of the same operations.

Java streams, however, are typically synchronous and work with a finite set of data. They're essentially a means of iterating over a collection with functions.

Reactive Streams support asynchronous processing of datasets of any size, including infinite datasets. They process data in real time, as it becomes available, with backpressure to avoid overwhelming their consumers.

On the other hand, JDK 9's Flow APIs correspond to Reactive Streams. The `Flow .Publisher`, `Flow.Subscriber`, `Flow.Subscription`, and `Flow.Processor` types in JDK 9 map directly to `Publisher`, `Subscriber`, `Subscription`, and `Processor` in Reactive Streams. That said, JDK 9's Flow APIs are not an actual implementation of Reactive Streams.

The Reactive Streams specification can be summed up by four interface definitions: `Publisher`, `Subscriber`, `Subscription`, and `Processor`. A `Publisher` produces data that it sends to a `Subscriber` per a `Subscription`. The `Publisher` interface declares a single method, `subscribe()`, through which a `Subscriber` can subscribe to the `Publisher`, as shown here:

```
public interface Publisher<T> {
  void subscribe(Subscriber<? super T> subscriber);
}
```

Once a `Subscriber` has subscribed, it can receive events from the `Publisher`. Those events are sent via methods on the `Subscriber` interface as follows:

```
public interface Subscriber<T> {
  void onSubscribe(Subscription sub);
  void onNext(T item);
  void onError(Throwable ex);
  void onComplete();
}
```

The first event that the `Subscriber` will receive is through a call to `onSubscribe()`. When the `Publisher` calls `onSubscribe()`, it passes a `Subscription` object to the `Subscriber`. It's through the `Subscription` that the `Subscriber` can manage its subscription, as shown next:

```
public interface Subscription {
  void request(long n);
  void cancel();
}
```

The Subscriber can call request() to request that data be sent, or it can call cancel() to indicate that it's no longer interested in receiving data and is canceling the subscription. When calling request(), the Subscriber passes in a long value to indicate how many data items it's willing to accept. This is where backpressure comes in, preventing the Publisher from sending more data than the Subscriber is able to handle. After the Publisher has sent as many items as were requested, the Subscriber can call request() again to request more.

Once the Subscriber has requested data, the data starts flowing through the stream. For every item that's published by the Publisher, the onNext() method will be called to deliver the data to the Subscriber. If there are any errors, onError() is called. If the Publisher has no more data to send and isn't going to produce any more data, it will call onComplete() to tell the Subscriber that it's out of business.

As for the Processor interface, it's a combination of Subscriber and Publisher, as shown here:

```
public interface Processor<T, R>
        extends Subscriber<T>, Publisher<R> {}
```

As a Subscriber, a Processor will receive data and process it in some way. Then it will switch hats and act as a Publisher to publish the results to its Subscribers.

As you can see, the Reactive Streams specification is rather straightforward. It's fairly easy to see how you could build up a data processing pipeline that starts with a Publisher, pumps data through zero or more Processors, and then drops the final results off to a Subscriber.

What the Reactive Streams interfaces don't lend themselves to, however, is composing such a stream in a functional way. Project Reactor is an implementation of the Reactive Streams specification that provides a functional API for composing Reactive Streams. As you'll see in the following chapters, Reactor is the foundation for Spring's reactive programming model. In the remainder of this chapter, we're going to explore (and, dare I say, have a lot of fun with) Project Reactor.

11.2 *Getting started with Reactor*

Reactive programming requires us to think in a very different way from imperative programming. Rather than describe a set of steps to be taken, reactive programming means building a pipeline through which data will flow. As data passes through the pipeline, it can be altered or used in some way.

For example, suppose you want to take a person's name, change all of the letters to uppercase, use it to create a greeting message, and then finally print it. In an imperative programming model, the code would look something like this:

```
String name = "Craig";
String capitalName = name.toUpperCase();
String greeting = "Hello, " + capitalName + "!";
System.out.println(greeting);
```

In the imperative model, each line of code performs a step, one right after the other, and definitely in the same thread. Each step blocks the executing thread from moving to the next step until complete.

In contrast, functional, reactive code could achieve the same thing like this:

```
Mono.just("Craig")
    .map(n -> n.toUpperCase())
    .map(cn -> "Hello, " + cn + "!")
    .subscribe(System.out::println);
```

Don't worry too much about the details of this example; we'll talk all about the just(), map(), and subscribe() operations soon enough. For now, it's important to understand that although the reactive example still seems to follow a step-by-step model, it's really a pipeline that data flows through. At each phase of the pipeline, the data is tweaked somehow, but no assumption can be made about which thread any of the operations are performed on. They may be the same thread . . . or they may not be.

The Mono in the example is one of Reactor's two core types. Flux is the other. Both are implementations of Reactive Streams' Publisher. A Flux represents a pipeline of zero, one, or many (potentially infinite) data items. A Mono is a specialized reactive type that's optimized for when the dataset is known to have no more than one data item.

> ### Reactor vs. RxJava (ReactiveX)
>
> If you're already familiar with RxJava or ReactiveX, you may be thinking that Mono and Flux sound a lot like Observable and Single. In fact, they're approximately equivalent semantically. They even offer many of the same operations.
>
> Although we focus on Reactor in this book, you may be happy to know that it's possible to convert between Reactor and RxJava types. Moreover, as you'll see in the following chapters, Spring can also work with RxJava types.

The previous example actually contains three Mono objects. The just() operation creates the first one. When the Mono emits a value, that value is given to the map() operation to be capitalized and used to create another Mono. When the second Mono publishes its data, it's given to the second map() operation to do some String concatenation, the results of which are used to create the third Mono. Finally, the call to subscribe() subscribes to the Mono, receives the data, and prints it.

11.2.1 *Diagramming reactive flows*

Reactive flows are often illustrated with marble diagrams. Marble diagrams, in their simplest form, depict a timeline of data as it flows through a `Flux` or `Mono` at the top, an operation in the middle, and the timeline of the resulting `Flux` or `Mono` at the bottom. Figure 11.1 shows a marble diagram template for a `Flux`. As you can see, as data flows through the original `Flux`, it's processed through some operation, resulting in a new `Flux` through which the processed data flows.

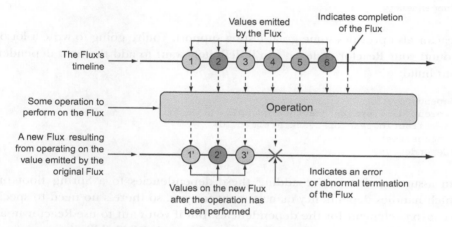

Figure 11.1 Marble diagram illustrating the basic flow of a `Flux`

Figure 11.2 shows a similar marble diagram, but for a `Mono`. As you can see, the key difference is that a `Mono` will have either zero or one data item, or an error.

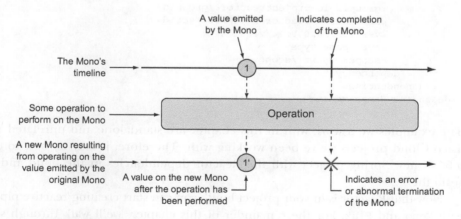

Figure 11.2 Marble diagram illustrating the basic flow of a `Mono`

In section 11.3, we'll explore many operations supported by Flux and Mono, and we'll use marble diagrams to visualize how they work.

11.2.2   *Adding Reactor dependencies*

To get started with Reactor, add the following dependency to the project build:

```
<dependency>
  <groupId>io.projectreactor</groupId>
  <artifactId>reactor-core</artifactId>
</dependency>
```

Reactor also provides some great testing support. You're going to write a lot of tests around your Reactor code, so you'll definitely want to add the next dependency to your build:

```
<dependency>
  <groupId>io.projectreactor</groupId>
  <artifactId>reactor-test</artifactId>
  <scope>test</scope>
</dependency>
```

I'm assuming that you're adding these dependencies to a Spring Boot project, which handles dependency management for you, so there's no need to specify the <version> element for the dependencies. But if you want to use Reactor in a non–Spring Boot project, you'll need to set up Reactor's BOM (bill of materials) in the build. The following dependency management entry adds Reactor's 2020.0.4 release to the build:

```
<dependencyManagement>
    <dependencies>
        <dependency>
            <groupId>io.projectreactor</groupId>
            <artifactId>reactor-bom</artifactId>
            <version>2020.0.4</version>
            <type>pom</type>
            <scope>import</scope>
        </dependency>
    </dependencies>
</dependencyManagement>
```

The examples we'll work with in this chapter are standalone and unrelated to the Taco Cloud projects we've been working with. Therefore, it may be best to create a fresh new Spring project with the Reactor dependencies in the build and work from there.

Now that Reactor is in your project build, you can start creating reactive pipelines with Mono and Flux. For the remainder of this chapter, we'll walk through several operations offered by Mono and Flux.

11.3 *Applying common reactive operations*

Flux and Mono are the most essential building blocks provided by Reactor, and the operations those two reactive types offer are the mortar that binds them together to create pipelines through which data can flow. Flux and Mono offer more than 500 operations, which can be loosely categorized as follows:

- Creation
- Combination
- Transformation
- Logic

As much fun as it would be to poke at each of the 500 operations to see how they tick, there's simply not enough room in this chapter. I've selected a few of the most useful operations to experiment with in this section. We'll start with creation operations.

> **NOTE** Where are the Mono examples? Mono and Flux share many of the same operations, so it's mostly unnecessary to show the same operation twice, once for Mono and again for Flux. Moreover, although the Mono operations are useful, they're slightly less interesting to look at than the same operations when given a Flux. Most of the examples we'll work with will involve Flux. Just know that Mono often has equivalent operations.

11.3.1 *Creating reactive types*

Often when working with reactive types in Spring, you'll be given a Flux or a Mono from a repository or a service, so you won't need to create one yourself. But occasionally you'll need to create a new reactive publisher.

Reactor provides several operations for creating a Flux or Mono. In this section, we'll look at a few of the most useful creation operations.

CREATING FROM OBJECTS

If you have one or more objects from which you'd like to create a Flux or Mono, you can use the static just() method on Flux or Mono to create a reactive type whose data is driven by those objects. For example, the following test method creates a Flux from five String objects:

```
@Test
public void createAFlux_just() {
  Flux<String> fruitFlux = Flux
      .just("Apple", "Orange", "Grape", "Banana", "Strawberry");
}
```

At this point, the Flux has been created, but it has no subscribers. Without any subscribers, data won't flow. Thinking of the garden hose analogy, you've attached the garden hose to the spigot, and there's water from the utility company on the other side—but until you turn on the spigot, water won't flow. Subscribing to a reactive type is how you turn on the flow of data.

To add a subscriber, you can call the subscribe() method on the Flux as follows:

```
fruitFlux.subscribe(
  f -> System.out.println("Here's some fruit: " + f)
);
```

The lambda given to subscribe() here is actually a java.util.Consumer that's used to create a Reactive Streams Subscriber. Upon calling subscribe(), the data starts flowing. In this example, there are no intermediate operations, so the data flows directly from the Flux to the Subscriber.

Printing the entries from a Flux or Mono to the console is a good way to see the reactive type in action. But a better way to actually test a Flux or a Mono is to use Reactor's StepVerifier. Given a Flux or Mono, StepVerifier subscribes to the reactive type and then applies assertions against the data as it flows through the stream, finally verifying that the stream completes as expected.

For example, to verify that the prescribed data flows through the fruitFlux, you can write a test that looks like this:

```
StepVerifier.create(fruitFlux)
    .expectNext("Apple")
    .expectNext("Orange")
    .expectNext("Grape")
    .expectNext("Banana")
    .expectNext("Strawberry")
    .verifyComplete();
```

In this case, StepVerifier subscribes to the Flux and then asserts that each item matches the expected fruit name. Finally, it verifies that after Strawberry is produced by the Flux, the Flux is complete.

For the remainder of the examples in this chapter, you'll use StepVerifier to write learning tests—tests that verify behavior and help you understand how something works—to get to know some of Reactor's most useful operations.

CREATING FROM COLLECTIONS

A Flux can also be created from an array, Iterable, or Java Stream. Figure 11.3 illustrates how this works with a marble diagram.

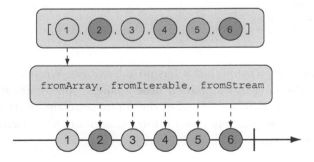

Figure 11.3 A Flux can be created from an array, Iterable, or Stream.

To create a `Flux` from an array, call the static `fromArray()` method, passing in the source array like so:

```
@Test
public void createAFlux_fromArray() {
  String[] fruits = new String[] {
      "Apple", "Orange", "Grape", "Banana", "Strawberry" };

  Flux<String> fruitFlux = Flux.fromArray(fruits);

  StepVerifier.create(fruitFlux)
      .expectNext("Apple")
      .expectNext("Orange")
      .expectNext("Grape")
      .expectNext("Banana")
      .expectNext("Strawberry")
      .verifyComplete();
}
```

Because the source array contains the same fruit names you used when creating a `Flux` from a list of objects, the data emitted by the `Flux` will have the same values. Thus, you can use the same `StepVerifier` as before to verify this `Flux`.

If you need to create a `Flux` from a `java.util.List`, `java.util.Set`, or any other implementation of `java.lang.Iterable`, you can pass it into the static `fromIterable()` method, as shown here:

```
@Test
public void createAFlux_fromIterable() {
  List<String> fruitList = new ArrayList<>();
  fruitList.add("Apple");
  fruitList.add("Orange");
  fruitList.add("Grape");
  fruitList.add("Banana");
  fruitList.add("Strawberry");

  Flux<String> fruitFlux = Flux.fromIterable(fruitList);

  StepVerifier.create(fruitFlux)
      .expectNext("Apple")
      .expectNext("Orange")
      .expectNext("Grape")
      .expectNext("Banana")
      .expectNext("Strawberry")
      .verifyComplete();
}
```

Or, if you happen to have a Java `Stream` that you'd like to use as the source for a `Flux`, `fromStream()` is the method you'll use, as shown next:

```
@Test
 public void createAFlux_fromStream() {
   Stream<String> fruitStream =
        Stream.of("Apple", "Orange", "Grape", "Banana", "Strawberry");
```

```
    Flux<String> fruitFlux = Flux.fromStream(fruitStream);

    StepVerifier.create(fruitFlux)
        .expectNext("Apple")
        .expectNext("Orange")
        .expectNext("Grape")
        .expectNext("Banana")
        .expectNext("Strawberry")
        .verifyComplete();
}
```

Again, you can use the same `StepVerifier` as before to verify the data published by the `Flux`.

GENERATING FLUX DATA

Sometimes you don't have any data to work with and just need `Flux` to act as a counter, emitting a number that increments with each new value. To create a counter `Flux`, you can use the static `range()` method. The diagram in figure 11.4 illustrates how `range()` works.

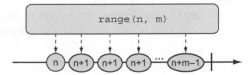

Figure 11.4   Creating a `Flux` from a range results in a counter-style publishing of messages.

The following test method demonstrates how to create a range `Flux`:

```
@Test
public void createAFlux_range() {
  Flux<Integer> intervalFlux =
      Flux.range(1, 5);

  StepVerifier.create(intervalFlux)
      .expectNext(1)
      .expectNext(2)
      .expectNext(3)
      .expectNext(4)
      .expectNext(5)
      .verifyComplete();
}
```

In this example, the range `Flux` is created with a starting value of 1 and an ending value of 5. The `StepVerifier` proves that it will publish five items, which are the integers 1 through 5.

Another `Flux`-creation method that's similar to `range()` is `interval()`. Like the `range()` method, `interval()` creates a `Flux` that emits an incrementing value. But what makes `interval()` special is that instead of you giving it a starting and ending value, you specify a duration or how often a value should be emitted. Figure 11.5 shows a marble diagram for the interval() creation method.

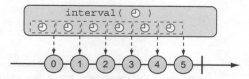

Figure 11.5 A Flux created from an interval has a periodic entry published to it.

For example, to create an interval Flux that emits a value every second, you can use the static interval() method as follows:

```
@Test
public void createAFlux_interval() {
  Flux<Long> intervalFlux =
      Flux.interval(Duration.ofSeconds(1))
          .take(5);

  StepVerifier.create(intervalFlux)
      .expectNext(0L)
      .expectNext(1L)
      .expectNext(2L)
      .expectNext(3L)
      .expectNext(4L)
      .verifyComplete();
}
```

Notice that the value emitted by an interval Flux starts with 0 and increments on each successive item. Also, because interval() isn't given a maximum value, it will potentially run forever. Therefore, you also use the take() operation to limit the results to the first five entries. We'll talk more about the take() operation in the next section.

11.3.2 Combining reactive types

You may find yourself with two reactive types that you need to somehow merge together. Or, in other cases, you may need to split a Flux into more than one reactive type. In this section, we'll examine operations that combine and split Reactor's Flux and Mono.

MERGING REACTIVE TYPES

Suppose you have two Flux streams and need to create a single resulting Flux that will produce data as it becomes available from either of the upstream Flux streams. To merge one Flux with another, you can use the mergeWith() operation, as illustrated with the marble diagram in figure 11.6.

For example, suppose you have a Flux whose values are the names of TV and movie characters, and you have a second Flux whose values are the names of foods

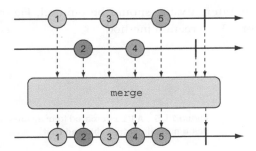

Figure 11.6   Merging two `Flux` streams interleaves their messages into a new `Flux`.

that those characters enjoy eating. The following test method shows how you could merge the two `Flux` objects with the `mergeWith()` method:

```
@Test
public void mergeFluxes() {

    Flux<String> characterFlux = Flux
        .just("Garfield", "Kojak", "Barbossa")
        .delayElements(Duration.ofMillis(500));
    Flux<String> foodFlux = Flux
        .just("Lasagna", "Lollipops", "Apples")
        .delaySubscription(Duration.ofMillis(250))
        .delayElements(Duration.ofMillis(500));

    Flux<String> mergedFlux = characterFlux.mergeWith(foodFlux);

    StepVerifier.create(mergedFlux)
        .expectNext("Garfield")
        .expectNext("Lasagna")
        .expectNext("Kojak")
        .expectNext("Lollipops")
        .expectNext("Barbossa")
        .expectNext("Apples")
        .verifyComplete();
}
```

Normally, a `Flux` will publish data as quickly as it possibly can. Therefore, you use a `delayElements()` operation on both of the created `Flux` streams to slow them down a little—emitting an entry only every 500 ms. Furthermore, so that the food `Flux` starts streaming after the character `Flux`, you apply a `delaySubscription()` operation to the food `Flux` so that it won't emit any data until 250 ms have passed following a subscription.

After merging the two `Flux` objects, a new merged `Flux` is created. When `Step-Verifier` subscribes to the merged `Flux`, it will, in turn, subscribe to the two source `Flux` streams, starting the flow of data.

The order of items emitted from the merged `Flux` aligns with the timing of how they're emitted from the sources. Because both `Flux` objects are set to emit at regular rates, the values will be interleaved through the merged Flux, resulting in a character, followed by a food, followed by a character, and so forth. If the timing of either Flux were to change, it's possible that you might see two character items or two food items published one after the other.

Because mergeWith() can't guarantee a perfect back and forth between its sources, you may want to consider the zip() operation instead. When two Flux objects are zipped together, it results in a new Flux that produces a tuple of items, where the tuple contains one item from each source Flux. Figure 11.7 illustrates how two Flux objects can be zipped together.

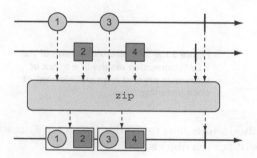

Figure 11.7   Zipping two Flux **streams results in a** Flux **containing tuples of one element from each** Flux**.**

To see the zip() operation in action, consider the following test method, which zips the character Flux and the food Flux together:

```
@Test
public void zipFluxes() {
  Flux<String> characterFlux = Flux
      .just("Garfield", "Kojak", "Barbossa");
  Flux<String> foodFlux = Flux
      .just("Lasagna", "Lollipops", "Apples");

  Flux<Tuple2<String, String>> zippedFlux =
      Flux.zip(characterFlux, foodFlux);

  StepVerifier.create(zippedFlux)
      .expectNextMatches(p ->
          p.getT1().equals("Garfield") &&
          p.getT2().equals("Lasagna"))
      .expectNextMatches(p ->
          p.getT1().equals("Kojak") &&
          p.getT2().equals("Lollipops"))
      .expectNextMatches(p ->
          p.getT1().equals("Barbossa") &&
          p.getT2().equals("Apples"))
      .verifyComplete();
}
```

Notice that unlike mergeWith(), the zip() operation is a static creation operation. The created Flux has a perfect alignment between characters and their favorite foods.

Each item emitted from the zipped `Flux` is a `Tuple2` (a container object that carries two other objects) containing items from each source `Flux`, in the order that they're published.

If you'd rather not work with a `Tuple2` and would rather work with some other type, you can provide a `Function` to `zip()` that produces any object you'd like, given the two items (as shown in the marble diagram in figure 11.8).

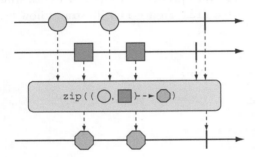

Figure 11.8   An alternative form of the `zip()` operation results in a `Flux` of messages created from one element of each incoming `Flux`.

For example, the following test method shows how to zip the character `Flux` with the food `Flux` so that it results in a `Flux` of `String` objects:

```
@Test
public void zipFluxesToObject() {
  Flux<String> characterFlux = Flux
      .just("Garfield", "Kojak", "Barbossa");
  Flux<String> foodFlux = Flux
      .just("Lasagna", "Lollipops", "Apples");

  Flux<String> zippedFlux =
      Flux.zip(characterFlux, foodFlux, (c, f) -> c + " eats " + f);

  StepVerifier.create(zippedFlux)
        .expectNext("Garfield eats Lasagna")
        .expectNext("Kojak eats Lollipops")
        .expectNext("Barbossa eats Apples")
        .verifyComplete();
}
```

The `Function` given to `zip()` (given here as a lambda) simply concatenates the two items into a sentence to be emitted by the zipped `Flux`.

SELECTING THE FIRST REACTIVE TYPE TO PUBLISH

Suppose you have two `Flux` objects, and rather than merge them together, you merely want to create a new `Flux` that emits the values from the first `Flux` that produces a value. As shown in figure 11.9, the `firstWithSignal()` operation picks the first of two `Flux` objects and echoes the values it publishes.

The following test method creates a fast `Flux` and a slow `Flux` (where "slow" means that it will not publish an item until 100 ms after subscription). Using `firstWithSignal()`,

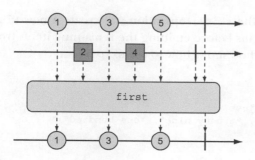

Figure 11.9 The `first()` operation chooses the first `Flux` to emit a message and thereafter produces messages only from that `Flux`.

it creates a new `Flux` that will publish values only from the first source `Flux` to publish a value.

```
@Test
public void firstWithSignalFlux() {

    Flux<String> slowFlux = Flux.just("tortoise", "snail", "sloth")
        .delaySubscription(Duration.ofMillis(100));
    Flux<String> fastFlux = Flux.just("hare", "cheetah", "squirrel");

    Flux<String> firstFlux = Flux.firstWithSignal(slowFlux, fastFlux);

    StepVerifier.create(firstFlux)
        .expectNext("hare")
        .expectNext("cheetah")
        .expectNext("squirrel")
        .verifyComplete();
}
```

In this case, because the slow `Flux` won't publish any values until 100 ms after the fast `Flux` has started publishing, the newly created `Flux` will simply ignore the slow `Flux` and publish values only from the fast `Flux`.

11.3.3 *Transforming and filtering reactive streams*

As data flows through a stream, you'll likely need to filter out some values and modify other values. In this section, we'll look at operations that transform and filter the data flowing through a reactive stream.

FILTERING DATA FROM REACTIVE TYPES

One of the most basic ways of filtering data as it flows from a `Flux` is to simply disregard the first so many entries. The `skip()` operation, illustrated in figure 11.10, does exactly that.

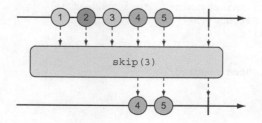

Figure 11.10 The `skip()` operation skips a specified number of messages before passing the remaining messages on to the resulting `Flux`.

Given a `Flux` with several entries, the `skip()` operation will create a new `Flux` that skips over a specified number of items before emitting the remaining items from the source `Flux`. The following test method shows how to use `skip()`:

```
@Test
public void skipAFew() {
  Flux<String> countFlux = Flux.just(
      "one", "two", "skip a few", "ninety nine", "one hundred")
      .skip(3);

  StepVerifier.create(countFlux)
      .expectNext("ninety nine", "one hundred")
      .verifyComplete();
}
```

In this case, you have a `Flux` of five `String` items. Calling `skip(3)` on that `Flux` produces a new `Flux` that skips over the first three items and publishes only the last two items.

But maybe you don't want to skip a specific number of items but instead need to skip the first so many items until some duration has passed. An alternate form of the `skip()` operation, illustrated in figure 11.11, produces a `Flux` that waits until some specified time has passed before emitting items from the source `Flux`.

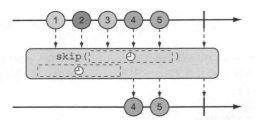

Figure 11.11   An alternative form of the `skip()` operation waits until some duration has passed before passing messages on to the resulting `Flux`.

The test method that follows uses `skip()` to create a `Flux` that waits 4 seconds before emitting any values. Because that `Flux` was created from a `Flux` that has a 1-second delay between items (using `delayElements()`), only the last two items will be emitted.

```
@Test
public void skipAFewSeconds() {
  Flux<String> countFlux = Flux.just(
      "one", "two", "skip a few", "ninety nine", "one hundred")
      .delayElements(Duration.ofSeconds(1))
      .skip(Duration.ofSeconds(4));

  StepVerifier.create(countFlux)
      .expectNext("ninety nine", "one hundred")
      .verifyComplete();
}
```

You've already seen an example of the take() operation, but in light of the skip() operation, take() can be thought of as the opposite of skip(). Whereas skip() skips the first few items, take() emits only the first so many items (as illustrated by the marble diagram in figure 11.12):

```
@Test
public void take() {
  Flux<String> nationalParkFlux = Flux.just(
      "Yellowstone", "Yosemite", "Grand Canyon", "Zion", "Acadia")
      .take(3);

  StepVerifier.create(nationalParkFlux)
      .expectNext("Yellowstone", "Yosemite", "Grand Canyon")
      .verifyComplete();
}
```

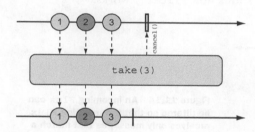

Figure 11.12 The take() operation passes only the first so many messages from the incoming Flux and then cancels the subscription.

Like skip(), take() also has an alternative form that's based on a duration rather than an item count. It will take and emit as many items as pass through the source Flux until some period of time has passed, after which the Flux completes. This is illustrated in figure 11.13.

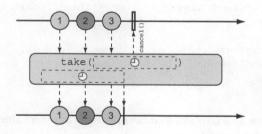

Figure 11.13 An alternative form of the take() operation passes messages on to the resulting Flux until some duration has passed.

The following test method uses the alternative form of take() to emit as many items as it can in the first 3.5 seconds after subscription:

```
@Test
public void takeForAwhile() {
```

```
    Flux<String> nationalParkFlux = Flux.just(
        "Yellowstone", "Yosemite", "Grand Canyon", "Zion", "Grand Teton")
        .delayElements(Duration.ofSeconds(1))
        .take(Duration.ofMillis(3500));

    StepVerifier.create(nationalParkFlux)
        .expectNext("Yellowstone", "Yosemite", "Grand Canyon")
        .verifyComplete();
}
```

The `skip()` and `take()` operations can be thought of as filter operations where the filter criteria are based on a count or a duration. For more general-purpose filtering of `Flux` values, you'll find the `filter()` operation quite useful.

Given a `Predicate` that decides whether an item will pass through the `Flux`, the `filter()` operation lets you selectively publish based on whatever criteria you want. The marble diagram in figure 11.14 shows how `filter()` works.

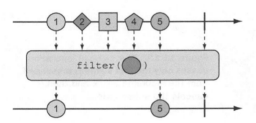

Figure 11.14   An incoming `Flux` can be filtered so that the resulting `Flux` receives only messages that match a given predicate.

To see `filter()` in action, consider the following test method:

```
@Test+
public void filter() {
  Flux<String> nationalParkFlux = Flux.just(
      "Yellowstone", "Yosemite", "Grand Canyon", "Zion", "Grand Teton")
      .filter(np -> !np.contains(" "));

  StepVerifier.create(nationalParkFlux)
      .expectNext("Yellowstone", "Yosemite", "Zion")
      .verifyComplete();
}
```

Here, `filter()` is given a `Predicate` as a lambda that accepts only `String` values that don't have any spaces. Consequently, `"Grand Canyon"` and `"Grand Teton"` are filtered out of the resulting `Flux`.

Perhaps the filtering you need is to filter out any items that you've already received. The `distinct()` operation, as illustrated in figure 11.15, results in a `Flux` that publishes only items from the source `Flux` that haven't already been published.

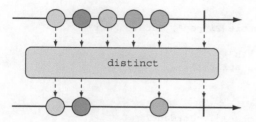

Figure 11.15 The distinct() operation filters out any duplicate messages.

In the following test, only unique String values will be emitted from the distinct Flux:

```
@Test
public void distinct() {
  Flux<String> animalFlux = Flux.just(
      "dog", "cat", "bird", "dog", "bird", "anteater")
      .distinct();

  StepVerifier.create(animalFlux)
      .expectNext("dog", "cat", "bird", "anteater")
      .verifyComplete();
}
```

Although "dog" and "bird" are each published twice from the source Flux, the distinct Flux publishes them only once.

MAPPING REACTIVE DATA

One of the most common operations you'll use on either a Flux or a Mono is to transform published items to some other form or type. Reactor's types offer map() and flatMap() operations for that purpose.

The map() operation creates a Flux that simply performs a transformation as prescribed by a given Function on each object it receives before republishing it. Figure 11.16 illustrates how the map() operation works.

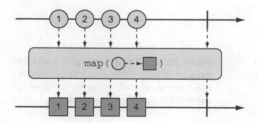

Figure 11.16 The map() operation performs a transformation of incoming messages into new messages on the resulting stream.

In the following test method, a Flux of String values representing basketball players is mapped to a new Flux of Player objects:

```
@Test
public void map() {
```

```
Flux<Player> playerFlux = Flux
  .just("Michael Jordan", "Scottie Pippen", "Steve Kerr")
  .map(n -> {
    String[] split = n.split("\\s");
    return new Player(split[0], split[1]);
  });

StepVerifier.create(playerFlux)
    .expectNext(new Player("Michael", "Jordan"))
    .expectNext(new Player("Scottie", "Pippen"))
    .expectNext(new Player("Steve", "Kerr"))
    .verifyComplete();
}

@Data
private static class Player {
  private final String firstName;
  private final String lastName;
}
```

The Function given to map() (as a lambda) splits the incoming String at a space
and uses the resulting String array to create a Player object. Although the Flux
created with just() carried String objects, the Flux resulting from map() carries
Player objects.

What's important to understand about map() is that the mapping is performed synchronously, as each item is published by the source Flux. If you want to perform the
mapping asynchronously, you should consider the flatMap() operation.

The flatMap() operation requires some thought and practice to acquire full profi-
ciency. As shown in figure 11.17, instead of simply mapping one object to another, as
in the case of map(), flatMap() maps each object to a new Mono or Flux. The results
of the Mono or Flux are flattened into a new resulting Flux. When used along with
subscribeOn(), flatMap() can unleash the asynchronous power of Reactor's types.

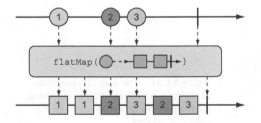

Figure 11.17 The flatMap() operation
uses an intermediate Flux to perform a
transformation, consequently allowing for
asynchronous transformations.

The following test method demonstrates the use of flatMap() and subscribeOn():

```
@Test
public void flatMap() {
  Flux<Player> playerFlux = Flux
    .just("Michael Jordan", "Scottie Pippen", "Steve Kerr")
```

```
    .flatMap(n -> Mono.just(n)
        .map(p -> {
            String[] split = p.split("\\s");
            return new Player(split[0], split[1]);
        })
        .subscribeOn(Schedulers.parallel())
    );

List<Player> playerList = Arrays.asList(
    new Player("Michael", "Jordan"),
    new Player("Scottie", "Pippen"),
    new Player("Steve", "Kerr"));

StepVerifier.create(playerFlux)
    .expectNextMatches(p -> playerList.contains(p))
    .expectNextMatches(p -> playerList.contains(p))
    .expectNextMatches(p -> playerList.contains(p))
    .verifyComplete();
}
```

Notice that flatMap() is given a lambda Function that transforms the incoming String into a Mono of type String. A map() operation is then applied to the Mono to transform the String into a Player. After the String is mapped to a Player on each internal Flux, they are published into a single Flux returned by flatMap(), thus completing the flattening of the results.

If you stopped right there, the resulting Flux would carry Player objects, produced synchronously in the same order as with the map() example. But the last thing you do with the Mono is call subscribeOn() to indicate that each subscription should take place in a parallel thread. Consequently, the mapping operations for multiple incoming String objects can be performed asynchronously and in parallel.

Although subscribeOn() is named similarly to subscribe(), they're quite different. Whereas subscribe() is a verb, subscribing to a reactive flow and effectively kicking it off, subscribeOn() is more descriptive, specifying *how* a subscription should be handled concurrently. Reactor doesn't force any particular concurrency model; it's through subscribeOn() that you can specify the concurrency model, using one of the static methods from Schedulers, that you want to use. In this example, you used parallel(), which uses worker threads from a fixed pool (sized to the number of CPU cores). But Schedulers supports several concurrency models, such as those described in table 11.1.

Table 11.1 Concurrency models for Schedulers

Schedulers method	Description
.immediate()	Executes the subscription in the current thread.
.single()	Executes the subscription in a single, reusable thread. Reuses the same thread for all callers.
.newSingle()	Executes the subscription in a per-call dedicated thread.

Table 11.1   Concurrency models for `Schedulers` *(continued)*

Schedulers method	Description
`.elastic()`	Executes the subscription in a worker pulled from an unbounded, elastic pool. New worker threads are created as needed, and idle workers are disposed of (by default, after 60 seconds).
`.parallel()`	Executes the subscription in a worker pulled from a fixed-size pool, sized to the number of CPU cores.

The upside to using `flatMap()` and `subscribeOn()` is that you can increase the throughput of the stream by splitting the work across multiple parallel threads. But because the work is being done in parallel, with no guarantees on which will finish first, there's no way to know the order of items emitted in the resulting `Flux`. Therefore, `Step-Verifier` is able to verify only that each item emitted exists in the expected list of `Player` objects and that there will be three such items before the `Flux` completes.

BUFFERING DATA ON A REACTIVE STREAM

In the course of processing the data flowing through a `Flux`, you might find it helpful to break the stream of data into bite-size chunks. The `buffer()` operation, shown in figure 11.18, can help with that.

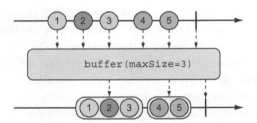

Figure 11.18   The `buffer()` **operation results in a** `Flux` **of lists of a given maximum size that are collected from the incoming** `Flux`.

Given a `Flux` of `String` values, each containing the name of a fruit, you can create a new `Flux` of `List` collections, where each `List` has no more than a specified number of elements as follows:

```
@Test
public void buffer() {
  Flux<String> fruitFlux = Flux.just(
      "apple", "orange", "banana", "kiwi", "strawberry");

  Flux<List<String>> bufferedFlux = fruitFlux.buffer(3);

  StepVerifier
     .create(bufferedFlux)
     .expectNext(Arrays.asList("apple", "orange", "banana"))
     .expectNext(Arrays.asList("kiwi", "strawberry"))
     .verifyComplete();
}
```

In this case, the `Flux` of `String` elements is buffered into a new `Flux` of `List` collections containing no more than three items each. Consequently, the original `Flux` that emits five `String` values will be converted to a `Flux` that emits two `List` collections, one containing three fruits and the other with two fruits.

So what? Buffering values from a reactive `Flux` into nonreactive `List` collections seems counterproductive. But when you combine `buffer()` with `flatMap()`, it enables each of the `List` collections to be processed in parallel, as shown next:

```
@Test
public void bufferAndFlatMap() throws Exception {
  Flux.just(
      "apple", "orange", "banana", "kiwi", "strawberry")
      .buffer(3)
      .flatMap(x ->
        Flux.fromIterable(x)
          .map(y -> y.toUpperCase())
          .subscribeOn(Schedulers.parallel())
          .log()
      ).subscribe();
}
```

In this new example, you still buffer a `Flux` of five `String` values into a new `Flux` of `List` collections. But then you apply `flatMap()` to that `Flux` of `List` collections. This takes each `List` buffer and creates a new `Flux` from its elements, and then applies a `map()` operation on it. Consequently, each buffered `List` is further processed in parallel in individual threads.

To prove that it works, I've also included a `log()` operation to be applied to each sub-`Flux`. The `log()` operation simply logs all Reactive Streams events, so that you can see what's really happening. As a result, the following entries are written to the log (with the time component removed for brevity's sake):

```
[main] INFO reactor.Flux.SubscribeOn.1 -
                 onSubscribe(FluxSubscribeOn.SubscribeOnSubscriber)
[main] INFO reactor.Flux.SubscribeOn.1 - request(32)
[main] INFO reactor.Flux.SubscribeOn.2 -
                 onSubscribe(FluxSubscribeOn.SubscribeOnSubscriber)
[main] INFO reactor.Flux.SubscribeOn.2 - request(32)
[parallel-1] INFO reactor.Flux.SubscribeOn.1 - onNext(APPLE)
[parallel-2] INFO reactor.Flux.SubscribeOn.2 - onNext(KIWI)
[parallel-1] INFO reactor.Flux.SubscribeOn.1 - onNext(ORANGE)
[parallel-2] INFO reactor.Flux.SubscribeOn.2 - onNext(STRAWBERRY)
[parallel-1] INFO reactor.Flux.SubscribeOn.1 - onNext(BANANA)
[parallel-1] INFO reactor.Flux.SubscribeOn.1 - onComplete()
[parallel-2] INFO reactor.Flux.SubscribeOn.2 - onComplete()
```

As the log entries clearly show, the fruits in the first buffer (apple, orange, and banana) are handled in the `parallel-1` thread. Meanwhile, the fruits in the second buffer (kiwi and strawberry) are processed in the `parallel-2` thread. As is apparent by the fact that the log entries from each buffer are woven together, the two buffers are processed in parallel.

If, for some reason, you need to collect everything that a Flux emits into a List, you can call buffer() with no arguments as follows:

```
Flux<List<String>> bufferedFlux = fruitFlux.buffer();
```

This results in a new Flux that emits a List that contains all the items published by the source Flux. You can achieve the same thing with the collectList() operation, illustrated by the marble diagram in figure 11.19.

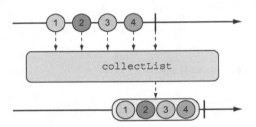

Figure 11.19   The collectList() operation results in a Mono containing a list of all messages emitted by the incoming Flux.

Rather than produce a Flux that publishes a List, collectList() produces a Mono that publishes a List. The following test method shows how it might be used:

```
@Test
public void collectList() {
  Flux<String> fruitFlux = Flux.just(
      "apple", "orange", "banana", "kiwi", "strawberry");

  Mono<List<String>> fruitListMono = fruitFlux.collectList();

  StepVerifier
      .create(fruitListMono)
      .expectNext(Arrays.asList(
          "apple", "orange", "banana", "kiwi", "strawberry"))
      .verifyComplete();
}
```

An even more interesting way of collecting items emitted by a Flux is to collect them into a Map. As shown in figure 11.20, the collectMap() operation results in a Mono

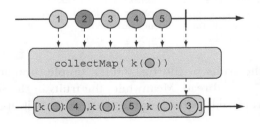

Figure 11.20   The collectMap() operation results in a Mono containing a map of messages emitted by the incoming Flux, where the key is derived from some characteristic of the incoming messages.

that publishes a `Map` that's populated with entries whose key is calculated by a given `Function`.

To see `collectMap()` in action, have a look at the following test method:

```java
@Test
public void collectMap() {
  Flux<String> animalFlux = Flux.just(
      "aardvark", "elephant", "koala", "eagle", "kangaroo");

  Mono<Map<Character, String>> animalMapMono =
      animalFlux.collectMap(a -> a.charAt(0));

  StepVerifier
      .create(animalMapMono)
      .expectNextMatches(map -> {
        return
            map.size() == 3 &&
            map.get('a').equals("aardvark") &&
            map.get('e').equals("eagle") &&
            map.get('k').equals("kangaroo");
      })
      .verifyComplete();
}
```

The source `Flux` emits the names of a handful of animals. From that `Flux`, you use `collectMap()` to create a new `Mono` that emits a `Map`, where the key value is determined by the first letter of the animal name and the value is the animal name itself. In the event that two animal names start with the same letter (as with *elephant* and *eagle* or *koala* and *kangaroo*), the last entry flowing through the stream overrides any earlier entries.

11.3.4 *Performing logic operations on reactive types*

Sometimes you just need to know if the entries published by a `Mono` or `Flux` match some criteria. The `all()` and `any()` operations perform such logic. Figures 11.21 and 11.22 illustrate how `all()` and `any()` work.

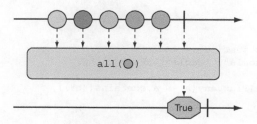

Figure 11.21 A `Flux` can be tested to ensure that all messages meet some condition with the `all()` operation.

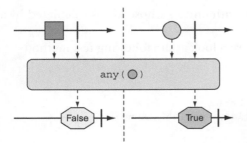

Figure 11.22 A `Flux` **can be tested to ensure that at least one message meets some condition with the** `any()` **operation.**

Suppose you want to know that every `String` published by a `Flux` contains the letter *a* or the letter *k*. The following test shows how to use `all()` to check for that condition:

```
@Test
public void all() {
  Flux<String> animalFlux = Flux.just(
      "aardvark", "elephant", "koala", "eagle", "kangaroo");

  Mono<Boolean> hasAMono = animalFlux.all(a -> a.contains("a"));
  StepVerifier.create(hasAMono)
    .expectNext(true)
    .verifyComplete();

  Mono<Boolean> hasKMono = animalFlux.all(a -> a.contains("k"));
  StepVerifier.create(hasKMono)
    .expectNext(false)
    .verifyComplete();
}
```

In the first `StepVerifier`, you check for the letter *a*. The all operation is applied to the source `Flux`, resulting in a `Mono` of type `Boolean`. In this case, all of the animal names contain the letter *a*, so `true` is emitted from the resulting `Mono`. But in the second `StepVerifier`, the resulting `Mono` will emit `false` because not all of the animal names contain a *k*.

Rather than perform an all-or-nothing check, maybe you're satisfied if at least one entry matches. In that case, the `any()` operation is what you want. This new test case uses `any()` to check for the letters *t* and *z*:

```
@Test
public void any() {
  Flux<String> animalFlux = Flux.just(
      "aardvark", "elephant", "koala", "eagle", "kangaroo");

  Mono<Boolean> hasTMono = animalFlux.any(a -> a.contains("t"));

  StepVerifier.create(hasTMono)
    .expectNext(true)
    .verifyComplete();
```

```
Mono<Boolean> hasZMono = animalFlux.any(a -> a.contains("z"));
StepVerifier.create(hasZMono)
  .expectNext(false)
  .verifyComplete();
}
```

In the first StepVerifier, you see that the resulting Mono emits true, because at least one animal name has the letter *t* (specifically, *elephant*). In the second case, the resulting Mono emits false, because none of the animal names contain z.

Summary

- Reactive programming involves creating pipelines through which data flows.
- The Reactive Streams specification defines four types: Publisher, Subscriber, Subscription, and Transformer (which is a combination of Publisher and Subscriber).
- Project Reactor implements Reactive Streams and abstracts stream definitions into two primary types, Flux and Mono, each of which offers several hundred operations.
- Spring leverages Reactor to create reactive controllers, repositories, REST clients, and other reactive framework support.

Developing reactive APIs

Now that you've had a good introduction to reactive programming and Project Reactor, you're ready to start applying those techniques in your Spring applications. In this chapter, we're going to revisit some of the controllers you wrote in chapter 7 to take advantage of Spring's reactive programming model.

More specifically, we're going to take a look at Spring's reactive web framework—Spring WebFlux. As you'll quickly discover, Spring WebFlux is remarkably similar to Spring MVC, making it easy to apply, along with what you already know about building REST APIs in Spring.

12.1 Working with Spring WebFlux

Typical servlet web frameworks, such as Spring MVC, are blocking and multithreaded in nature, using a single thread per connection. As requests are handled, a worker thread is pulled from a thread pool to process the request. Meanwhile, the request thread is blocked until it's notified by the worker thread that it's finished.

Consequently, blocking web frameworks won't scale effectively under heavy request volume. Latency in slow worker threads makes things even worse because it'll take longer for the worker thread to be returned to the pool, ready to handle another request. In some use cases, this arrangement is perfectly acceptable. In fact, this is largely how most web applications have been developed for well over a decade. But times are changing.

The clients of those web applications have grown from people occasionally viewing websites to people frequently consuming content and using applications that coordinate with HTTP APIs. And these days, the so-called *Internet of Things* (where humans aren't even involved) yields cars, jet engines, and other nontraditional clients constantly exchanging data with web APIs. With an increasing number of clients consuming web applications, scalability is more important than ever.

Asynchronous web frameworks, in contrast, achieve higher scalability with fewer threads—generally one per CPU core. By applying a technique known as *event looping* (as illustrated in figure 12.1), these frameworks are able to handle many requests per thread, making the per-connection cost more economical.

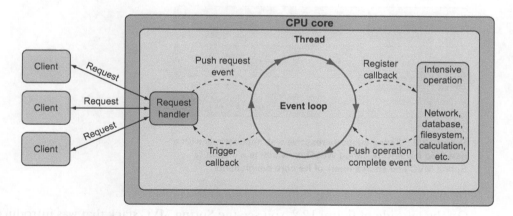

Figure 12.1 Asynchronous web frameworks apply event looping to handle more requests with fewer threads.

In an event loop, everything is handled as an event, including requests and callbacks from intensive operations like database and network operations. When a costly operation is needed, the event loop registers a callback for that operation to be performed in parallel, while it moves on to handle other events.

When the operation is complete, it's treated as an event by the event loop, the same as requests. As a result, asynchronous web frameworks are able to scale better under heavy request volume with fewer threads, resulting in reduced overhead for thread management.

Spring offers a nonblocking, asynchronous web framework based largely on its Project Reactor to address the need for greater scalability in web applications and APIs. Let's take a look at Spring WebFlux—a reactive web framework for Spring.

12.1.1   Introducing Spring WebFlux

As the Spring team was considering how to add a reactive programming model to the web layer, it quickly became apparent that it would be difficult to do so without a great deal of work in Spring MVC. That would involve branching code to decide whether or not to handle requests reactively. In essence, the result would be two web frameworks packaged as one, with `if` statements to separate the reactive from the nonreactive.

Instead of trying to shoehorn a reactive programming model into Spring MVC, the Spring team decided to create a separate reactive web framework, borrowing as much from Spring MVC as possible. Spring WebFlux is the result. Figure 12.2 illustrates the complete web development stack available in Spring.

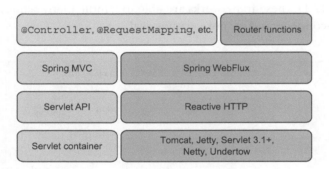

Figure 12.2   Spring supports reactive web applications with a new web framework called WebFlux, which is a sibling to Spring MVC and shares many of its core components.

On the left side of figure 12.2, you see the Spring MVC stack that was introduced in version 2.5 of the Spring Framework. Spring MVC (covered in chapters 2 and 7) sits atop the Java Servlet API, which requires a servlet container (such as Tomcat) to execute on.

By contrast, Spring WebFlux (on the right side) doesn't have ties to the Servlet API, so it builds on top of a Reactive HTTP API, which is a reactive approximation of the same functionality provided by the Servlet API. And because Spring WebFlux isn't coupled to the Servlet API, it doesn't require a servlet container to run on. Instead, it can run on any nonblocking web container including Netty, Undertow, Tomcat, Jetty, or any Servlet 3.1 or higher container.

What's most noteworthy about figure 12.2 is the top-left box, which represents the components that are common between Spring MVC and Spring WebFlux, primarily the annotations used to define controllers. Because Spring MVC and Spring WebFlux share the same annotations, Spring WebFlux is, in many ways, indistinguishable from Spring MVC.

The box in the top-right corner represents an alternative programming model that defines controllers with a functional programming paradigm instead of using annotations. We'll talk more about Spring's functional web programming model in section 12.2.

The most significant difference between Spring MVC and Spring WebFlux boils down to which dependency you add to your build. When working with Spring Web-Flux, you'll need to add the Spring Boot WebFlux starter dependency instead of the standard web starter (e.g., `spring-boot-starter-web`). In the project's pom.xml file, it looks like this:

```
<dependency>
    <groupId>org.springframework.boot</groupId>
    <artifactId>spring-boot-starter-webflux</artifactId>
</dependency>
```

> **NOTE** As with most of Spring Boot's starter dependencies, this starter can also be added to a project by checking the Reactive Web check box in the Initializr.

An interesting side effect of using WebFlux instead of Spring MVC is that the default embedded server for WebFlux is Netty instead of Tomcat. Netty is one of a handful of asynchronous, event-driven servers and is a natural fit for a reactive web framework like Spring WebFlux.

Aside from using a different starter dependency, Spring WebFlux controller methods usually accept and return reactive types, like `Mono` and `Flux`, instead of domain types and collections. Spring WebFlux controllers can also deal with RxJava types like `Observable`, `Single`, and `Completable`.

REACTIVE SPRING MVC?

Although Spring WebFlux controllers typically return `Mono` and `Flux`, that doesn't mean that Spring MVC doesn't get to have some fun with reactive types. Spring MVC controller methods can also return a `Mono` or `Flux`, if you'd like.

The difference is in how those types are used. Whereas Spring WebFlux is a truly reactive web framework, allowing for requests to be handled in an event loop, Spring MVC is servlet-based, relying on multithreading to handle multiple requests.

Let's put Spring WebFlux to work by rewriting some of Taco Cloud's API controllers to take advantage of Spring WebFlux.

12.1.2 *Writing reactive controllers*

You may recall that in chapter 7, you created a few controllers for Taco Cloud's REST API. Those controllers had request-handling methods that dealt with input and output in terms of domain types (such as TacoOrder and Taco) or collections of those domain types. As a reminder, consider the following snippet from TacoController that you wrote back in chapter 7:

```
@RestController
@RequestMapping(path="/api/tacos",
                produces="application/json")
@CrossOrigin(origins="*")
public class TacoController {

...

  @GetMapping(params="recent")
  public Iterable<Taco> recentTacos() {
    PageRequest page = PageRequest.of(
            0, 12, Sort.by("createdAt").descending());
    return tacoRepo.findAll(page).getContent();
  }

...

}
```

As written, the recentTacos() controller handles HTTP GET requests for /api/tacos?recent to return a list of recently created tacos. More specifically, it returns an Iterable of type Taco. That's primarily because that's what's returned from the repository's findAll() method, or, more accurately, from the getContent() method on the Page object returned from findAll().

That works fine, but Iterable isn't a reactive type. You won't be able to apply any reactive operations on it, nor can you let the framework take advantage of it as a reactive type to split any work over multiple threads. What you'd like is for recentTacos() to return a Flux<Taco>.

A simple but somewhat limited option here is to rewrite recentTacos() to convert the Iterable to a Flux. And, while you're at it, you can do away with the paging code and replace it with a call to take() on the Flux as follows:

```
@GetMapping(params="recent")
public Flux<Taco> recentTacos() {
  return Flux.fromIterable(tacoRepo.findAll()).take(12);
}
```

Using Flux.fromIterable(), you convert the Iterable<Taco> to a Flux<Taco>. And now that you're working with a Flux, you can use the take() operation to limit the returned Flux to 12 Taco objects at most. Not only is the code simpler, it also deals with a reactive Flux rather than a plain Iterable.

Writing reactive code has been a winning move so far. But it would be even better if the repository gave you a Flux to start with so that you wouldn't need to do the conversion. If that were the case, then recentTacos() could be written to look like this:

```
@GetMapping(params="recent")
public Flux<Taco> recentTacos() {
  return tacoRepo.findAll().take(12);
}
```

That's even better! Ideally, a reactive controller will be the tip of a stack that's reactive end to end, including controllers, repositories, the database, and any services that may sit in between. Such an end-to-end reactive stack is illustrated in figure 12.3.

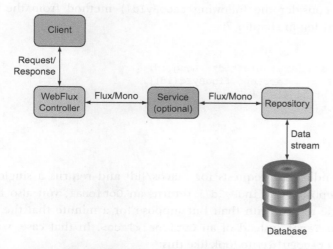

Figure 12.3   To maximize the benefit of a reactive web framework, it should be part of a full end-to-end reactive stack.

Such an end-to-end stack requires that the repository be written to return a Flux instead of an Iterable. We'll look into writing reactive repositories in the next chapter, but here's a sneak peek at what a reactive TacoRepository might look like:

```
package tacos.data;

import org.springframework.data.repository.reactive.ReactiveCrudRepository;
import tacos.Taco;

public interface TacoRepository
        extends ReactiveCrudRepository<Taco, Long> {
}
```

What's most important to note at this point, however, is that aside from working with a Flux instead of an Iterable, as well as how you obtain that Flux, the programming model for defining a reactive WebFlux controller is no different than for a nonreactive Spring MVC controller. Both are annotated with `@RestController` and a high-level `@RequestMapping` at the class level. And both have request-handling functions that are annotated with `@GetMapping` at the method level. It's truly a matter of what type the handler methods return.

Another important observation to make is that although you're getting a `Flux<Taco>` back from the repository, you can return it without calling `subscribe()`. Indeed, the framework will call `subscribe()` for you. This means that when a request for /api/tacos?recent is handled, the `recentTacos()` method will be called and will return before the data is even fetched from the database!

RETURNING SINGLE VALUES

As another example, consider the following `tacoById()` method from the `TacoController` as it was written in chapter 7:

```
@GetMapping("/{id}")
public Taco tacoById(@PathVariable("id") Long id) {
  Optional<Taco> optTaco = tacoRepo.findById(id);
  if (optTaco.isPresent()) {
    return optTaco.get();
  }
  return null;
}
```

Here, this method handles GET requests for /tacos/{id} and returns a single `Taco` object. Because the repository's `findById()` returns an `Optional`, you also had to write some clunky code to deal with that. But suppose for a minute that the `findById()` returns a `Mono<Taco>` instead of an `Optional<Taco>`. In that case, you can rewrite the controller's `tacoById()` to look like this:

```
@GetMapping("/{id}")
public Mono<Taco> tacoById(@PathVariable("id") Long id) {
  return tacoRepo.findById(id);
}
```

Wow! That's a lot simpler. What's more important, however, is that by returning a `Mono<Taco>` instead of a `Taco`, you're enabling Spring WebFlux to handle the response in a reactive manner. Consequently, your API will scale better in response to heavy loads.

WORKING WITH RXJAVA TYPES

It's worth pointing out that although Reactor types like `Flux` and `Mono` are a natural choice when working with Spring WebFlux, you can also choose to work with RxJava types like `Observable` and `Single`. For example, suppose there's a service sitting between `TacoController` and the backend repository that deals in terms of RxJava types. In that case, you might write the `recentTacos()` method like this:

```
@GetMapping(params = "recent")
public Observable<Taco> recentTacos() {
  return tacoService.getRecentTacos();
}
```

Similarly, the `tacoById()` method could be written to deal with an RxJava `Single` rather than a `Mono`, as shown next:

```
@GetMapping("/{id}")
public Single<Taco> tacoById(@PathVariable("id") Long id) {
  return tacoService.lookupTaco(id);
}
```

In addition, Spring WebFlux controller methods can also return RxJava's `Completable`, which is equivalent to a `Mono<Void>` in Reactor. WebFlux can also return RxJava's `Flowable` as an alternative to `Observable` or Reactor's `Flux`.

HANDLING INPUT REACTIVELY

So far, we've concerned ourselves only with what reactive types the controller methods return. But with Spring WebFlux, you can also accept a `Mono` or a `Flux` as an input to a handler method. To demonstrate, consider the original implementation of `postTaco()` from `TacoController`, shown here:

```
@PostMapping(consumes="application/json")
@ResponseStatus(HttpStatus.CREATED)
public Taco postTaco(@RequestBody Taco taco) {
  return tacoRepo.save(taco);
}
```

As originally written, `postTaco()` not only returns a simple `Taco` object but also accepts a `Taco` object that's bound to the content in the body of the request. This means that `postTaco()` can't be invoked until the request payload has been fully resolved and used to instantiate a `Taco` object. It also means `postTaco()` can't return until the blocking call to the repository's `save()` method returns. In short, the request is blocked twice: as it enters `postTaco()` and again, inside of `postTaco()`. But by applying a little reactive coding to `postTaco()`, shown next, you can make it a fully nonblocking, request-handling method:

```
@PostMapping(consumes = "application/json")
@ResponseStatus(HttpStatus.CREATED)
public Mono<Taco> postTaco(@RequestBody Mono<Taco> tacoMono) {
  return tacoRepo.saveAll(tacoMono).next();
}
```

Here, `postTaco()` accepts a `Mono<Taco>` and calls the repository's `saveAll()` method, which accepts any implementation of Reactive Streams `Publisher`, including `Mono` or `Flux`. The `saveAll()` method returns a `Flux<Taco>`, but because you started with a

Mono, you know there's at most one Taco that will be published by the Flux. You can therefore call next() to obtain a Mono<Taco> that will return from postTaco().

By accepting a Mono<Taco> as input, the method is invoked immediately without waiting for the Taco to be resolved from the request body. And because the repository is also reactive, it'll accept a Mono and immediately return a Flux<Taco>, from which you call next() and return the resulting Mono<Taco> . . . all before the request is even processed!

Alternatively, you could also implement postTaco() like this:

```
@PostMapping(consumes = "application/json")
@ResponseStatus(HttpStatus.CREATED)
public Mono<Taco> postTaco(@RequestBody Mono<Taco> tacoMono) {
  return tacoMono.flatMap(tacoRepo::save);
}
```

This approach flips things around so that the tacoMono is the driver of the action. The Taco contained within tacoMono is handed to the repository's save() method via flatMap(), resulting in a new Mono<Taco> that is returned.

Either way works well, and there are probably several other ways that you could write postTaco(). Choose whichever way works best and makes the most sense to you.

Spring WebFlux is a fantastic alternative to Spring MVC, offering the option of writing reactive web applications using the same development model as Spring MVC. But Spring has another new trick up its sleeve. Let's take a look at how to create reactive APIs using Spring's functional programming style.

12.2   *Defining functional request handlers*

Spring MVC's annotation-based programming model has been around since Spring 2.5 and is widely popular. It comes with a few downsides, however.

First, any annotation-based programming involves a split in the definition of *what* the annotation is supposed to do and *how* it's supposed to do it. Annotations themselves define the what; the how is defined elsewhere in the framework code. This division complicates the programming model when it comes to any sort of customization or extension because such changes require working in code that's external to the annotation. Moreover, debugging such code is tricky because you can't set a breakpoint on an annotation.

Also, as Spring continues to grow in popularity, developers new to Spring from other languages and frameworks may find annotation-based Spring MVC (and Web-Flux) quite unlike what they already know. As an alternative to WebFlux, Spring offers a functional programming model for defining reactive APIs.

This new programming model is used more like a library and less like a framework, letting you map requests to handler code without annotations. Writing an API using Spring's functional programming model involves the following four primary types:

- *RequestPredicate*—Declares the kind(s) of requests that will be handled
- *RouterFunction*—Declares how a matching request should be routed to the handler code
- *ServerRequest*—Represents an HTTP request, including access to header and body information
- *ServerResponse*—Represents an HTTP response, including header and body information

As a simple example that pulls all of these types together, consider the following Hello World example:

```
package hello;

import static org.springframework.web
                .reactive.function.server.RequestPredicates.GET;
import static org.springframework.web
                .reactive.function.server.RouterFunctions.route;
import static org.springframework.web
                .reactive.function.server.ServerResponse.ok;
import static reactor.core.publisher.Mono.just;
import org.springframework.context.annotation.Bean;
import org.springframework.context.annotation.Configuration;
import org.springframework.web.reactive.function.server.RouterFunction;

@Configuration
public class RouterFunctionConfig {

  @Bean
  public RouterFunction<?> helloRouterFunction() {
    return route(GET("/hello"),
        request -> ok().body(just("Hello World!"), String.class))
      ;
  }

}
```

The first thing to notice is that you've chosen to statically import a few helper classes that you can use to create the aforementioned functional types. You've also statically imported Mono to keep the rest of the code easier to read and understand.

In this @Configuration class, you have a single @Bean method of type Router-Function<?>. As mentioned, a RouterFunction declares mappings between one or more RequestPredicate objects and the functions that will handle the matching request(s).

The route() method from RouterFunctions accepts two parameters: a Request-Predicate and a function to handle matching requests. In this case, the GET() method from RequestPredicates declares a RequestPredicate that matches HTTP GET requests for the /hello path.

As for the handler function, it's written as a lambda, although it can also be a method reference. Although it isn't explicitly declared, the handler lambda accepts a

ServerRequest as a parameter. It returns a ServerResponse using ok() from Server-Response and body() from BodyBuilder, which was returned from ok(). This was done to create a response with an HTTP 200 (OK) status code and a body payload that says "Hello World!"

As written, the helloRouterFunction() method declares a RouterFunction that handles only a single kind of request. But if you need to handle a different kind of request, you don't have to write another @Bean method, although you can. You only need to call andRoute() to declare another RequestPredicate to function mapping. For example, here's how you might add another handler for GET requests for /bye:

```
@Bean
public RouterFunction<?> helloRouterFunction() {
  return route(GET("/hello"),
      request -> ok().body(just("Hello World!"), String.class))
      .andRoute(GET("/bye"),
      request -> ok().body(just("See ya!"), String.class))
    ;
}
```

Hello World samples are fine for dipping your toes into something new. But let's amp it up a bit and see how to use Spring's functional web programming model to handle requests that resemble real-world scenarios.

To demonstrate how the functional programming model might be used in a real-world application, let's reinvent the functionality of TacoController in the functional style. The following configuration class is a functional analog to TacoController:

```
package tacos.web.api;

import static org.springframework.web.reactive.function.server
    .RequestPredicates.GET;
import static org.springframework.web.reactive.function.server
    .RequestPredicates.POST;
import static org.springframework.web.reactive.function.server
    .RequestPredicates.queryParam;
import static org.springframework.web.reactive.function.server
    .RouterFunctions.route;

import java.net.URI;

import org.springframework.beans.factory.annotation.Autowired;
import org.springframework.context.annotation.Bean;
import org.springframework.context.annotation.Configuration;
import org.springframework.web.reactive.function.server.RouterFunction;
import org.springframework.web.reactive.function.server.ServerRequest;
import org.springframework.web.reactive.function.server.ServerResponse;

import reactor.core.publisher.Mono;
import tacos.Taco;
import tacos.data.TacoRepository;
```

```java
@Configuration
public class RouterFunctionConfig {

  @Autowired
  private TacoRepository tacoRepo;

  @Bean
  public RouterFunction<?> routerFunction() {
    return route(GET("/api/tacos").
            and(queryParam("recent", t->t != null )),
            this::recents)
        .andRoute(POST("/api/tacos"), this::postTaco);
  }

  public Mono<ServerResponse> recents(ServerRequest request) {
    return ServerResponse.ok()
        .body(tacoRepo.findAll().take(12), Taco.class);
  }

  public Mono<ServerResponse> postTaco(ServerRequest request) {
    return request.bodyToMono(Taco.class)
        .flatMap(taco -> tacoRepo.save(taco))
        .flatMap(savedTaco -> {
            return ServerResponse
                .created(URI.create(
                    "http://localhost:8080/api/tacos/" +
                    savedTaco.getId()))
                .body(savedTaco, Taco.class);
        });
  }
}
```

As you can see, the routerFunction() method declares a RouterFunction<?> bean, like the Hello World example. But it differs in what types of requests are handled and how they're handled. In this case, the RouterFunction is created to handle GET requests for /api/tacos?recent and POST requests for /api/tacos.

What stands out even more is that the routes are handled by method references. Lambdas are great when the behavior behind a RouterFunction is relatively simple and brief. In many cases, however, it's better to extract that functionality into a separate method (or even into a separate method in a separate class) to maintain code readability.

For your needs, GET requests for /api/tacos?recent will be handled by the recents() method. It uses the injected TacoRepository to fetch a Flux<Taco>, from which it takes 12 items. It then wraps the Flux<Taco> in a Mono<ServerResponse> so that we can ensure that the response has an HTTP 200 (OK) status by calling ok() on the ServerResponse. It's important to understand that even though up to 12 tacos are returned, there is only one server response—that's why it is returned in a Mono and not a Flux. Internally, Spring will still stream the Flux<Taco> to the client as a Flux.

Meanwhile, POST requests for /api/tacos are handled by the postTaco() method, which extracts a Mono<Taco> from the body of the incoming ServerRequest. The postTaco() method then uses a series of flatMap() operations to save that taco to the TacoRepository and create a ServerResponse with an HTTP 201 (CREATED) status code and the saved Taco object in the response body.

The flatMap() operations are used to ensure that at each step in the flow, the result of the mapping is wrapped in a Mono, starting with a Mono<Taco> after the first flatMap() and ultimately ending with a Mono<ServerResponse> that is returned from postTaco().

12.3   Testing reactive controllers

When it comes to testing reactive controllers, Spring hasn't left us in the lurch. Indeed, Spring has introduced WebTestClient, a new test utility that makes it easy to write tests for reactive controllers written with Spring WebFlux. To see how to write tests with WebTestClient, let's start by using it to test the recentTacos() method from the TacoController that you wrote in section 12.1.2.

12.3.1   Testing GET requests

One thing we'd like to assert about the recentTacos() method is that if an HTTP GET request is issued for the path /api/tacos?recent, then the response will contain a JSON payload with no more than 12 tacos. The test class in the next listing is a good start.

> **Listing 12.1   Using WebTestClient to test TacoController**

```
package tacos.web.api;
import static org.mockito.ArgumentMatchers.any;
import static org.mockito.Mockito.when;
import java.util.ArrayList;
import java.util.List;
import org.junit.jupiter.api.Test;
import org.mockito.Mockito;
import org.springframework.http.MediaType;
import org.springframework.test.web.reactive.server.WebTestClient;
import reactor.core.publisher.Flux;
import reactor.core.publisher.Mono;
import tacos.Ingredient;
import tacos.Ingredient.Type;
import tacos.Taco;
import tacos.data.TacoRepository;

public class TacoControllerTest {

  @Test
  public void shouldReturnRecentTacos() {
    Taco[] tacos = {
        testTaco(1L), testTaco(2L),
        testTaco(3L), testTaco(4L),            ◄───┐  Creates some
        testTaco(5L), testTaco(6L),                │  test data
        testTaco(7L), testTaco(8L),
```

```
        testTaco(9L), testTaco(10L),
        testTaco(11L), testTaco(12L),
        testTaco(13L), testTaco(14L),
        testTaco(15L), testTaco(16L)};
    Flux<Taco> tacoFlux = Flux.just(tacos);

    TacoRepository tacoRepo = Mockito.mock(TacoRepository.class);
    when(tacoRepo.findAll()).thenReturn(tacoFlux);              ◄─┐ Mocks the
                                                                 │ TacoRepository
    WebTestClient testClient = WebTestClient.bindToController(
        new TacoController(tacoRepo))
        .build();                     ◄──────── Creates a WebTestClient

    testClient.get().uri("/api/tacos?recent")     ─┐ Requests
        .exchange()                                ◄─┘ recent tacos
        .expectStatus().isOk()              ◄──┐ Verifies the expected
        .expectBody()                          ┘ response
        .jsonPath("$").isArray()
        .jsonPath("$").isNotEmpty()
        .jsonPath("$[0].id").isEqualTo(tacos[0].getId().toString())
        .jsonPath("$[0].name").isEqualTo("Taco 1")
        .jsonPath("$[1].id").isEqualTo(tacos[1].getId().toString())
        .jsonPath("$[1].name").isEqualTo("Taco 2")
        .jsonPath("$[11].id").isEqualTo(tacos[11].getId().toString())
        .jsonPath("$[11].name").isEqualTo("Taco 12")
        .jsonPath("$[12]").doesNotExist();
    }
    ...

}
```

The first thing that the shouldReturnRecentTacos() method does is set up test data in the form of a Flux<Taco>. This Flux is then provided as the return value from the findAll() method of a mock TacoRepository.

With regard to the Taco objects that will be published by Flux, they're created with a utility method named testTaco() that, when given a number, produces a Taco object whose ID and name are based on that number. The testTaco() method is implemented as follows:

```
private Taco testTaco(Long number) {
  Taco taco = new Taco();
  taco.setId(number != null ? number.toString(): "TESTID");
  taco.setName("Taco " + number);
  List<Ingredient> ingredients = new ArrayList<>();
  ingredients.add(
      new Ingredient("INGA", "Ingredient A", Type.WRAP));
  ingredients.add(
      new Ingredient("INGB", "Ingredient B", Type.PROTEIN));
  taco.setIngredients(ingredients);
  return taco;
}
```

For the sake of simplicity, all test tacos will have the same two ingredients. But their ID and name will be determined by the given number.

Meanwhile, back in the `shouldReturnRecentTacos()` method, you instantiated a `TacoController`, injecting the mock `TacoRepository` into the constructor. The controller is given to `WebTestClient.bindToController()` to create an instance of `WebTestClient`.

With all of the setup complete, you're now ready to use `WebTestClient` to submit a GET request to /api/tacos?recent and verify that the response meets your expectations. Calling `get().uri("/api/tacos?recent")` describes the request you want to issue. Then a call to `exchange()` submits the request, which will be handled by the controller that `WebTestClient` is bound to—the `TacoController`.

Finally, you can affirm that the response is as expected. By calling `expectStatus()`, you assert that the response has an HTTP 200 (OK) status code. After that, you see several calls to `jsonPath()` that assert that the JSON in the response body has the values it should have. The final assertion checks that the 12th element (in a zero-based array) is nonexistent, because the result should never have more than 12 elements.

If the JSON returns are complex, with a lot of data or highly nested data, it can be tedious to use `jsonPath()`. In fact, I left out many of the calls to `jsonPath()` in listing 12.1 to conserve space. For those cases where it may be clumsy to use `jsonPath()`, `WebTestClient` offers `json()`, which accepts a `String` parameter containing the JSON to compare the response against.

For example, suppose that you've created the complete response JSON in a file named recent-tacos.json and placed it in the classpath under the path /tacos. Then you can rewrite the `WebTestClient` assertions to look like this:

```
ClassPathResource recentsResource =
    new ClassPathResource("/tacos/recent-tacos.json");
String recentsJson = StreamUtils.copyToString(
    recentsResource.getInputStream(), Charset.defaultCharset());

testClient.get().uri("/api/tacos?recent")
  .accept(MediaType.APPLICATION_JSON)
  .exchange()
  .expectStatus().isOk()
  .expectBody()
    .json(recentsJson);
```

Because `json()` accepts a `String`, you must first load the classpath resource into a `String`. Thankfully, Spring's `StreamUtils` makes this easy with `copyToString()`. The `String` that's returned from `copyToString()` will contain the entire JSON you expect in the response to your request. Giving it to the `json()` method ensures that the controller is producing the correct output.

Another option offered by `WebTestClient` allows you to compare the response body with a list of values. The `expectBodyList()` method accepts either a `Class` or a `ParameterizedTypeReference` indicating the type of elements in the list and returns a ListBodySpec object to make assertions against. Using expectBodyList(), you can rewrite the test to use a subset of the same test data you used to create the mock TacoRepository, as shown here:

```
testClient.get().uri("/api/tacos?recent")
  .accept(MediaType.APPLICATION_JSON)
  .exchange()
  .expectStatus().isOk()
  .expectBodyList(Taco.class)
    .contains(Arrays.copyOf(tacos, 12));
```

Here you assert that the response body contains a list that has the same elements as the first 12 elements of the original Taco array you created at the beginning of the test method.

12.3.2 Testing POST requests

WebTestClient can do more than just test GET requests against controllers. It can also be used to test any kind of HTTP method. Table 12.1 maps HTTP methods to Web-TestClient methods.

Table 12.1 WebTestClient tests any kind of request against Spring WebFlux controllers.

HTTP method	WebTestClient method
GET	.get()
POST	.post()
PUT	.put()
PATCH	.patch()
DELETE	.delete()
HEAD	.head()

As an example of testing another HTTP method request against a Spring WebFlux controller, let's look at another test against TacoController. This time, you'll write a test of your API's taco creation endpoint by submitting a POST request to /api/tacos as follows:

```
@SuppressWarnings("unchecked")
@Test
public void shouldSaveATaco() {
  TacoRepository tacoRepo = Mockito.mock(          ← Mocks the
          TacoRepository.class);                      TacoRepository

  WebTestClient testClient = WebTestClient.bindToController(     ←
      new TacoController(tacoRepo)).build();

                                              Creates a WebTestClient
```

```
Mono<Taco> unsavedTacoMono = Mono.just(testTaco(1L));
Taco savedTaco = testTaco(1L);
Flux<Taco> savedTacoMono = Flux.just(savedTaco);          Sets up test data

when(tacoRepo.saveAll(any(Mono.class))).thenReturn(savedTacoMono);  ⟵

                                POSTs a taco
testClient.post()          ⟵
    .uri("/api/tacos")
    .contentType(MediaType.APPLICATION_JSON)
    .body(unsavedTacoMono, Taco.class)
    .exchange()
    .expectStatus().isCreated()      ⟵    Verifies the
    .expectBody(Taco.class)                response
    .isEqualTo(savedTaco);
}
```

As with the previous test method, shouldSaveATaco() starts by mocking Taco-Repository, building a WebTestClient that's bound to the controller, and setting up some test data. Then, it uses the WebTestClient to submit a POST request to /api/tacos, with a body of type application/json and a payload that's a JSON-serialized form of the Taco in the unsaved Mono. After performing exchange(), the test asserts that the response has an HTTP 201 (CREATED) status and a payload in the body equal to the saved Taco object.

12.3.3 *Testing with a live server*

The tests you've written so far have relied on a mock implementation of the Spring WebFlux framework so that a real server wouldn't be necessary. But you may need to test a WebFlux controller in the context of a server like Netty or Tomcat and maybe with a repository or other dependencies. That is to say, you may want to write an integration test.

   To write a WebTestClient integration test, you start by annotating the test class with @RunWith and @SpringBootTest like any other Spring Boot integration test, as shown here:

```
package tacos;

import java.io.IOException;
import org.junit.jupiter.api.Test;
import org.junit.jupiter.api.extension.ExtendWith;
import org.springframework.beans.factory.annotation.Autowired;
import org.springframework.boot.test.context.SpringBootTest;
import org.springframework.boot.test.context.SpringBootTest.WebEnvironment;
import org.springframework.http.MediaType;
import org.springframework.test.context.junit.jupiter.SpringExtension;
import org.springframework.test.web.reactive.server.WebTestClient;

@ExtendWith(SpringExtension.class)
@SpringBootTest(webEnvironment=WebEnvironment.RANDOM_PORT)
public class TacoControllerWebTest {
```

```
@Autowired
private WebTestClient testClient;

}
```

By setting the `webEnvironment` attribute to `WebEnvironment.RANDOM_PORT`, you're asking Spring to start a running server listening on a randomly chosen port.[1]

You'll notice that you've also autowired a `WebTestClient` into the test class. This not only means that you'll no longer have to create one in your test methods but also that you won't need to specify a full URL when making requests. That's because the `WebTestClient` will be rigged to know which port the test server is running on. Now you can rewrite `shouldReturnRecentTacos()` as an integration test that uses the autowired `WebTestClient` as follows:

```
@Test
public void shouldReturnRecentTacos() throws IOException {
  testClient.get().uri("/api/tacos?recent")
    .accept(MediaType.APPLICATION_JSON).exchange()
    .expectStatus().isOk()
    .expectBody()
        .jsonPath("$").isArray()
        .jsonPath("$.length()").isEqualTo(3)
        .jsonPath("$[?(@.name == 'Carnivore')]").exists()
        .jsonPath("$[?(@.name == 'Bovine Bounty')]").exists()
        .jsonPath("$[?(@.name == 'Veg-Out')]").exists();
}
```

You've no doubt noticed that this new version of `shouldReturnRecentTacos()` has much less code. You no longer need to create a `WebTestClient` because you'll be making use of the autowired instance. And you don't have to mock `TacoRepository` because Spring will create an instance of `TacoController` and inject it with a real `TacoRepository`. In this new version of the test method, you use JSONPath expressions to verify values served from the database.

`WebTestClient` is useful when, in the course of a test, you need to consume the API exposed by a WebFlux controller. But what about when your application itself consumes some other API? Let's turn our attention to the client side of Spring's reactive web story and see how `WebClient` provides a REST client that deals in reactive types such as `Mono` and `Flux`.

12.4 Consuming REST APIs reactively

In chapter 8, you used `RestTemplate` to make client requests to the Taco Cloud API. `RestTemplate` is an old-timer, having been introduced in Spring version 3.0. In its time, it has been used to make countless requests on behalf of the applications that employ it.

---

[1] You could have also set `webEnvironment` to `WebEnvironment.DEFINED_PORT` and specified a port with the properties attribute, but that's generally inadvisable. Doing so opens the risk of a port clash with a concurrently running server.

But all of the methods provided by RestTemplate deal in nonreactive domain types and collections. This means that if you want to work with a response's data in a reactive way, you'll need to wrap it with a Flux or Mono. And if you already have a Flux or Mono and you want to send it in a POST or PUT request, then you'll need to extract the data into a nonreactive type before making the request.

It would be nice if there was a way to use RestTemplate natively with reactive types. Fear not. Spring offers WebClient as a reactive alternative to RestTemplate. WebClient lets you both send and receive reactive types when making requests to external APIs.

Using WebClient is quite different from using RestTemplate. Rather than having several methods to handle different kinds of requests, WebClient has a fluent builder-style interface that lets you describe and send requests. The general usage pattern for working with WebClient follows:

- Create an instance of WebClient (or inject a WebClient bean)
- Specify the HTTP method of the request to send
- Specify the URI and any headers that should be in the request
- Submit the request
- Consume the response

Let's look at several examples of WebClient in action, starting with how to use Web-Client to send HTTP GET requests.

12.4.1 *GETting resources*

As an example of WebClient usage, suppose that you need to fetch an Ingredient object by its ID from the Taco Cloud API. Using RestTemplate, you might use the get-ForObject() method. But with WebClient, you build the request, retrieve a response, and then extract a Mono that publishes the Ingredient object, as shown here:

```
Mono<Ingredient> ingredient = WebClient.create()
    .get()
    .uri("http://localhost:8080/ingredients/{id}", ingredientId)
    .retrieve()
    .bodyToMono(Ingredient.class);

ingredient.subscribe(i -> { ... });
```

Here you create a new WebClient instance with create(). Then you use get() and uri() to define a GET request to http://localhost:8080/ingredients/{id}, where the {id} placeholder will be replaced by the value in ingredientId. The retrieve() method executes the request. Finally, a call to bodyToMono() extracts the response's body payload into a Mono<Ingredient> on which you can continue applying additional Mono operations.

To apply additional operations on the Mono returned from bodyToMono(), it's important to subscribe to it before the request will even be sent. Making requests that can return a collection of values is easy. For example, the following snippet of code fetches all ingredients:

```
Flux<Ingredient> ingredients = WebClient.create()
    .get()
    .uri("http://localhost:8080/ingredients")
    .retrieve()
    .bodyToFlux(Ingredient.class);

ingredients.subscribe(i -> { ... });
```

For the most part, fetching multiple items is the same as making a request for a single item. The big difference is that instead of using bodyToMono() to extract the response's body into a Mono, you use bodyToFlux() to extract it into a Flux.

As with bodyToMono(), the Flux returned from bodyToFlux() hasn't yet been subscribed to. This allows additional operations (filters, maps, and so forth) to be applied to the Flux before the data starts flowing through it. Therefore, it's important to subscribe to the resulting Flux, or else the request will never even be sent.

MAKING REQUESTS WITH A BASE URI

You may find yourself using a common base URI for many different requests. In that case, it can be useful to create a WebClient bean with a base URI and inject it anywhere it's needed. Such a bean could be declared like this (in any @Configuration-annotated class):

```
@Bean
public WebClient webClient() {
  return WebClient.create("http://localhost:8080");
}
```

Then, anywhere you need to make requests using that base URI, the WebClient bean can be injected and used like this:

```
@Autowired
WebClient webClient;

public Mono<Ingredient> getIngredientById(String ingredientId) {
  Mono<Ingredient> ingredient = webClient
    .get()
    .uri("/ingredients/{id}", ingredientId)
    .retrieve()
    .bodyToMono(Ingredient.class);

  ingredient.subscribe(i -> { ... });
}
```

Because the WebClient had already been created, you're able to get right to work by calling get(). As for the URI, you need to specify only the path relative to the base URI when calling uri().

TIMING OUT ON LONG-RUNNING REQUESTS

One thing that you can count on is that networks aren't always reliable or as fast as you'd expect them to be. Or maybe a remote server is sluggish in handling a request. Ideally, a request to a remote service will return in a reasonable amount of time. But if not, it would be great if the client didn't get stuck waiting on a response for too long.

To avoid having your client requests held up by a sluggish network or service, you can use the `timeout()` method from `Flux` or `Mono` to put a limit on how long you'll wait for data to be published. As an example, consider how you might use `timeout()` when fetching ingredient data, as shown in the next code sample:

```
Flux<Ingredient> ingredients = webclient
    .get()
    .uri("/ingredients")
    .retrieve()
    .bodyToFlux(Ingredient.class);

ingredients
  .timeout(Duration.ofSeconds(1))
  .subscribe(
      i -> { ... },
      e -> {
        // handle timeout error
      });
```

As you can see, before subscribing to the `Flux`, you called `timeout()`, specifying a duration of 1 second. If the request can be fulfilled in less than 1 second, then there's no problem. But if the request is taking longer than 1 second, it'll time-out, and the error handler given as the second parameter to `subscribe()` is invoked.

12.4.2 *Sending resources*

Sending data with `WebClient` isn't much different from receiving data. As an example, let's say that you have a `Mono<Ingredient>` and want to send a `POST` request with the `Ingredient` that's published by the `Mono` to the URI with a relative path of /ingredients. All you must do is use the `post()` method instead of `get()` and specify that the `Mono` is to be used to populate the request body by calling `body()` as follows:

```
Mono<Ingredient> ingredientMono = Mono.just(
    new Ingredient("INGC", "Ingredient C", Ingredient.Type.VEGGIES));

Mono<Ingredient> result = webClient
  .post()
  .uri("/ingredients")
  .body(ingredientMono, Ingredient.class)
  .retrieve()
  .bodyToMono(Ingredient.class);

result.subscribe(i -> { ... });
```

If you don't have a Mono or Flux to send, but instead have the raw domain object on hand, you can use bodyValue(). For example, suppose that instead of a Mono <Ingredient>, you have an Ingredient that you want to send in the request body, as shown next:

```
Ingredient ingredient = ...;

Mono<Ingredient> result = webClient
  .post()
  .uri("/ingredients")
  .bodyValue(ingredient)
  .retrieve()
  .bodyToMono(Ingredient.class);

result.subscribe(i -> { ... });
```

Instead of a POST request, if you want to update an Ingredient with a PUT request, you call put() instead of post() and adjust the URI path accordingly, like so:

```
Mono<Void> result = webClient
  .put()
  .uri("/ingredients/{id}", ingredient.getId())
  .bodyValue(ingredient)
  .retrieve()
  .bodyToMono(Void.class);

result.subscribe();
```

PUT requests typically have empty response payloads, so you must ask bodyToMono() to return a Mono of type Void. On subscribing to that Mono, the request will be sent.

12.4.3 Deleting resources

WebClient also allows the removal of resources by way of its delete() method. For example, the following code deletes an ingredient for a given ID:

```
Mono<Void> result = webClient
  .delete()
  .uri("/ingredients/{id}", ingredientId)
  .retrieve()
  .bodyToMono(Void.class);

result.subscribe();
```

As with PUT requests, DELETE requests don't typically have a payload. Once again, you return and subscribe to a Mono<Void> to send the request.

12.4.4 Handling errors

All of the WebClient examples thus far have assumed a happy ending; there were no responses with 400-level or 500-level status codes. Should either kind of error statuses be returned, WebClient will log the failure and move on without incident.

If you need to handle such errors, then a call to onStatus() can be used to specify how various HTTP status codes should be dealt with. onStatus() accepts two functions: a predicate function, which is used to match the HTTP status, and a function that, given a ClientResponse object, returns a Mono<Throwable>.

To demonstrate how onStatus() can be used to create a custom error handler, consider the following use of WebClient that aims to fetch an ingredient given its ID:

```
Mono<Ingredient> ingredientMono = webClient
    .get()
    .uri("http://localhost:8080/ingredients/{id}", ingredientId)
    .retrieve()
    .bodyToMono(Ingredient.class);
```

As long as the value in ingredientId matches a known ingredient resource, then the resulting Mono will publish the Ingredient object when it's subscribed to. But what would happen if there were no matching ingredient?

When subscribing to a Mono or Flux that might end in an error, it's important to register an error consumer as well as a data consumer in the call to subscribe() as follows:

```
ingredientMono.subscribe(
    ingredient -> {
      // handle the ingredient data
      ...
    },
    error-> {
      // deal with the error
      ...
    });
```

If the ingredient resource is found, then the first lambda (the data consumer) given to subscribe() is invoked with the matching Ingredient object. But if it isn't found, then the request responds with a status code of HTTP 404 (NOT FOUND), which results in the second lambda (the error consumer) being given by default a Web-ClientResponseException.

The biggest problem with WebClientResponseException is that it's rather nonspecific as to what may have gone wrong to cause the Mono to fail. Its name suggests that there was an error in the response from a request made by WebClient, but you'll need to dig into WebClientResponseException to know what went wrong. And in any event, it would be nice if the exception given to the error consumer were more domain-specific instead of WebClient-specific.

By adding a custom error handler, you can provide code that translates a status code to a Throwable of your own choosing. Let's say that you want a failed request for an ingredient resource to cause the Mono to complete in error with an Unknown-IngredientException. You can add the following call to onStatus() after the call to retrieve() to achieve that:

```
Mono<Ingredient> ingredientMono = webClient
    .get()
    .uri("http://localhost:8080/ingredients/{id}", ingredientId)
    .retrieve()
    .onStatus(HttpStatus::is4xxClientError,
            response -> Mono.just(new UnknownIngredientException())))
    .bodyToMono(Ingredient.class);
```

The first argument in the onStatus() call is a predicate that's given an HttpStatus and returns true if the status code is one you want to handle. And if the status code matches, then the response will be returned to the function in the second argument to handle as it sees fit, ultimately returning a Mono of type Throwable.

In the example, if the status code is a 400-level status code (e.g., a client error), then a Mono will be returned with an UnknownIngredientException. This causes the ingredientMono to fail with that exception.

Note that HttpStatus::is4xxClientError is a method reference to the is4xx-ClientError method of HttpStatus. It's this method that will be invoked on the given HttpStatus object. If you want, you can use another method on HttpStatus as a method reference; or you can provide your own function in the form of a lambda or method reference that returns a boolean.

For example, you can get even more precise in your error handling, checking specifically for an HTTP 404 (NOT FOUND) status by changing the call to onStatus() to look like this:

```
Mono<Ingredient> ingredientMono = webClient
    .get()
    .uri("http://localhost:8080/ingredients/{id}", ingredientId)
    .retrieve()
    .onStatus(status -> status == HttpStatus.NOT_FOUND,
            response -> Mono.just(new UnknownIngredientException())))
    .bodyToMono(Ingredient.class);
```

It's also worth noting that you can have as many calls to onStatus() as you need to handle any variety of HTTP status codes that might come back in the response.

12.4.5 Exchanging requests

Up to this point, you've used the retrieve() method to signify sending a request when working with WebClient. In those cases, the retrieve() method returned an object of type ResponseSpec, through which you were able to handle the response with calls to methods such as onStatus(), bodyToFlux(), and bodyToMono(). Working with ResponseSpec is fine for simple cases, but it's limited in a few ways. If you need access to the response's headers or cookie values, for example, then ResponseSpec isn't going to work for you.

When ResponseSpec comes up short, you can try calling exchangeToMono() or exchangeToFlux() instead of retrieve(). The exchangeToMono() method returns a Mono of type ClientResponse, on which you can apply reactive operations to inspect and use data from the entire response, including the payload, headers, and cookies. The exchangeToFlux() method works much the same way but returns a Flux of type ClientResponse for working with multiple data items in the response.

Before we look at what makes exchangeToMono() and exchangeToFlux() different from retrieve(), let's start by looking at how similar they are. The following snippet of code uses a WebClient and exchangeToMono() to fetch a single ingredient by the ingredient's ID:

```
Mono<Ingredient> ingredientMono = webClient
    .get()
    .uri("http://localhost:8080/ingredients/{id}", ingredientId)
    .exchangeToMono(cr -> cr.bodyToMono(Ingredient.class));
```

This is roughly equivalent to the next example that uses retrieve():

```
Mono<Ingredient> ingredientMono = webClient
    .get()
    .uri("http://localhost:8080/ingredients/{id}", ingredientId)
    .retrieve()
    .bodyToMono(Ingredient.class);
```

In the exchangeToMono() example, rather than use the ResponseSpec object's body-ToMono() to get a Mono<Ingredient>, you get a Mono<ClientResponse> on which you can apply a flat-mapping function to map the ClientResponse to a Mono<Ingredient>, which is flattened into the resulting Mono.

Let's see what makes exchangeToMono() different from retrieve(). Let's suppose that the response from the request might include a header named X_UNAVAILABLE with a value of true to indicate that (for some reason) the ingredient in question is unavailable. And for the sake of discussion, suppose that if that header exists, you want the resulting Mono to be empty—to not return anything. You can achieve this scenario by adding another call to flatMap(), but now it's simpler with a WebClient call like this:

```
Mono<Ingredient> ingredientMono = webClient
    .get()
    .uri("http://localhost:8080/ingredients/{id}", ingredientId)
    .exchangeToMono(cr -> {
      if (cr.headers().header("X_UNAVAILABLE").contains("true")) {
        return Mono.empty();
      }
      return Mono.just(cr);
    })
    .flatMap(cr -> cr.bodyToMono(Ingredient.class));
```

The new flatMap() call inspects the given ClientRequest object's headers, looking for a header named X_UNAVAILABLE with a value of true. If found, it returns an empty Mono. Otherwise, it returns a new Mono that contains the ClientResponse. In either event, the Mono returned will be flattened into the Mono that the next flatMap() call will operate on.

12.5 Securing reactive web APIs

For as long as there has been Spring Security (and even before that, when it was known as Acegi Security), its web security model has been built around servlet filters. After all, it just makes sense. If you need to intercept a request bound for a servlet-based web framework to ensure that the requester has proper authority, a servlet filter is an obvious choice. But Spring WebFlux puts a kink into that approach.

When writing a web application with Spring WebFlux, there's no guarantee that servlets are even involved. In fact, a reactive web application is debatably more likely to be built on Netty or some other nonservlet server. Does this mean that the servlet filter–based Spring Security can't be used to secure Spring WebFlux applications?

It's true that using servlet filters isn't an option when securing a Spring WebFlux application. But Spring Security is still up to the task. Starting with version 5.0.0, you can use Spring Security to secure both servlet-based Spring MVC and reactive Spring WebFlux applications. It does this using Spring's `WebFilter`, a Spring-specific analog to servlet filters that doesn't demand dependence on the servlet API.

What's even more remarkable, though, is that the configuration model for reactive Spring Security isn't much different from what you saw in chapter 4. In fact, unlike Spring WebFlux, which has a separate dependency from Spring MVC, Spring Security comes as the same Spring Boot security starter, regardless of whether you intend to use it to secure a Spring MVC web application or one written with Spring WebFlux. As a reminder, here's what the security starter looks like:

```
<dependency>
  <groupId>org.springframework.boot</groupId>
  <artifactId>spring-boot-starter-security</artifactId>
</dependency>
```

That said, a few small differences exist between Spring Security's reactive and nonreactive configuration models. It's worth taking a quick look at how the two configuration models compare.

12.5.1 Configuring reactive web security

As a reminder, configuring Spring Security to secure a Spring MVC web application typically involves creating a new configuration class that extends `WebSecurity-ConfigurerAdapter` and is annotated with `@EnableWebSecurity`. Such a configuration class would override a `configuration()` method to specify web security specifics such as what authorizations are required for certain request paths. The following simple Spring Security configuration class serves as a reminder of how to configure security for a nonreactive Spring MVC application:

```
@Configuration
@EnableWebSecurity
public class SecurityConfig extends WebSecurityConfigurerAdapter {
```

```
@Override
protected void configure(HttpSecurity http) throws Exception {
  http
    .authorizeRequests()
      .antMatchers("/api/tacos", "/orders").hasAuthority("USER")
      .antMatchers("/**").permitAll();
}

}
```

Now let's see what this same configuration might look like for a reactive Spring Web-Flux application. The following listing shows a reactive security configuration class that's roughly equivalent to the simple security configuration from before.

Listing 12.2   Configuring Spring Security for a Spring WebFlux application

```
@Configuration
@EnableWebFluxSecurity
public class SecurityConfig {

  @Bean
  public SecurityWebFilterChain securityWebFilterChain(
                                    ServerHttpSecurity http) {
    return http
        .authorizeExchange()
          .pathMatchers("/api/tacos", "/orders").hasAuthority("USER")
          .anyExchange().permitAll()
      .and()
        .build();
  }

}
```

As you can see, there's a lot that's familiar, though, at the same time, much is different. Rather than @EnableWebSecurity, this new configuration class is annotated with @EnableWebFluxSecurity. What's more, the configuration class doesn't extend Web-SecurityConfigurerAdapter or any other base class whatsoever. Therefore, it also doesn't override any configure() methods.

In place of a configure() method, you declare a bean of type SecurityWeb-FilterChain with the securityWebFilterChain() method. The body of securityWeb-FilterChain() isn't much different from the previous configuration's configure() method, but there are some subtle changes.

Primarily, the configuration is declared using a given ServerHttpSecurity object instead of an HttpSecurity object. Using the given ServerHttpSecurity, you can call authorizeExchange(), which is roughly equivalent to authorizeRequests(), to declare request-level security.

NOTE   ServerHttpSecurity is new to Spring Security 5 and is the reactive analog to HttpSecurity.

When matching paths, you can still use Ant-style wildcard paths, but do so with the `pathMatchers()` method instead of `antMatchers()`. And as a convenience, you no longer need to specify a catchall Ant-style path of `/**` because the `anyExchange()` returns the catchall you need.

Finally, because you're declaring the `SecurityWebFilterChain` as a bean instead of overriding a framework method, you must call the `build()` method to assemble all of the security rules into the `SecurityWebFilterChain` to be returned.

Aside from those small differences, configuring web security isn't that different for Spring WebFlux than for Spring MVC. But what about user details?

12.5.2 *Configuring a reactive user details service*

When extending `WebSecurityConfigurerAdapter`, you override one `configure()` method to declare web security rules and another `configure()` method to configure authentication logic, typically by defining a `UserDetails` object. As a reminder of what this looks like, consider the following overridden `configure()` method that uses an injected `UserRepository` object in an anonymous implementation of `UserDetailsService` to look up a user by username:

```
@Autowired
UserRepository userRepo;

@Override
protected void
    configure(AuthenticationManagerBuilder auth)
    throws Exception {
  auth
  .userDetailsService(new UserDetailsService() {
    @Override
    public UserDetails loadUserByUsername(String username)
                          throws UsernameNotFoundException {
      User user = userRepo.findByUsername(username)
      if (user == null) {
        throw new UsernameNotFoundException(
                  username " + not found")
      }
      return user.toUserDetails();
    }
  });
}
```

In this nonreactive configuration, you override the only method required by `UserDetailsService`: `loadUserByUsername()`. Inside of that method, you use the given `UserRepository` to look up the user by the given username. If the name isn't found, you throw a `UsernameNotFoundException`. But if it's found, then you call a helper method, `toUserDetails()`, to return the resulting `UserDetails` object.

In a reactive security configuration, you don't override a `configure()` method. Instead, you declare a `ReactiveUserDetailsService` bean. `ReactiveUserDetails-Service` is the reactive equivalent to `UserDetailsService`. Like `UserDetailsService`,

ReactiveUserDetailsService requires implementation of only a single method. Specifically, the findByUsername() method returns a Mono<UserDetails> instead of a raw UserDetails object.

In the following example, the ReactiveUserDetailsService bean is declared to use a given UserRepository, which is presumed to be a reactive Spring Data repository (which we'll talk more about in the next chapter):

```
@Bean
public ReactiveUserDetailsService userDetailsService(
                                        UserRepository userRepo) {
  return new ReactiveUserDetailsService() {
    @Override
    public Mono<UserDetails> findByUsername(String username) {
      return userRepo.findByUsername(username)
        .map(user -> {
          return user.toUserDetails();
        });
    }
  };
}
```

Here, a Mono<UserDetails> is returned as required, but the UserRepository.findByUsername() method returns a Mono<User>. Because it's a Mono, you can chain operations on it, such as a map() operation to map the Mono<User> to a Mono<UserDetails>.

In this case, the map() operation is applied with a lambda that calls the helper toUserDetails() method on the User object published by the Mono. This converts the User to a UserDetails. As a consequence, the .map() operation returns a Mono<UserDetails>, which is precisely what the ReactiveUserDetailsService.findByUsername() requires. If findByUsername() can't find a matching user, then the Mono returned will be empty, indicating no match and resulting in a failure to authenticate.

Summary

- Spring WebFlux offers a reactive web framework whose programming model mirrors that of Spring MVC and even shares many of the same annotations.
- Spring also offers a functional programming model as an alternative to Spring WebFlux's annotation-based programming model.
- Reactive controllers can be tested with WebTestClient.
- On the client side, Spring offers WebClient, a reactive analog to Spring's RestTemplate.
- Although WebFlux has some significant implications for the underlying mechanisms for securing a web application, Spring Security 5 supports reactive security with a programming model that isn't dramatically different from nonreactive Spring MVC applications.

Persisting data reactively 13

This chapter covers

- Reactive relational persistence with R2DBC
- Defining reactive repositories for MongoDB and Cassandra
- Testing reactive repositories

If we've learned one thing from science fiction, it's that if you want to improve upon past experiences, all you need is a little time travel. It worked in *Back to the Future*, several episodes of various Star Trek shows, *Avengers: Endgame*, and Stephen King's *11/22/63*. (OK, well maybe that last one didn't turn out better. But you get the idea.)

In this chapter, we're going to rewind back to chapters 3 and 4, revisiting the repositories we created for relational databases, MongoDB, and Cassandra. This time, we're going to improve on them by taking advantage of some of Spring Data's reactive repository support, allowing us to work with those repositories in a non-blocking fashion.

Let's start by looking at Spring Data R2DBC, a reactive alternative to Spring Data JDBC for persistence to relational databases.

13.1   *Working with R2DBC*

Reactive Relational Database Connectivity, or R2DBC (https://r2dbc.io/) as it is commonly known, is a relatively new option for working with relational data using reactive types. It is effectively a reactive alternative to JDBC, enabling nonblocking persistence against conventional relational databases such as MySQL, PostgreSQL, H2, and Oracle. Because it's built on Reactive Streams, it is quite different from JDBC and is a separate specification, unrelated to Java SE.

Spring Data R2DBC is a subproject of Spring Data that offers automatic repository support for R2DBC, much the same as Spring Data JDBC, which we looked at in chapter 3. Unlike Spring Data JDBC, however, Spring Data R2DBC doesn't require strict adherence to domain-driven design concepts. In fact, as you'll soon see, attempting to persist data through an aggregate root requires a bit more work with Spring Data R2DBC than with Spring Data JDBC.

To use Spring Data R2DBC, you'll need to add a starter dependency to your project's build. For a Maven-built project, the dependency looks like this:

```
<dependency>
    <groupId>org.springframework.boot</groupId>
    <artifactId>spring-boot-starter-data-r2dbc</artifactId>
</dependency>
```

Or, if you're using the Initializr, select the Spring Data R2DBC check box when creating your project.

You'll also need a relational database to persist data to, along with a corresponding R2DBC driver. For our project, we'll be using an in-memory H2 database. Therefore, we need to add two dependencies: the H2 database library itself and the H2 R2DBC driver. The Maven dependencies follow:

```
<dependency>
    <groupId>com.h2database</groupId>
    <artifactId>h2</artifactId>
    <scope>runtime</scope>
</dependency>
<dependency>
    <groupId>io.r2dbc</groupId>
    <artifactId>r2dbc-h2</artifactId>
    <scope>runtime</scope>
</dependency>
```

If you're using a different database, then you'll need to add the corresponding R2BDC driver dependency for the database of your choice.

Now that the dependencies are in place, let's see how Spring Data R2DBC works. Let's start by defining the domain entities.

13.1.1 Defining domain entities for R2DBC

To get to know Spring Data R2DBC, we'll recreate just the persistence layer of the Taco Cloud application, focusing only on the components that are necessary for persisting taco and order data. This includes creating domain entities for `TacoOrder`, `Taco`, and `Ingredient`, along with corresponding repositories for each.

The first domain entity class we'll create is the `Ingredient` class. It will look something like the next code listing.

Listing 13.1 The `Ingredient` entity class for R2DBC persistence

```
package tacos;

import org.springframework.data.annotation.Id;
import lombok.Data;
import lombok.EqualsAndHashCode;
import lombok.NoArgsConstructor;
import lombok.NonNull;
import lombok.RequiredArgsConstructor;

@Data
@NoArgsConstructor
@RequiredArgsConstructor
@EqualsAndHashCode(exclude = "id")
public class Ingredient {

  @Id
  private Long id;

  private @NonNull String slug;

  private @NonNull String name;
  private @NonNull Type type;

  public enum Type {
    WRAP, PROTEIN, VEGGIES, CHEESE, SAUCE
  }

}
```

As you can see, this isn't much different from other incarnations of the `Ingredient` class that we've created before. Note the following two noteworthy differences:

- Spring Data R2DBC requires that properties have setter methods, so rather than define most properties as `final`, they have to be non-`final`. But to help Lombok create a required arguments constructor, we annotate most of the properties with `@NonNull`. This will cause Lombok and the `@RequiredArgsConstructor` annotation to include those properties in the constructor.
- When saving an object through a Spring Data R2DBC repository, if the object's ID property is non-null, it is treated as an update. In the case of `Ingredient`, the `id` property was previously typed as `String` and specified at

creation time. But doing that with Spring Data R2DBC results in an error. So, here we shift that String ID to a new property named slug, which is just a pseudo-ID for the Ingredient, and use a Long ID property with a value generated by the database.

The corresponding database table is defined in schema.sql like this:

```
create table Ingredient (
  id identity,
  slug varchar(4) not null,
  name varchar(25) not null,
  type varchar(10) not null
);
```

The Taco entity class is also quite similar to its Spring Data JDBC counterpart, as shown in the next code.

Listing 13.2   The Taco entity class for R2DBC persistence

```
package tacos;

import java.util.HashSet;
import java.util.Set;
import org.springframework.data.annotation.Id;
import lombok.Data;
import lombok.NoArgsConstructor;
import lombok.NonNull;
import lombok.RequiredArgsConstructor;

@Data
@NoArgsConstructor
@RequiredArgsConstructor
public class Taco {

  @Id
  private Long id;

  private @NonNull String name;

  private Set<Long> ingredientIds = new HashSet<>();

  public void addIngredient(Ingredient ingredient) {
    ingredientIds.add(ingredient.getId());
  }

}
```

As with the Ingredient class, we have to allow for setter methods on the entity's fields, thus the use of @NonNull instead of final.

But what's especially interesting here is that instead of having a collection of Ingredient objects, Taco has a Set<Long> referencing the IDs of Ingredient objects that are part of this taco. Set was chosen over List to guarantee uniqueness. But why must we use a Set<Long> and not a Set<Ingredient> for the ingredient collection?

Unlike other Spring Data projects, Spring Data R2DBC doesn't currently support direct relationships between entities (at least not at this time). As a relatively new project, Spring Data R2DBC is still working through some of the challenges of handling relationships in a nonblocking way. This may change in future versions of Spring Data R2DBC.

Until then, we can't have Taco referencing a collection of Ingredient and expect persistence to just work. Instead, we have the following options when it comes to dealing with relationships:

- *Define entities with references to the IDs of related objects.* In this case, the corresponding column in the database table must be defined with an array type, if possible. H2 and PostgreSQL are two databases that support array columns, but many others do not. Also, even if the database supports array columns, it may not be possible to define the entries as foreign keys to the referenced table, making it impossible to enforce referential integrity.
- *Define entities and their corresponding tables to match each other perfectly.* For collections, this would mean that the referred object would have a column mapping back to the referring table. For example, the table for Taco objects would need to have a column that points back to the TacoOrder that the Taco is a part of.
- *Serialize referenced entities to JSON and store the JSON in a large VARCHAR column.* This works especially well if there's no need to query through to the referenced objects. It does, however, have potential limits to how big the JSON-serialized object(s) can be due to limits to the length of the corresponding VARCHAR column. Moreover, we won't have any way to leverage the database schema to guarantee referential integrity, because the referenced objects will be stored as a simple string value (which could contain anything).

Although none of these options are ideal, after weighing them, we'll choose the first option for the Taco object. The Taco class has a Set<Long> that references one or more Ingredient IDs. This means that the corresponding table must have an array column to store those IDs. For the H2 database, the Taco table is defined like this:

```
create table Taco (
  id identity,
  name varchar(50) not null,
  ingredient_ids array
);
```

The array type used on the ingredient_ids column is specific to H2. For PostgreSQL, that column might be defined as integer[]. Consult your chosen database documentation for details on how to define array columns. Note that not all database implementations support array columns, so you may need to choose one of the other options for modeling relationships.

Finally, the `TacoOrder` class, as shown in the next listing, is defined using many of the things we've already employed in defining our domain entities for persistence with Spring Data R2DBC.

Listing 13.3   The `TacoOrder` entity class for R2DBC persistence

```java
package tacos;

import java.util.LinkedHashSet;
import java.util.Set;
import org.springframework.data.annotation.Id;
import lombok.Data;

@Data
public class TacoOrder {

  @Id
  private Long id;

  private String deliveryName;
  private String deliveryStreet;
  private String deliveryCity;
  private String deliveryState;
  private String deliveryZip;
  private String ccNumber;
  private String ccExpiration;
  private String ccCVV;

  private Set<Long> tacoIds = new LinkedHashSet<>();

  private List<Taco> tacos = new ArrayList<>();
  public void addTaco(Taco taco) {
    tacos.add(taco);
  }

}
```

As you can see, aside from having a few more properties, the `TacoOrder` class follows the same pattern as the `Taco` class. It references its child `Taco` objects via a `Set<Long>`. A little later, though, we'll see how to get complete `Taco` objects into a `TacoOrder`, even though Spring Data R2DBC doesn't directly support relationships in that way.

The database schema for the `Taco_Order` table looks like this:

```sql
create table Taco_Order (
  id identity,
  delivery_name varchar(50) not null,
  delivery_street varchar(50) not null,
  delivery_city varchar(50) not null,
  delivery_state varchar(2) not null,
  delivery_zip varchar(10) not null,
  cc_number varchar(16) not null,
  cc_expiration varchar(5) not null,
```

```
    cc_cvv varchar(3) not null,
    taco_ids array
);
```

Just like the `Taco` table, which references ingredients with an array column, the `Taco-Order` table references its child `Tacos` with a `taco_ids` column defined as an array column. Again, this schema is for an H2 database; consult your database documentation for details on support and creation of array columns.

Oftentimes, a production application already has its schema defined through other means, and such scripts aren't desirable except for tests. Therefore, this bean is defined in a configuration that is loaded only when running automated tests and isn't available in the runtime application context. We'll see an example of such a test for testing R2DBC repositories after we have defined those services.

What's more, notice that this bean uses only the schema.sql file from the root of the classpath (under src/main/resources in the project). If you'd like other SQL scripts to be included as part of the database initialization, add more `Resource-DatabasePopulator` objects in the call to `populator.addPopulators()`.

Now that we've defined our entities and their corresponding database schemas, let's create the repositories through which we'll save and fetch taco data.

13.1.2 *Defining reactive repositories*

In chapters 3 and 4, we defined our repositories as interfaces that extend Spring Data's `CrudRepository` interface. But that base repository interface dealt with singular objects and `Iterable` collections. In contrast, we'd expect that a reactive repository would deal in `Mono` and `Flux` objects.

That's why Spring Data offers `ReactiveCrudRepository` for defining reactive repositories. `ReactiveCrudRepository` operates very much like `CrudRepository`. To create a repository, define an interface that extends `ReactiveCrudRepository`, such as this:

```
package tacos.data;

import org.springframework.data.repository.reactive.ReactiveCrudRepository;

import tacos.TacoOrder;

public interface OrderRepository
        extends ReactiveCrudRepository<TacoOrder, Long> {
}
```

On the surface, the only difference between this `OrderRepository` and the ones we defined in chapters 3 and 4 is that it extends `ReactiveCrudRepository` instead of `CrudRepository`. But what's significantly different is that its methods return `Mono` and `Flux` types instead of a single `TacoOrder` or `Iterable<TacoOrder>`. Two examples include the `findById()` method, which returns a `Mono<TacoOrder>`, and `findAll()`, which returns a `Flux<TacoOrder>`.

To see how this reactive repository might work in action, suppose that you want to fetch all `TacoOrder` objects and print their delivery names to standard output. In that case, you might write some code like the next snippet.

Listing 13.4 Calling a reactive repository method

```
@Autowired
OrderRepository orderRepo;

...

orderRepository.findAll()
    .doOnNext(order -> {
      System.out.println(
          "Deliver to: " + order.getDeliveryName());
    })
    .subscribe();
```

Here, the call to `findAll()` returns a `Flux<TacoOrder>` on which we have added a `doOnNext()` to print the delivery name. Finally, the call to `subscribe()` kicks off the flow of data through the `Flux`.

In the Spring Data JDBC example from chapter 3, `TacoOrder` was the aggregate root, with `Taco` being a child in that aggregate. Therefore, `Taco` objects were persisted as part of a `TacoOrder`, and there was no need to define a repository dedicated to `Taco` persistence. But Spring Data R2DBC doesn't support proper aggregate roots this way, so we'll need a `TacoRepository` through which `Taco` objects are persisted. See the next listing for such a repository.

Listing 13.5 Persisting Taco objects with a reactive repository

```
package tacos.data;

import org.springframework.data.repository.reactive.ReactiveCrudRepository;
import tacos.Taco;

public interface TacoRepository
        extends ReactiveCrudRepository<Taco, Long> {
}
```

As you can see, `TacoRepository` isn't much different from `OrderRepository`. It extends `ReactiveCrudRepository` to give us reactive types when working with `Taco` persistence. There aren't many surprises here.

On the other hand, `IngredientRepository` is slightly more interesting, as shown next.

Listing 13.6 Persisting `Ingredient` objects with a reactive repository

```
package tacos.data;

import org.springframework.data.repository.reactive.ReactiveCrudRepository;
```

```
import reactor.core.publisher.Mono;
import tacos.Ingredient;

public interface IngredientRepository
        extends ReactiveCrudRepository<Ingredient, Long> {

  Mono<Ingredient> findBySlug(String slug);

}
```

As with our other two reactive repositories, `IngredientRepository` extends `Reactive-CrudRepository`. But because we might need a way to look up `Ingredient` objects based on a slug value, `IngredientRepository` includes a `findBySlug()` method that returns a `Mono<Ingredient>`.[1]

Now let's see how to write tests to verify that our repositories work.

13.1.3 *Testing R2DBC repositories*

Spring Data R2DBC includes support for writing integration tests for R2DBC repositories. Specifically, the `@DataR2dbcTest` annotation, when placed on a test class, causes Spring to create an application context with the generated Spring Data R2DBC repositories as beans that can be injected into the test class. Along with `StepVerifier`, which we've used in previous chapters, this enables us to write automated tests against all of the repositories we've created.

For the sake of brevity, we'll focus solely on a single test class: `Ingredient-RepositoryTest`. This will test `IngredientRepository`, verifying that it can save `Ingredient` objects, fetch a single `Ingredient`, and fetch all saved `Ingredient` objects. The next code sample shows this test class.

Listing 13.7 Testing a Spring Data R2DBC repository

```
package tacos.data;

import static org.assertj.core.api.Assertions.assertThat;

import java.util.ArrayList;

import org.junit.jupiter.api.BeforeEach;
import org.junit.jupiter.api.Test;
import org.springframework.beans.factory.annotation.Autowired;
import org.springframework.boot.test.autoconfigure.data.r2dbc.DataR2dbcTest;

import reactor.core.publisher.Flux;
import reactor.test.StepVerifier;
import tacos.Ingredient;
import tacos.Ingredient.Type;
```

---

[1] This method wasn't necessary in chapter 3's JDBC-based repository because we were able to have the `id` field serve double duty as both an ID and a slug.

```
@DataR2dbcTest
public class IngredientRepositoryTest {

  @Autowired
  IngredientRepository ingredientRepo;

  @BeforeEach
  public void setup() {
      Flux<Ingredient> deleteAndInsert = ingredientRepo.deleteAll()
          .thenMany(ingredientRepo.saveAll(
              Flux.just(
                  new Ingredient("FLTO", "Flour Tortilla", Type.WRAP),
                  new Ingredient("GRBF", "Ground Beef", Type.PROTEIN),
                  new Ingredient("CHED", "Cheddar Cheese", Type.CHEESE)
          )));

      StepVerifier.create(deleteAndInsert)
                  .expectNextCount(3)
                  .verifyComplete();
  }

  @Test
  public void shouldSaveAndFetchIngredients() {

      StepVerifier.create(ingredientRepo.findAll())
          .recordWith(ArrayList::new)
          .thenConsumeWhile(x -> true)
          .consumeRecordedWith(ingredients -> {
            assertThat(ingredients).hasSize(3);
            assertThat(ingredients).contains(
                new Ingredient("FLTO", "Flour Tortilla", Type.WRAP));
            assertThat(ingredients).contains(
                new Ingredient("GRBF", "Ground Beef", Type.PROTEIN));
            assertThat(ingredients).contains(
                new Ingredient("CHED", "Cheddar Cheese", Type.CHEESE));
          })
          .verifyComplete();

      StepVerifier.create(ingredientRepo.findBySlug("FLTO"))
          .assertNext(ingredient -> {
              ingredient.equals(new Ingredient("FLTO", "Flour Tortilla",
      Type.WRAP));
          });
  }

}
```

The setup() method starts by creating a Flux of test Ingredient objects and then saving them via the saveAll() method on the injected IngredientRepository. It then
uses a StepVerifier to verify that, in fact, three ingredients were saved and no
more. Internally, the StepVerifier subscribes to the ingredient Flux to open the
flow of data.

In the `shouldSaveAndFetchIngredients()` test method, another `StepVerifier` is used to verify the ingredients returned from the repository's `findAll()` method. It does this by collecting the ingredients into an `ArrayList` via the `recordWith()` method. Then in the lambda passed to `consumeRecordedWith()` method, it simply inspects the contents of the `ArrayList` and verifies that it contains the expected `Ingredient` objects.

At the end of `shouldSaveAndFetchIngredients()`, the `findBySlug()` repository method is tested against a single ingredient by passing `"FLTO"` into `findBySlug()` to create a `Mono<Ingredient>` and then using `StepVerifier` to assert that the next item emitted by the Mono is a flour tortilla `Ingredient` object.

Although we focused only on testing the `IngredientRepository`, the same techniques can be used to test any Spring Data R2BDC–generated repository.

So far, so good. We now have defined our domain types and their respective repositories. And we've written a test to verify that they work. We can use them as is if we like. But these repositories make persistence of a `TacoOrder` inconvenient in that we must first create and persist `Taco` objects that are part of that order and then persist the `TacoOrder` object that references the child `Taco` objects. And when reading the `TacoOrder`, we'll receive only a collection of `Taco` IDs and not fully defined `Taco` objects.

It would be nice if we could persist `TacoOrder` as an aggregate root and have its child `Taco` objects be persisted along with it. Likewise, it would be great if we could fetch a `TacoOrder` and have it fully defined with complete `Taco` objects and not just the IDs. Let's define a service-level class that sits in front of `OrderRepository` and `TacoRepository` to mimic the persistence behavior of chapter 3's `OrderRepository`.

13.1.4 *Defining an OrderRepository aggregate root service*

The first step toward persisting `TacoOrder` and `Taco` objects together such that `TacoOrder` is the aggregate root is to add a `Taco` collection property to the `TacoOrder` class. This is shown next.

Listing 13.8 Adding a `Taco` collection to `TacoOrder`

```
@Data
public class TacoOrder {

  ...

  @Transient
  private transient List<Taco> tacos = new ArrayList<>();

  public void addTaco(Taco taco) {
    tacos.add(taco);
    if (taco.getId() != null) {
      tacoIds.add(taco.getId());
    }
  }

}
```

Aside from adding a new List<Taco> property named tacos to the TacoOrder class, the addTaco() method now adds the given Taco to that list (as well as adding its id to the tacoIds set as before).

Notice, however, that the tacos property is annotated with @Transient (as well as marked with Java's transient keyword). This indicates that Spring Data R2DBC shouldn't attempt to persist this property. Without the @Transient annotation, Spring Data R2DBC would try to persist it and result in an error, due to it not supporting such relationships.

When a TacoOrder is saved, only the tacoIds property will be written to the database, and the tacos property will be ignored. Even so, at least now TacoOrder has a place to hold Taco objects. That will come in handy both for saving Taco objects when a TacoOrder is saved and also to read in Taco objects when a TacoOrder is fetched.

Now we can create a service bean that saves and reads TacoOrder objects along with their respective Taco objects. Let's start with saving a TacoOrder. The TacoOrder-AggregateService class defined in the next code listing has a save() method that does precisely that.

Listing 13.9 Saving TacoOrders and Tacos as an aggregate

```
package tacos.web.api;

import java.util.ArrayList;
import java.util.List;

import org.springframework.stereotype.Service;

import lombok.RequiredArgsConstructor;
import reactor.core.publisher.Mono;
import tacos.Taco;
import tacos.TacoOrder;
import tacos.data.OrderRepository;
import tacos.data.TacoRepository;

@Service
@RequiredArgsConstructor
public class TacoOrderAggregateService {

  private final TacoRepository tacoRepo;
  private final OrderRepository orderRepo;

  public Mono<TacoOrder> save(TacoOrder tacoOrder) {
    return Mono.just(tacoOrder)
      .flatMap(order -> {
        List<Taco> tacos = order.getTacos();
        order.setTacos(new ArrayList<>());
        return tacoRepo.saveAll(tacos)
          .map(taco -> {
            order.addTaco(taco);
            return order;
          }).last();
```

```
        })
        .flatMap(orderRepo::save);
    }

}
```

Although there aren't many lines in listing 13.9, there's a lot going on in the `save()` method that requires some explanation. Firstly, the `TacoOrder` that is received as a parameter is wrapped in a `Mono` using the `Mono.just()` method. This allows us to work with it as a reactive type throughout the rest of the `save()` method.

The next thing we do is apply a `flatMap()` to the `Mono<TacoOrder>` we just created. Both `map()` and `flatMap()` are options for doing transformations on a data object passing through a `Mono` or `Flux`, but because the operations we perform in the course of doing the transformation will result in a `Mono<TacoOrder>`, the `flatMap()` operation ensures that we continue working with a `Mono<TacoOrder>` after the mapping and not a `Mono<Mono<TacoOrder>>`, as would be the case if we used `map()` instead.

The purpose of the mapping is to ensure that the `TacoOrder` ends up with the IDs of the child `Taco` objects and saves those `Taco` objects along the way. Each `Taco` object's ID is probably `null` initially for a new `TacoOrder`, and we won't know the IDs until after the `Taco` objects have been saved.

After fetching the `List<Taco>` from the `TacoOrder`, which we'll use when saving `Taco` objects, we reset the `tacos` property to an empty list. We'll be rebuilding that list with new `Taco` objects that have been assigned IDs after having been saved.

A call to the `saveAll()` method on the injected `TacoRepository` saves all of our `Taco` objects. The `saveAll()` method returns a `Flux<Taco>` that we then cycle through by way of the `map()` method. In this case, the transformation operation is secondary to the fact that each `Taco` object is being added back to the `TacoOrder`. But to ensure that it's a `TacoOrder` and not a `Taco` that ends up on the resulting `Flux`, the mapping operation returns the `TacoOrder` instead of the `Taco`. A call to `last()` ensures that we won't have duplicate `TacoOrder` objects (one for each `Taco`) as a result of the mapping operation.

At this point, all `Taco` objects should have been saved and then pushed back into the parent `TacoOrder` object, along with their newly assigned IDs. All that's left is to save the `TacoOrder`, which is what the final `flatMap()` call does. Again, we choose `flatMap()` here to ensure that the `Mono<TacoOrder>` returned from the call to `OrderRepository.save()` doesn't get wrapped in another `Mono`. We want our `save()` method to return a `Mono<TacoOrder>`, not a `Mono<Mono<TacoOrder>>`.

Now let's have a look at a method that will read a `TacoOrder` by its ID, reconstituting all of the child `Taco` objects. The following code sample shows a new `findById()` method for that purpose.

Listing 13.10 Reading `TacoOrders` and `Tacos` as an aggregate

```
public Mono<TacoOrder> findById(Long id) {
    return orderRepo
```

```
        .findById(id)
        .flatMap(order -> {
          return tacoRepo.findAllById(order.getTacoIds())
            .map(taco -> {
              order.addTaco(taco);
              return order;
          }).last();
        });
}
```

The new findById() method is a bit shorter than the save() method. But we still have a lot to unpack in this small method.

The first thing to do is fetch the TacoOrder by calling the findById() method on the OrderRepository. This returns a Mono<TacoOrder> that is then flat-mapped to transform it from a TacoOrder that has only Taco IDs into a TacoOrder that includes complete Taco objects.

The lambda given to the flatMap() method makes a call to the TacoRepository .findAllById() method to fetch all Taco objects referenced in the tacoIds property at once. This results in a Flux<Taco> that is cycled over via map(), adding each Taco to the parent TacoOrder, much like we did in the save() method after saving all Taco objects with saveAll().

Again, the map() operation is used more as a means of iterating over the Taco objects rather than as a transformation. But the lambda given to map() returns the parent TacoOrder each time so that we end up with a Flux<TacoOrder> instead of a Flux<Taco>. The call to last() takes the last entry in that Flux and returns a Mono<TacoOrder>, which is what we return from the findById() method.

The code in the save() and findById() methods may be a little confusing if you're not already in a reactive mind-set. Reactive programming requires a different mindset and can be confusing at first, but you'll come to recognize it as quite elegant as your reactive programming skills get stronger.

As with any code—but especially code that may appear confusing like that in Taco-OrderAggregateService—it's a good idea to write tests to ensure that it works as expected. The test will also serve as an example of how the TacoOrderAggregateService can be used. The following code listing shows a test for TacoOrderAggregateService.

Listing 13.11   Testing the TacoOrderAggregateService

```
package tacos.web.api;

import static org.assertj.core.api.Assertions.assertThat;

import org.junit.jupiter.api.BeforeEach;
import org.junit.jupiter.api.Test;
import org.springframework.beans.factory.annotation.Autowired;
import org.springframework.boot.test.autoconfigure.data.r2dbc.DataR2dbcTest;
import org.springframework.test.annotation.DirtiesContext;
```

```java
import reactor.test.StepVerifier;
import tacos.Taco;
import tacos.TacoOrder;
import tacos.data.OrderRepository;
import tacos.data.TacoRepository;

@DataR2dbcTest
@DirtiesContext
public class TacoOrderAggregateServiceTests {

  @Autowired
  TacoRepository tacoRepo;

  @Autowired
  OrderRepository orderRepo;

  TacoOrderAggregateService service;

  @BeforeEach
  public void setup() {
    this.service = new TacoOrderAggregateService(tacoRepo, orderRepo);
  }

  @Test
  public void shouldSaveAndFetchOrders() {
    TacoOrder newOrder = new TacoOrder();
    newOrder.setDeliveryName("Test Customer");
    newOrder.setDeliveryStreet("1234 North Street");
    newOrder.setDeliveryCity("Notrees");
    newOrder.setDeliveryState("TX");
    newOrder.setDeliveryZip("79759");
    newOrder.setCcNumber("4111111111111111");
    newOrder.setCcExpiration("12/24");
    newOrder.setCcCVV("123");

    newOrder.addTaco(new Taco("Test Taco One"));
    newOrder.addTaco(new Taco("Test Taco Two"));

    StepVerifier.create(service.save(newOrder))
      .assertNext(this::assertOrder)
      .verifyComplete();

    StepVerifier.create(service.findById(1L))
      .assertNext(this::assertOrder)
      .verifyComplete();
  }

  private void assertOrder(TacoOrder savedOrder) {
    assertThat(savedOrder.getId()).isEqualTo(1L);
    assertThat(savedOrder.getDeliveryName()).isEqualTo("Test Customer");
    assertThat(savedOrder.getDeliveryName()).isEqualTo("Test Customer");
    assertThat(savedOrder.getDeliveryStreet()).isEqualTo("1234 North Street");
    assertThat(savedOrder.getDeliveryCity()).isEqualTo("Notrees");
    assertThat(savedOrder.getDeliveryState()).isEqualTo("TX");
    assertThat(savedOrder.getDeliveryZip()).isEqualTo("79759");
```

```
        assertThat(savedOrder.getCcNumber()).isEqualTo("4111111111111111");
        assertThat(savedOrder.getCcExpiration()).isEqualTo("12/24");
        assertThat(savedOrder.getCcCVV()).isEqualTo("123");
        assertThat(savedOrder.getTacoIds()).hasSize(2);
        assertThat(savedOrder.getTacos().get(0).getId()).isEqualTo(1L);
        assertThat(savedOrder.getTacos().get(0).getName())
                .isEqualTo("Test Taco One");
        assertThat(savedOrder.getTacos().get(1).getId()).isEqualTo(2L);
        assertThat(savedOrder.getTacos().get(1).getName())
                .isEqualTo("Test Taco Two");
    }

}
```

Listing 13.11 contains a lot of lines, but much of it is asserting the contents of a TacoOrder in the assertOrder() method. We'll focus on the other parts as we review this test.

The test class is annotated with @DataR2dbcTest to have Spring create an application context with all of our repositories as beans. @DataR2dbcTest seeks out a configuration class annotated with @SpringBootConfiguration to define the Spring application context. In a single-module project, the bootstrap class annotated with @SpringBoot-Application (which itself is annotated with @SpringBootConfiguration) serves this purpose. But in our multimodule project, this test class isn't in the same project as the bootstrap class, so we'll need a simple configuration class like this one:

```
package tacos;

import org.springframework.boot.SpringBootConfiguration;
import org.springframework.boot.autoconfigure.EnableAutoConfiguration;

@SpringBootConfiguration
@EnableAutoConfiguration
public class TestConfig {

}
```

Not only does this satisfy the need for a @SpringBootConfiguration-annotated class, but it also enables autoconfiguration, ensuring that (among other things) the repository implementations will be created.

On its own, TacoOrderAggregateServiceTests should pass fine. But in an IDE that may share JVMs and Spring application contexts between test runs, running this test alongside other persistence tests may result in conflicting data being written to the in-memory H2 database. The @DirtiesContext annotation is used here to ensure that the Spring application context is reset between test runs, resulting in a new and empty H2 database on each run.

The setup() method creates an instance of TacoOrderAggregateService using the TacoRepository and OrderRepository objects injected into the test class. The TacoOrderAggregateService is assigned to an instance variable so that the test method(s) can use it.

Now we're finally ready to test our aggregation service. The first several lines of shouldSaveAndFetchOrders() builds up a TacoOrder object and populates it with a couple of test Taco objects. Then the TacoOrder is saved via the save() method from TacoOrderAggregateService, which returns a Mono<TacoOrder> representing the saved order. Using StepVerifier, we assert that the TacoOrder in the returned Mono matches our expectations, including that it contains the child Taco objects.

Next, we call the service's findById() method, which also returns a Mono<TacoOrder>. As with the call to save(), a StepVerifier is used to step through each TacoOrder in the returned Mono (there should be only one) and asserts that it meets our expectations.

In both StepVerifier situations, a call to verifyComplete() ensures that there are no more objects in the Mono and that the Mono is complete.

It's worth noting that although we could apply a similar aggregation operation to ensure that Taco objects always contain fully defined Ingredient objects, we choose not to, given that Ingredient is its own aggregate root, likely being referenced by multiple Taco objects. Therefore, every Taco will carry only a Set<Long> to reference Ingredient IDs, which can then be looked up separately via IngredientRepository.

Although it may require a bit more work to aggregate entities, Spring Data R2DBC provides a way of working with relational data in a reactive way. But it's not the only reactive persistence option provided by Spring. Let's have a look at how to work with MongoDB using reactive Spring Data repositories.

13.2 *Persisting document data reactively with MongoDB*

In chapter 4, we used Spring Data MongoDB to define document-based persistence against a MongoDB document database. In this section, we're going to revisit MongoDB persistence using Spring Data's reactive support for MongoDB.

To get started, you'll need to create a project with the Spring Data Reactive MongoDB starter. That is, in fact, the name of the check box to select when creating the project with the Initalizr. Or you can add it manually to your Maven build with the following dependency:

```
<dependency>
    <groupId>org.springframework.boot</groupId>
    <artifactId>spring-boot-starter-data-mongodb-reactive</artifactId>
</dependency>
```

In chapter 4, we also leaned on the Flapdoodle embedded MongoDB database for testing. Unfortunately, Flapdoodle doesn't behave quite as well when fronted with reactive repositories. When it comes to running the tests, you'll need to have an actual Mongo database running and listening on port 27017.

Now we're ready to start writing code for reactive MongoDB persistence. We'll start with the document types that make up our domain.

13.2.1 *Defining domain document types*

As before, we'll need to create the classes that define our application's domain. As we do, we'll need to annotate them with Spring Data MongoDB's @Document annotation, just as we did in chapter 4, to indicate that they are documents to be stored in MongoDB. Let's start with the Ingredient class, shown here.

Listing 13.12 An Ingredient class annotated for Mongo persistence

```
package tacos;

import org.springframework.data.annotation.Id;
import org.springframework.data.mongodb.core.mapping.Document;

import lombok.AccessLevel;
import lombok.AllArgsConstructor;
import lombok.Data;
import lombok.NoArgsConstructor;

@Data
@AllArgsConstructor
@NoArgsConstructor(access=AccessLevel.PRIVATE, force=true)
@Document
public class Ingredient {

  @Id
  private String id;
  private String name;
  private Type type;

  public enum Type {
    WRAP, PROTEIN, VEGGIES, CHEESE, SAUCE
  }

}
```

A keen eye will notice that this Ingredient class is identical to the one we created in chapter 4. In fact, MongoDB @Document classes are the same whether being persisted through a reactive or nonreactive repository. That means that the Taco and TacoOrder classes are going to be the same as the ones we created in chapter 4. But for the sake of completeness—and so that you won't need to turn back to chapter 4—we'll repeat them here.

A similarly annotated Taco class is shown next.

Listing 13.13 A Taco class annotated for Mongo persistence

```
package tacos;

import java.util.ArrayList;
import java.util.Date;
import java.util.List;
```

```
import javax.validation.constraints.NotNull;
import javax.validation.constraints.Size;

import org.springframework.data.annotation.Id;
import org.springframework.data.mongodb.core.mapping.Document;
import org.springframework.data.rest.core.annotation.RestResource;

import lombok.Data;

@Data
@RestResource(rel = "tacos", path = "tacos")
@Document
public class Taco {

  @Id
  private String id;

  @NotNull
  @Size(min = 5, message = "Name must be at least 5 characters long")
  private String name;

  private Date createdAt = new Date();

  @Size(min=1, message="You must choose at least 1 ingredient")
  private List<Ingredient> ingredients = new ArrayList<>();

  public void addIngredient(Ingredient ingredient) {
    this.ingredients.add(ingredient);
  }

}
```

Notice that, unlike `Ingredient`, the `Taco` class isn't annotated with `@Document`. That's because it isn't saved as a document in itself and is instead saved as part of the `Taco-Order` aggregate root. On the other hand, because `TacoOrder` is an aggregate root, it is annotated with `@Document` as shown in the next code.

Listing 13.14 A `TacoOrder` class annotated for Mongo persistence

```
package tacos;

import java.io.Serializable;
import java.util.ArrayList;
import java.util.Date;
import java.util.List;

import org.springframework.data.annotation.Id;
import org.springframework.data.mongodb.core.mapping.Document;

import lombok.Data;

@Data
@Document
```

```
public class TacoOrder implements Serializable {
  private static final long serialVersionUID = 1L;

  @Id
  private String id;
  private Date placedAt = new Date();

  private User user;

  private String deliveryName;

  private String deliveryStreet;

  private String deliveryCity;

  private String deliveryState;

  private String deliveryZip;

  private String ccNumber;

  private String ccExpiration;

  private String ccCVV;


  private List<Taco> tacos = new ArrayList<>();

  public void addTaco(Taco taco) {
    tacos.add(taco);
  }

}
```

Again, the domain document classes are no different for reactive MongoDB repositories than they would be for nonreactive repositories. As you'll see next, reactive MongoDB repositories themselves differ very slightly from their nonreactive counterparts.

13.2.2 *Defining reactive MongoDB repositories*

Now we'll need to define two repositories, one for the `TacoOrder` aggregate root and another for `Ingredient`. We won't need a repository for `Taco` because it is a child of the `TacoOrder` root.

The `IngredientRepository` interface, shown here, should be familiar to you by now:

```
package tacos.data;

import org.springframework.data.repository.reactive.ReactiveCrudRepository;
import org.springframework.web.bind.annotation.CrossOrigin;

import tacos.Ingredient;
@CrossOrigin(origins="http://localhost:8080")
```

```
public interface IngredientRepository
        extends ReactiveCrudRepository<Ingredient, String> {

}
```

This `IngredientRepository` interface is only slightly different from the one we defined in chapter 4 in that it extends `ReactiveCrudRepository` instead of `Crud-Repository`. And it differs from the one we created for Spring Data R2DBC persistence only in that it doesn't include the `findBySlug()` method.

Likewise, `OrderRepository` is all but identical to the same MongoDB repository we created in chapter 4, shown next:

```
package tacos.data;

import org.springframework.data.domain.Pageable;
import org.springframework.data.repository.reactive.ReactiveCrudRepository;

import reactor.core.publisher.Flux;
import tacos.TacoOrder;
import tacos.User;

public interface OrderRepository
        extends ReactiveCrudRepository<TacoOrder, String> {

  Flux<TacoOrder> findByUserOrderByPlacedAtDesc(
          User user, Pageable pageable);

}
```

Ultimately, the only difference between reactive and nonreactive MongoDB repositories is whether they extend `ReactiveCrudRepository` or `CrudRepository`. In choosing to extend `ReactiveCrudRepository`, however, clients of these repositories must be prepared to deal with reactive types like `Flux` and `Mono`. That becomes apparent as we write tests for the reactive repositories, which is what we'll do next.

13.2.3 *Testing reactive MongoDB repositories*

The key to writing tests for MongoDB repositories is to annotate the test class with `@DataMongoTest`. This annotation performs a function similar to the `@DataR2dbcTest` annotation that we used earlier in this chapter. It ensures that a Spring application context is created with the generated repositories available as beans to be injected into the test. From there, the test can use those injected repositories to set up test data and perform other operations against the database.

For example, consider `IngredientRepositoryTest` in the next listing, which tests `IngredientRepository`, asserting that `Ingredient` objects can be written to and read from the database.

Listing 13.15 Testing a reactive Mongo repository

```java
package tacos.data;

import static org.assertj.core.api.Assertions.assertThat;
import java.util.ArrayList;

import org.junit.jupiter.api.BeforeEach;
import org.junit.jupiter.api.Test;
import org.springframework.beans.factory.annotation.Autowired;
import org.springframework.boot.test.autoconfigure.data.mongo.DataMongoTest;
import reactor.core.publisher.Flux;
import reactor.test.StepVerifier;
import tacos.Ingredient;
import tacos.Ingredient.Type;

@DataMongoTest
public class IngredientRepositoryTest {

  @Autowired
  IngredientRepository ingredientRepo;

  @BeforeEach
  public void setup() {
    Flux<Ingredient> deleteAndInsert = ingredientRepo.deleteAll()
        .thenMany(ingredientRepo.saveAll(
            Flux.just(
                new Ingredient("FLTO", "Flour Tortilla", Type.WRAP),
                new Ingredient("GRBF", "Ground Beef", Type.PROTEIN),
                new Ingredient("CHED", "Cheddar Cheese", Type.CHEESE)
        )));

    StepVerifier.create(deleteAndInsert)
                .expectNextCount(3)
                .verifyComplete();
  }

  @Test
  public void shouldSaveAndFetchIngredients() {

    StepVerifier.create(ingredientRepo.findAll())
        .recordWith(ArrayList::new)
        .thenConsumeWhile(x -> true)
        .consumeRecordedWith(ingredients -> {
          assertThat(ingredients).hasSize(3);
          assertThat(ingredients).contains(
              new Ingredient("FLTO", "Flour Tortilla", Type.WRAP));
          assertThat(ingredients).contains(
              new Ingredient("GRBF", "Ground Beef", Type.PROTEIN));
          assertThat(ingredients).contains(
              new Ingredient("CHED", "Cheddar Cheese", Type.CHEESE));
        })
        .verifyComplete();
```

```
     StepVerifier.create(ingredientRepo.findById("FLTO"))
         .assertNext(ingredient -> {
             ingredient.equals(new Ingredient("FLTO", "Flour Tortilla",
   Type.WRAP));
         });
   }

}
```

This test is similar to, but still slightly different from, the R2DBC-based repository test we wrote earlier in this chapter. It starts by writing three `Ingredient` objects to the database. Then, it employs two `StepVerifier` instances to verify that `Ingredient` objects can be read through the repository, first as a collection of all `Ingredient` objects and then fetching a single `Ingredient` by its ID.

Also, just as with the R2DBC-based test from earlier, the `@DataMongoTest` annotation will seek out a `@SpringBootConfiguration`-annotated class for creating the application context. A test just like the one created earlier will work here, too.

What's unique here is that the first `StepVerifier` collects all of the `Ingredient` objects into an `ArrayList` and then asserts that the `ArrayList` contains each `Ingredient`. The `findAll()` method doesn't guarantee a consistent ordering of the resulting documents, which makes the use of `assertNext()` or `expectNext()` prone to fail. By collecting all resulting `Ingredient` objects into a list, we can assert that the list has all three objects, regardless of their order.

A test for `OrderRepository` looks quite similar, as shown here.

Listing 13.16 Testing the Mongo `OrderRepository`

```
package tacos.data;

import org.junit.jupiter.api.BeforeEach;
import org.junit.jupiter.api.Test;
import org.springframework.beans.factory.annotation.Autowired;
import org.springframework.boot.test.autoconfigure.data.mongo.DataMongoTest;

import reactor.test.StepVerifier;
import tacos.Ingredient;
import tacos.Taco;
import tacos.TacoOrder;
import tacos.Ingredient.Type;

@DataMongoTest
public class OrderRepositoryTest {

  @Autowired
  OrderRepository orderRepo;

  @BeforeEach
  public void setup() {
    orderRepo.deleteAll().subscribe();
  }
```

```
@Test
public void shouldSaveAndFetchOrders() {
  TacoOrder order = createOrder();

  StepVerifier
    .create(orderRepo.save(order))
    .expectNext(order)
    .verifyComplete();

  StepVerifier
    .create(orderRepo.findById(order.getId()))
    .expectNext(order)
    .verifyComplete();

  StepVerifier
    .create(orderRepo.findAll())
    .expectNext(order)
    .verifyComplete();
}

private TacoOrder createOrder() {
  TacoOrder order = new TacoOrder();
    ...
  return order;
}

}
```

The first thing that the shouldSaveAndFetchOrders() method does is construct an order, complete with customer and payment information and a couple of tacos. (For brevity's sake, I've left out the details of the createOrder() method.) It then uses a StepVerifier to save the TacoOrder object and assert that the save() method returns the saved TacoOrder. It then attempts to fetch the order by its ID and asserts that it receives the full TacoOrder. Finally, it fetches all TacoOrder objects—there should be only one—and asserts it is the expected TacoOrder.

As mentioned earlier, you'll need a MongoDB server available and listening on port 27017 to run this test. The Flapdoodle embedded MongoDB doesn't work well with reactive repositories. If you have Docker installed on your machine, you can easily start a MongoDB server exposed on port 27017 like this:

```
$ docker run -p27017:27017 mongo
```

Other ways to get a MongoDB setup are possible. Consult the documentation at https://www.mongodb.com/ for more details.

Now that we've seen how to create reactive repositories for R2BDC and MongoDB, let's have a look at one more Spring Data option for reactive persistence: Cassandra.

13.3   *Reactively persisting data in Cassandra*

To get started with reactive persistence against a Cassandra database, you'll need to add the following starter dependency to your project build. This dependency is in lieu of any Mongo or R2DBC dependencies we've used earlier.

```
<dependency>
    <groupId>org.springframework.boot</groupId>
    <artifactId>spring-boot-starter-data-cassandra-reactive</artifactId>
</dependency>
```

Then, you'll need to declare some details about the Cassandra keyspace and how the schema should be managed. In your application.yml file, add the following lines:

```
spring:
  data:
    rest:
      base-path: /data-api
    cassandra:
      keyspace-name: tacocloud
      schema-action: recreate
      local-datacenter: datacenter1
```

This is the same YAML configuration we used in chapter 4 when working with nonreactive Cassandra repositories. The key thing to take note of is the keyspace-name. It is important that you create a keyspace with that name in your Cassandra cluster.

     You'll also need to have a Cassandra cluster running on your local machine listening on port 9042. The easiest way to do that is with Docker, as follows:

```
$ docker network create cassandra-net
$ docker run --name my-cassandra --network cassandra-net \
        -p 9042:9042 -d cassandra:latest
```

If your Cassandra cluster is on another machine or port, you'll need to specify the contact points and port in application.yml, as shown in chapter 4. To create the keyspace, run the CQL shell and use the create keyspace command like this:

```
$ docker run -it --network cassandra-net --rm cassandra cqlsh my-cassandra
cqlsh> create keyspace tacocloud
WITH replication = {'class': 'SimpleStrategy', 'replication_factor' : 1};
```

Now that you have a Cassandra cluster, a new tacocloud keyspace, and the Spring Data Cassandra Reactive starter in your project, you're ready to start defining the domain classes.

13.3.1 *Defining domain classes for Cassandra persistence*

As was the case when persisting with Mongo, the choice of reactive versus nonreactive Cassandra persistence makes absolutely no difference in how you define your domain classes. The domain classes for `Ingredient`, `Taco`, and `TacoOrder` we'll use are identical to the ones we created in chapter 4. A Cassandra-annotated `Ingredient` class is shown here.

Listing 13.17 Annotating `Ingredient` for Cassandra persistence

```java
package tacos;

import org.springframework.data.cassandra.core.mapping.PrimaryKey;
import org.springframework.data.cassandra.core.mapping.Table;

import lombok.AccessLevel;
import lombok.AllArgsConstructor;
import lombok.Data;
import lombok.NoArgsConstructor;

@Data
@AllArgsConstructor
@NoArgsConstructor(access=AccessLevel.PRIVATE, force=true)
@Table("ingredients")
public class Ingredient {

  @PrimaryKey
  private String id;
  private String name;
  private Type type;

  public enum Type {
    WRAP, PROTEIN, VEGGIES, CHEESE, SAUCE
  }

}
```

As for the `Taco` class, it is defined with similar Cassandra persistence annotations in the next code listing.

Listing 13.18 Annotating `Taco` for Cassandra persistence

```java
package tacos;

import java.util.ArrayList;
import java.util.Date;
import java.util.List;
import java.util.UUID;

import javax.validation.constraints.NotNull;
import javax.validation.constraints.Size;

import org.springframework.data.cassandra.core.cql.Ordering;
import org.springframework.data.cassandra.core.cql.PrimaryKeyType;
```

```
import org.springframework.data.cassandra.core.mapping.Column;
import org.springframework.data.cassandra.core.mapping.PrimaryKeyColumn;
import org.springframework.data.cassandra.core.mapping.Table;
import org.springframework.data.rest.core.annotation.RestResource;

import com.datastax.oss.driver.api.core.uuid.Uuids;

import lombok.Data;

@Data
@RestResource(rel = "tacos", path = "tacos")
@Table("tacos")
public class Taco {

  @PrimaryKeyColumn(type=PrimaryKeyType.PARTITIONED)
  private UUID id = Uuids.timeBased();

  @NotNull
  @Size(min = 5, message = "Name must be at least 5 characters long")
  private String name;

  @PrimaryKeyColumn(type=PrimaryKeyType.CLUSTERED,
                    ordering=Ordering.DESCENDING)
  private Date createdAt = new Date();

  @Size(min=1, message="You must choose at least 1 ingredient")
  @Column("ingredients")
  private List<IngredientUDT> ingredients = new ArrayList<>();

  public void addIngredient(Ingredient ingredient) {
      this.ingredients.add(new IngredientUDT(ingredient.getName(),
      ingredient.getType()));
  }

}
```

Because `Taco` refers to `Ingredient` objects via a user-defined type, you'll also need the
`IngredientUDT` class, as shown next.

Listing 13.19 An `Ingredient` user-defined type for Cassandra persistence

```
package tacos;

import org.springframework.data.cassandra.core.mapping.UserDefinedType;

import lombok.AccessLevel;
import lombok.AllArgsConstructor;
import lombok.Data;
import lombok.NoArgsConstructor;

@Data
@AllArgsConstructor
@NoArgsConstructor(access = AccessLevel.PRIVATE, force = true)
@UserDefinedType("ingredient")
```

```
public class IngredientUDT {
  private String name;
  private Ingredient.Type type;
}
```

The final of our three domain classes, `TacoOrder` is annotated for Cassandra persistence as shown in the following listing.

Listing 13.20   Annotating `TacoOrder` for Cassandra persistence

```java
package tacos;

import java.io.Serializable;
import java.util.ArrayList;
import java.util.Date;
import java.util.List;
import java.util.UUID;

import org.springframework.data.cassandra.core.mapping.Column;
import org.springframework.data.cassandra.core.mapping.PrimaryKey;
import org.springframework.data.cassandra.core.mapping.Table;

import com.datastax.oss.driver.api.core.uuid.Uuids;

import lombok.Data;

@Data
@Table("tacoorders")
public class TacoOrder implements Serializable {
  private static final long serialVersionUID = 1L;

  @PrimaryKey
  private UUID id = Uuids.timeBased();
  private Date placedAt = new Date();

  @Column("user")
  private UserUDT user;

  private String deliveryName;

  private String deliveryStreet;

  private String deliveryCity;

  private String deliveryState;

  private String deliveryZip;

  private String ccNumber;

  private String ccExpiration;

  private String ccCVV;
```

```
@Column("tacos")
private List<TacoUDT> tacos = new ArrayList<>();

public void addTaco(Taco taco) {
  addTaco(new TacoUDT(taco.getName(), taco.getIngredients()));
}

public void addTaco(TacoUDT tacoUDT) {
  tacos.add(tacoUDT);
}

}
```

And, just like how `Taco` refers to `Ingredient` via a user-defined type, `TacoOrder` refers to `Taco` via the `TacoUDT` class, which is shown next.

Listing 13.21 An `Taco` user-defined type for Cassandra persistence

```
package tacos;

import java.util.List;

import org.springframework.data.cassandra.core.mapping.UserDefinedType;

import lombok.Data;

@Data
@UserDefinedType("taco")
public class TacoUDT {

  private final String name;
  private final List<IngredientUDT> ingredients;

}
```

It bears repeating that these are identical to their nonreactive counterparts. I've only repeated them here so that you don't have to flip back 11 chapters to remember what they look like.

Now let's define the repositories that persist these objects.

13.3.2 *Creating reactive Cassandra repositories*

By now you may already be expecting the reactive Cassandra repositories to look a lot like the equivalent nonreactive repositories. If so, then great! You're catching on that Spring Data, wherever possible, attempts to maintain a similar programming model regardless of whether or not repositories are reactive.

You may have already guessed that the only key difference that makes the repositories reactive is that the interfaces extend `ReactiveCrudRepository`, as shown here in the `IngredientRepository` interface:

```
package tacos.data;

import org.springframework.data.repository.reactive.ReactiveCrudRepository;

import tacos.Ingredient;

public interface IngredientRepository
        extends ReactiveCrudRepository<Ingredient, String> {

}
```

Naturally, the same holds true for OrderRepository, as shown next:

```
package tacos.data;

import java.util.UUID;

import org.springframework.data.domain.Pageable;
import org.springframework.data.repository.reactive.ReactiveCrudRepository;

import reactor.core.publisher.Flux;
import tacos.TacoOrder;
import tacos.User;

public interface OrderRepository
        extends ReactiveCrudRepository<TacoOrder, UUID> {

  Flux<TacoOrder> findByUserOrderByPlacedAtDesc(
          User user, Pageable pageable);

}
```

In fact, not only are these repositories reminiscent of their nonreactive counterparts, they also do not differ greatly from the MongoDB repositories we wrote earlier in this chapter. Aside from Cassandra using UUID as an ID type instead of String for Taco-Order, they are virtually identical. This once again demonstrates the consistency employed (where possible) across Spring Data projects.

Let's wrap up our look at writing reactive Cassandra repositories by writing a couple of tests to verify that they work.

13.3.3 *Testing reactive Cassandra repositories*

At this point, it may not come as a surprise that testing reactive Cassandra repositories is quite similar to how you test reactive MongoDB repositories. For example, take a look at IngredientRepositoryTest in the next listing, and see if you can spot how it differs from listing 13.15.

Listing 13.22   Testing the Cassandra IngredientRepository

```
package tacos.data;

import static org.assertj.core.api.Assertions.assertThat;
```

```java
import java.util.ArrayList;

import org.junit.jupiter.api.BeforeEach;
import org.junit.jupiter.api.Test;
import org.springframework.beans.factory.annotation.Autowired;
import org.springframework.boot.test.autoconfigure.data.cassandra
    .DataCassandraTest;

import reactor.core.publisher.Flux;
import reactor.test.StepVerifier;
import tacos.Ingredient;
import tacos.Ingredient.Type;

@DataCassandraTest
public class IngredientRepositoryTest {

  @Autowired
  IngredientRepository ingredientRepo;

  @BeforeEach
  public void setup() {
    Flux<Ingredient> deleteAndInsert = ingredientRepo.deleteAll()
        .thenMany(ingredientRepo.saveAll(
            Flux.just(
                new Ingredient("FLTO", "Flour Tortilla", Type.WRAP),
                new Ingredient("GRBF", "Ground Beef", Type.PROTEIN),
                new Ingredient("CHED", "Cheddar Cheese", Type.CHEESE)
        )));

    StepVerifier.create(deleteAndInsert)
                .expectNextCount(3)
                .verifyComplete();
  }

  @Test
  public void shouldSaveAndFetchIngredients() {

    StepVerifier.create(ingredientRepo.findAll())
        .recordWith(ArrayList::new)
        .thenConsumeWhile(x -> true)
        .consumeRecordedWith(ingredients -> {
          assertThat(ingredients).hasSize(3);
          assertThat(ingredients).contains(
              new Ingredient("FLTO", "Flour Tortilla", Type.WRAP));
          assertThat(ingredients).contains(
              new Ingredient("GRBF", "Ground Beef", Type.PROTEIN));
          assertThat(ingredients).contains(
              new Ingredient("CHED", "Cheddar Cheese", Type.CHEESE));
        })
        .verifyComplete();

    StepVerifier.create(ingredientRepo.findById("FLTO"))
        .assertNext(ingredient -> {
            ingredient.equals(new Ingredient("FLTO", "Flour Tortilla",
    Type.WRAP));
```

```
            });
    }

}
```

Did you see it? Where the MongoDB version was annotated with @DataMongoTest, this new Cassandra version is annotated with @DataCassandraTest. That's it! Otherwise, the tests are identical.

The same is true for OrderRepositoryTest. Replace @DataMongoTest with @Data-CassandraTest, and everything else is the same, as shown here:

```
@DataCassandraTest
public class OrderRepositoryTest {
    ...
}
```

Once again, consistency between various Spring Data projects extends even into how the tests are written. This makes it easy to switch between projects that persist to different kinds of databases without having to think much differently about how they are developed.

Summary

- Spring Data supports reactive persistence for a variety of database types, including relational databases (with R2DBC), MongoDB, and Cassandra.
- Spring Data R2DBC offers a reactive option for relational persistence but doesn't yet directly support relationships in domain classes.
- For lack of direct relationship support, Spring Data R2DBC repositories require a different approach to domain and database table design.
- Spring Data MongoDB and Spring Data Cassandra offer a near-identical programming model for writing reactive repositories for MongoDB and Cassandra databases.
- Using Spring Data test annotations along with StepVerifier, you can test automatically created reactive repositories from the Spring application context.

Working with RSocket 14

This chapter covers

- Reactive network communication with RSocket
- Working with each of RSocket's four communication models
- Transporting RSocket over WebSocket

There was a time, before telephones and modern electronics, when the best way to communicate with friends and family that live far away involved writing a letter and dropping it in the mail. It wasn't a quick form of communication, taking several days or even weeks before you'd receive a response, but it was effective and truly the only option available.

Thanks to Alexander Graham Bell, the telephone offered a new way to talk with distant friends and family, giving near-real-time, synchronous communication The telephone has evolved quite a bit since Mr. Bell's first invention, but it's still a popular means of keeping in touch, making letter-writing nearly a lost art.

When it comes to communication between applications, the request-response model offered by HTTP and REST services is quite common, but it has limitations. Much like letter-writing, request-response involves sending a message and then waiting for a response. It doesn't easily allow for asynchronous communication in which a server might respond with a stream of responses or allow for an open bidirectional channel on which a client and server can repeatedly send data to each other.

In this chapter, we're going to look at RSocket, a relatively new protocol for inter-application communication that allows for more than simple request-response communication. And because it's reactive in nature, it can be far more efficient than blocking HTTP requests.

Along the way, we'll see how to develop RSocket communication in Spring. But first, let's take a high-level look at RSocket to see what makes it different from HTTP-based communication.

14.1 *Introducing RSocket*

RSocket (https://rsocket.io/) is a binary application protocol that is asynchronous and based on Reactive Streams. Put another way, RSocket offers asynchronous communication between applications that supports a reactive model consistent with reactive types like `Flux` and `Mono` that we learned about in chapter 12.

As an alternative to HTTP-based communication, it is more flexible, providing four distinct communication models: request-response, request-stream, fire-and-forget, and channel.

Request-response is the most familiar communication model from RSocket, mimicking how typical HTTP communication works. In the request-response model, a client issues a single request to the server, and the server responds with a single response. This is illustrated in figure 14.1, using Reactor's `Mono` type to define the request and response.

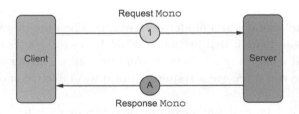

Figure 14.1   RSocket's request-response communication model

Although the request-response model may appear to be equivalent to the communication model offered by HTTP, it's important to understand that RSocket is fundamentally nonblocking and based on reactive types. Although the client will still wait for a reply from the server, under the covers everything is nonblocking and reactive, making more efficient use of threads.

The *request-stream* communication model is similar to request-response, except that after the client has sent a single request to the server, the server responds with a stream of zero-to-many values in a stream. Figure 14.2 illustrates the request-stream model using `Mono` for the request and `Flux` for the response.

Request-stream

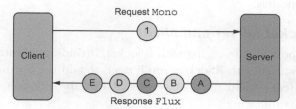

Figure 14.2 RSocket's request-stream
communication model

In some cases, the client may need to send data to the server but doesn't need a response. RSocket provides the *fire-and-forget* model for those situations, as illustrated in figure 14.3.

Fire-and-forget

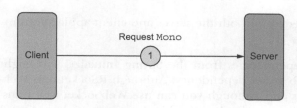

Figure 14.3 RSocket's fire-and-forget
communication model

In the fire-and-forget model, a client sends a request to the server, but the server doesn't send a response back.

Finally, the most flexible of RSocket's communication models is the *channel* model. In the channel model, the client opens a bidirectional channel with the server, and each can send data to the other at any time. Figure 14.4 illustrates the channel communication style.

Channel

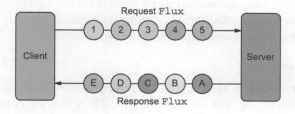

Figure 14.4 RSocket's channel
communication model

RSocket is supported on a variety of languages and platforms, including Java, Java-Script, Kotlin, .NET, Go, and C++.[1] Recent versions of Spring offer first-class support for RSocket, making it easy to create servers and clients using familiar Spring idioms.

---

[1] This is just a short list of languages that are listed on the RSocket website, but there may be community-led implementations of RSocket for other languages.

Let's dive in and see how to create RSocket servers and clients that work with each of the four communication models.

14.2   *Creating a simple RSocket server and client*

Spring offers incredible support for messaging with RSocket, including all four communication models. To get started with RSocket, you'll need to add the Spring Boot RSocket starter to your project's build. In a Maven POM file, the RSocket starter dependency looks like this the following.

Listing 14.1   Spring Boot's RSocket starter dependency

```
<dependency>
    <groupId>org.springframework.boot</groupId>
    <artifactId>spring-boot-starter-rsocket</artifactId>
</dependency>
```

This same dependency is needed for both the server and client applications involved in RSocket communication.

> **NOTE**   When choosing dependencies from the Spring Initializr, you might see a similarly named WebSocket dependency. Although RSocket and Web-Socket have similar names and although you can use WebSocket as a transport for RSocket (and we'll cover that later in this chapter), you do not need to select the WebSocket dependency when working with RSocket.

Next, you'll need to decide which communication model is best for your application. There's no clear answer that fits every situation, so you'll want to weigh the choice against the desired communication behavior of your application. However, as you'll see in the next several examples, the development model isn't much different for each of the communication models, so it'll be easy to switch if you choose wrong.

Let's see how to create an RSocket server and client in Spring using each of the communication models. Because each of RSocket's communication models is different and is best suited for specific use-case scenarios, we'll set the Taco Cloud application aside for now and see how to apply RSocket on different problem domains. We'll start by seeing how to apply the request-response communication model.

14.2.1   *Working with request-response*

Creating an RSocket server in Spring is as simple as creating a controller class, much the same as you would for a web application or REST service. The following controller is an example of an RSocket service that handles greetings from the client and responds with another greeting.

Listing 14.2   A simple RSocket request-response server

```
package rsocket;
import org.springframework.messaging.handler.annotation.MessageMapping;
import org.springframework.stereotype.Controller;
```

```
import lombok.extern.slf4j.Slf4j;
import reactor.core.publisher.Mono;

@Controller
@Slf4j
public class GreetingController {

    @MessageMapping("greeting")
    public Mono<String> handleGreeting(Mono<String> greetingMono) {
        return greetingMono
            .doOnNext(greeting ->
                log.info("Received a greeting: {}", greeting))
            .map(greeting -> "Hello back to you!");
    }

}
```

As you can see, the key difference between a web controller and an RSocket controller is that instead of handling HTTP requests for a given path (using @GetMapping or @Post-Mapping), an RSocket controller handles incoming messages on a given route with the @MessageMapping annotation. In this example, the handleGreeting() method is invoked when a request is sent from the client to the route named "greeting".

The handleGreeting() method receives the message payload from the client in a Mono<String> parameter. In this case, the greeting is simple enough that a String is sufficient, but the incoming payload could be a more complex type, if needed. Upon receiving the Mono<String>, the method simply logs the fact that it received the greeting and then uses the map() function on the Mono to create a new Mono<String> to carry the response that is returned to the client.

Although RSocket controllers aren't handling HTTP requests for a path, the route name can be made to have a pathlike appearance, including variable placeholders that can be passed into the handler method. For example, consider the following twist on the handleGreeting() method:

```
@MessageMapping("greeting/{name}")
public Mono<String> handleGreeting(
        @DestinationVariable("name") String name,
        Mono<String> greetingMono) {

    return greetingMono
        .doOnNext(greeting ->
            log.info("Received a greeting from {} : {}", name, greeting))
        .map(greeting -> "Hello to you, too, " + name);
}
```

In this case, the route specified in @MessageMapping contains a placeholder variable named "name". It is denoted by curly braces, the same way as path variables in a Spring MVC controller. Likewise, the method accepts a String parameter annotated with @DestinationVariable that references the placeholder variable. Just like Spring

MVC's `@PathVariable` annotation, `@DestinationVariable` is used to extract the value specified in the route's placeholder and pass it into the handler method. Once inside this new version of `handleGreeting()`, the name specified in the route will be used to return a more personalized greeting to the client.

There's one more thing you must remember to do when creating an RSocket server: specify the port to listen on. By default, RSocket services are TCP-based and are their own server listening on a specific port. The `spring.rsocket.server.port` configuration property sets the port for the RSocket server, as shown here:

```
spring:
  rsocket:
    server:
      port: 7000
```

The `spring.rsocket.server.port` property serves two purposes: enabling a server and specifying which port the server should listen on. If it is not set, then Spring will assume that your application will be acting as a client only, and no server port will be listening. In this case, we're starting a server, so setting the `spring.rsocket.server.port` property as shown in the previous code will start a server listening on port 7000.

Now let's turn our attention to the RSocket client. In Spring, RSocket clients are implemented using an `RSocketRequester`. Spring Boot autoconfiguration for RSocket will automatically create a bean of type `RSocketRequester.Builder` in the Spring application context. You can inject that builder bean into any other bean you need to create an instance of `RSocketRequester`.

For example, here's the start of an `ApplicationRunner` bean that is injected with an `RSocketRequester.Builder`:

```java
package rsocket;
import org.springframework.boot.ApplicationRunner;
import org.springframework.context.annotation.Bean;
import org.springframework.context.annotation.Configuration;
import org.springframework.messaging.rsocket.RSocketRequester;

@Configuration
@Slf4j
public class RSocketClientConfiguration {

  @Bean
  public ApplicationRunner sender(RSocketRequester.Builder requesterBuilder)
    {
    return args -> {
      RSocketRequester tcp = requesterBuilder.tcp("localhost", 7000);

      // ... send messages with RSocketRequester ...

    };
  }

}
```

In this case, the builder is used to create an RSocketRequester that listens on local-host, port 7000. The resulting RSocketRequester can then be used to send messages to the server.

In a request-response model, the request will need to (at least) specify the route and the data payload. As you'll recall, our server's controller is handling requests for the route named "greeting" and expects a String input. It also returns a String output. The following complete listing of client code shows how to send a greeting to the server and handle the response.

Listing 14.3 Sending a request from a client

```
RSocketRequester tcp = requesterBuilder.tcp("localhost", 7000);

// ... send messages with RSocketRequester ...
tcp
  .route("greeting")
  .data("Hello RSocket!")
  .retrieveMono(String.class)
  .subscribe(response -> log.info("Got a response: {}", response));
```

This sends a greeting of "Hello RSocket!" to the server on the "greeting" route. Notice that it also expects a Mono<String> in return, as specified in the call to retrieveMono(). The subscribe() method subscribes to the returned Mono and handles its payload by logging the value.

Now let's say you want to send a greeting to the other route that accepts a variable value in its route. The client-side code works pretty much the same, except that you include the variable placeholder in the value given to route() along with the value it should contain as follows:

```
String who = "Craig";
tcp
  .route("greeting/{name}", who)
  .data("Hello RSocket!")
  .retrieveMono(String.class)
  .subscribe(response -> log.info("Got a response: {}", response));
```

Here, the message will be sent to the route named "greeting/Craig", which will be handled by the controller handler method whose @MessageMapping specified the route "greeting/{name}". Although you could also hardcode the name in the route or use String concatenation to create the route name, using a placeholder in the client makes it really easy to drop in a value without the messiness of String concatenation.

Although the request-response model is probably the easiest of RSocket's communication models to wrap your head around, it's just the beginning. Let's see how to handle requests that could potentially return several responses with the request-stream model.

14.2.2 *Handling request-stream messaging*

Not all interactions feature a single request and a single response. In a stock quote scenario, for example, it may be useful to request a stream of stock quotes for a given stock symbol. In a request-response model, the client would need to repeatedly poll for the current stock price. But in a request-stream model, the client need ask for the stock price only once and then subscribe to a stream of periodic updates.

To illustrate the request-stream model, let's implement the server and client for the stock quote scenario. First, we'll need to define an object that can carry the stock quote information. The StockQuote class in the next listing will serve this purpose.

Listing 14.4   A model class representing a stock quote

```
package rsocket;
import java.math.BigDecimal;
import java.time.Instant;

import lombok.AllArgsConstructor;
import lombok.Data;

@Data
@AllArgsConstructor
public class StockQuote {

    private String symbol;
    private BigDecimal price;
    private Instant timestamp;

}
```

As you can see, a StockQuote carries the stock symbol, the price, and a timestamp that the price was valid. For brevity's sake, we're using Lombok to help with constructors and accessor methods.

Now let's write a controller to handle requests for stock quotes. You'll find that the StockQuoteController in the next snippet is quite similar to the GreetingController from the previous section.

Listing 14.5   An RSocket controller to stream stock quotes

```
package rsocket;
import java.math.BigDecimal;
import java.time.Duration;
import java.time.Instant;

import org.springframework.messaging.handler.annotation.DestinationVariable;
import org.springframework.messaging.handler.annotation.MessageMapping;
import org.springframework.stereotype.Controller;

import reactor.core.publisher.Flux;
```

```
@Controller
public class StockQuoteController {

    @MessageMapping("stock/{symbol}")
    public Flux<StockQuote> getStockPrice(
            @DestinationVariable("symbol") String symbol) {
        return Flux
            .interval(Duration.ofSeconds(1))
            .map(i -> {
                BigDecimal price = BigDecimal.valueOf(Math.random() * 10);
                return new StockQuote(symbol, price, Instant.now());
            });
    }
}
```

Here, the getStockPrice() method handles incoming requests on the "stock/{symbol}" route, accepting the stock symbol from the route with the @DestinationVariable annotation. For simplicity's sake, rather than look up actual stock prices, the price is calculated as a random value (which may or may not accurately model the volatility of some actual stocks).

What's most notable about getStockPrice(), however, is that it returns a Flux<StockQuote> instead of a Mono<StockQuote>. This is a clue to Spring that this handler method supports the request-stream model. Internally, the Flux is created initially as an interval that fires every one second, but that Flux is mapped to another Flux that produces the random StockQuote. Put simply, a single request handled by the getStockPrice() method returns multiple values, once every second.

A client of a request-stream service is similar to one for a request-response service. The only key difference is that instead of calling retrieveMono() on the requester, it should call retreiveFlux(). The client of the stock quote service might look like this:

```
String stockSymbol = "XYZ";

RSocketRequester tcp = requesterBuilder.tcp("localhost", 7000);
tcp
    .route("stock/{symbol}", stockSymbol)
    .retrieveFlux(StockQuote.class)
    .doOnNext(stockQuote ->
        log.info(
                "Price of {} : {} (at {})",
                stockQuote.getSymbol(),
                stockQuote.getPrice(),
                stockQuote.getTimestamp())
    )
    .subscribe();
```

At this point, we've seen how to create RSocket servers and clients that handle single and multiple responses. But what if the server doesn't have a response to send or the client doesn't need a response? Let's see how to deal with the fire-and-forget communication model.

14.2.3 *Sending fire-and-forget messages*

Imagine that you're on a starship that has just come under attack from an enemy vessel. You sound a ship-wide "red alert" so that all hands are in battle mode. You don't need to wait for a response from the ship's computers affirming the alert status, nor do you have time to wait for and read any kind of response in this situation. You set the alert and then move on to more critical matters.

This is an example of fire-and-forget. Although you may not forget that you're at red alert, given the circumstances, it's more important that you deal with the battle crisis than it is for you to handle a response from setting the alert.

To simulate this scenario, we'll create an RSocket server that handles alert statuses but doesn't return anything. First, we'll need to define a class that defines the request payload, such as the `Alert` class in the following code listing.

Listing 14.6   A model class representing an alert

```
package rsocket;

import java.time.Instant;

import lombok.AllArgsConstructor;
import lombok.Data;

@Data
@AllArgsConstructor
public class Alert {

    private Level level;
    private String orderedBy;
    private Instant orderedAt;

    public enum Level {
        YELLOW, ORANGE, RED, BLACK
    }
}
```

The `Alert` object captures the alert level, who ordered the alert, and a timestamp for when the alert was ordered (defined as an `Instant`). Again, we're using Lombok for constructors and accessor methods in the interest of keeping the listing short.

On the server side, the `AlertController` in the following listing will handle `Alert` messages.

Listing 14.7   An RSocket controller to handle alert updates

```
package rsocket;
import org.springframework.messaging.handler.annotation.MessageMapping;
import org.springframework.stereotype.Controller;
import lombok.extern.slf4j.Slf4j;
import reactor.core.publisher.Mono;
```

```
@Controller
@Slf4j
public class AlertController {

    @MessageMapping("alert")
    public Mono<Void> setAlert(Mono<Alert> alertMono) {
        return alertMono
            .doOnNext(alert ->
                log.info("{} alert ordered by {} at {}",
                        alert.getLevel(),
                        alert.getOrderedBy(),
                        alert.getOrderedAt())
            )
            .thenEmpty(Mono.empty());
    }

}
```

The setAlert() method handles Alert messages on the "alert" route. To keep things simple (albeit useless in an actual battle situation), it logs only the alerts. But what's important is that it returns a Mono<Void>, indicating that there is no response, and, therefore, this handler method supports the fire-and-forget model.

In the client, the code isn't much different from the request-response or request-stream models, as shown here:

```
RSocketRequester tcp = requesterBuilder.tcp("localhost", 7000);
tcp
    .route("alert")
    .data(new Alert(
            Alert.Level.RED, "Craig", Instant.now()))
    .send()
    .subscribe();
log.info("Alert sent");
```

Notice, however, that instead of calling retrieveMono() or retrieveFlux(), the client merely calls send() with no expectation of a response.

Now let's take a look at how to handle the channel communication model in which both the server and the client send multiple messages to each other.

14.2.4 *Sending messages bidirectionally*

In all of the communication models we've seen thus far, the client sends a single request, and the server responds with zero, one, or many responses. In the request-stream model, the server was able to stream back multiple responses to the client, but the client was still limited to sending only a single request. But why should the server have all of the fun? Why can't the client send multiple requests?

That's where the channel communication model comes in handy. In the channel communication model, the client can stream multiple requests to the server, which may also stream back multiple responses in a bidirectional conversation between both sides. It's the most flexible of RSocket's communication models, although also the most complex.

To demonstrate how to work with RSocket channel communication in Spring, let's create a service that calculates gratuity on a bill, receiving a `Flux` of requests and responding with a `Flux` of responses. First, we'll need to define the model objects that represent the request and the response. The `GratuityIn` class, shown next, represents the request sent by the client and received by the server.

Listing 14.8   A model representing an inbound gratuity request

```
package rsocket;

import java.math.BigDecimal;

import lombok.AllArgsConstructor;
import lombok.Data;

@Data
@AllArgsConstructor
public class GratuityIn {

    private BigDecimal billTotal;
    private int percent;

}
```

`GratuityIn` carries two essential pieces of information required to calculate gratuity: the bill total and a percentage. The `GratuityOut` class shown in the next code snippet represents the response, echoing the values given in `GratuityIn`, along with a gratuity property containing the calculated gratuity amount.

Listing 14.9   A model representing an outbound gratuity response

```
package rsocket;

import java.math.BigDecimal;

import lombok.AllArgsConstructor;
import lombok.Data;

@Data
@AllArgsConstructor
public class GratuityOut {

    private BigDecimal billTotal;
    private int percent;
    private BigDecimal gratuity;

}
```

The `GratuityController` in the next code listing handles the gratuity request and looks a lot like the controllers we've written earlier in this chapter.

Listing 14.10 An RSocket controller that handles multiple messages on a channel

```java
package rsocket;
import java.math.BigDecimal;
import org.springframework.messaging.handler.annotation.MessageMapping;
import org.springframework.stereotype.Controller;

import lombok.extern.slf4j.Slf4j;
import reactor.core.publisher.Flux;


@Controller
@Slf4j
public class GratuityController {

    @MessageMapping("gratuity")
    public Flux<GratuityOut> calculate(Flux<GratuityIn> gratuityInFlux) {
        return gratuityInFlux
            .doOnNext(in -> log.info("Calculating gratuity:  {}", in))
            .map(in -> {
                double percentAsDecimal = in.getPercent() / 100.0;
                BigDecimal gratuity = in.getBillTotal()
                        .multiply(BigDecimal.valueOf(percentAsDecimal));
                return new GratuityOut(
                        in.getBillTotal(), in.getPercent(), gratuity);
            });
    }

}
```

There is, however, one significant difference between the previous example and the earlier ones: not only does this code return a Flux, but it also accepts a Flux as input. As with the request-stream model, the Flux returned enables the controller to stream multiple values to the client. But the Flux parameter is what differentiates the channel model from the request-stream model. The Flux parameter coming in allows the controller to handle a stream of requests from the client coming into the handler method.

The client side of the channel model differs from the client of the request-stream model only in that it sends a Flux<GratuityIn> to the server instead of a Mono<GratuityIn>, as shown here.

Listing 14.11 A client that sends and receives multiple messages over an open channel

```java
RSocketRequester tcp = requesterBuilder.tcp("localhost", 7000);

Flux<GratuityIn> gratuityInFlux =
        Flux.fromArray(new GratuityIn[] {
                new GratuityIn(BigDecimal.valueOf(35.50), 18),
                new GratuityIn(BigDecimal.valueOf(10.00), 15),
                new GratuityIn(BigDecimal.valueOf(23.25), 20),
                new GratuityIn(BigDecimal.valueOf(52.75), 18),
```

```
            new GratuityIn(BigDecimal.valueOf(80.00), 15)
    })
    .delayElements(Duration.ofSeconds(1));


tcp
    .route("gratuity")
    .data(gratuityInFlux)
    .retrieveFlux(GratuityOut.class)
    .subscribe(out ->
        log.info(out.getPercent() + "% gratuity on "
                + out.getBillTotal() + " is "
                + out.getGratuity())));
```

In this case, the Flux<GratuityIn> is created statically using the fromArray() method, but it could be a Flux created from any source of data, perhaps retrieved from a reactive data repository.

You may have observed a pattern in how the reactive types accepted and returned by the server controller's handler methods determine the RSocket communication model supported. Table 14.1 summarizes the relationship between the server's input/output types and the RSocket communication models.

Table 14.1 The supported RSocket model is determined by the handler method's parameter and return types.

RSocket model	Handler parameter	Handler returns
Request-response	Mono	Mono
Request-stream	Mono	Flux
Fire-and-forget	Mono	Mono<Void>
Channel	Flux	Flux

You may wonder whether it's possible for a server to accept a Flux and return a Mono. In short, that's not an option. Although you may imagine handling multiple requests on an incoming Flux and responding with a Mono<Void> in a weird mashup of the channel and fire-and-forget models, there is no RSocket model that maps to that scenario. Therefore, it's not supported.

14.3 *Transporting RSocket over WebSocket*

By default, RSocket communication takes place over a TCP socket. But in some cases, TCP isn't an option. Consider the following two situations:

- The client is written in JavaScript and is running in a user's web browser.
- The client must cross a gateway or firewall boundary to get to the server, and the firewall doesn't allow communication over arbitrary ports.

Moreover, WebSocket itself lacks any support for routing, requiring that routing details be defined at the application level. By layering RSocket over WebSocket, WebSocket will benefit from RSocket's built-in routing support.

In these situations, RSocket can be transported over WebSocket. WebSocket communication takes place over HTTP, which is the primary means of communication in all web browsers and is usually allowed through firewalls.

To switch from the TCP transport to the WebSocket transport, you need to make only a few minor changes in the server and client. To start, because WebSocket is carried over HTTP, you need to be sure that the server-side application supports handling HTTP requests. Put simply, you need to add the following WebFlux starter dependency to the project build (if it's not already there):

```
<dependency>
    <groupId>org.springframework.boot</groupId>
    <artifactId>spring-boot-starter-webflux</artifactId>
</dependency>
```

You also need to specify that you want to use the WebSocket transport in the server-side configuration by setting the `spring.rsocket.server.transport` property. Also, you need to set the HTTP path that the RSocket communication will take place on by setting `spring.rsocket.server.mapping-path`. The server's configuration will look like this in application.yml:

```
spring:
  rsocket:
    server:
      transport: websocket
      mapping-path: /rsocket
```

Unlike the TCP transport, which communicates over a specific port, the WebSocket transport works over a specific HTTP path. Thus, there is no need to set `spring.rsocket.server.port` as with RSocket over TCP.

That's all you'll need to do on the server side to enable WebSocket transport for RSocket. Everything else will work exactly the same as with TCP.

On the client side, only one small change is required. Rather than create a TCP-based requester, you want to create a WebSocket-based requester by calling the `websocket()` method on the `RSocketRequester.Builder` like so:

```
RSocketRequester requester = requesterBuilder.websocket(
                  URI.create("ws://localhost:8080/rsocket"));

requester
  .route("greeting")
  .data("Hello RSocket!")
  .retrieveMono(String.class)
  .subscribe(response -> log.info("Got a response: {}", response));
```

And that's all there is to transporting RSocket over WebSocket!

Summary

- RSocket is an asynchronous binary protocol that offers four communication models: request-response, request-stream, fire-and-forget, and channel.
- Spring supports RSocket on the server through controllers and handler methods annotated with `@MessageMapping`.
- The `RSocketRequester` enables client-side communication with RSocket.
- In both cases, Spring's RSocket support works through Reactor's `Flux` and `Mono` reactive types for fully reactive communication.
- RSocket communication takes place over TCP by default but can also be transported over WebSocket to deal with firewall constraints and browser clients.

Part 4

Deployed Spring

In part 4, you'll ready an application for production and see how to deploy it. Chapter 15 introduces the Spring Boot Actuator, an extension to Spring Boot that exposes the internals of a running Spring application as REST endpoints and JMX MBeans. In chapter 16, you'll see how to use Spring Boot Admin to put a user-friendly browser-based administrative application on top of the Actuator. You'll also see how to register client applications with and secure the Admin Server. Chapter 17 discusses how to expose and consume Spring beans as JMX MBeans. Finally, in chapter 18, you'll see how to deploy your Spring application in a variety of production environments, including containerized Spring applications that can run in Kubernetes.

15

Working with
Spring Boot Actuator

This chapter covers

- Enabling Actuator in Spring Boot projects
- Exploring Actuator endpoints
- Customizing Actuator
- Securing Actuator

Have you ever tried to guess what's inside a wrapped gift? You shake it, weigh it, and measure it. And you might even have a solid idea as to what's inside. But until you open it up, there's no way of knowing for sure.

A running application is kind of like a wrapped gift. You can poke at it and make reasonable guesses as to what's going on under the covers. But how can you know for sure? If only there were some way that you could peek inside a running application, see how it's behaving, check on its health, and maybe even trigger operations that influence how it runs!

In this chapter, we're going to explore Spring Boot Actuator. Actuator offers production-ready features such as monitoring and metrics to Spring Boot applications. Actuator's features are provided by way of several endpoints, which are made available over HTTP as well as through JMX MBeans. This chapter focuses primarily on HTTP endpoints, saving JMX endpoints for chapter 18.

387

15.1 *Introducing Actuator*

In a machine, an actuator is a component that's responsible for controlling and moving a mechanism. In a Spring Boot application, the Spring Boot Actuator plays that same role, enabling us to see inside of a running application and, to some degree, control how the application behaves.

Using endpoints exposed by Actuator, we can ask things about the internal state of a running Spring Boot application, such as the following:

- What configuration properties are available in the application environment?
- What are the logging levels of various packages in the application?
- How much memory is being consumed by the application?
- How many times has a given HTTP endpoint been requested?
- What is the health of the application and any external services it coordinates with?

To enable Actuator in a Spring Boot application, you simply need to add Actuator's starter dependency to your build. In any Spring Boot application Maven pom.xml file, the following <dependency> entry does the trick:

```
<dependency>
  <groupId>org.springframework.boot</groupId>
  <artifactId>spring-boot-starter-actuator</artifactId>
</dependency>
```

Once the Actuator starter is part of the project build, the application will be equipped with several out-of-the-box Actuator endpoints, including those described in table 15.1.

Table 15.1   Actuator endpoints for peeking inside and manipulating the state of a running Spring Boot application

HTTP method	Path	Description
GET	/auditevents	Produces a report of any audit events that have been fired
GET	/beans	Describes all the beans in the Spring application context
GET	/conditions	Produces a report of autoconfiguration conditions that either passed or failed, leading to the beans created in the application context
GET	/configprops	Describes all configuration properties along with the current values
GET, POST, DELETE	/env	Produces a report of all property sources and their properties available to the Spring application
GET	/env/{toMatch}	Describes the value of a single environment property
GET	/health	Returns the aggregate health of the application and (possibly) the health of external dependent applications
GET	/heapdump	Downloads a heap dump

Table 15.1 Actuator endpoints for peeking inside and manipulating the state of a running Spring Boot application *(continued)*

HTTP method	Path	Description
GET	/httptrace	Produces a trace of the most recent 100 requests
GET	/info	Returns any developer-defined information about the application
GET	/loggers	Produces a list of packages in the application along with their configured and effective logging levels
GET, POST	/loggers/{name}	Returns the configured and effective logging level of a given logger; the effective logging level can be set with a POST request
GET	/mappings	Produces a report of all HTTP mappings and their corresponding handler methods
GET	/metrics	Returns a list of all metrics categories
GET	/metrics/{name}	Returns a multidimensional set of values for a given metric
GET	/scheduledtasks	Lists all scheduled tasks
GET	/threaddump	Returns a report of all application threads

In addition to HTTP endpoints, all of the Actuator endpoints in table 15.1, with the lone exception of /heapdump, are also exposed as JMX MBeans. We'll look at the JMX side of Actuator in chapter 17.

15.1.1 Configuring Actuator's base path

By default, the paths for all the endpoints shown in table 15.1 are prefixed with /actuator. This mean that, for example, if you wish to retrieve health information about your application from Actuator, then issuing a GET request for /actuator/health will return the information you need.

The Actuator prefix path can be changed by setting the management.endpoint .web.base-path property. For example, if you'd rather the prefix be /management, you would set the management.endpoints.web.base-path property like this:

```
management:
  endpoints:
    web:
      base-path: /management
```

With this property set as shown, you'd need to make a GET request for /management/ health to obtain the application's health information.

Whether or not you decide to change the Actuator base path, all Actuator endpoints in this chapter will be referred to without the base path for the sake of brevity. For example, when the /health endpoint is mentioned, it is the /{base path}/health endpoint that is intended, or more precisely, the /actuator/health endpoint if the base path hasn't been changed.

15.1.2 *Enabling and disabling Actuator endpoints*

You may have noticed that only the /health endpoint is enabled by default. Most Actuator endpoints carry sensitive information and should be secured. You can use Spring Security to lock down Actuator, but because Actuator isn't secured on its own, most of the endpoints are disabled by default, requiring you to opt in for the endpoints you wish to expose.

Two configuration properties, `management.endpoints.web.exposure.include` and `management.endpoints.web.exposure.exclude`, can be used to control which endpoints are exposed. Use `management.endpoints.web.exposure.include` to specify which endpoints you want to expose. For example, if you wish to expose only the /health, /info, /beans, and /conditions endpoints, you can specify that with the following configuration:

```
management:
  endpoints:
    web:
      exposure:
        include: health,info,beans,conditions
```

The `management.endpoints.web.exposure.include` property also accepts an asterisk (*) as a wildcard to indicate that all Actuator endpoints should be exposed, as shown here:

```
management:
  endpoints:
    web:
      exposure:
        include: '*'
```

If you want to expose all but a few endpoints, it's typically easier to include them all with a wildcard and then explicitly exclude a few. For example, to expose all Actuator endpoints except for /threaddump and /heapdump, you could set both the `management.endpoints.web.exposure.include` and `management.endpoints.web.exposure.exclude` properties like this:

```
management:
  endpoints:
    web:
      exposure:
        include: '*'
        exclude: threaddump,heapdump
```

Should you decide to expose more than /health and /info, it's probably a good idea to configure Spring Security to restrict access to the other endpoints. We'll look at how to secure Actuator endpoints in section 15.4. For now, though, let's look at how you can consume the HTTP endpoints exposed by Actuator.

15.2 *Consuming Actuator endpoints*

Actuator can bestow a veritable treasure trove of interesting and useful information about a running application by way of the HTTP endpoints listed in table 15.1. As HTTP endpoints, these can be consumed like any REST API, using whatever HTTP client you wish, including Spring's `RestTemplate` and `WebClient`, from a JavaScript application, or simply with the `curl` command-line client.

For the sake of exploring Actuator endpoints, we'll use the `curl` command-line client in this chapter. In chapter 16, I'll introduce you to Spring Boot Admin, which layers a user-friendly web application on top of an application's Actuator endpoints.

To get some idea of what endpoints Actuator has to offer, a GET request to Actuator's base path will provide HATEOAS links for each of the endpoints. Using `curl` to make a request to /actuator, you might get a response something like this (abridged to save space):

```
$ curl localhost:8080/actuator
{
  "_links": {
    "self": {
      "href": "http://localhost:8080/actuator",
      "templated": false
    },
    "auditevents": {
      "href": "http://localhost:8080/actuator/auditevents",
      "templated": false
    },
    "beans": {
      "href": "http://localhost:8080/actuator/beans",
      "templated": false
    },
    "health": {
      "href": "http://localhost:8080/actuator/health",
      "templated": false
    },
    ...
  }
}
```

Because different libraries may contribute additional Actuator endpoints of their own, and because some endpoints may be not be exported, the actual results may vary from application to application.

In any event, the set of links returned from Actuator's base path serve as a map to all that Actuator has to offer. Let's begin our exploration of the Actuator landscape with the two endpoints that provide essential information about an application: the /health and /info endpoints.

15.2.1 *Fetching essential application information*

At the beginning of a typical visit to the doctor, we're usually asked two very basic questions: who are you and how do you feel? Although the words chosen by the doctor or nurse may be different, they ultimately want to know a little bit about the person they're treating and why you're seeing them.

Those same essential questions are what Actuator's /info and /health endpoints answer for a Spring Boot application. The /info endpoint tells you a little about the application, and the /health endpoint tells you how healthy the application is.

ASKING FOR INFORMATION ABOUT AN APPLICATION

To learn a little bit of information about a running Spring Boot application, you can ask the /info endpoint. By default, however, the /info endpoint isn't very informative. Here's what you might see when you make a request for it using `curl`:

```
$ curl localhost:8080/actuator/info
{}
```

Although it may seem that the /info endpoint isn't very useful, it's best to think of it as a clean canvas on which you may paint any information you'd like to present.

We have several ways to supply information for the /info endpoint to return, but the most straightforward way is to create one or more configuration properties where the property name is prefixed with `info`. For example, suppose that you want the response from the /info endpoint to include support contact information, including an email address and phone number. To do that, you can configure the following properties in the application.yml file:

```
info:
  contact:
    email: support@tacocloud.com
    phone: 822-625-6831
```

Neither the `info.contact.email` property nor the `info.contact.phone` property has any special meaning to Spring Boot or any bean that may be in the application context. However, by virtue of the fact that it's prefixed with *info*, the /info endpoint will now echo the value of the property in its response as follows:

```
{
  "contact": {
    "email": "support@tacocloud.com",
    "phone": "822-625-6831"
  }
}
```

In section 15.3.1, we'll look at a few other ways to populate the /info endpoint with useful information about an application.

INSPECTING APPLICATION HEALTH

Issuing an HTTP GET request for the /health endpoint results in a simple JSON response with the health status of your application. For example, here's what you might see when using curl to fetch the /health endpoint:

```
$ curl localhost:8080/actuator/health
{"status":"UP"}
```

You may be wondering how useful it is to have an endpoint that reports that the application is UP. What would it report if the application were down?

As it turns out, the status shown here is an aggregate status of one or more health indicators. Health indicators report the health of external systems that the application interacts with, such as databases, message brokers, and even Spring Cloud components such as Eureka and the Config Server. The health status of each indicator could be one of the following:

- *UP*—The external system is up and is reachable.
- *DOWN*—The external system is down or unreachable.
- *UNKNOWN*—The status of the external system is unclear.
- *OUT_OF_SERVICE*—The external system is reachable but is currently unavailable.

The health statuses of all health indicators are then aggregated into the application's overall health status, applying the following rules:

- If all health indicators are UP, then the application health status is UP.
- If one or more health indicators are DOWN, then the application health status is DOWN.
- If one or more health indicators are OUT_OF_SERVICE, then the application health status is OUT_OF_SERVICE.
- UNKNOWN health statuses are ignored and aren't rolled into the application's aggregate health.

By default, only the aggregate status is returned in response to a request for /health. You can configure the management.endpoint.health.show-details property, however, to show the full details of all health indicators, as shown next:

```
management:
  endpoint:
    health:
      show-details: always
```

The management.endpoint.health.show-details property defaults to never, but it can also be set to always to always show the full details of all health indicators, or to when-authorized to show the full details only when the requesting client is fully authorized.

Now when you issue a GET request to the /health endpoint, you get full health indicator details. Here's a sample of what that might look like for a service that integrates with the Mongo document database:

```
{
  "status": "UP",
  "details": {
    "mongo": {
      "status": "UP",
      "details": {
        "version": "3.5.5"
      }
    },
    "diskSpace": {
      "status": "UP",
      "details": {
        "total": 499963170816,
        "free": 177284784128,
        "threshold": 10485760
      }
    }
  }
}
```

All applications, regardless of any other external dependencies, will have a health indicator for the filesystem named diskSpace. The diskSpace health indicator indicates the health of the filesystem (hopefully, UP), which is determined by how much free space is remaining. If the available disk space drops below the threshold, it will report a status of DOWN.

In the preceding example, there's also a mongo health indicator, which reports the status of the Mongo database. Details shown include the Mongo database version.

Autoconfiguration ensures that only health indicators that are pertinent to an application will appear in the response from the /health endpoint. In addition to the mongo and diskSpace health indicators, Spring Boot also provides health indicators for several other external databases and systems, including the following:

- Cassandra
- Config Server
- Couchbase
- Eureka
- Hystrix
- JDBC data sources
- Elasticsearch
- InfluxDB
- JMS message brokers
- LDAP
- Email servers

- Neo4j
- Rabbit message brokers
- Redis
- Solr

Additionally, third-party libraries may contribute their own health indicators. We'll look at how to write a custom health indicator in section 15.3.2.

As you've seen, the /health and /info endpoints provide general information about the running application. Meanwhile, other Actuator endpoints provide insight into the application configuration. Let's look at how Actuator can show how an application is configured.

15.2.2 Viewing configuration details

Beyond receiving general information about an application, it can be enlightening to understand how an application is configured. What beans are in the application context? What autoconfiguration conditions passed or failed? What environment properties are available to the application? How are HTTP requests mapped to controllers? What logging level are one or more packages or classes set to?

These questions are answered by Actuator's /beans, /conditions, /env, /config-props, /mappings, and /loggers endpoints. And in some cases, such as /env and /loggers, you can even adjust the configuration of a running application on the fly. We'll look at how each of these endpoints gives insight into the configuration of a running application, starting with the /beans endpoint.

GETTING A BEAN WIRING REPORT

The most essential endpoint for exploring the Spring application context is the /beans endpoint. This endpoint returns a JSON document describing every single bean in the application context, its Java type, and any of the other beans it's injected with.

A complete response from a GET request to /beans could easily fill this entire chapter. Instead of examining the complete response from /beans, let's consider the following snippet, which focuses on a single bean entry:

```
{
  "contexts": {
    "application-1": {
      "beans": {
...
        "ingredientsController": {
          "aliases": [],
          "scope": "singleton",
          "type": "tacos.ingredients.IngredientsController",
          "resource": "file [/Users/habuma/Documents/Workspaces/
            TacoCloud/ingredient-service/target/classes/tacos/
            ingredients/IngredientsController.class]",
          "dependencies": [
            "ingredientRepository"
```

```
            ]
          },
    ...
        },
        "parentId": null
      }
    }
}
```

At the root of the response is the contexts element, which includes one subelement for each Spring application context in the application. Within each application context is a beans element that holds details for all the beans in the application context.

In the preceding example, the bean shown is the one whose name is ingredients-Controller. You can see that it has no aliases, is scoped as a singleton, and is of type tacos.ingredients.IngredientsController. Moreover, the resource property gives the path to the class file that defines the bean. And the dependencies property lists all other beans that are injected into the given bean. In this case, the ingredients-Controller bean is injected with a bean whose name is ingredientRepository.

EXPLAINING AUTOCONFIGURATION

As you've seen, autoconfiguration is one of the most powerful things that Spring Boot offers. Sometimes, however, you may wonder why something has been autoconfigured. Or you may expect something to have been autoconfigured and are left wondering why it hasn't been. In that case, you can make a GET request to /conditions to get an explanation of what took place in autoconfiguration.

The autoconfiguration report returned from /conditions is divided into three parts: positive matches (conditional configuration that passed), negative matches (conditional configuration that failed), and unconditional classes. The following snippet from the response to a request to /conditions shows an example of each section:

```
{
  "contexts": {
    "application-1": {
      "positiveMatches": {
    ...
        "MongoDataAutoConfiguration#mongoTemplate": [
          {
            "condition": "OnBeanCondition",
            "message": "@ConditionalOnMissingBean (types:
                org.springframework.data.mongodb.core.MongoTemplate;
                SearchStrategy: all) did not find any beans"
          }
        ],
    ...
      },
      "negativeMatches": {
    ...
        "DispatcherServletAutoConfiguration": {
          "notMatched": [
```

```
    {
        "condition": "OnClassCondition",
        "message": "@ConditionalOnClass did not find required
            class 'org.springframework.web.servlet.
                                            DispatcherServlet'"
    }
    ],
    "matched": []
},
...
},
"unconditionalClasses": [
...
    "org.springframework.boot.autoconfigure.context.
                    ConfigurationPropertiesAutoConfiguration",
...
    ]
    }
}
}
```

Under the positiveMatches section, you see that a MongoTemplate bean was configured by autoconfiguration because one didn't already exist. The autoconfiguration that caused this includes a @ConditionalOnMissingBean annotation, which passes off the bean to be configured if it hasn't already been explicitly configured. But in this case, no beans of type MongoTemplate were found, so autoconfiguration stepped in and configured one.

Under negativeMatches, Spring Boot autoconfiguration considered configuring a DispatcherServlet. But the @ConditionalOnClass conditional annotation failed because DispatcherServlet couldn't be found.

Finally, a ConfigurationPropertiesAutoConfiguration bean was configured unconditionally, as seen under the unconditionalClasses section. Configuration properties are foundational to how Spring Boot operates, so you should autoconfigure any configuration pertaining to configuration properties without any conditions.

INSPECTING THE ENVIRONMENT AND CONFIGURATION PROPERTIES

In addition to knowing how your application beans are wired together, you might also be interested in learning what environment properties are available and what configuration properties were injected into the beans.

When you issue a GET request to the /env endpoint, you'll receive a rather lengthy response that includes properties from all property sources in play in the Spring application. This includes properties from environment variables, JVM system properties, application.properties and application.yml files, and even the Spring Cloud Config Server (if the application is a client of the Config Server).

The following listing shows a greatly abridged example of the kind of response you might get from the /env endpoint, to give you some idea of the kind of information it provides.

Listing 15.1   The results from the /env endpoint

```
$ curl localhost:8080/actuator/env
{
  "activeProfiles": [
    "development"
  ],
  "propertySources": [
...
    {
      "name": "systemEnvironment",
      "properties": {
        "PATH": {
          "value": "/usr/bin:/bin:/usr/sbin:/sbin",
          "origin": "System Environment Property \"PATH\""
        },
...
        "HOME": {
          "value": "/Users/habuma",
          "origin": "System Environment Property \"HOME\""
        }
      }
    },
    {
      "name": "applicationConfig: [classpath:/application.yml]",
      "properties": {
        "spring.application.name": {
          "value": "ingredient-service",
          "origin": "class path resource [application.yml]:3:11"
        },
        "server.port": {
          "value": 8080,
          "origin": "class path resource [application.yml]:9:9"
        },
...
      }
    },
...
  ]
}
```

Although the full response from /env provides even more information, what's shown in listing 15.1 contains a few noteworthy elements. First, notice that near the top of the response is a field named `activeProfiles`. In this case, it indicates that the development profile is active. If any other profiles were active, those would be listed as well.

Next, the `propertySources` field is an array containing an entry for every property source in the Spring application environment. In listing 15.1, only the system-Environment and an `applicationConfig` property source referencing the application.yml file are shown.

Within each property source is a listing of all properties provided by that source, paired with their values. In the case of the application.yml property source, the `origin` field for each property tells exactly where the property is set, including the line and column within application.yml.

The /env endpoint can also be used to fetch a specific property when that property's name is given as the second element of the path. For example, to examine the server.port property, submit a GET request for /env/server.port, as shown here:

```
$ curl localhost:8080/actuator/env/server.port
{
  "property": {
    "source": "systemEnvironment", "value": "8080"
  },
  "activeProfiles": [ "development" ],
  "propertySources": [
    { "name": "server.ports" },
    { "name": "mongo.ports" },
    { "name": "systemProperties" },
    { "name": "systemEnvironment",
      "property": {
        "value": "8080",
        "origin": "System Environment Property \"SERVER_PORT\""
      }
    },
    { "name": "random" },
    { "name": "applicationConfig: [classpath:/application.yml]",
      "property": {
        "value": 0,
        "origin": "class path resource [application.yml]:9:9"
      }
    },
    { "name": "springCloudClientHostInfo" },
    { "name": "refresh" },
    { "name": "defaultProperties" },
    { "name": "Management Server" }
  ]
}
```

As you can see, all property sources are still represented, but only those that set the specified property will contain any additional information. In this case, both the systemEnvironment property source and the application.yml property source had values for the server.port property. Because the systemEnvironment property source takes precedence over any of the property sources listed below it, its value of 8080 wins. The winning value is reflected near the top under the property field.

The /env endpoint can be used for more than just reading property values. By submitting a POST request to the /env endpoint, along with a JSON document with name and value fields, you can also set properties in the running application. For example, to set a property named tacocloud.discount.code to TACOS1234, you can use curl to submit the POST request at the command line like this:

```
$ curl localhost:8080/actuator/env \
       -d'{"name":"tacocloud.discount.code","value":"TACOS1234"}' \
```

```
       -H "Content-type: application/json"
{"tacocloud.discount.code":"TACOS1234"}
```

After submitting the property, the newly set property and its value are returned in the response. Later, should you decide you no longer need that property, you can submit a DELETE request to the /env endpoint as follows to delete all properties created through that endpoint:

```
$ curl localhost:8080/actuator/env -X DELETE
{"tacocloud.discount.code":"TACOS1234"}
```

As useful as setting properties through Actuator's API can be, it's important to be aware that any properties set with a POST request to the /env endpoint apply only to the application instance receiving the request, are temporary, and will be lost when the application restarts.

NAVIGATING HTTP REQUEST MAPPINGS

Although Spring MVC's (and Spring WebFlux's) programming model makes it easy to handle HTTP requests by simply annotating methods with request-mapping annotations, it can sometimes be challenging to get a big-picture understanding of all the kinds of HTTP requests that an application can handle and what kinds of components handle those requests.

Actuator's /mappings endpoint offers a one-stop view of every HTTP request handler in an application, whether it be from a Spring MVC controller or one of Actuator's own endpoints. To get a complete list of all the endpoints in a Spring Boot application, make a GET request to the /mappings endpoint, and you might receive something that's a little bit like the abridged response shown next.

Listing 15.2   HTTP mappings as shown by the /mappings endpoint

```
$ curl localhost:8080/actuator/mappings | jq
{
  "contexts": {
    "application-1": {
      "mappings": {
        "dispatcherHandlers": {
          "webHandler": [
...
            {
              "predicate": "{[/ingredients],methods=[GET]}",
              "handler": "public
reactor.core.publisher.Flux<tacos.ingredients.Ingredient>
tacos.ingredients.IngredientsController.allIngredients()",
              "details": {
                "handlerMethod": {
                  "className": "tacos.ingredients.IngredientsController",
                  "name": "allIngredients",
                  "descriptor": "()Lreactor/core/publisher/Flux;"
                },
```

```
          "handlerFunction": null,
          "requestMappingConditions": {
            "consumes": [],
            "headers": [],
            "methods": [
              "GET"
            ],
            "params": [],
            "patterns": [
              "/ingredients"
            ],
            "produces": []
          }
        }
      },
...
      ]
    }
  },
  "parentId": "application-1"
},
  "bootstrap": {
    "mappings": {
      "dispatcherHandlers": {}
    },
    "parentId": null
  }
}
}
```

Here, the response from the curl command line is piped to a utility called jq (https://stedolan.github.io/jq/), which, among other things, pretty-prints the JSON returned from the request in an easily readable format. For the sake of brevity, this response has been abridged to show only a single request handler. Specifically, it shows that GET requests for /ingredients will be handled by the allIngredients() method of IngredientsController.

MANAGING LOGGING LEVELS

Logging is an important feature of any application. Logging can provide a means of auditing as well as a crude means of debugging.

Setting logging levels can be quite a balancing act. If you set the logging level to be too verbose, there may be too much noise in the logs, and finding useful information may be difficult. On the other hand, if you set logging levels to be too slack, the logs may not be of much value in understanding what an application is doing.

Logging levels are typically applied on a package-by-package basis. If you're ever wondering what logging levels are set in your running Spring Boot application, you can issue a GET request to the /loggers endpoint. The following JSON code shows an excerpt from a response to /loggers:

```
{
  "levels": [ "OFF", "ERROR", "WARN", "INFO", "DEBUG", "TRACE" ],
  "loggers": {
    "ROOT": {
      "configuredLevel": "INFO", "effectiveLevel": "INFO"
    },
...
    "org.springframework.web": {
      "configuredLevel": null, "effectiveLevel": "INFO"
    },
...
    "tacos": {
      "configuredLevel": null, "effectiveLevel": "INFO"
    },
    "tacos.ingredients": {
      "configuredLevel": null, "effectiveLevel": "INFO"
    },
    "tacos.ingredients.IngredientServiceApplication": {
      "configuredLevel": null, "effectiveLevel": "INFO"
    }
  }
}
```

The response starts off with a list of all valid logging levels. After that, the `loggers` element lists logging-level details for each package in the application. The `configured-Level` property shows the logging level that has been explicitly configured (or `null` if it hasn't been explicitly configured). The `effectiveLevel` property gives the effective logging level, which may have been inherited from a parent package or from the root logger.

Although this excerpt shows logging levels only for the root logger and four packages, the complete response will include logging-level entries for every single package in the application, including those for libraries that are in use. If you'd rather focus your request on a specific package, you can specify the package name as an extra path component in the request.

For example, if you just want to know what logging levels are set for the `tacocloud.ingredients` package, you can make a request to /loggers/tacos.ingredients as follows:

```
{
  "configuredLevel": null,
  "effectiveLevel": "INFO"
}
```

Aside from returning the logging levels for the application packages, the /loggers endpoint also allows you to change the configured logging level by issuing a POST request. For example, suppose you want to set the logging level of the `tacocloud.ingredients` package to `DEBUG`. The following `curl` command will achieve that:

```
$ curl localhost:8080/actuator/loggers/tacos/ingredients \
       -d'{"configuredLevel":"DEBUG"}' \
       -H"Content-type: application/json"
```

Now that the logging level has been changed, you can issue a GET request to /loggers/tacos/ingredients as shown here to see that it has been changed:

```
{
  "configuredLevel": "DEBUG",
  "effectiveLevel": "DEBUG"
}
```

Notice that where the configuredLevel was previously null, it's now DEBUG. That change carries over to the effectiveLevel as well. But what's most important is that if any code in that package logs anything at debug level, the log files will include that debug-level information.

15.2.3 *Viewing application activity*

It can be useful to keep an eye on activity in a running application, including the kinds of HTTP requests that the application is handling and the activity of all of the threads in the application. For this, Actuator provides the /httptrace, /threaddump, and /heapdump endpoints.

The /heapdump endpoint is perhaps the most difficult Actuator endpoint to describe in any detail. Put succinctly, it downloads a gzip-compressed HPROF heap dump file that can be used to track down memory or thread issues. For the sake of space and because use of the heap dump is a rather advanced feature, I'm going to limit coverage of the /heapdump endpoint to this paragraph.

TRACING HTTP ACTIVITY

The /httptrace endpoint reports details on the most recent 100 requests handled by an application. Details included are the request method and path, a timestamp indicating when the request was handled, headers from both the request and the response, and the time taken handling the request.

The following snippet of JSON code shows a single entry from the response of the /httptrace endpoint:

```
{
  "traces": [
    {
      "timestamp": "2020-06-03T23:41:24.494Z",
      "principal": null,
      "session": null,
      "request": {
        "method": "GET",
        "uri": "http://localhost:8080/ingredients",
        "headers": {
          "Host": ["localhost:8080"],
          "User-Agent": ["curl/7.54.0"],
          "Accept": ["*/*"]
        },
        "remoteAddress": null
      },
```

```
      "response": {
        "status": 200,
        "headers": {
          "Content-Type": ["application/json;charset=UTF-8"]
        }
      },
      "timeTaken": 4
    },
...
  ]
}
```

Although this information may be useful for debugging purposes, it's even more interesting when the trace data is tracked over time, providing insight into how busy the
application was at any given time as well as how many requests were successful compared to how many failed, based on the value of the response status. In chapter 16,
you'll see how Spring Boot Admin captures this information into a running graph that
visualizes the HTTP trace information over a period of time.

MONITORING THREADS

In addition to HTTP request tracing, thread activity can also be useful in determining
what's going on in a running application. The /threaddump endpoint produces a
snapshot of current thread activity. The following snippet from a /threaddump response
gives a taste of what this endpoint provides:

```
{
  "threadName": "reactor-http-nio-8",
  "threadId": 338,
  "blockedTime": -1,
  "blockedCount": 0,
  "waitedTime": -1,
  "waitedCount": 0,
  "lockName": null,
  "lockOwnerId": -1,
  "lockOwnerName": null,
  "inNative": true,
  "suspended": false,
  "threadState": "RUNNABLE",
  "stackTrace": [
    {
      "methodName": "kevent0",
      "fileName": "KQueueArrayWrapper.java",
      "lineNumber": -2,
      "className": "sun.nio.ch.KQueueArrayWrapper",
      "nativeMethod": true
    },
    {
      "methodName": "poll",
      "fileName": "KQueueArrayWrapper.java",
      "lineNumber": 198,
      "className": "sun.nio.ch.KQueueArrayWrapper",
```

```
        "nativeMethod": false
      },
  ...
    ],
    "lockedMonitors": [
      {
        "className": "io.netty.channel.nio.SelectedSelectionKeySet",
        "identityHashCode": 1039768944,
        "lockedStackDepth": 3,
        "lockedStackFrame": {
          "methodName": "lockAndDoSelect",
          "fileName": "SelectorImpl.java",
          "lineNumber": 86,
          "className": "sun.nio.ch.SelectorImpl",
          "nativeMethod": false
        }
      },
  ...
    ],
    "lockedSynchronizers": [],
    "lockInfo": null
}
```

The complete thread dump report includes every thread in the running application. To save space, the thread dump here shows an abridged entry for a single thread. As you can see, it includes details regarding the blocking and locking status of the thread, among other thread specifics. There's also a stack trace that gives some insight into which area of the code the thread is spending time on.

Because the /threaddump endpoint provides a snapshot of thread activity only at the time it was requested, it can be difficult to get a full picture of how threads are behaving over time. In chapter 16, you'll see how Spring Boot Admin can monitor the /threaddump endpoint in a live view.

15.2.4 *Tapping runtime metrics*

The /metrics endpoint can report many metrics produced by a running application, including memory, processor, garbage collection, and HTTP requests. Actuator provides more than two dozen categories of metrics out of the box, as evidenced by the following list of metrics categories returned when issuing a GET request to /metrics:

```
$ curl localhost:8080/actuator/metrics | jq
{
  "names": [
    "jvm.memory.max",
    "process.files.max",
    "jvm.gc.memory.promoted",
    "http.server.requests",
    "system.load.average.1m",
    "jvm.memory.used",
    "jvm.gc.max.data.size",
    "jvm.memory.committed",
```

```
      "system.cpu.count",
      "logback.events",
      "jvm.buffer.memory.used",
      "jvm.threads.daemon",
      "system.cpu.usage",
      "jvm.gc.memory.allocated",
      "jvm.threads.live",
      "jvm.threads.peak",
      "process.uptime",
      "process.cpu.usage",
      "jvm.classes.loaded",
      "jvm.gc.pause",
      "jvm.classes.unloaded",
      "jvm.gc.live.data.size",
      "process.files.open",
      "jvm.buffer.count",
      "jvm.buffer.total.capacity",
      "process.start.time"
   ]
}
```

So many metrics are covered that it would be impossible to discuss them all in any meaningful way in this chapter. Instead, let's focus on one category of metrics, `http.server.requests`, as an example of how to consume the /metrics endpoint.

If instead of simply requesting /metrics, you were to issue a GET request for /metrics/{metrics name}, you'd receive more detail about the metrics for that category. In the case of `http.server.requests`, a GET request for /metrics/ http.server .requests returns data that looks like the following:

```
$ curl localhost:8080/actuator/metrics/http.server.requests
{
  "name": "http.server.requests",
  "measurements": [
    { "statistic": "COUNT", "value": 2103 },
    { "statistic": "TOTAL_TIME", "value": 18.086334315 },
    { "statistic": "MAX", "value": 0.028926313 }
  ],
  "availableTags": [
    { "tag": "exception",
      "values": [ "ResponseStatusException",
                  "IllegalArgumentException", "none" ] },
    { "tag": "method", "values": [ "GET" ] },
    { "tag": "uri",
      "values": [
        "/actuator/metrics/{requiredMetricName}",
        "/actuator/health", "/actuator/info", "/ingredients",
        "/actuator/metrics", "/**" ] },
    { "tag": "status", "values": [ "404", "500", "200" ] }
  ]
}
```

The most significant portion of this response is the `measurements` section, which includes all the metrics for the requested category. In this case, it reports that there have been 2,103 HTTP requests. The total time spent handling those requests is 18.086334315 seconds, and the maximum time spent processing any request is 0.028926313 seconds.

Those generic metrics are interesting, but you can narrow down the results further by using the tags listed under `availableTags`. For example, you know that there have been 2,103 requests, but what's unknown is how many of them resulted in an HTTP 200 versus an HTTP 404 or HTTP 500 response status. Using the status tag, you can get metrics for all requests resulting in an HTTP 404 status like this:

```
$ curl localhost:8080/actuator/metrics/http.server.requests? \
                                    tag=status:404
{
  "name": "http.server.requests",
  "measurements": [
    { "statistic": "COUNT", "value": 31 },
    { "statistic": "TOTAL_TIME", "value": 0.522061212 },
    { "statistic": "MAX", "value": 0 }
  ],
  "availableTags": [
    { "tag": "exception",
      "values": [ "ResponseStatusException", "none" ] },
    { "tag": "method", "values": [ "GET" ] },
    { "tag": "uri",
      "values": [
        "/actuator/metrics/{requiredMetricName}", "/**" ] }
  ]
}
```

By specifying the tag name and value with the `tag` request attribute, you now see metrics specifically for requests that resulted in an HTTP 404 response. This shows that there were 31 requests resulting in a 404, and it took 0.522061212 seconds to serve them all. Moreover, it's clear that some of the failing requests were GET requests for /actuator/metrics/{requiredMetricsName} (although it's unclear what the {required-MetricsName} path variable resolved to). And some were for some other path, captured by the /** wildcard path.

Hmmm . . . what if you want to know how many of those HTTP 404 responses were for the /** path? All you need to do to filter this further is to specify the `uri` tag in the request, like this:

```
% curl "localhost:8080/actuator/metrics/http.server.requests? \
                                    tag=status:404&tag=uri:/**"
{
  "name": "http.server.requests",
  "measurements": [
    { "statistic": "COUNT", "value": 30 },
    { "statistic": "TOTAL_TIME", "value": 0.519791548 },
    { "statistic": "MAX", "value": 0 }
  ],
  "availableTags": [
    { "tag": "exception", "values": [ "ResponseStatusException" ] },
```

```
    { "tag": "method", "values": [ "GET" ] }
  ]
}
```

Now you can see that there were 30 requests for some path that matched /** that resulted in an HTTP 404 response, and it took a total of 0.519791548 seconds to handle those requests.

You'll also notice that as you refine the request, the available tags are more limited. The tags offered are only those that match the requests captured by the displayed metrics. In this case, the exception and method tags each have only a single value; it's obvious that all 30 of the requests were GET requests that resulted in a 404 because of a ResponseStatusException.

Navigating the /metrics endpoint can be a tricky business, but with a little practice, it's not impossible to get the data you're looking for. In chapter 16, you'll see how Spring Boot Admin makes consuming data from the /metrics endpoint much easier.

Although the information presented by Actuator endpoints offers useful insight into the inner workings of a running Spring Boot application, it's not well suited for human consumption. Because Actuator endpoints are REST endpoints, the data they provide is intended for consumption by some other application, perhaps a UI. With that in mind, let's see how you can present Actuator information in a user-friendly web application.

15.3   Customizing Actuator

One of the greatest features of Actuator is that it can be customized to meet the specific needs of an application. A few of the endpoints themselves allow for customization. Meanwhile, Actuator itself allows you to create custom endpoints.

Let's look at a few ways that Actuator can be customized, starting with ways to add information to the /info endpoint.

15.3.1   Contributing information to the /info endpoint

As you saw in section 15.2.1, the /info endpoint starts off empty and uninformative. But you can easily add data to it by creating properties that are prefixed with info.

Although prefixing properties with info. is a very easy way to get custom data into the /info endpoint, it's not the only way. Spring Boot offers an interface named Info-Contributor that allows you to programmatically add any information you want to the /info endpoint response. Spring Boot even comes ready with a couple of useful implementations of InfoContributor that you'll no doubt find useful.

Let's see how you can write your own InfoContributor to add some custom info to the /info endpoint.

CREATING A CUSTOM INFOCONTRIBUTOR

Suppose you want to add some simple statistics regarding Taco Cloud to the /info endpoint. For example, let's say you want to include information about how many

tacos have been created. To do that, you can write a class that implements Info-
Contributor, inject it with TacoRepository, and then publish whatever count that
TacoRepository gives you as information to the /info endpoint. The next listing
shows how you might implement such a contributor.

Listing 15.3   A custom implementation of InfoContributor

```
package tacos.actuator;

import java.util.HashMap;
import java.util.Map;

import org.springframework.boot.actuate.info.Info.Builder;
import org.springframework.boot.actuate.info.InfoContributor;
import org.springframework.stereotype.Component;

import tacos.data.TacoRepository;

@Component
public class TacoCountInfoContributor implements InfoContributor {
  private TacoRepository tacoRepo;

  public TacoCountInfoContributor(TacoRepository tacoRepo) {
    this.tacoRepo = tacoRepo;
  }

  @Override
  public void contribute(Builder builder) {
    long tacoCount = tacoRepo.count().block();
    Map<String, Object> tacoMap = new HashMap<String, Object>();
    tacoMap.put("count", tacoCount);
    builder.withDetail("taco-stats", tacoMap);
  }
}
```

By implementing InfoContributor, TacoCountInfoContributor is required to implement the contribute() method. This method is given a Builder object on which the
contribute() method makes a call to withDetail() to add info details. In your
implementation, you consult TacoRepository by calling its count() method to find
out how many tacos have been created. In this particular case, you're working with a
reactive repository, so you need to call block() to get the count out of the returned
Mono<Long>. Then you put that count into a Map, which you then give to the builder
with the label taco-stats. The results of the /info endpoint will include that count,
as shown here:

```
{
  "taco-stats": {
    "count": 44
  }
}
```

As you can see, an implementation of `InfoContributor` is able to use whatever means necessary to contribute information. This is in contrast to simply prefixing a property with `info.`, which, although simple, is limited to static values.

INJECTING BUILD INFORMATION INTO THE /INFO ENDPOINT

Spring Boot comes with a few built-in implementations of `InfoContributor` that automatically add information to the results of the /info endpoint. Among them is `Build-InfoContributor`, which adds information from the project build file into the /info endpoint results. The basic information includes the project version, the timestamp of the build, and the host and user who performed the build.

To enable build information to be included in the results of the /info endpoint, add the `build-info` goal to the Spring Boot Maven Plugin executions, as follows:

```xml
<build>
  <plugins>
    <plugin>
      <groupId>org.springframework.boot</groupId>
      <artifactId>spring-boot-maven-plugin</artifactId>
      <executions>
        <execution>
          <goals>
            <goal>build-info</goal>
          </goals>
        </execution>
      </executions>
    </plugin>
  </plugins>
</build>
```

If you're using Gradle to build your project, you can simply add the following lines to your build.gradle file:

```groovy
springBoot {
  buildInfo()
}
```

In either event, the build will produce a file named build-info.properties in the distributable JAR or WAR file that `BuildInfoContributor` will consume and contribute to the /info endpoint. The following snippet from the /info endpoint response shows the build information that's contributed:

```json
{
  "build": {
    "artifact": "tacocloud",
    "name": "taco-cloud",
    "time": "2021-08-08T23:55:16.379Z",
    "version": "0.0.15-SNAPSHOT",
    "group": "sia"
  },
}
```

This information is useful for understanding exactly which version of an application is running and when it was built. By performing a GET request to the /info endpoint, you'll know whether you're running the latest and greatest build of the project.

EXPOSING GIT COMMIT INFORMATION

Assuming that your project is kept in Git for source code control, you may want to include Git commit information in the /info endpoint. To do that, you'll need to add the following plugin in the Maven project pom.xml:

```
<build>
  <plugins>
...
    <plugin>
      <groupId>pl.project13.maven</groupId>
      <artifactId>git-commit-id-plugin</artifactId>
    </plugin>
  </plugins>
</build>
```

If you're a Gradle user, don't worry. There's an equivalent plugin for you to add to your build.gradle file, shown here:

```
plugins {
  id "com.gorylenko.gradle-git-properties" version "2.3.1"
}
```

Both of these plugins do essentially the same thing: they generate a build-time artifact named git.properties that contains all of the Git metadata for the project. A special InfoContributor implementation discovers that file at runtime and exposes its contents as part of the /info endpoint.

Of course, to generate the git.properties file, the project needs to have Git commit metadata. That is, it must be a clone of a Git repository or be a newly initialized local Git repository with at least one commit. If not, then either of these plugins will fail. You can, however, configure them to ignore the missing Git metadata. For the Maven plugin, set the failOnNoGitDirectory property to false like this:

```
<build>
  <plugins>
...
    <plugin>
      <groupId>pl.project13.maven</groupId>
      <artifactId>git-commit-id-plugin</artifactId>
      <configuration>
        <failOnNoGitDirectory>false</failOnNoGitDirectory>
      </configuration>
    </plugin>
  </plugins>
</build>
```

Similarly, you can set the `failOnNoGitDirectory` property in Gradle by specifying it under `gitProperties` like this:

```
gitProperties {
  failOnNoGitDirectory = false
}
```

In its simplest form, the Git information presented in the /info endpoint includes the Git branch, commit hash, and timestamp that the application was built against, as shown here:

```
{
  "git": {
    "branch": "main",
    "commit": {
      "id": "df45505",
      "time": "2021-08-08T21:51:12Z"
    }
  },
  ...
}
```

This information is quite definitive in describing the state of the code when the project was built. But by setting the `management.info.git.mode` property to `full`, you can get extremely detailed information about the Git commit that was in play when the project was built, as shown in the next code sample:

```
management:
  info:
    git:
      mode: full
```

The following listing shows a sample of what the full Git info might look like.

Listing 15.4   Full Git commit info exposed through the /info endpoint

```
"git": {
  "local": {
    "branch": {
      "ahead": "8",
      "behind": "0"
    }
  },
  "commit": {
    "id": {
      "describe-short": "df45505-dirty",
      "abbrev": "df45505",
      "full": "df455055daaf3b1347b0ad1d9dca4ebbc6067810",
      "describe": "df45505-dirty"
    },
    "message": {
      "short": "Apply chapter 18 edits",
```

```json
      "full": "Apply chapter 18 edits"
    },
    "user": {
      "name": "Craig Walls",
      "email": "craig@habuma.com"
    },
    "author": {
      "time": "2021-08-08T15:51:12-0600"
    },
    "committer": {
      "time": "2021-08-08T15:51:12-0600"
    },
    "time": "2021-08-08T21:51:12Z"
  },
  "branch": "master",
  "build": {
    "time": "2021-08-09T00:13:37Z",
    "version": "0.0.15-SNAPSHOT",
    "host": "Craigs-MacBook-Pro.local",
    "user": {
      "name": "Craig Walls",
      "email": "craig@habuma.com"
    }
  },
  "tags": "",
  "total": {
    "commit": {
      "count": "196"
    }
  },
  "closest": {
    "tag": {
      "commit": {
        "count": ""
      },
      "name": ""
    }
  },
  "remote": {
    "origin": {
      "url": "git@github.com:habuma/spring-in-action-6-samples.git"
    }
  },
  "dirty": "true"
},
```

In addition to the timestamp and abbreviated Git commit hash, the full version includes the name and email of the user who committed the code as well as the commit message and other information, allowing you to pinpoint exactly what code was used to build the project. In fact, notice that the `dirty` field in listing 15.4 is true, indicating that some uncommitted changes existed in the build directory when the project was built. It doesn't get much more definitive than that!

15.3.2 *Defining custom health indicators*

Spring Boot comes with several out-of-the-box health indicators that provide health information for many common external systems that a Spring application may integrate with. But at some point, you may find that you're interacting with some external system that Spring Boot neither anticipated nor provided a health indicator for.

For instance, your application may integrate with a legacy mainframe application, and the health of your application may be affected by the health of the legacy system. To create a custom health indicator, all you need to do is create a bean that implements the HealthIndicator interface.

As it turns out, the Taco Cloud services have no need for a custom health indicator, because the ones provided by Spring Boot are more than sufficient. But to demonstrate how you can develop a custom health indicator, consider the next listing, which shows a simple implementation of HealthIndicator in which health is determined somewhat randomly by the time of day.

Listing 15.5   An unusual implementation of HealthIndicator

```
package tacos.actuator;

import java.util.Calendar;
import org.springframework.boot.actuate.health.Health;
import org.springframework.boot.actuate.health.HealthIndicator;
import org.springframework.stereotype.Component;


@Component
public class WackoHealthIndicator
        implements HealthIndicator {
  @Override
  public Health health() {
    int hour = Calendar.getInstance().get(Calendar.HOUR_OF_DAY);
    if (hour > 12) {
      return Health
          .outOfService()
          .withDetail("reason",
                "I'm out of service after lunchtime")
          .withDetail("hour", hour)
          .build();
    }

    if (Math.random() <= 0.1) {
      return Health
          .down()
          .withDetail("reason", "I break 10% of the time")
          .build();
    }
    return Health
        .up()
        .withDetail("reason", "All is good!")
```

```
        .build();
    }
}
```

This crazy health indicator first checks what the current time is, and if it's after noon, returns a health status of OUT_OF_SERVICE, with a few details explaining the reason for that status. Even if it's before lunch, there's a 10% chance that the health indicator will report a DOWN status, because it uses a random number to decide whether or not it's up. If the random number is less than 0.1, the status will be reported as DOWN. Otherwise, the status will be UP.

Obviously, the health indicator in listing 15.5 isn't going to be very useful in any real-world applications. But imagine that instead of consulting the current time or a random number, it were to make a remote call to some external system and determine the status based on the response it receives. In that case, it would be a very useful health indicator.

15.3.3 *Registering custom metrics*

In section 15.2.4, we looked at how you could navigate the /metrics endpoint to consume various metrics published by Actuator, with a focus on metrics pertaining to HTTP requests. The metrics provided by Actuator are very useful, but the /metrics endpoint isn't limited to only those built-in metrics.

Ultimately, Actuator metrics are implemented by Micrometer (https://micrometer .io/), a vendor-neutral metrics facade that makes it possible for applications to publish any metrics they want and to display them in the third-party monitoring system of their choice, including support for Prometheus, Datadog, and New Relic, among others.

The most basic means of publishing metrics with Micrometer is through Micrometer's MeterRegistry. In a Spring Boot application, all you need to do to publish metrics is inject a MeterRegistry wherever you may need to publish counters, timers, or gauges that capture the metrics for your application.

As an example of publishing custom metrics, suppose you want to keep counters for the numbers of tacos that have been created with different ingredients. That is, you want to track how many tacos have been made with lettuce, ground beef, flour tortillas, or any of the available ingredients. The TacoMetrics bean in the next listing shows how you might use MeterRegistry to gather that information.

Listing 15.6 TacoMetrics registers metrics around taco ingredients

```
package tacos.actuator;

import java.util.List;
import org.springframework.data.rest.core.event.AbstractRepositoryEventListener;
import org.springframework.stereotype.Component;
import io.micrometer.core.instrument.MeterRegistry;
import tacos.Ingredient;
import tacos.Taco;
```

```
@Component
public class TacoMetrics extends AbstractRepositoryEventListener<Taco> {
  private MeterRegistry meterRegistry;

  public TacoMetrics(MeterRegistry meterRegistry) {
    this.meterRegistry = meterRegistry;
  }

  @Override
  protected void onAfterCreate(Taco taco) {
    List<Ingredient> ingredients = taco.getIngredients();
    for (Ingredient ingredient : ingredients) {
      meterRegistry.counter("tacocloud",
          "ingredient", ingredient.getId()).increment();
    }
  }
}
```

As you can see, `TacoMetrics` is injected through its constructor with a `MeterRegistry`.
It also extends `AbstractRepositoryEventListener`, a Spring Data class that enables
the interception of repository events and overrides the `onAfterCreate()` method so
that it can be notified any time a new `Taco` object is saved.

Within `onAfterCreate()`, a counter is declared for each `ingredient` where the tag
name is ingredient and the tag value is equal to the ingredient ID. If a counter with
that tag already exists, it will be reused. The counter is incremented, indicating that
another taco has been created for the ingredient.

After a few tacos have been created, you can start querying the /metrics endpoint
for ingredient counts. A GET request to /metrics/tacocloud yields some unfiltered
metric counts, as shown next:

```
$ curl localhost:8080/actuator/metrics/tacocloud
{
  "name": "tacocloud",
  "measurements": [ { "statistic": "COUNT", "value": 84 }
  ],
  "availableTags": [
    {
      "tag": "ingredient",
      "values": [ "FLTO", "CHED", "LETC", "GRBF",
                  "COTO", "JACK", "TMTO", "SLSA"]
    }
  ]
}
```

The count value under measurements doesn't mean much here, because it's a sum
of all the counts for all ingredients. But let's suppose you want to know how many
tacos have been created with flour tortillas (FLTO). All you need to do is specify the
ingredient tag with a value of FLTO as follows:

```
$ curl localhost:8080/actuator/metrics/tacocloud?tag=ingredient:FLTO
```

```
{
  "name": "tacocloud",
  "measurements": [
    { "statistic": "COUNT", "value": 39 }
  ],
  "availableTags": []
}
```

Now it's clear that 39 tacos have had flour tortillas as one of their ingredients.

15.3.4 *Creating custom endpoints*

At first glance, you might think that Actuator's endpoints are implemented as nothing more than Spring MVC controllers. But as you'll see in chapter 17, the endpoints are also exposed as JMX MBeans as well as through HTTP requests. Therefore, there must be something more to these endpoints than just a controller class.

In fact, Actuator endpoints are defined quite differently from controllers. Instead of a class that's annotated with `@Controller` or `@RestController`, Actuator endpoints are defined with classes that are annotated with `@Endpoint`.

What's more, instead of using HTTP-named annotations such as `@GetMapping`, `@PostMapping`, or `@DeleteMapping`, Actuator endpoint operations are defined by methods annotated with `@ReadOperation`, `@WriteOperation`, and `@DeleteOperation`. These annotations don't imply any specific communication mechanism and, in fact, allow Actuator to communicate by any variety of communication mechanisms, HTTP, and JMX out of the box. To demonstrate how to write a custom Actuator endpoint, consider `NotesEndpoint` in the next listing.

Listing 15.7 A custom endpoint for taking notes

```
package tacos.actuator;

import java.util.ArrayList;
import java.util.Date;
import java.util.List;
import org.springframework.boot.actuate.endpoint.annotation.DeleteOperation;
import org.springframework.boot.actuate.endpoint.annotation.Endpoint;
import org.springframework.boot.actuate.endpoint.annotation.ReadOperation;
import org.springframework.boot.actuate.endpoint.annotation.WriteOperation;
import org.springframework.stereotype.Component;

@Component
@Endpoint(id="notes", enableByDefault=true)
public class NotesEndpoint {

  private List<Note> notes = new ArrayList<>();

  @ReadOperation
  public List<Note> notes() {
```

```
    return notes;
  }

@WriteOperation
public List<Note> addNote(String text) {
  notes.add(new Note(text));
  return notes;
}

@DeleteOperation
public List<Note> deleteNote(int index) {
  if (index < notes.size()) {
    notes.remove(index);
  }
  return notes;
}

class Note {
  private Date time = new Date();
  private final String text;

  public Note(String text) {
    this.text = text;
  }

  public Date getTime() {
    return time;
  }

  public String getText() {
    return text;
  }
}
}
```

This endpoint is a simple note-taking endpoint, wherein one can submit a note with a write operation, read the list of notes with a read operation, and remove a note with the delete operation. Admittedly, this endpoint isn't very useful as far as Actuator endpoints go. But when you consider that the out-of-the-box Actuator endpoints cover so much ground, it's difficult to come up with a practical example of a custom Actuator endpoint.

At any rate, the NotesEndpoint class is annotated with @Component so that it will be picked up by Spring's component scanning and instantiated as a bean in the Spring application context. But more relevant to this discussion, it's also annotated with @Endpoint, making it an Actuator endpoint with an ID of notes. And it's enabled by default so that you won't need to explicitly enable it by including it in the management.web.endpoints.web.exposure.include configuration property.

As you can see, NotesEndpoint offers one of each kind of operation:

- The notes() method is annotated with @ReadOperation. When invoked, it will return a list of available notes. In HTTP terms, this means it will handle an HTTP GET request for /actuator/notes and respond with a JSON list of notes.

- The `addNote()` method is annotated with `@WriteOperation`. When invoked, it will create a new note from the given text and add it to the list. In HTTP terms, it handles a `POST` request where the body of the request is a JSON object with a `text` property. It finishes by responding with the current state of the notes list.
- The `deleteNote()` method is annotated with `@DeleteOperation`. When invoked, it will delete the note at the given index. In HTTP terms, this endpoint handles `DELETE` requests where the index is given as a request parameter.

To see this in action, you can use `curl` to poke about with this new endpoint. First, add a couple of notes, using two separate `POST` requests, as shown here:

```
$ curl localhost:8080/actuator/notes \
              -d'{"text":"Bring home milk"}' \
              -H"Content-type: application/json"
[{"time":"2020-06-08T13:50:45.085+0000","text":"Bring home milk"}]

$ curl localhost:8080/actuator/notes \
              -d'{"text":"Take dry cleaning"}' \
              -H"Content-type: application/json"
[{"time":"2021-07-03T12:39:13.058+0000","text":"Bring home milk"},
 {"time":"2021-07-03T12:39:16.012+0000","text":"Take dry cleaning"}]
```

As you can see, each time a new note is posted, the endpoint responds with the newly appended list of notes. But if later you want to view the list of notes, you can do a simple `GET` request like so:

```
$ curl localhost:8080/actuator/notes
[{"time":"2021-07-03T12:39:13.058+0000","text":"Bring home milk"},
 {"time":"2021-07-03T12:39:16.012+0000","text":"Take dry cleaning"}]
```

If you decide to remove one of the notes, a `DELETE` request with an `index` request parameter, shown next, should do the trick:

```
$ curl localhost:8080/actuator/notes?index=1 -X DELETE
[{"time":"2021-07-03T12:39:13.058+0000","text":"Bring home milk"}]
```

It's important to note that although I've shown only how to interact with the endpoint using HTTP, it will also be exposed as an MBean that can be accessed using whatever JMX client you choose. But if you want to limit it to only exposing an HTTP endpoint, you can annotate the endpoint class with `@WebEndpoint` instead of `@Endpoint` as follows:

```
@Component
@WebEndpoint(id="notes", enableByDefault=true)
public class NotesEndpoint {
  ...
}
```

Likewise, if you prefer an MBean-only endpoint, annotate the class with `@JmxEndpoint`.

15.4   *Securing Actuator*

The information presented by Actuator is probably not something that you would want prying eyes to see. Moreover, because Actuator provides a few operations that let you change environment properties and logging levels, it's probably a good idea to secure Actuator so that only clients with proper access will be allowed to consume its endpoints.

Even though it's important to secure Actuator, security is outside of Actuator's responsibilities. Instead, you'll need to use Spring Security to secure Actuator. And because Actuator endpoints are just paths in the application like any other path in the application, there's nothing unique about securing Actuator versus any other application path. Everything we discussed in chapter 5 applies when securing Actuator endpoints.

Because all Actuator endpoints are gathered under a common base path of /actuator (or possibly some other base path if the `management.endpoints.web.base-path` property is set), it's easy to apply authorization rules to all Actuator endpoints across the board. For example, to require that a user have `ROLE_ADMIN` authority to invoke Actuator endpoints, you might override the `configure()` method of `WebSecurity-ConfigurerAdapter` like this:

```
@Override
protected void configure(HttpSecurity http) throws Exception {
  http
    .authorizeRequests()
      .antMatchers("/actuator/**").hasRole("ADMIN")

    .and()

    .httpBasic();
}
```

This requires that all requests be from an authenticated user with `ROLE_ADMIN` authority. It also configures HTTP basic authentication so that client applications can submit encoded authentication information in their request `Authorization` headers.

The only real problem with securing Actuator this way is that the path to the endpoints is hardcoded as /actuator/**. If this were to change because of a change to the `management.endpoints.web.base-path` property, it would no longer work. To help with this, Spring Boot also provides `EndpointRequest`—a request matcher class that makes this even easier and less dependent on a given `String` path. Using `Endpoint-Request`, you can apply the same security requirements for Actuator endpoints without hardcoding the /actuator/** path, as shown here:

```
@Override
protected void configure(HttpSecurity http) throws Exception {
  http
    .requestMatcher(EndpointRequest.toAnyEndpoint())
      .authorizeRequests()
```

The `EndpointRequest.toAnyEndpoint()` method returns a request matcher that matches any Actuator endpoint. If you'd like to exclude some of the endpoints from the request matcher, you can call `excluding()`, specifying them by name as follows:

```
@Override
protected void configure(HttpSecurity http) throws Exception {
  http
    .requestMatcher(
        EndpointRequest.toAnyEndpoint()
                      .excluding("health", "info"))
    .authorizeRequests()
      .anyRequest().hasRole("ADMIN")
  .and()
    .httpBasic();
}
```

On the other hand, should you wish to apply security to only a handful of Actuator endpoints, you can specify those endpoints by name by calling `to()` instead of `toAnyEndpoint()`, like this:

```
@Override
protected void configure(HttpSecurity http) throws Exception {
  http
    .requestMatcher(EndpointRequest.to(
            "beans", "threaddump", "loggers"))
    .authorizeRequests()
      .anyRequest().hasRole("ADMIN")
  .and()
    .httpBasic();
}
```

This limits Actuator security to only the /beans, /threaddump, and /loggers endpoints. All other Actuator endpoints are left wide open.

Summary

- Spring Boot Actuator provides several endpoints, both as HTTP and JMX MBeans, that let you peek into the inner workings of a Spring Boot application.
- Most Actuator endpoints are disabled by default but can be selectively exposed by setting `management.endpoints.web.exposure.include` and `management.endpoints.web.exposure.exclude`.
- Some endpoints, such as the /loggers and /env endpoints, allow for write operations to change a running application's configuration on the fly.
- Details regarding an application's build and Git commit can be exposed in the /info endpoint.

- An application's health can be influenced by a custom health indicator, tracking the health of an externally integrated application.
- Custom application metrics can be registered through Micrometer, which affords Spring Boot applications instant integration with several popular metrics engines such as Datadog, New Relic, and Prometheus.
- Actuator web endpoints can be secured using Spring Security, much like any other endpoint in a Spring application.

Administering Spring

This chapter covers

- Setting up Spring Boot Admin
- Registering client applications
- Working with Actuator endpoints
- Securing the Admin server

A picture is worth a thousand words (or so they say), and for many application users, a user-friendly web application is worth a thousand API calls. Don't get me wrong, I'm a command-line junkie and a big fan of using `curl` and HTTPie to consume REST APIs. But sometimes, manually typing the command line to invoke a REST endpoint and then visually inspecting the results can be less efficient than simply clicking a link and reading the results in a web browser.

In the previous chapter, we explored all of the HTTP endpoints exposed by the Spring Boot Actuator. As HTTP endpoints that return JSON responses, there's no limit to how those can be used. In this chapter, we'll see how to put a frontend user interface (UI) on top of the Actuator to make it easier to use, as well as capture live data that would be difficult to consume from Actuator directly.

16.1   *Using Spring Boot Admin*

I've been asked several times if it'd make sense and, if so, how hard it'd be to develop a web application that consumes Actuator endpoints and serves them up in an easy-to-view UI. I respond that it's just a REST API, and, therefore, anything is possible. But why bother creating your own UI for the Actuator when the good folks at codecentric AG (https://www.codecentric.de/), a software and consulting company based in Germany, have already done the work for you?

Spring Boot Admin is an administrative frontend web application that makes Actuator endpoints more consumable by humans. It's split into two primary components: the Spring Boot Admin server and its clients. The Admin server collects and displays Actuator data that's fed to it from one or more Spring Boot applications, which are identified as Spring Boot Admin clients, as illustrated in figure 16.1.

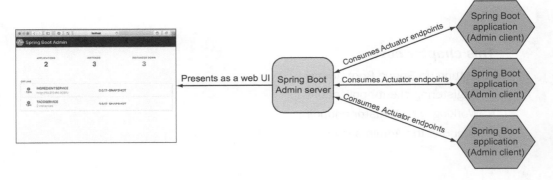

Figure 16.1   The Spring Boot Admin server consumes Actuator endpoints from one or more Spring Boot applications and presents the data in a web-based UI.

You'll need to register each of your applications with the Spring Boot Admin server, including the Taco Cloud application. But first, you'll set up the Spring Boot Admin server to receive each client's Actuator information.

16.1.1   *Creating an Admin server*

To enable the Admin server, you'll first need to create a new Spring Boot application and add the Admin server dependency to the project's build. The Admin server is generally used as a standalone application, separate from any other application. Therefore, the easiest way to get started is to use the Spring Boot Initializr to create a new Spring Boot project and select the check box labeled Spring Boot Admin (Server). This results in the following dependency being included in the <dependencies> block:

```
<dependency>
  <groupId>de.codecentric</groupId>
  <artifactId>spring-boot-admin-starter-server</artifactId>
</dependency>
```

Next, you'll need to enable the Admin server by annotating the main configuration class with @EnableAdminServer as shown here:

```
package tacos.admin;

import org.springframework.boot.SpringApplication;
import org.springframework.boot.autoconfigure.SpringBootApplication;

import de.codecentric.boot.admin.server.config.EnableAdminServer;

@EnableAdminServer
@SpringBootApplication
public class AdminServerApplication {

    public static void main(String[] args) {
        SpringApplication.run(AdminServerApplication.class, args);
    }

}
```

Finally, because the Admin server won't be the only application running locally as it's developed, you should set it to listen in on a unique port, but one you can easily access (not port 0, for example). Here, I've chosen port 9090 as the port for the Spring Boot Admin server:

```
server:
  port: 9090
```

Now your Admin server is ready. If you were to fire it up at this point and navigate to http://localhost:9090 in your web browser, you'd see something like what's shown in figure 16.2.

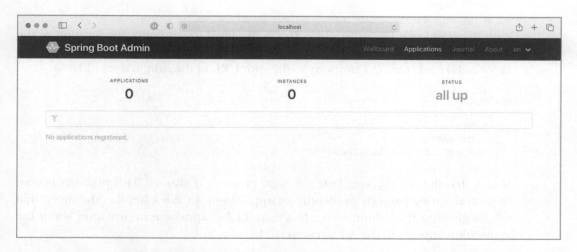

Figure 16.2   A newly created server displayed in the Spring Boot Admin UI. No applications are registered yet.

As you can see, the Spring Boot Admin shows that zero instances of zero applications are all up. But that's meaningless information when you consider the message below those counts that states No Applications Registered. For the Admin server to be useful, you'll need to register some applications with it.

16.1.2 *Registering Admin clients*

Because the Admin server is an application separate from other Spring Boot application(s) for which it presents Actuator data, you must somehow make the Admin server aware of the applications it should display. Two ways to register Spring Boot Admin clients with the Admin server follow:

- Each application explicitly registers itself with the Admin server.
- The Admin server discovers applications through the Eureka service registry.

We'll focus on how to configure individual Boot applications as Spring Boot Admin clients so that they can register themselves with the Admin server. For more information about working with Eureka, see the Spring Cloud documentation at https://docs .spring.io/spring-cloud-netflix/docs/current/reference/html/ or *Spring Microservices in Action, 2nd Edition*, by John Carnell and Illary Huaylupo Sánchez.

For a Spring Boot application to register itself as a client of the Admin server, you must include the Spring Boot Admin client starter in its build. You can easily add this dependency to your build by selecting the check box labeled Spring Boot Admin (Client) in the Initializr, or you can set the following <dependency> for a Maven-built Spring Boot application:

```
<dependency>
  <groupId>de.codecentric</groupId>
  <artifactId>spring-boot-admin-starter-client</artifactId>
</dependency>
```

With the client-side library in place, you'll also need to configure the location of the Admin server so that the client can register itself. To do that, you'll set the spring .boot.admin.client.url property to the root URL of the Admin server like so:

```
spring:
  boot:
    admin:
      client:
        url: http://localhost:9090
```

Notice that the spring.application.name property is also set. This property is used by several Spring projects to identify an application. In this case, it is the name that will be given to the Admin server to use as a label anywhere information about the application appears in the Admin server.

Although there isn't much information about the Taco Cloud application shown in figure 16.3, it does show the application's uptime, whether the Spring Boot Maven plugin has the `build-info` goal configured (as we discussed in section 15.3.1), and the build version. Rest assured that you'll see plenty of other runtime details after you click the application in the Admin server.

Figure 16.3   The Spring Boot Admin UI displays a single registered application.

Now that you have the Taco Cloud application registered with the Admin server, let's see what the Admin server has to offer.

16.2   *Exploring the Admin server*

Once you've registered all of the Spring Boot applications as Admin server clients, the Admin server makes a wealth of information available for seeing what's going on inside each application, including the following:

- General health and information
- Any metrics published through Micrometer and the /metrics endpoint
- Environment properties
- Logging levels for packages and classes

In fact, almost anything that the Actuator exposes can be viewed in the Admin server, albeit in a much more human-friendly format. This includes graphs and filters to help distill the information. The amount of information presented in the Admin server is far richer than the space we'll have in this chapter to cover it in detail. But let me use the rest of this section to share a few of the highlights of the Admin server.

16.2.1 *Viewing general application health and information*

As discussed in section 15, some of the most basic information provided by the Actuator is health and general application information via the /health and /info endpoints. The Admin server displays that information under the Details menu item as shown in figure 16.4.

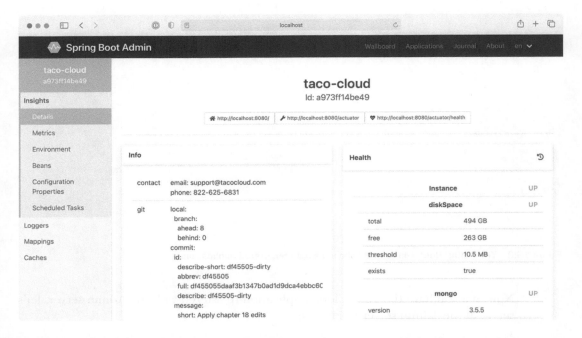

Figure 16.4   The Details screen of the Spring Boot Admin UI displays general health and information about an application.

If you scroll past the Health and Info sections in the Details screen, you'll find useful statistics from the application's JVM, including graphs displaying memory, thread, and processor usage (see figure 16.5).

The information displayed in the graphs, as well as the metrics under Processes and Garbage Collection Pauses, can provide useful insights into how your application uses JVM resources.

16.2.2 *Watching key metrics*

The information presented by the /metrics endpoint is perhaps the least human-readable of all of the Actuator's endpoints. But the Admin server makes it easy for us mere mortals to consume the metrics produced in an application with its UI under the Metrics menu item.

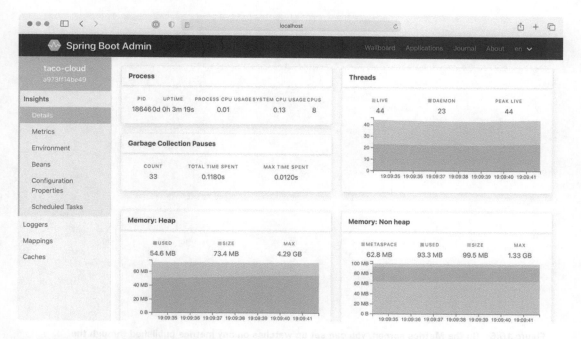

Figure 16.5 As you scroll down on the Details screen, you can view additional JVM internal information, including processor, thread, and memory statistics.

Initially, the Metrics screen doesn't display any metrics whatsoever. But the form at the top lets you set up one or more watches on any metrics you want to keep an eye on.

In figure 16.6, I've set up two watches on metrics under the http.server.requests category. The first reports metrics anytime an HTTP GET request is received and the return status is 200 (OK). The second reports metrics for any request that results in an HTTP 404 (NOT FOUND) response.

What's nice about these metrics (and, in fact, almost anything displayed in the Admin server) is that they show live data—they'll automatically update without the need to refresh the page.

16.2.3 Examining environment properties

The Actuator's /env endpoint returns all environment properties available to a Spring Boot application from all of its property sources. And although the JSON response from the endpoint isn't all that difficult to read, the Admin server presents it in a much more aesthetically pleasing form under the Environment menu item, shown in figure 16.7.

Because there can be hundreds of properties, you can filter the list of available properties by either property name or value. Figure 16.7 shows properties filtered by those whose name and/or values contain the text "spring.". The Admin server also

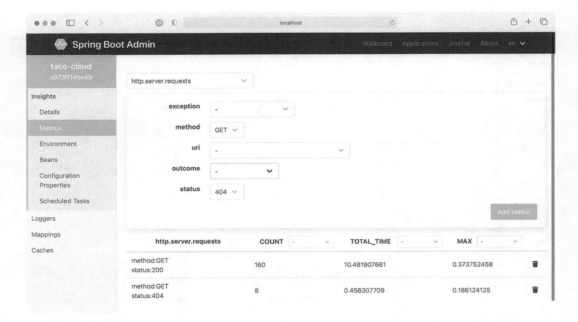

Figure 16.6   On the Metrics screen, you can set up watches on any metrics published through the application's /metrics endpoint.

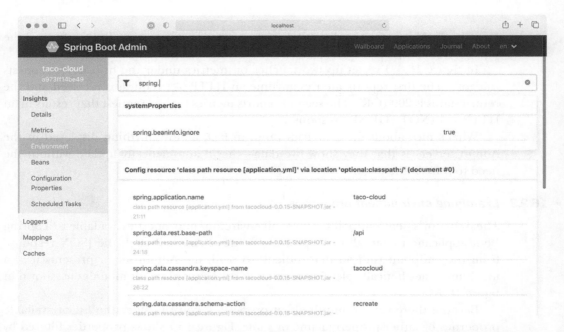

Figure 16.7   The Environment screen displays environment properties and includes options to override and filter those values.

allows you to set or override environment properties using the form under the Environment Manager header.

16.2.4 *Viewing and setting logging levels*

The Actuator's /loggers endpoint is helpful in understanding and overriding logging levels in a running application. The Admin server's Loggers screen adds an easy-to-use UI on top of the /loggers endpoint to make simple work of managing logging in an application. Figure 16.8 shows the list of loggers filtered by the name org.springframework.boot.

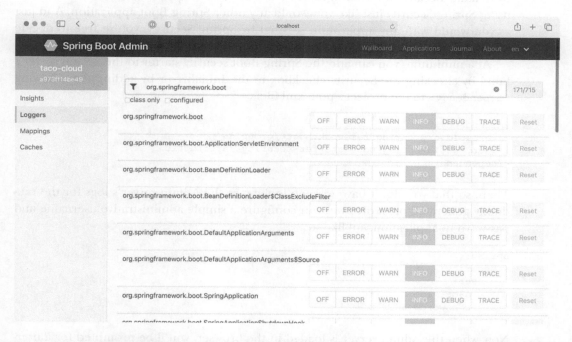

Figure 16.8   The Loggers screen displays logging levels for packages and classes in the application and lets you override those levels.

By default, the Admin server displays logging levels for all packages and classes. Those can be filtered by name (for classes only) and/or logging levels that are explicitly configured versus inherited from the root logger.

16.3   *Securing the Admin server*

As we discussed in the previous chapter, the information exposed by the Actuator's endpoints isn't intended for general consumption. They contain information that exposes details about an application that only an application administrator should see. Moreover, some of the endpoints allow changes that certainly shouldn't be exposed to just anyone.

Just as security is important to the Actuator, it's also important to the Admin server. What's more, if the Actuator endpoints require authentication, then the Admin server needs to know the credentials to be able to access those endpoints. Let's see how to add a little security to the Admin server. We'll start by requiring authentication.

16.3.1 *Enabling login in the Admin server*

It's probably a good idea to add security to the Admin server because it's not secured by default. Because the Admin server is a Spring Boot application, you can secure it using Spring Security just like you would any other Spring Boot application. And just as you would with any application secured by Spring Security, you're free to decide which security scheme fits your needs best.

At a minimum, you can add the Spring Boot security starter to the Admin server's build by checking the Security checkbox in the Initializr or by adding the following <dependency> to the project's pom.xml file:

```
<dependency>
  <groupId>org.springframework.boot</groupId>
  <artifactId>spring-boot-starter-security</artifactId>
</dependency>
```

Then, so that you don't have to keep looking at the Admin server's logs for the randomly generated password, you can configure a simple administrative username and password in application.yml like so:

```
spring:
  security:
    user:
      name: admin
      password: 53cr3t
```

Now when the Admin server is loaded in the browser, you'll be prompted for a username and password with Spring Security's default login form. As in the code snippet, entering admin and 53cr3t will get you in.

By default, Spring Security will enable CSRF on the Spring Boot Admin server, which will prevent client applications from registering with the Admin Server. Therefore, we will need a small bit of security configuration to disable CSRF, as shown here:

```
package tacos.admin;

import org.springframework.context.annotation.Bean;
import org.springframework.security.config.annotation.web.reactive
    .EnableWebFluxSecurity;
import org.springframework.security.config.web.server.ServerHttpSecurity;
import org.springframework.security.web.server.SecurityWebFilterChain;
```

```
@EnableWebFluxSecurity
public class SecurityConfig {

    @Bean
    public SecurityWebFilterChain filterChain(ServerHttpSecurity http) throws
      Exception {
      return http
            .csrf()
                .disable()
                .build();
    }

}
```

Of course, this security configuration is extremely basic. I recommend that you consult chapter 5 for ways of configuring Spring Security for a richer security scheme around the Admin server.

16.3.2 *Authenticating with the Actuator*

In section 15.4, we discussed how to secure Actuator endpoints with HTTP Basic authentication. By doing so, you'll be able to keep out everyone who doesn't know the username and password you assigned to the Actuator endpoints. Unfortunately, that also means that the Admin server won't be able to consume Actuator endpoints unless it provides the username and password. But how will the Admin server get those credentials?

If the application registers directly with the Admin server, then it can send its credentials to the server at registration time. You'll need to configure a few properties to enable that.

The `spring.boot.admin.client.username` and `spring.boot.admin.client.password` properties specify the credentials that the Admin server can use to access an application's Actuator endpoints. The following snippet from application.yml shows how you might set those properties:

```
spring:
  boot:
    admin:
      client:
        url: http://localhost:9090
        username: admin
        password: 53cr3t
```

The username and password properties must be set in each application that registers itself with the Admin server. The values given must match the username and password that's required in an HTTP Basic authentication header to the Actuator endpoints. In this example, they're set to admin and password, which are the credentials configured to access the Actuator endpoints.

Summary

- The Spring Boot Admin server consumes the Actuator endpoints from one or more Spring Boot applications and presents the data in a user-friendly web application.
- Spring Boot applications can either register themselves as clients to the Admin server or the Admin server can discover them through Eureka.
- Unlike the Actuator endpoints that capture a snapshot of an application's state, the Admin server is able to display a live view into the inner workings of an application.
- The Admin server makes it easy to filter Actuator results and, in some cases, display data visually in a graph.
- Because it's a Spring Boot application, the Admin server can be secured by any means available through Spring Security.

Monitoring Spring with JMX

This chapter covers

- Working with Actuator endpoint MBeans
- Exposing Spring beans as MBeans
- Publishing notifications

For over a decade and a half, Java Management Extensions (JMX) has been the standard means of monitoring and managing Java applications. By exposing managed components known as MBeans (managed beans), an external JMX client can manage an application by invoking operations, inspecting properties, and monitoring events from MBeans.

We'll start exploring Spring and JMX by looking at how Actuator endpoints are exposed as MBeans.

17.1 Working with Actuator MBeans

By default, all Actuator endpoints are exposed as MBeans. But, starting with Spring Boot 2.2, JMX itself is disabled by default. To enable JMX in your Spring Boot application, you can set `spring.jmx.enabled` to `true`. In application.yml, this would look like this:

```
spring:
  jmx:
    enabled: true
```

With that property set, Spring support for JMX is enabled. And with it, the Actuator endpoints are all exposed as MBeans. You can use any JMX client you wish to connect with Actuator endpoint MBeans. Using JConsole, which comes with the Java Development Kit, you'll find Actuator MBeans listed under the `org.springframework.boot` domain, as shown in figure 17.1.

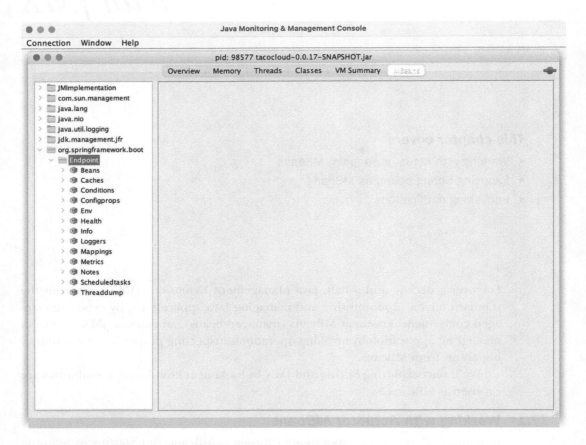

Figure 17.1   Actuator endpoints are automatically exposed as JMX MBeans.

One thing that's nice about Actuator MBean endpoints is that they're all exposed by default. There's no need to explicitly include any of them, as you had to do with HTTP. You can, however, choose to narrow down the choices by setting `management .endpoints.jmx.exposure.include` and `management.endpoints.jmx.exposure .exclude`. For example, to limit Actuator endpoint MBeans to only the /health,

/info, /bean, and /conditions endpoints, set `management.endpoints.jmx.exposure`
`.include` like this:

```
management:
  endpoints:
    jmx:
      exposure:
        include: health,info,bean,conditions
```

Or, if there are only a few you want to exclude, you can set `management.end-`
`points.jmx.exposure.exclude` like this:

```
management:
  endpoints:
    jmx:
      exposure:
        exclude: env,metrics
```

Here, you use `management.endpoints.jmx.exposure.exclude` to exclude the /env
and /metrics endpoints. All other Actuator endpoints will still be exposed as MBeans.

To invoke the managed operations on one of the Actuator MBeans in JConsole,
expand the endpoint MBean in the left-hand tree, and then select the desired operation under Operations.

For example, if you'd like to inspect the logging levels for the `tacos.ingredients`
package, expand the `Loggers` MBean and click on the operation named `logger-`
`Levels`, as shown in figure 17.2. In the form at the top right, fill in the Name field with
the package name (`org.springframework.web`, for example), and then click the
`loggerLevels` button.

After you click the `loggerLevels` button, a dialog box will pop up, showing you the
response from the /loggers endpoint MBean. It might look a little like figure 17.3.

Although the JConsole UI is a bit clumsy to work with, you should be able to get
the hang of it and use it to explore any Actuator endpoint in much the same way. If
you don't like JConsole, that's fine—there are plenty of other JMX clients to
choose from.

17.2 Creating your own MBeans

Spring makes it easy to expose any bean you want as a JMX MBean. All you must do is
annotate the bean class with `@ManagedResource` and then annotate any methods or
properties with `@ManagedOperation` or `@ManagedAttribute`. Spring will take care of
the rest.

For example, suppose you want to provide an MBean that tracks how many tacos
have been ordered through Taco Cloud. You can define a service bean that keeps a
running count of how many tacos have been created. The following listing shows what
such a service might look like.

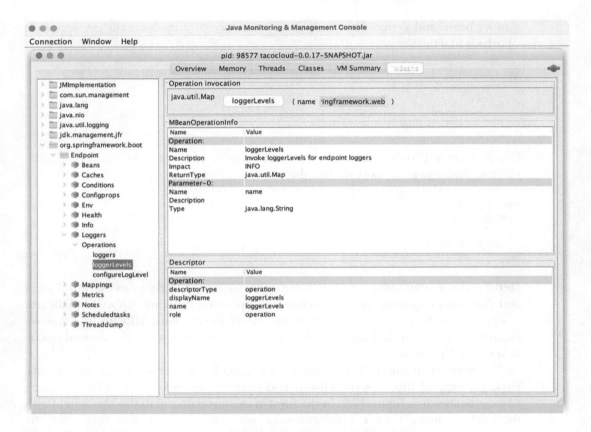

Figure 17.2   Using JConsole to display logging levels from a Spring Boot application

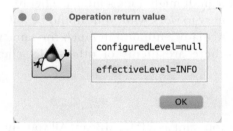

Figure 17.3   Logging levels from the /loggers endpoint MBean displayed in JConsole

---

Listing 17.1   An MBean that counts how many tacos have been created

```
package tacos.jmx;

import java.util.concurrent.atomic.AtomicLong;
import org.springframework.data.rest.core.event.AbstractRepositoryEventListener;
import org.springframework.jmx.export.annotation.ManagedAttribute;
import org.springframework.jmx.export.annotation.ManagedOperation;
```

```
import org.springframework.jmx.export.annotation.ManagedResource;
import org.springframework.stereotype.Service;
import tacos.Taco;
import tacos.data.TacoRepository;

@Service
@ManagedResource
public class TacoCounter
        extends AbstractRepositoryEventListener<Taco> {

  private AtomicLong counter;
  public TacoCounter(TacoRepository tacoRepo) {
    tacoRepo
        .count()
        .subscribe(initialCount -> {
            this.counter = new AtomicLong(initialCount);
        });
  }

  @Override
  protected void onAfterCreate(Taco entity) {
    counter.incrementAndGet();
  }

  @ManagedAttribute
  public long getTacoCount() {
    return counter.get();
  }

  @ManagedOperation
  public long increment(long delta) {
    return counter.addAndGet(delta);
  }

}
```

The TacoCounter class is annotated with @Service so that it will be picked up by component scanning and an instance will be registered as a bean in the Spring application context. But it's also annotated with @ManagedResource to indicate that this bean should also be an MBean. As an MBean, it will expose one attribute and one operation. The getTacoCount() method is annotated with @ManagedAttribute so that it will be exposed as an MBean attribute, whereas the increment() method is annotated with @ManagedOperation, exposing it as an MBean operation. Figure 17.4 shows how the TacoCounter MBean appears in JConsole.

TacoCounter has another trick up its sleeve, although it has nothing to do with JMX. Because it extends AbstractRepositoryEventListener, it will be notified of any persistence events when a Taco is saved through TacoRepository. In this particular case, the onAfterCreate() method will be invoked anytime a new Taco object is created and saved, and it will increment the counter by one. But AbstractRepository-EventListener also offers several methods for handling events both before and after objects are created, saved, or deleted.

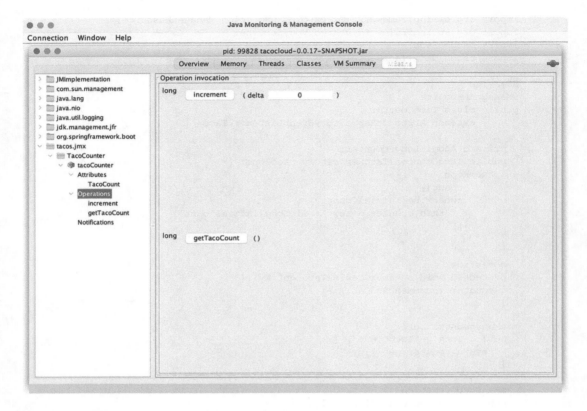

Figure 17.4   `TacoCounter`'s operations and attributes as seen in JConsole

Working with MBean operations and attributes is largely a pull operation. That is, even if the value of an MBean attribute changes, you won't know until you view the attribute through a JMX client. Let's turn the tables and see how you can push notifications from an MBean to a JMX client.

17.3   *Sending notifications*

MBeans can push notifications to interested JMX clients with Spring's `Notification-Publisher`. `NotificationPublisher` has a single `sendNotification()` method that, when given a `Notification` object, publishes the notification to any JMX clients that have subscribed to the MBean.

For an MBean to be able to publish notifications, it must implement the `NotificationPublisherAware` interface, which requires that a `setNotification-Publisher()` method be implemented. For example, suppose you want to publish a notification for every 100 tacos that are created. You can change the `TacoCounter` class so that it implements `NotificationPublisherAware` and uses the injected `NotificationPublisher` to send notifications for every 100 tacos that are created.

The following listing shows the changes that must be made to TacoCounter to enable such notifications.

Listing 17.2 Sending notifications for every 100 tacos

```java
package tacos.jmx;

import java.util.concurrent.atomic.AtomicLong;
import org.springframework.data.rest.core.event.AbstractRepositoryEventListener;
import org.springframework.jmx.export.annotation.ManagedAttribute;
import org.springframework.jmx.export.annotation.ManagedOperation;
import org.springframework.jmx.export.annotation.ManagedResource;
import org.springframework.stereotype.Service;

import org.springframework.jmx.export.notification.NotificationPublisher;
import org.springframework.jmx.export.notification.NotificationPublisherAware;
import javax.management.Notification;

import tacos.Taco;
import tacos.data.TacoRepository;

@Service
@ManagedResource
public class TacoCounter
        extends AbstractRepositoryEventListener<Taco>
        implements NotificationPublisherAware {

  private AtomicLong counter;
  private NotificationPublisher np;

  @Override
  public void setNotificationPublisher(NotificationPublisher np) {
    this.np = np;
  }

  ...

  @ManagedOperation
  public long increment(long delta) {
    long before = counter.get();
    long after = counter.addAndGet(delta);
    if ((after / 100) > (before / 100)) {
      Notification notification = new Notification(
          "taco.count", this,
          before, after + "th taco created!");
      np.sendNotification(notification);
    }
    return after;
  }

}
```

In the JMX client, you'll need to subscribe to the TacoCounter MBean to receive notifications. Then, as tacos are created, the client will receive notifications for each century count. Figure 17.5 shows how the notifications may appear in JConsole.

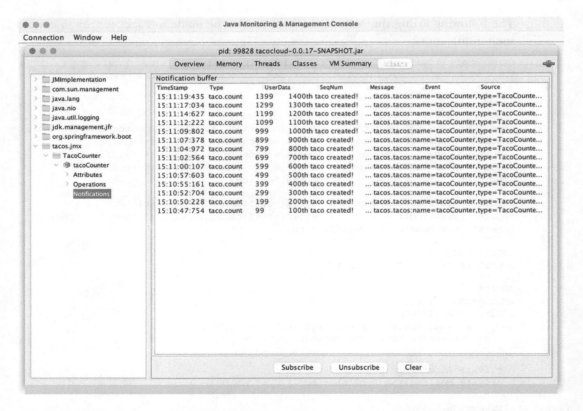

Figure 17.5   JConsole, subscribed to the `TacoCounter` MBean, receives a notification for every 100 tacos that are created.

Notifications are a great way for an application to actively send data and alerts to a monitoring client without requiring the client to poll managed attributes or invoke managed operations.

Summary

- Most Actuator endpoints are available as MBeans that can be consumed using any JMX client.
- Spring automatically enables JMX for monitoring beans in the Spring application context.
- Spring beans can be exposed as MBeans by annotating them with `@Managed-Resource`. Their methods and properties can be exposed as managed operations and attributes by annotating the bean class with `@ManagedOperation` and `@ManagedAttribute`.
- Spring beans can publish notifications to JMX clients using `Notification-Publisher`.

Deploying Spring

This chapter covers

- Building Spring applications as either WAR or JAR files
- Building Spring applications as container images
- Deploying Spring applications in Kubernetes

Think of your favorite action movie. Now imagine going to see that movie in the theater and being taken on a thrilling audiovisual ride with high-speed chases, explosions, and battles, only to have it come to a sudden halt before the good guys take down the bad guys. Instead of seeing the movie's conflict resolved, when the theater lights come on, everyone is ushered out the door. Although the lead-up was exciting, it's the climax of the movie that's important. Without it, it's action for action's sake.

Now imagine developing applications and putting a lot of effort and creativity into solving the business problem, but then never deploying the application for others to use and enjoy. Sure, most applications we write don't involve car chases or explosions (at least I hope not), but there's a certain rush you get along the way. Not every line of code you write is destined for production, but it'd be a big letdown if none of it ever was deployed.

Up to this point, we've focused on using the features of Spring Boot that help us develop an application. There have been some exciting steps along the way, but it's all for nothing if you don't cross the finish line and deploy the application.

In this chapter, we're going to step beyond developing applications with Spring Boot and look at how to deploy those applications. Although this may seem obvious for anyone who has ever deployed a Java-based application, Spring Boot and related Spring projects have some features you can draw on that make deploying Spring Boot applications unique.

In fact, unlike most Java web applications, which are typically deployed to an application server as WAR files, Spring Boot offers several deployment options. Before we look at how to deploy a Spring Boot application, let's consider all the options and choose a few that suit your needs best.

18.1 *Weighing deployment options*

You can build and run Spring Boot applications in several ways, including the following:

- Running the application directly in the IDE with either Spring Tool Suite or IntelliJ IDEA
- Running the application from the command line using the Maven `spring-boot:run` goal or Gradle `bootRun` task
- Using Maven or Gradle to produce an executable JAR file that can be run at the command line or be deployed in the cloud
- Using Maven or Gradle to produce a WAR file that can be deployed to a traditional Java application server
- Using Maven or Gradle to produce a container image that can be deployed anywhere that containers are supported, including Kubernetes environments.

Any of these choices is suitable for running the application while you're still developing it. But what about when you're ready to deploy the application into a production or other nondevelopment environment?

Although running an application from the IDE or via Maven or Gradle isn't considered a production-ready option, executable JAR files and traditional Java WAR files are certainly valid options for deploying applications to a production environment. Given the options of deploying a WAR file, a JAR file, or a container image, how do you choose? In general, the choice comes down to whether you plan to deploy your application to a traditional Java application server or a cloud platform, as described here:

- *Deploying to a Platform as a Service (PaaS) cloud*—If you're planning to deploy your application to a PaaS cloud platform such as Cloud Foundry (https:// www.cloudfoundry.org/), then an executable JAR file is a fine choice. Even if the cloud platform supports WAR deployment, the JAR file format is much simpler than the WAR format, which is designed for application server deployment.

- *Deploying to Java application servers*—If you must deploy your application to Tomcat, WebSphere, WebLogic, or any other traditional Java application server, you really have no choice but to build your application as a WAR file.
- *Deploying to Kubernetes*—Modern cloud platforms are increasingly based on Kubernetes (https://kubernetes.io/). When deploying to Kubernetes, which is itself a container-orchestration system, the obvious choice is to build your application into a container image.

In this chapter, we'll focus on the following three deployment scenarios:

- Building a Spring Boot application as an executable JAR file, which can possibly be pushed to a PaaS platform
- Deploying a Spring Boot application as a WAR file to a Java application server such as Tomcat
- Packaging a Spring Boot application as a Docker container image for deployment to any platform that supports Docker deployments

To get started, let's take a look at what is perhaps the most common way of building a Spring Boot application: as an executable JAR file.

18.2 Building executable JAR files

Building a Spring application into an executable JAR file is rather straightforward. Assuming that you chose JAR packaging when initializing your project, then you should be able to produce an executable JAR file with the following Maven command:

```
$ mvnw package
```

After a successful build, the resulting JAR file will be placed into the target directory with a name and version based on the <artifactId> and <version> entries in the project's pom.xml file (e.g., tacocloud-0.0.19-SNAPSHOT.jar).

Or, if you're using Gradle, then this will do the trick:

```
$ gradlew build
```

For Gradle builds, the resulting JAR will be found in the build/libs directory. The name of the JAR file will be based on the rootProject.name property in the settings .gradle file along with the version property in build.gradle.

Once you have the executable JAR file, you can run it with java -jar like this:

```
$ java -jar tacocloud-0.0.19-SNAPSHOT.jar
```

The application will run and, assuming it is a web application, start up an embedded server (Netty or Tomcat, depending on whether or not the project is a reactive web project) and start listening for requests on the configured server.port (8080 by default).

That's great for running the application locally. But how can you deploy an executable JAR file?

That really depends on where you'll be deploying the application. But if you are deploying to a Cloud Foundry foundation, you can push the JAR file using the `cf` command-line tool as follows:

```
$ cf push tacocloud -p target/tacocloud-0.0.19-SNAPSHOT.jar
```

The first argument to `cf push` is the name given to the application in Cloud Foundry. This name is used to reference the application in Cloud Foundry and the `cf` CLI, as well as used as a subdomain at which the application is hosted. For example, if the application domain for your Cloud Foundry foundation is cf.myorg.com, then the Taco Cloud application will be available at https://tacocloud.cf.myorg.com.

Another way to deploy executable JAR files is to package them in a Docker container and run them in Docker or Kubernetes. Let's see how to do that next.

18.3 *Building container images*

Docker (https://www.docker.com/) has become the de facto standard for distributing applications of all kinds for deployment in the cloud. Many different cloud environments, including AWS, Microsoft Azure, and Google Cloud Platform (to name a few) accept Docker containers for deploying applications.

The idea of containerized applications, such as those created with Docker, draws analogies from real-world intermodal containers that are used to ship items all over the world. Intermodal containers all have a standard size and format, regardless of their contents. Because of that, intermodal containers are easily stacked on ships, carried on trains, or pulled by trucks. In a similar way, containerized applications share a common container format that can be deployed and run anywhere, regardless of the application inside.

The most basic way to create an image from your Spring Boot application is to use the `docker build` command and a Dockerfile that copies the executable JAR file from the project build into the container image. The following extremely simple Dockerfile does exactly that:

```
FROM openjdk:11.0.12-jre
ARG JAR_FILE=target/*.jar
COPY ${JAR_FILE} app.jar
ENTRYPOINT ["java","-jar","/app.jar"]
```

The Dockerfile describes how the container image will be created. Because it's so brief, let's examine this Dockerfile line by line:

- *Line 1*—Declares that the image we create will be based on a predefined container image that provides (among other things) the Open JDK 11 Java runtime.
- *Line 2*—Creates a variable that references all JAR files in the project's target/ directory. For most Maven builds, there should be only one JAR file in there. By using a wildcard, however, we decouple the Dockerfile definition from the JAR

file's name and version. The path to the JAR file assumes that the Dockerfile is in the root of the Maven project.

- *Line 3*—Copies the JAR file from the project's target/ directory into the container image with a generic name of app.jar.
- *Line 4*—Defines an entry point—that is, defines a command to run when a container created from this image starts—to run the JAR file with `java -jar /app.jar`.

With this Dockerfile in hand, you can create the image using the Docker command-line tool like this:

```
$ docker build . -t habuma/tacocloud:0.0.19-SNAPSHOT
```

The `.` in this command references the relative path to the location of the Dockerfile. If you are running `docker build` from a different path, replace the `.` with the path to the Dockerfile (without the filename). For example, if you are running `docker build` from the parent of the project, you will use `docker build` like this:

```
$ docker build tacocloud -t habuma/tacocloud:0.0.19-SNAPSHOT
```

The value given after the `-t` argument is the image tag, which is made up of a name and version. In this case, the image name is habuma/tacocloud and the version is 0.0.19-SNAPSHOT. If you'd like to try it out, you can use `docker run` to run this newly created image:

```
$ docker run -p8080:8080 habuma/tacocloud:0.0.19-SNAPSHOT
```

The `-p8080:8080` forwards requests to port 8080 on the host machine (e.g., your machine where you're running Docker) to the container's port 8080 (where Tomcat or Netty is listening for requests).

While building a Docker image this way is easy enough if you already have an executable JAR file handy, it's not the easiest way to create an image from a Spring Boot application. Beginning with Spring Boot 2.3.0, you can build container images without adding any special dependencies or configuration files, or editing your project in any way. That's because the Spring Boot build plugins for both Maven and Gradle support the building of container images directly. To build your Maven-built Spring project into a container image, you use the `build-image` goal from the Spring Boot Maven plugin like this:

```
$ mvnw spring-boot:build-image
```

Likewise, a Gradle-built project can be built into a container image like this:

```
$ gradlew bootBuildImage
```

This builds an image with a default tag based on the `<artifactId>` and `<version>` properties in the pom.xml file. For the Taco Cloud application, this will be something like library/tacocloud:0.0.19-SNAPSHOT. We'll see in a moment how to specify a custom image tag.

Spring Boot's build plugins rely on Docker to create images. Therefore, you'll need to have the Docker runtime installed on the machine building the image. But once the image has been created, you can run it like this:

```
$ docker run -p8080:8080 library/tacocloud:0.0.19-SNAPSHOT
```

This runs the image and exposes the image's port 8080 (which the embedded Tomcat or Netty server is listening on) to the host machine's port 8080.

The default format of the tag is docker.io/library/ ${project.artifactId}:${project.version}, which explains why the tag began with "library." That's fine if you'll only ever be running the image locally. But you'll most likely want to push the image to an image registry such as DockerHub and will need the image to be built with a tag that references your image repository's name.

For example, suppose that your organization's repository name in DockerHub is tacocloud. In that case, you'll want the image name to be tacocloud/tacocloud:0.0.19-SNAPSHOT, effectively replacing the "library" default prefix with "tacocloud." To make that happen, you just need to specify a build property when building the image. For Maven, you'll specify the image name using the spring-boot.build-image.image-Name JVM system property like this:

```
$ mvnw spring-boot:build-image \
    -Dspring-boot.build-image.imageName=tacocloud/tacocloud:0.0.19-SNAPSHOT
```

For a Gradle-built project, it's slightly simpler. You specify the image name using an --imageName parameter like this:

```
$ gradlew bootBuildImage --imageName=tacocloud/tacocloud:0.0.19-SNAPSHOT
```

Either of these ways of specifying the image name requires you to remember to do them when building the image and requires that you not make a mistake. To make things even easier, you can specify the image name as part of the build itself.

In Maven, you specify the image name as a configuration entry in the Spring Boot Maven Plugin. For example, the following snippet from the project's pom.xml file shows how to specify the image name as a <configuration> block:

```
<plugin>
 <groupId>org.springframework.boot</groupId>
 <artifactId>spring-boot-maven-plugin</artifactId>
 <configuration>
   <image>
     <name>tacocloud/${project.artifactId}:${project.version}</name>
   </image>
 </configuration>
</plugin>
```

Notice, that rather than hardcoding the artifact ID and version, we can leverage build variables to make those values reference what is already specified elsewhere in the build. This removes any need to manually bump the version number in the image name as a project evolves. For a Gradle-built project, the following entry in build.gradle achieves the same effect:

```
bootBuildImage {
  imageName = "habuma/${rootProject.name}:${version}"
}
```

With this configuration in place in the project build specification, you can build the image at the command line without specifying the image name, as we did earlier. At this point, you can run the image with docker run as before (referencing the image by its new name) or you can use docker push to push the image to an image registry such as DockerHub, as shown here:

```
$ docker push habuma/tacocloud:0.0.19-SNAPSHOT
```

Once the image is in an image registry, it can be pulled and run from any environment that has access to that registry. An increasingly common place to run images is in Kubernetes. Let's take a look at how to run an image in Kubernetes.

18.3.1 *Deploying to Kubernetes*

Kubernetes is an amazing container-orchestration platform that runs images, handles scaling containers up and down as necessary, and reconciles broken containers for increased robustness, among many other things.

Kubernetes is a powerful platform on which to deploy applications—so powerful, in fact, that there's no way we'll be able to cover it in detail in this chapter. Instead, we'll focus solely on the tasks required to deploy a Spring Boot application, built into a container image, into a Kubernetes cluster. For a more detailed understanding of Kubernetes, check out *Kubernetes in Action, 2nd Edition,* by Marko Lukša.

Kubernetes has earned a reputation of being difficult to use (perhaps unfairly), but deploying a Spring application that has been built as a container image in Kubernetes is really easy and is worth the effort given all of the benefits afforded by Kubernetes.

You'll need a Kubernetes environment into which to deploy your application. Several options are available, including Amazon's AWS EKS and the Google Kubernetes Engine (GKE). For experimentation locally, you can also run Kubernetes clusters using a variety of Kubernetes implementations such as MiniKube (https://minikube .sigs.k8s.io/docs/), MicroK8s (https://microk8s.io/), and my personal favorite, Kind (https://kind.sigs.k8s.io/).

The first thing you'll need to do is create a deployment manifest. The deployment manifest is a YAML file that describes how an image should be deployed. As a simple example, consider the following deployment manifest that deploys the Taco Cloud image created earlier in a Kubernetes cluster:

```
apiVersion: apps/v1
kind: Deployment
metadata:
  name: taco-cloud-deploy
  labels:
    app: taco-cloud
spec:
  replicas: 3
  selector:
    matchLabels:
      app: taco-cloud
  template:
    metadata:
      labels:
        app: taco-cloud
    spec:
      containers:
      - name: taco-cloud-container
        image: tacocloud/tacocloud:latest
```

This manifest can be named anything you like. But for the sake of discussion, let's assume you named it deploy.yaml and placed it in a directory named k8s at the root of the project.

Without diving into the details of how a Kubernetes deployment specification works, the key things to notice here are that our deployment is named taco-cloud-deploy and (near the bottom) is set to deploy and start a container based on the image whose name is tacocloud/tacocloud:latest. By giving "latest" as the version rather than "0.0.19-SNAPSHOT," we can know that the very latest image pushed to the container registry will be used.

Another thing to notice is that the `replicas` property is set to 3. This tells the Kubernetes runtime that there should be three instances of the container running. If, for any reason, one of those three instances fails, then Kubernetes will automatically reconcile the problem by starting a new instance in its place. To apply the deployment, you can use the `kubectl` command-line tool like this:

```
$ kubectl apply -f deploy.yaml
```

After a moment or so, you should be able to use `kubectl get all` to see the deployment in action, including three *pods*, each one running a container instance. Here's a sample of what you might see:

```
$ kubectl get all
NAME                                         READY   STATUS    RESTARTS   AGE
pod/taco-cloud-deploy-555bd8fdb4-dln45       1/1     Running   0          20s
pod/taco-cloud-deploy-555bd8fdb4-n455b       1/1     Running   0          20s
pod/taco-cloud-deploy-555bd8fdb4-xp756       1/1     Running   0          20s
```

```
NAME                                  READY    UP-TO-DATE   AVAILABLE   AGE
deployment.apps/taco-cloud-deploy     3/3      3            3           20s


NAME                                         DESIRED   CURRENT   READY   AGE
replicaset.apps/taco-cloud-deploy-555bd8fdb4 3         3         3       20s
```

The first section shows three pods, one for each instance we requested in the `replicas` property. The middle section is the deployment resource itself. And the final section is a `ReplicaSet` resource, a special resource that Kubernetes uses to remember how many replicas of the application should be maintained.

If you want to try out the application, you'll need to expose a port from one of the pods on your machine. To do that, the `kubectl port-forward` command, shown next, comes in handy:

```
$ kubectl port-forward pod/taco-cloud-deploy-555bd8fdb4-dln45 8080:8080
```

In this case, I've chosen the first of the three pods listed from `kubectl get all` and asked to forward requests from the host machine's (the machine on which the Kubernetes cluster is running) port 8080 to the pod's port 8080. With that in place, you should be able to point your browser at http://localhost:8080 to see the Taco Cloud application running on the specified pod.

18.3.2 Enabling graceful shutdown

We have several ways in which to make Spring applications Kubernetes friendly, but the two most essential things you'll want to do are to enable graceful shutdown as well as liveness and readiness probes.

At any time, Kubernetes may decide to shut down one or more of the pods that your application is running in. That may be because it senses a problem, or it might be because someone has explicitly requested that the pod be shut down or restarted. Whatever the reason, if the application on that pod is in the process of handling a request, it's poor form for the pod to immediately shut down, leaving the request unhandled. Doing so will result in an error response to the client and require that the client make the request again.

Instead of burdening the client with an error, you can enable graceful shutdown in your Spring application by simply setting the `server.shutdown` property to `"graceful"`. This can be done in any of the property sources discussed in chapter 6, including in application.yml like this:

```
server:
  shutdown: graceful
```

By enabling graceful shutdown, Spring will hold off on allowing the application to shut down for up to 30 seconds, allowing any in-progress requests to be handled. After all pending requests have been completed or the shutdown time-out expires, the application will be allowed to shut down.

The shutdown time-out is 30 seconds by default, but you can override that by setting the `spring.lifecycle.timeout-per-shutdown-phase` property. For example, to change the time-out to 20 seconds, you would set the property like this:

```
spring:
  lifecycle.timeout-per-shutdown-phase: 20s
```

While the shutdown is pending, the embedded server will stop accepting new requests. This allows for all in-flight requests to be drained before shutdown occurs.

Shutdown isn't the only time when the application may not be able to handle requests. During startup, for example, an application may need a moment to be prepared to handle traffic. One of the ways that a Spring application can indicate to Kubernetes that it isn't ready to handle traffic is with a readiness probe. Next up, we'll take a look at how to enable liveness and readiness probes in a Spring application.

18.3.3 *Working with application liveness and readiness*

As we saw in chapter 15, the Actuator's health endpoint provides a status on the health of an application. But that health is only in relation to the health of any external dependencies that the application relies on, such as a database or message broker. Even if an application is perfectly healthy with regard to its database connection, that doesn't necessarily mean that it's ready to handle requests or that it is even healthy enough to remain running in its current state.

Kubernetes supports the notion of liveness and readiness probes: indicators of an application's health that help Kubernetes determine whether traffic should be sent to the application, or if the application should be restarted to resolve some issue. Spring Boot supports liveness and readiness probes via the Actuator health endpoint as subsets of the health endpoint known as *health groups*.

Liveness is an indicator of whether an application is healthy enough to continue running without being restarted. If an application indicates that its liveness indicator is down, then the Kubernetes runtime can react to that by terminating the pod that the application is running in and starting a new one in its place.

Readiness, on the other hand, tells Kubernetes whether the application is ready to handle traffic. During startup, for instance, an application may need to perform some initialization before it can start handling requests. During this time, the application's readiness may show that it's down. During this time, the application is still alive, so Kubernetes won't restart it. But Kubernetes will honor the readiness indicator by not sending requests to the application. Once the application has completed initialization, it can set the readiness probe to indicate that it is up, and Kubernetes will be able to route traffic to it.

ENABLING LIVENESS AND READINESS PROBES

To enable liveness and readiness probes in your Spring Boot application, you must set `management.health.probes.enabled` to `true`. In an application.yml file, that will look like this:

```
management:
  health:
    probes:
      enabled: true
```

Once the probes are enabled, a request to the Actuator health endpoint will look something like this (assuming that the application is perfectly healthy):

```
{
  "status": "UP",
  "groups": [
    "liveness",
    "readiness"
  ]
}
```

On its own, the base health endpoint doesn't tell us much about the liveness or readiness of an application. But a request to /actuator/health/liveness or /actuator/health/readiness will provide the liveness and readiness state of the application. In either case, an up status will look like this:

```
{
  "status": "UP"
}
```

On the other hand, if either readiness or liveness is down, then the result will look like this:

```
{
  "status": "DOWN"
}
```

In the case of a down readiness status, Kubernetes will not direct traffic to the application. If the liveness endpoint indicates a down status, then Kubernetes will attempt to remedy the situation by deleting the pod and starting a new instance in its place.

CONFIGURING LIVENESS AND READINESS PROBES IN THE DEPLOYMENT

With the Actuator producing liveness and readiness status on these two endpoints, all we need to do now is tell Kubernetes about them in the deployment manifest. The tail end of the following deployment manifest shows the configuration necessary to let Kubernetes know how to check on liveness and readiness:

```
apiVersion: apps/v1
kind: Deployment
metadata:
  name: taco-cloud-deploy
  labels:
    app: taco-cloud
spec:
  replicas: 3
```

```
selector:
  matchLabels:
    app: taco-cloud
template:
  metadata:
    labels:
      app: taco-cloud
  spec:
    containers:
    - name: taco-cloud-container
      image: tacocloud/tacocloud:latest
      livenessProbe:
        initialDelaySeconds: 2
        periodSeconds: 5
        httpGet:
          path: /actuator/health/liveness
          port: 8080
      readinessProbe:
        initialDelaySeconds: 2
        periodSeconds: 5
        httpGet:
          path: /actuator/health/readiness
          port: 8080
```

This tells Kubernetes, for each probe, to make a GET request to the given path on port 8080 to get the liveness or readiness status. As configured here, the first request should happen 2 seconds after the application pod is running and every 5 seconds thereafter.

MANAGING LIVENESS AND READINESS

How do the liveness and readiness statuses get set? Internally, Spring itself or some library that the application depends on can set the statuses by publishing an availability change event. But that ability isn't limited to Spring and its libraries; you can also write code in your application that publishes these events.

For example, suppose that you want to delay the readiness of your application until some initialization has taken place. Early on in the application lifecycle, perhaps in an ApplicationRunner or CommandLineRunner bean, you can publish a readiness state to refuse traffic like this:

```
@Bean
public ApplicationRunner disableLiveness(ApplicationContext context) {
  return args -> {
    AvailabilityChangeEvent.publish(context,
      ReadinessState.REFUSING_TRAFFIC);
  };
}
```

Here, the ApplicationRunner is given an instance of the Spring application context as a parameter to the @Bean method. This is necessary because the static publish()

method needs it to publish the event. Once initialization is complete, the application's readiness state can be updated to accept traffic in a similar way, as shown next:

```
AvailabilityChangeEvent.publish(context, ReadinessState.ACCEPTING_TRAFFIC);
```

Liveness status can be updated in very much the same way. The key difference is that instead of publishing ReadinessState.ACCEPTING_TRAFFIC or ReadinessState .REFUSING_TRAFFIC, you'll publish LivenessState.CORRECT or LivenessState .BROKEN. For example, if in your application code you detect an unrecoverable fatal error, your application can request that it be killed and restarted by publishing Liveness.BROKEN like this:

```
AvailabilityChangeEvent.publish(context, LivenessState.BROKEN);
```

Shortly after this event is published, the liveness endpoint will indicate that the application is down, and Kubernetes will take action by restarting the application. This gives you very little time to publish a LivenessState.CORRECT event. But if you determine that, in fact, the application is healthy after all, then you can undo the broken event by publishing a new event like this:

```
AvailabilityChangeEvent.publish(context, LivenessState.CORRECT);
```

As long as Kubernetes hasn't hit your liveness endpoint since you set the status to broken, your application can chalk this up as a close call and keep serving requests.

18.4 Building and deploying WAR files

Throughout the course of this book, as you've developed the applications that make up the Taco Cloud application, you've run them either in the IDE or from the command line as an executable JAR file. In either case, an embedded Tomcat server (or Netty, in the case of Spring WebFlux applications) has always been there to serve requests to the application.

Thanks in large part to Spring Boot autoconfiguration, you've been spared from having to create a web.xml file or servlet initializer class to declare Spring's Dispatcher-Servlet for Spring MVC. But if you're going to deploy the application to a Java application server, you're going to need to build a WAR file. And, so that the application server will know how to run the application, you'll also need to include a servlet initializer in that WAR file to play the part of a web.xml file and declare DispatcherServlet.

As it turns out, building a Spring Boot application into a WAR file isn't all that difficult. In fact, if you chose the WAR option when creating the application through the Initializr, then there's nothing more you need to do.

The Initializr ensures that the generated project will contain a servlet initializer class, and the build file will be geared to produce a WAR file. If, however, you chose to build a JAR file from the Initializr (or if you're curious as to what the pertinent differences are), then read on.

First, you'll need a way to configure Spring's `DispatcherServlet`. Although this could be done with a web.xml file, Spring Boot makes this even easier with `Spring-BootServletInitializr`. `SpringBootServletInitializer` is a special Spring Boot–aware implementation of Spring's `WebApplicationInitializer`. Aside from configuring Spring's `DispatcherServlet`, `SpringBootServletInitializer` also looks for any beans in the Spring application context that are of type `Filter`, `Servlet`, or `Servlet-ContextInitializer` and binds them to the servlet container.

To use `SpringBootServletInitializer`, create a subclass and override the `configure()` method to specify the Spring configuration class. The next code listing shows `TacoCloudServletInitializer`, a subclass of `SpringBootServletInitializer` that you'll use for the Taco Cloud application.

> **Listing 18.1   Enabling Spring web applications via Java**

```
package tacos;

import org.springframework.boot.builder.SpringApplicationBuilder;
import org.springframework.boot.context.web.SpringBootServletInitializer;

public class TacoCloudServletInitializer
        extends SpringBootServletInitializer {
  @Override
  protected SpringApplicationBuilder configure(
                                 SpringApplicationBuilder builder) {
    return builder.sources(TacoCloudApplication.class);
  }
}
```

As you can see, the `configure()` method is given a `SpringApplicationBuilder` as a parameter and returns it as a result. In between, it calls the `sources()` method that registers Spring configuration classes. In this case, it registers only the `TacoCloud-Application` class, which serves the dual purpose of a bootstrap class (for executable JARs) and a Spring configuration class.

Even though the application has other Spring configuration classes, it's not necessary to register them all with the `sources()` method. The `TacoCloudApplication` class, annotated with `@SpringBootApplication`, implicitly enables component scanning. Component scanning discovers and pulls in any other configuration classes that it finds.

For the most part, `SpringBootServletInitializer`'s subclass is boilerplate. It references the application's main configuration class. But aside from that, it'll be the same for every application where you'll be building a WAR file. And you'll almost never need to make any changes to it.

Now that you've written a servlet initializer class, you must make a few small changes to the project build. If you're building with Maven, the change required is as simple as ensuring that the `<packaging>` element in pom.xml is set to war, as shown here:

```
<packaging>war</packaging>
```

The changes required for a Gradle build are similarly straightforward. You must apply the war plugin in the build.gradle file as follows:

```
apply plugin: 'war'
```

Now you're ready to build the application. With Maven, you'll use the Maven wrapper script that the Initializr used to execute the package goal like so:

```
$ mvnw package
```

If the build is successful, then the WAR file can be found in the target directory. On the other hand, if you were using Gradle to build the project, you'd use the Gradle wrapper to execute the build task as follows:

```
$ gradlew build
```

Once the build completes, the WAR file will be in the build/libs directory. All that's left is to deploy the application. The deployment procedure varies across application servers, so consult the documentation for your application server's specific deployment procedure.

It may be interesting to note that although you've built a WAR file suitable for deployment to any Servlet 3.0 (or higher) servlet container, the WAR file can still be executed at the command line as if it were an executable JAR file as follows:

```
$ java -jar target/taco-cloud-0.0.19-SNAPSHOT.war
```

In effect, you get two deployment options out of a single deployment artifact!

18.5 *The end is where we begin*

Over the past several hundred pages, we've gone from a simple start—or start.spring.io, more specifically—to deploying an application in the cloud. I hope that you've had as much fun working through these pages as I've had writing them.

But while this book must come to an end, your Spring adventure is just beginning. Using what you've learned in these pages, go build something amazing with Spring. I can't wait to see what you come up with!

Summary

- Spring applications can be deployed in a number of different environments, including traditional application servers and PaaS environments like Cloud Foundry, or as Docker containers.
- Building as an executable JAR file allows a Spring Boot application to be deployed to several cloud platforms without the overhead of a WAR file.

- When building a WAR file, you should include a class that subclasses `Spring-BootServletInitializr` to ensure that Spring's `DispatcherServlet` is properly configured.
- Containerizing Spring applications is as simple as using the Spring Boot build plugin's support for building images. These images can then be deployed anywhere Docker containers can be deployed, including in Kubernetes clusters.

appendix
Bootstrapping
Spring applications

You can kick-start your Spring projects in a lot of ways, and which you choose is largely a matter of personal taste. Many of the choices will be decided by which IDE is your favorite.

All but one of these options are based on the Spring Initializr, which is a REST API that generates Spring Boot projects for you. The various IDE choices are nothing more than clients for that REST API. Additionally, you have a few ways to use the Spring Initializr API outside of your IDE. This appendix takes a quick look at all of these options.

A.1   Initializing a project with Spring Tool Suite

To initialize a new Spring project with Spring Tool Suite, choose the Spring Starter Project menu option from the File > New menu, as shown in figure A.1.

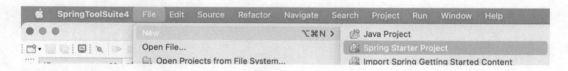

Figure A.1   Starting a new project in Spring Tool Suite

> **NOTE**   This is an abbreviated description of using Spring Tool Suite to initialize a Spring project. For a more detailed explanation, see section 1.2.1.

You'll be shown the first page of the project creation dialog box (figure A.2). On this page, you'll define basic project information, such as the project's name, coordinates

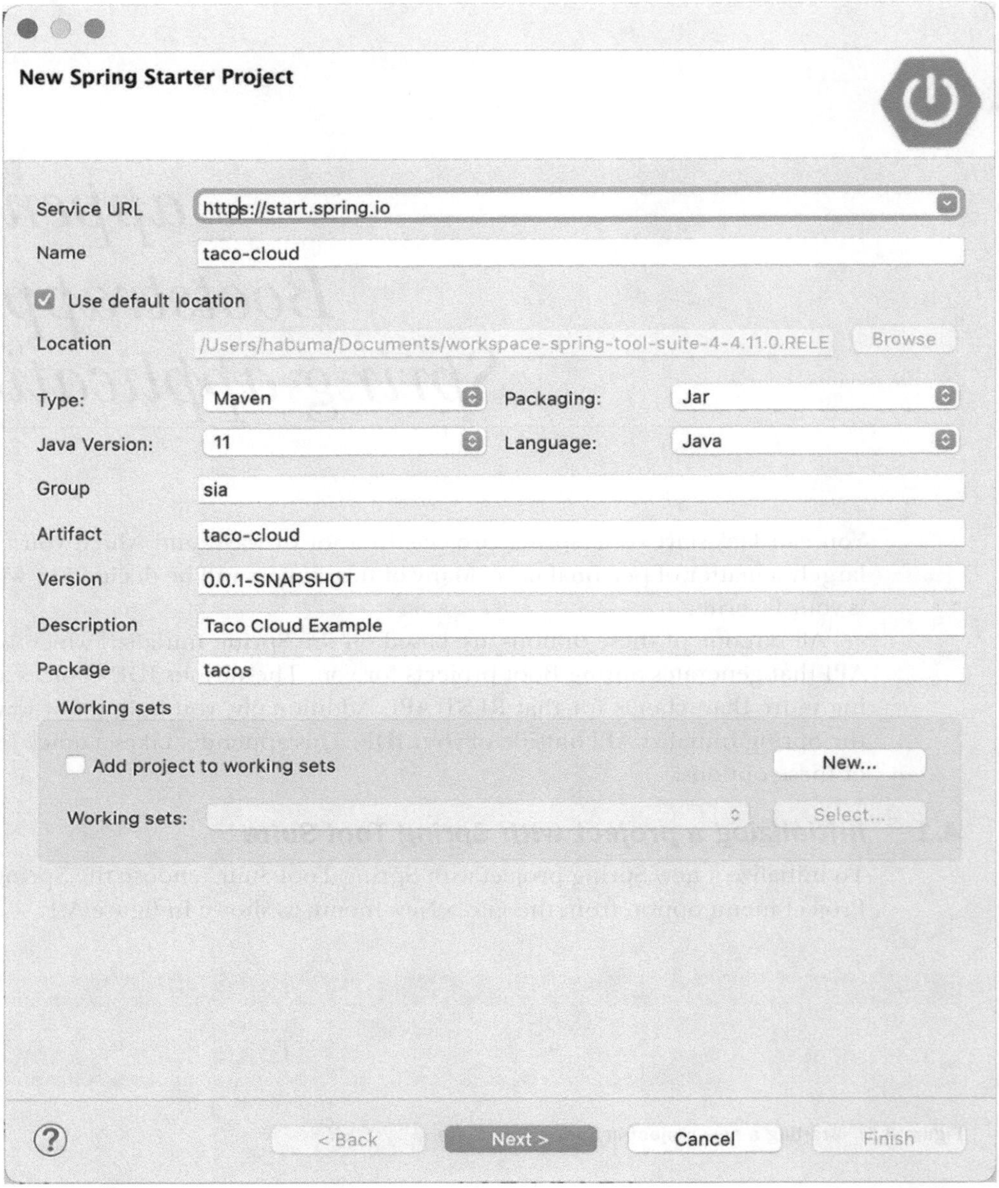

Figure A.2   Defining basic project information

(group ID and artifact ID), version, and base package name. You can also specify whether the project will be built with Maven or Gradle, whether the build will produce a JAR file or a WAR file, which version of Java to build with, and even an alternate JVM language to use, such as Groovy or Kotlin.

The first field on this page asks you to specify the location of the Spring Initializr service. If you're running or using a custom instance of the Initializr, you'll want to specify the base URL of the Initializr service here. Otherwise, you'll be fine leaving it with the default that points to http://start.spring.io.

After you've defined the basic project information, click Next to see the project dependencies page (see figure A.3).

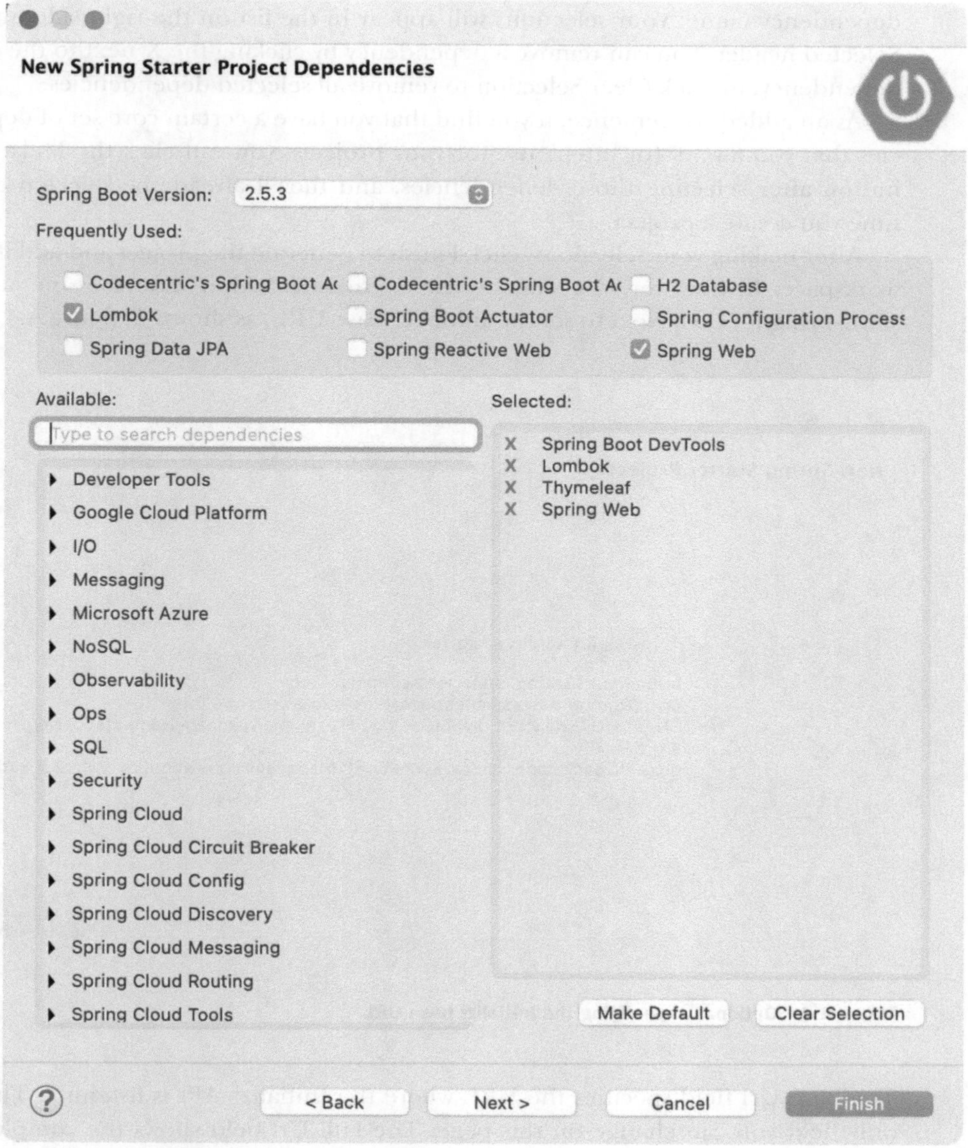

Figure A.3 Specifying project dependencies

On the project dependencies page, you can specify all of the dependencies your project will need. Many of these dependencies are Spring Boot Starter dependencies, although some other dependencies are commonly used in Spring projects.

The available dependencies are listed on the left side, organized in groups that can be expanded or collapsed. If you're having trouble finding a dependency, you can also search for dependencies to narrow down your choices.

To add a dependency to the generated project, select the check box next to the dependency name. Your selections will appear in the list on the right side under the Selected header. You can remove a dependency by clicking the X next to the selected dependency, or click Clear Selection to remove all selected dependencies.

As an added convenience, if you find that you have a certain core set of dependencies that you always (or often) use for your projects, you can click the Make Default button after selecting those dependencies, and they'll already be selected the next time you create a project.

After making your selections, click Finish to generate the project and add it to your workspace. If, however, you want to use an Initializr other than the one at http:// start.spring.io, click Next to set the Initializr base URL, as shown in figure A.4.

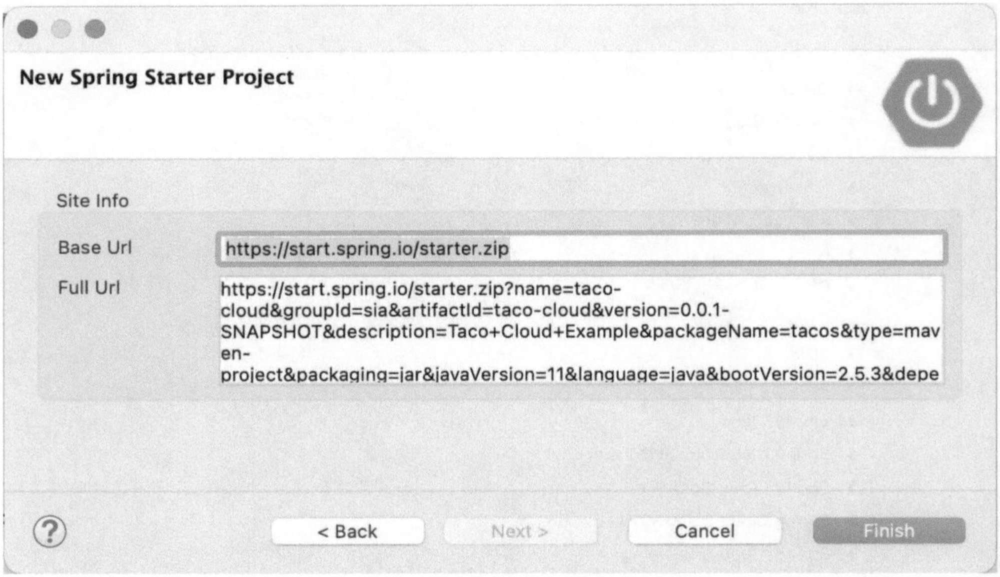

Figure A.4   Optionally specifying the Initializr base URL

The Base Url field specifies the URL where the Initializr API is listening. This is the only field you can change on this page. The Full Url field shows the complete URL that will be used to request a new project from the Initializr.

A.2   Initializing a project with IntelliJ IDEA

To get started on a new Spring project in IntelliJ IDEA, choose the Project menu item from the File > New menu, as shown in figure A.5.

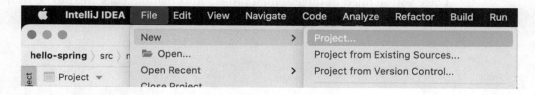

Figure A.5   Starting a new Spring project in IntelliJ IDEA

This opens up the first page of a new Spring Initializr project wizard. You'll be presented with a page that asks for essential project information, as shown in figure A.6.

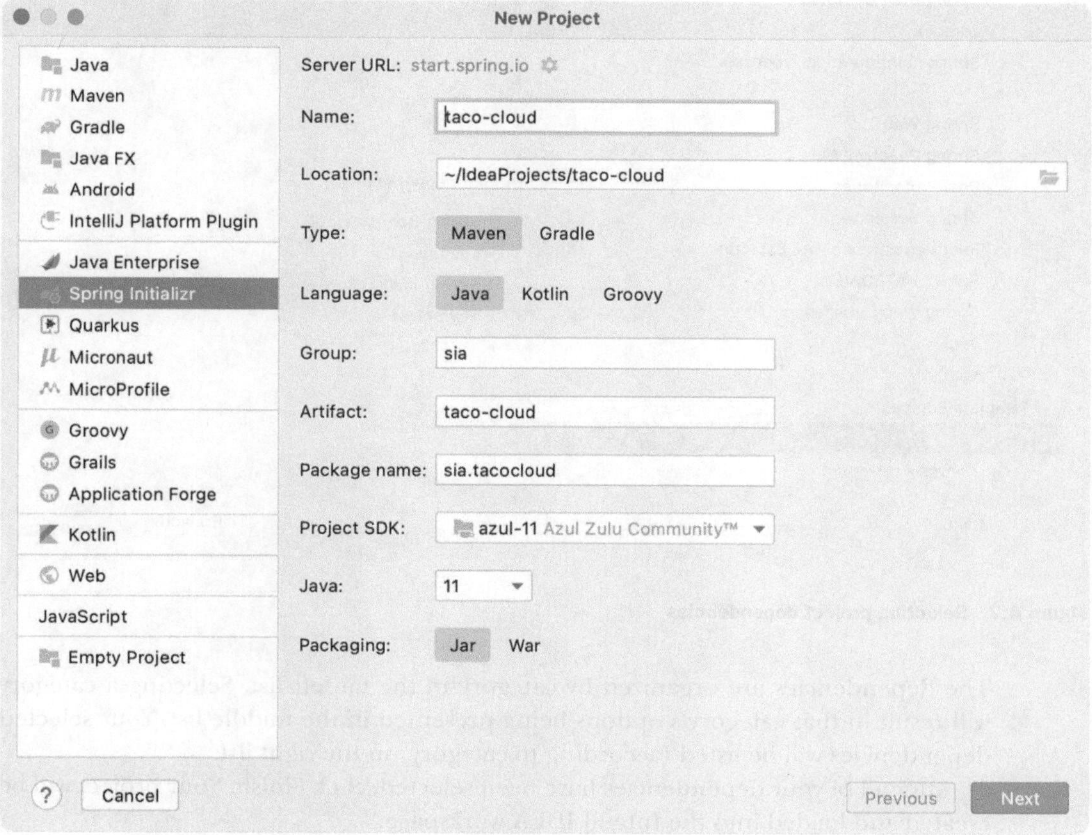

Figure A.6   Specifying essential project information in IntelliJ IDEA

You may recognize some of the fields on this page as information that might appear in a Maven pom.xml file—in fact, if you select Maven Project from the Type field, that's exactly how it will be used. You're welcome to choose Gradle Project instead if Gradle is your preference.

Once you've filled in the essential project information, click Next to be shown the project dependencies page (see figure A.7).

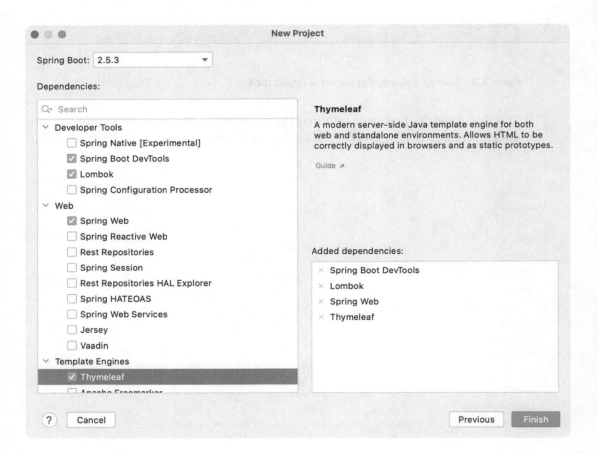

Figure A.7   Selecting project dependencies

The dependencies are organized by category in the far-left list. Selecting a category will result in that category's options being presented in the middle list. Your selected dependencies will be listed (according to category) in the right list.

After all of your dependencies have been selected, click Finish. Your project will be created and loaded into the IntelliJ IDEA workspace.

A.3 Initializing a project with NetBeans

Before you can create a new Spring Boot project in NetBeans, you need to install a plugin that enables Spring Boot development in NetBeans. The NB Spring Boot plugin adds features to NetBeans that are similar to those built into Spring ToolSuite and IntelliJ IDEA.

To install the plugin, select the Plugins option from the Tools menu, as shown in figure A.8.

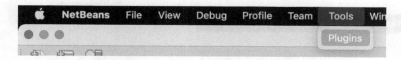

Figure A.8   The NetBeans Plugins menu item

You'll be shown a list of available plugins for NetBeans, including the NB Spring Boot plugin, as shown in figure A.9.

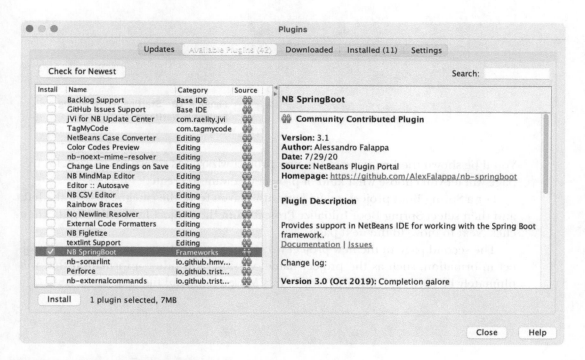

Figure A.9   Selecting the NB Spring Boot plugin

Click Install to begin the installation of the Spring Boot plugin. You'll be prompted with a handful of dialogs to confirm your decision and to acknowledge the plugin license agreement. Simply click Next through them all until you get to the last one, then click Install. Finally, you'll be prompted to restart NetBeans for the plugin to take effect.

After installing the Spring Boot plugin, you are ready to initialize a new Spring Boot project in NetBeans. To create a new Spring project in NetBeans, start by selecting the New Project menu item under the File menu, as shown in figure A.10.

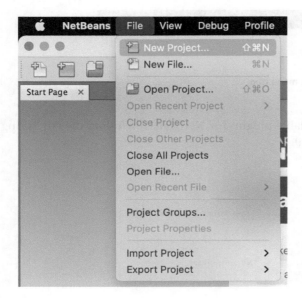

Figure A.10   Starting a new Spring project in NetBeans

You'll be shown the first page of the new project wizard. As shown in figure A.11, this page will let you choose what kind of project you want to create.

For a Spring Boot project, select Java with Maven from the category list on the left, and then select Spring Boot Initializr Project from the project list on the right. Then click Next to move to the next page.

The second page in the new project wizard (figure A.12) lets you set essential project information, such as the project name, version, and other information that will ultimately be used to define the project in a Maven pom.xml file.

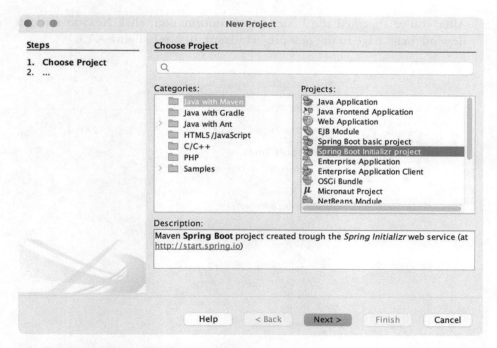

Figure A.11   Creating a new Spring Boot Initializr project

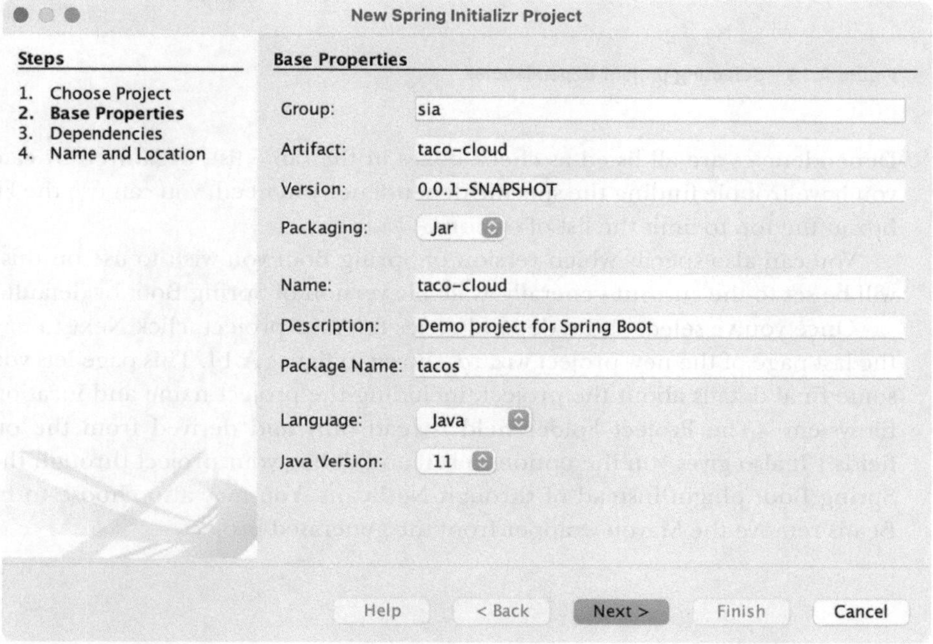

Figure A.12   Specifying essential project information

After you've specified the basic project information, click Next to navigate to the dependencies page in the new project wizard, shown in figure A.13.

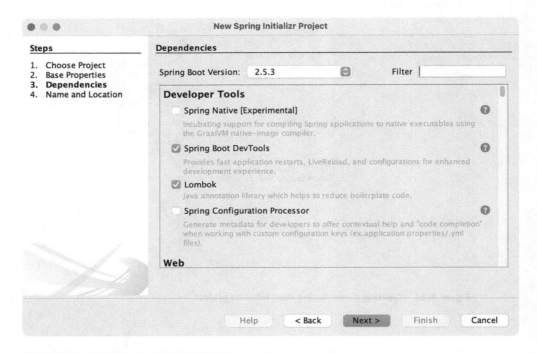

Figure A.13   Selecting project dependencies

Dependencies are all listed as check boxes in the same list, organized by category. If you have trouble finding the specific dependency you need, you can use the Filter text box at the top to limit the list of options.

You can also specify which version of Spring Boot you wish to use on this page. It will be set to the current generally available version of Spring Boot by default.

Once you've selected the dependencies for your project, click Next to navigate to the last page of the new project wizard, shown in figure A.14. This page lets you specify some final details about the project, including the project name and location on the filesystem. (The Project Folder field is read only and derived from the other two fields.) It also gives you the option to run and debug your project through the Maven Spring Boot plugin instead of through NetBeans. You may also choose to have Net-Beans remove the Maven wrapper from the generated project.

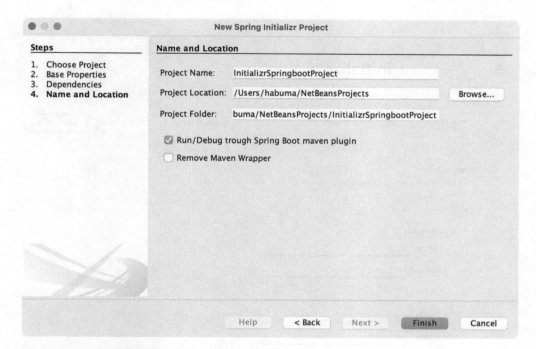

Figure A.14   Specifying the project's name and location

Once you've set the final bit of project information, click Finish to generate the project and have it added to your NetBeans workspace.

A.4   *Initializing a project at start.spring.io*

Although one of the IDE-based initialization options described thus far will likely suit your needs, it's possible that you may use a completely different IDE, or you might favor working with a simpler text editor. In that case, you can still take advantage of the Spring Initializr using the Initializr web-based interface.

To get started, direct your favorite web browser to https://start.spring.io. You should see the simple version of the Spring Initializr web user interface, shown in figure A.15.

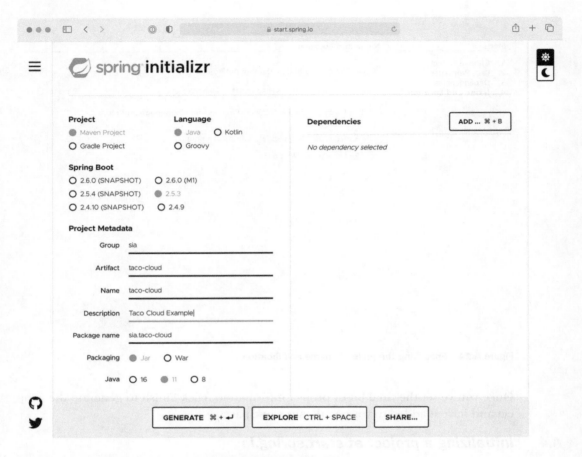

Figure A.15 The simple version of the Spring Initializr web interface

In the simple version of the Initializr web application, you're asked for some very basic information, including whether you want to build with Maven or Gradle, which language you want to develop the project with, which version of Spring Boot to build against, and the group and artifact IDs of the project.

You'll also have the option of specifying dependencies by typing search criteria in the search box. For example, as shown in figure A.16, you can type web to search for any dependencies where "web" is a keyword.

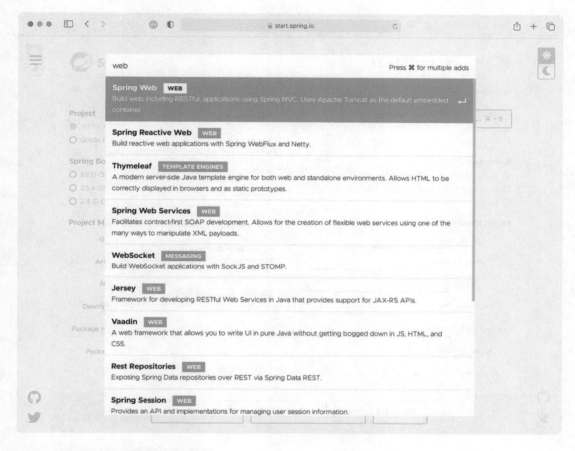

Figure A.16 Searching for dependencies

When you see the dependency you want, press Return on your keyboard to select it, and it will be added to the list of selected dependencies. The boxes beneath Selected Dependencies in figure A.17 show that the Web, Thymeleaf, DevTools, and Lombok dependencies have been selected.

If you decide you don't need a selected dependency, you can click the X to the right of the dependency entry to remove it. When you're finished, you can click Generate Project (or use the keyboard shortcut displayed on the button, which will vary by operating system) to have the Initializr generate the project and download it as a zip file. Then you can unzip the project and load it in whatever IDE or editor you choose.

Figure A.17   Selecting dependencies

Before clicking Generate Project, you can get a sneak peak of the project by clicking Explore. This will pull up a dialog with a project explorer, much like the one shown in figure A.18.

The project's build specification (either a Maven pom.xml file or Gradle build.gradle file) will be shown first. By clicking on items in the tree on the left, you can see what other artifacts will be included in the project.

A.5   *Initializing a project from the command line*

The IDE and browser-based user interfaces for the Spring Initializr are probably the most common way that you'll bootstrap your projects. They're all just clients of a REST service offered by the Initializr application. In some special cases (e.g., in a scripted scenario), you might find it useful to consume the Initializr service directly from the command line.

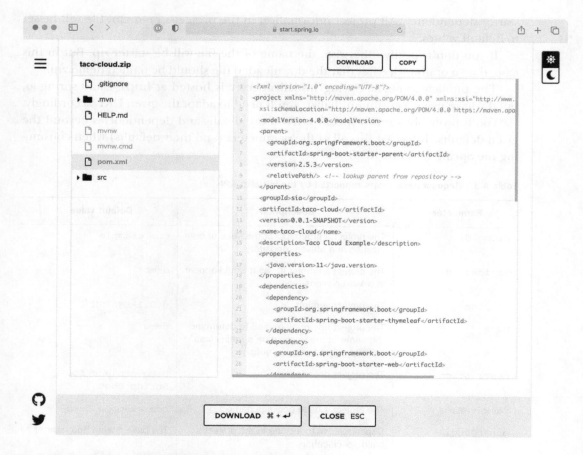

Figure A.18   The full version of the Initializr user interface

You can consume the API in the following two ways:

- Using the `curl` command (or some similar command-line REST client command)
- Using the Spring Boot command-line interface (aka, Spring Boot CLI)

Let's look at these options, starting with the `curl` command.

curl and the Initializr API

The simplest way to bootstrap a Spring project with `curl` is to consume the API like this:

```
% curl https://start.spring.io/starter.zip -o demo.zip
```

In this case, you're requesting the /starter.zip endpoint from the Initializr, which will generate a Spring project and download it as a zip file. The generated project will be Maven built and will have no dependencies other than the base Spring Boot starter dependency. All project information in the project's pom.xml file will be set to default values.

If you don't specify otherwise, the name of the file will be starter.zip. But in this case, the -o option specifies that the downloaded file should be named demo.zip.

The publicly available Spring Initializr server is hosted at https://start.spring.io, but if you're using a custom Initializr, you'll need to adapt the given URL accordingly.

You'll probably want to specify a few more details and dependencies beyond the given defaults. Table A.1 lists all of the parameters (and their defaults) when consuming the Spring Initializr REST service.

Table A.1   Request parameters supported by the Initializr API

Parameter	Description	Default value
groupId	The project's group ID, for the sake of organization in a Maven repository	com.example
artifactId	The project's artifact ID, as it would appear in a Maven repository	demo
version	The project version	0.0.1-SNAPSHOT
name	The project name; also used to determine the name of the application's main class (with an Application suffix)	demo
description	The project description	Demo project for Spring Boot
packageName	The project's base package name	com.example.demo
dependencies	Dependencies to include in the project's build specification	The base Spring Boot starter
type	The kind of project to generate: either maven-project or gradle-project	maven-project
javaVersion	The version of Java to build with	1.8
bootVersion	The version of Spring Boot to build against	The current GA version of Spring Boot
language	The programming language to use: java, groovy, or kotlin	java
packaging	How the project should be packaged: either jar or war	jar
applicationName	The name of the application	The value of the name parameter
baseDir	The name of the base directory in the generated archive	The root directory

You can also get this list of parameters, as well as a list of available dependencies, by making a simple request to the base Initializr URL as follows:

```
% curl https://start.spring.io
```

The `dependencies` parameter is the one you'll probably find the most useful. For example, suppose that you want to create a simple web project with Spring. The following command-line use of `curl` will produce a project zip with the web starter as a dependency:

```
% curl https://start.spring.io/starter.zip \
     -d dependencies=web \
     -o demo.zip
```

As a more complex example, suppose you wanted to develop a web application that uses Spring Data JPA for data persistence. You also want to build it with Gradle, and the project should be under a directory named my-dir within the zip file. And let's suppose that rather than just download a zip file, you want the project unpacked into your filesystem upon download. In that case, the following command should do the trick:

```
% curl https://start.spring.io/starter.tgz \
     -d dependencies=web,data-jpa \
     -d type=gradle-project
     -d baseDir=my-dir | tar -xzvf -
```

Here, the downloaded zip file is piped to the `tar` command for unpacking.

Spring Boot command-line interface

The Spring Boot CLI is another option for initializing Spring applications. You can install the Spring Boot CLI in many ways, but probably the easiest way (and my favorite) is to use SDKMAN (http://sdkman.io/), as shown next:

```
% sdk install springboot
```

Once the Spring Boot CLI is installed, you can start using it to generate projects, much like with `curl`. The command you'll use is `spring init`. In fact, the simplest way to use the Spring Boot CLI to generate a project is like this:

```
% spring init
```

This will result in a bare-bones Spring Boot project being downloaded in a zip file named demo.zip. However, you'll probably want to specify more details and dependencies. Table A.2 lists all of the parameters available to the `spring init` command.

Table A.2 Request parameters supported by the `spring init` command

Parameter	Description	Default value
group-id	The project's group ID, for the sake of organization in a Maven repository	com.example
artifact-id	The project's artifact ID, as it would appear in a Maven repository	demo
version	The project version	0.0.1-SNAPSHOT
name	The project name; also used to determine the name of the application's main class (with an Application suffix)	demo
description	The project description	Demo project for Spring Boot
package-name	The project's base package name	com.example.demo
dependencies	Dependencies to include in the project's build specification	The base Spring Boot starter
type	The kind of project to generate: either maven-project or gradle-project	maven-project
java-version	The version of Java to build with	11
boot-version	The version of Spring Boot to build against	The current GA version of Spring Boot
language	The programming language to use: java, groovy, or kotlin	java
packaging	How the project should be packaged: either jar or war	jar

You can also get this list of parameters, as well as a list of available dependencies, by using the --list parameter as follows:

```
% spring init --list
```

Suppose you wish to create a web application that builds against Java 1.7. The following command uses the --dependencies and --java parameters to make those choices:

```
% spring init --dependencies=web --java-version=1.7
```

Or suppose you want to create a web application with Spring Data JPA for persistence, and you'd like to use Gradle to perform the build instead of Maven. You'd use the following command:

```
% spring init --dependencies=web,jpa --type=gradle-project
```

You may also notice that many of the `spring init` parameters are the same as or similar to the parameters for the `curl` option. That said, the `spring init` command doesn't support all of the same parameters as the `curl` option (e.g., baseDir), and the parameters are hyphen-delimited instead of camelCase (e.g., `package-name` versus `packageName`).

A.6 *Building and running projects*

No matter how you initialize your project, you can always run the application from the command line with the `java -jar` command as follows:

```
% java -jar demo.jar
```

This will even work if you decide to create a WAR file distribution instead of a JAR file, as shown here:

```
% java -jar demo.war
```

You can also take advantage of the Spring Boot Maven and Gradle plugins to run your application. For example, if your project is built with Maven, you can run it like this:

```
% mvn spring-boot:run
```

If, on the other hand, you've chosen to build your project with Gradle, you can run your project like this:

```
% gradle bootRun
```

In either case, whether using Maven or Gradle, the build tool will first build your project (if it hasn't already been built) and run it.

index